Coping with Change

ERFURTER STUDIEN ZUR KULTURGESCHICHTE DES ORTHODOXEN CHRISTENTUMS

Herausgegeben von / Edited by
Vasilios N. Makrides

BAND 18

Zu Qualitätssicherung und Peer Review der vorliegenden Publikation

Die Qualität der in dieser Reihe erscheinenden Arbeiten wird vor der Publikation durch den Herausgeber der Reihe in Zusammenarbeit mit externen Gutachtern geprüft.

Note on the quality assurance and peer review of this publication

Prior to publication, the quality of the works published in this series is reviewed by the editor in collaboration with external referees.

Sebastian Rimestad & Vasilios N. Makrides (eds)

Coping with Change

Orthodox Christian Dynamics between Tradition, Innovation, and *Realpolitik*

PETER LANG

Bibliographic Information published by the Deutsche Nationalbibliothek
The Deutsche Nationalbibliothek lists this publication in the Deutsche Nationalbibliografie; detailed bibliographic data is available online at http://dnb.d-nb.de.

Library of Congress Cataloging-in-Publication Data
A CIP catalog record for this book has been applied for at the Library of Congress.

Cover illustration: St Anthony's Greek Orthodox Monastery, Florence, Arizona. Founded in 1995, it is the first of many Orthodox Christian monasteries established by the Athonite Elder Ephraim over the last decades across the USA. This was a novel development in the history and expansion of Athonite monasticism with far-reaching repercussions for Eastern Orthodoxy within the broad American religious landscape (Source: Wikimedia Commons).

Printed by CPI books GmbH, Leck

ISSN 1612-152X
ISBN 978-3-631-67146-7 (Print)
E-ISBN 978-3-653-07063-7 (E-PDF)
E-ISBN 978-3-631-71026-5 (EPUB)
E-ISBN 978-3-631-71027-2 (MOBI)
DOI 10.3726/978-3-653-07063-7

Peter Lang – Berlin · Bern · Bruxelles · New York · Oxford · Warszawa · Wien

This publication has been peer reviewed.

www.peterlang.com

Table of Contents

JURISDICTION

Orthodox Christianity Today: Charting Changes, Understanding Developments – An Introduction

Sebastian Rimestad / Vasilios N. Makrides

The world of Orthodox Christianity is in flux, especially in the current global context after the end of the bipolar world order. The famous German Protestant theologian Adolf von Harnack at the turn of the twentieth century argued that the Orthodox Church of his day had remained essentially unchanged for more than a millennium.[1] For Harnack, a proponent of the liberal *Kulturprotestantismus*, this was basically a negative assessment. In fact, mainstream Protestantism was then considered the pinnacle of Christian development across time, a vehicle for progress and fully compatible with modernity. In the frame of the *Kulturkampf* in Germany, Harnack's critique was also directed against Roman Catholicism and its antimodern stance at that time. But things were different with regard to Orthodox Christianity, which had already been massively criticised in the past by the Western Christian dominant discourse as a monolithic, backward, and stagnant religious system that bore no relevance to the modern age and its exigencies.[2] The discourses about Orthodox Christianity were "Orientalist" and "Balkanist", a trope that partly re-emerged in recent decades in the wake of the fall of the former Eastern Bloc.[3]

It is true that the Eastern Orthodox world did not develop in the same way and at the same pace as Western Latin Christianity has managed to do from the High Middle Ages onwards, mainly out of socio-political, cultural, and, last but not least, religious reasons. Interestingly enough, during the first centuries of the Christian era, it was the Byzantine (East Roman) East that initiated the major developments in church life, ranging from the Ecumenical Councils for the formulation and the consolidation of the mainstream Christian doctrine to the legitimation of the practice of icon painting and veneration. However, with the passing of time, traditionalist trends became stronger and more pervasive in the East, while special emphasis was put on preserving the true Orthodox faith, bequeathed by the Church Fathers and the Church Councils, unaltered and

1 Adolf von Harnack, *Das Wesen des Christentums* [1900], ed. by Claus-Dieter Osthövener, Second Edition, Tübingen 2007, 124–138.

2 Larry Wolff, *The Enlightenment and the Orthodox World: Western Perspectives on the Orthodox Church in Eastern Europe*, Athens 2001.

3 Elizabeth Prodromou, "Paradigms, Power, and Identity: Rediscovering Orthodoxy and Regionalizing Europe", *European Journal of Political Research* 30 (1996) 125–154; Christopher D. L. Johnson, "'He Has Made the Dry Bones Live': Orientalism's Attempted Resuscitation of Eastern Christianity", *Journal of the American Academy of Religion* 82 (2014) 811–840.

uncontaminated. In particular, the Orthodox used to look down upon later developments in the Latin West, considering them heretical and thus dangerous deviations from the pristine Orthodox faith. In fact, the Orthodox kept feeling superior to the West because they claimed to exclusively possess the true Christian faith. As a result, they often despised the overall development achieved in the West in mundane domains, especially in the course of modern times, as trivial and insignificant in comparison to the religious authenticity they claimed to represent. All this is hardly accidental, given that in Orthodox Christianity the past holds clear priority over the present and the future, an orientation that shows the excessive and normative value that tradition holds in our context.[4]

All this notwithstanding, it would still be a mistake to characterise Orthodox Christianity diachronically, collectively, and indistinctly as an immovable religious system and as a custodian of outdated religious knowledge. This does not only hold with reference to the past, but especially regarding the modern and contemporary situation. The principal difficulty stems from the way we view and define "tradition" and "change", both historically and with regard to modernity. For a long time, these terms were regarded as opposite, contradictory, and mutually exclusive while progress was mainly connected with Western modernity. However, more recently, in the context of postmodern and postcolonial approaches, these older perspectives have been radically reassessed and articulated anew.[5] Tradition is no longer a useless and arid remnant of the past, but is important for understanding various overlapping social processes and ongoing fermentations, both in the religious realm and beyond. Further, tradition is no longer seen as opposed to or surpassed completely by modernity, but as an element that coexists with it and complements it in numerous ways.[6] Breaking the long chain of tradition renders societies "amnesic", and this has tremendous implications, which is what happened in Western societies in the course of modern times due to the process of secularisation.[7]

---

4 Sabrina P. Ramet, "The Way we Were – and Should be Again? European Orthodox Churches and the 'Idyllic Past'", in Timothy A. Byrnes/Peter H. Katzenstein (eds), *Religion in an Expanding Europe*, Cambridge 2006, 148–175; Pantelis Kalaitzidis, "Challenges of Renewal and Reformation Facing the Orthodox Church", *The Ecumenical Review* 61 (2009) 136–164.

5 David Chidester, "Colonialism", in Willi Braun/Russell T. McCutcheon (eds), *Guide to the Study of Religion*, London/New York 2000, 423–437; Colin Campbell, "Modernity and Postmodernity", in Robert A. Segal (ed.), *The Blackwell Companion to the Study of Religions*, Malden 2006, 309–320.

6 Richard Weiss/Gregory P. Grieve (eds), *Historicizing "Tradition" in the Study of Religion*, Berlin 2005; James R. Lewis/Olav Hammer (eds), *The Invention of Sacred Tradition*, Cambridge 2007.

7 Danièle Hervieu-Léger, "Religion as Memory: Reference to Tradition and the Constitution of a Heritage of Belief in Modern Societies", in Jan G. Platvoet/Arie L. Molendijk (eds),

Given the intrinsic connection between religion and tradition, this new approach led to a significant re-evaluation of the role that religions play in today's world at different levels. Not the least, this also led to a fresh and more positive look at Orthodox Christianity. In this respect, the view of the Orthodox Church as a backward and reactionary force has changed. There certainly still are scholars and commentators looking at Orthodoxy from this angle, arguing that Orthodox Christianity did not foster various developments in the course of modern times and even delayed many of them. Although the latter argument contains certain seeds of truth, other scholars place more emphasis on the fact that Orthodox Christianity has had an encounter with modernity, even if it is a partial one, and that it seeks to find a suitable role for itself in the modern world. Any observed deficits or particularities in this process are considered normal and expectable.[8] Given the growing and interdisciplinary interest in the examination of religious dynamics,[9] the question is how exactly to understand and assess the numerous changes happening within Orthodox Christianity and the dynamics that transpire through these processes Do they show a fundamental compatibility of Orthodoxy with modernity in terms of innovation, development, and progress? Or do they also include elements and trajectories that point to a re-traditionalisation that is deemed necessary in the present global age?

Before discussing these questions, it should be mentioned that the modern world is the result of developments that mainly happened in Western Europe and North America, i.e., outside of the regions where Orthodox Christianity usually dominated and still survives today. Truth be told, in the context of postmodern and postcolonial approaches the constant interconnections and interferences between the Western and the non-Western worlds have gained in prominence and significance in a more global setting. Older, more static, Eurocentric theories and perspectives have been abandoned and new inclusive models of development (e.g., the multiple modernities approach[10]) have become more popular and widespread. Nonetheless, one cannot deny that, historically speaking, modernity has a "fundamental Western character", even if this feature tends to vanish in the present global melting pot. In religious and other terms, Western developments

---

The Pragmatics of Defining Religion: Concepts, Contexts and Contests, Leiden 1999, 73–92.

8 Vasilios N. Makrides, "Orthodox Christianity, Rationalization, Modernization: A Reassessment", in Victor Roudometof/Alexander Agadjanian/Jerry Pankhurst (eds), *Eastern Orthodoxy in a Global Age: Tradition Faces the Twenty-first Century*, Walnut Creek/CA 2005, 179–209; idem, "Orthodox Christianity, Modernity and Postmodernity: Overview, Analysis and Assessment", *Religion, State & Society* 40 (2012) 248–285.

9 Gerardo Martí, "New Concepts for New Dynamics: Generating Theory for the Study of Religious Innovation and Social Change", *Journal for the Scientific Study of Religion* 56 (2017) 6–18.

10 Shmuel N. Eisenstadt, "Multiple Modernities", *Daedalus* 129 (2000) 1–29.

were in fact an exception from broader global trends.[11] More importantly, this is evident in the way the Orthodox have always considered modernity, namely as something intrinsically "Western". This explains also why modernity and modern developments have always been viewed critically by Orthodox actors, namely as something foreign and external to their own culture. The Orthodox Church and tradition were never consciously viewed as being a part of modernity. In fact, Orthodox Christianity was often not even recognised as part of the Christian world, as can be seen in the frequent evocation of the term "*antemurale Christianitatis*" (bulwark of Christianity) in early modern Poland-Lithuania and Hungary. In many cases, the Orthodox Christians in South Eastern Europe or in Russia were not considered any better than the Muslim Ottomans that threatened Western Europe and Christianity.[12]

Nevertheless, since the late eighteenth century, modernity – and not only in terms of scientific and technological innovations – started to gain hold also within Orthodox Christian cultures. Especially enlightenment ideas and nationalism entered the Orthodox world and triggered a number of serious fermentations and subsequent transformations. This took place within the confines of the Orthodox world, which was thereby forced to find a *modus vivendi* under the new conditions. In other words, due to the intensification of globalisation, the modern world unavoidably came to the Orthodox Christians, and the latter had to find ways to accommodate it in their lives, albeit mostly not in the same way as in the West. At the same time, there was an excessive Orthodox critique of modernity, which was conceived of as a further stage in the long chain of Western Latin deviations. The critique was part of the phenomenon of Orthodox anti-Westernism that survives in numerous forms up to this day.[13] Despite this at times vociferous criticism, it remains a fact that Orthodox Christianity (exactly as many other religions worldwide[14]) has had an unavoidable encounter with globalised modernity and cannot be understood today without taking this crucial parameter into consideration.

Furthermore, Orthodox Christianity has encountered the modern world at other, more concrete levels. Whereas globalisation in the sense described above

---

11 Grace Davie, *Europe: The Exceptional Case. Parameters of Faith in the Modern World*, London 2002; Peter Berger/Grace Davie/Effie Fokas, *Religious America, Secular Europe? A Theme and Variations*, Farnham 2008.

12 Paul Srodecki, *Antemurale Christianitatis: Zur Genese der Bollwerksrhetorik im östlichen Mitteleuropa an der Schwelle vom Mittelalter zur Frühen Neuzeit*, Husum 2015.

13 Vasilios N. Makrides/Dirk Uffelmann, "Studying Eastern Orthodox Anti-Westernism: The Need for a Comparative Research Agenda", in Jonathan Sutton/Wil van den Bercken (eds), *Orthodox Christianity and Contemporary Europe*, Leuven 2003, 87–120; Aristotle Papanikolaou/George Demacopoulos (eds), *Orthodox Constructions of the West*, New York 2013.

14 Peter van der Veer (ed.), *Conversion to Modernities: The Globalization of Christianity*, London/New York 1996.

happened rather passively – with the Orthodox Christians reacting to the modern ideas and tenets that trickled into their societies –, this second sense relates to the active encounter with and the arrival of modern institutions and of a thorough modern frame to Orthodox cultures. This took place, on the one hand, every time Orthodox Christians moved from a predominantly Orthodox country to the West, either as voluntary migrants or as refugees from the wars that have ravaged the eastern part of the European continent over the twentieth century. As expected, these migrants brought with them their incomplete understanding of modernity. Consequently, they complemented it upon their arrival in the West or they clung to their Orthodox faith and tradition, in order not to get lost in what they perceived as a challenging and at times hostile modern world.[15] The Russian Orthodox diaspora in Western Europe and the USA after the October Revolution of 1917 is a case in point, given that Russian key Orthodox thinkers (e.g., Sergei Bulgakov, Nikolai Berdiayev) initiated a quite fruitful, albeit at times controversial, dialogue with Western modernity.[16]

On the other hand, and more importantly, it is about the political institutions of modernity, into which also predominantly Orthodox countries have been integrated during the last decades, especially after the fall of the "Iron Curtain". The most comprehensive of these is today's European Union (EU), which has four predominantly Orthodox member states at the moment: Greece (accessed 1981), Cyprus (2004), as well as Bulgaria and Romania (2007). The eastward EU enlargement process is a paramount example of the Orthodox arrival to modernity.[17] Hence, after several centuries under Muslim rule and many decades under communism, several Orthodox states of Eastern and South Eastern Europe have reached another level in their encounter with modernity. This is not to say that there was previously no integration of Orthodox states in the project of modernity at all. Yet, their entrance into the EU, even if a limited one up to now, is proof of a long process coming to fruition in terms of a more thorough interaction between Orthodoxy and modernity.[18]

---

15 George Demacopoulos, "'Traditional Orthodoxy' as a Postcolonial Movement", The *Journal of Religion* 97 (2017) 475–499; Sebastian Rimestad, "The Russian Orthodox Church in Western Europe: One or Many?", *Religion, State & Society* 43 (2015) 228–243. See also the contributions by Frances Kostarelos and Anna Karpathakis in this volume.

16 Kristina Stöckl, "Modernity and its Critique in 20th Century Russian Orthodox Thought", *Studies in East European Thought* 58 (2006) 243–269.

17 See also the contributions by Daniel Jianu, Georgios Trantas, and Dragan Šljivić in this volume.

18 Vasilios N. Makrides, "Orthodox Anti-Westernism Today: A Hindrance to European Integration?", *International Journal for the Study of the Christian Church* 9 (2009) 209–224; Tina Olteanu/Dorothée de Nève, "Eastern Orthodoxy and the Processes of European Integration", in Andrii Krawchuk/Thomas Bremer (eds), *Eastern Orthodox Encounters of Identity and Otherness: Values, Self-Reflection, Dialogue*, New York 2014, 179–206.

Despite these momentous changes, which may have been inconceivable a few decades earlier, the Orthodox world is far from uniform on this matter. The Ecumenical Patriarchate of Constantinople (based in Istanbul, Turkey) has shown a remarkable adaptation of the Orthodox tradition to the exigencies of modernity. Under the leadership of current Patriarch Bartholomew (in office since 1991), it has become a noted and respected global player with a huge geopolitical significance at different levels, despite the many domestic constraints it still faces in Turkey. Its position on the issue of modern human rights[19] or its most recent formulation of an "Orthodox social ethos" in 2020[20] are indicative of its overall spirit and orientation to attain a constructive relationship with modernity in the present global era.

The numerically largest Orthodox Church of today, namely the Russian one, headed by the Patriarchate of Moscow, has developed in post-communist times to an important domestic and global player as well, directly challenging the reactivated role of the Patriarchate of Constantinople. Backed by a powerful state and being part of Russia's "soft power" worldwide,[21] the Moscow Patriarchate has articulated a church agenda that has brought it into tension and even conflict with the basic tenets of modernity on numerous occasions.[22] The official documents on the "Social Concept" (2000)[23] and on modern human rights (2008)[24] attest to this, as they are permeated by a spirit that seeks to reverse various achievements of modernity and longs for a pre-modern, non-secular socio-political and religious order. Even if modernity itself has been self-reflective and allowed for internal critique and subsequent revisions in the frame of postmodernity,[25] the Russian Orthodox critique of modernity is formulated

19 Vasilios N. Makrides, "Orthodox Christianity and Modern Human Rights: Theorising their Nexus and Addressing Orthodox Specificities", in Giuseppe Giordan/Siniša Zrinščak (eds), *Global Eastern Orthodoxy: Politics, Religion, and Human Rights*, Cham 2020, 13–39.

20 "For the Life of the World: Toward a Social Ethos of the Orthodox Church", URL: https://www.goarch.org/social-ethos [30.04.2020].

21 Dmitrii Sidorov, "Post-Imperial Third Romes: Resurrections of a Russian Orthodox Geopolitical Metaphor", *Geopolitics* 11 (2011) 317–347; Mikhail D. Suslov, "Holy Rus: The Geopolitical Imagination in the Contemporary Russian Orthodox Church", *Russian Politics and Law* 56/3 (2015) 43–62.

22 Regina Elsner, *Die Russische Orthodoxe Kirche vor der Herausforderung Moderne. Historische Wegmarken und theologische Optionen im Spannungsfeld von Einheit und Vielfalt*, Würzburg 2018.

23 Alexander Agadjanian, "Breakthrough to Modernity, Apologia for Traditionalism: The Russian Orthodox View of Society and Culture in Comparative Perspective", *Religion, State & Society* 31 (2003) 327–346.

24 Kristina Stoeckl, *The Russian Orthodox Church and Human Rights,* London/New York 2014.

25 Margaret S. Archer, *The Reflexive Imperative in Late Modernity*, Cambridge/New York, 2012.

from another angle and has different goals.[26] In fact, Constantinople's and Moscow's positions on modernity diverge significantly and attest to the existing internal variation within the wider Orthodox Church body. The quest for greater Orthodox unity on such matters is more pressing than ever, and Pan-Orthodox attempts, such as the Holy and Great Council of the Orthodox Church in 2016, did not bear the expected results.[27] In all these cases, we are dealing with changes that constantly take place within Orthodox Christianity, trigger various dynamics, and need a pertinent explanation and contextualisation.

In this context, the specific case of Ukraine is highly interesting one, as it is about a predominantly Orthodox country between East and West with a related turbulent political and religious history that experienced tremendous changes in recent years. The Orthodox Church in Ukraine was divided among several church structures, variously recognised by world Orthodoxy since the end of the Soviet Union. Since the summer of 2018, however, there was a serious development, which was also politically backed, towards a greater internal unity and independence of Ukrainian Orthodoxy from Moscow. This process ended with the official declaration of the autocephaly of the Ukrainian Orthodox Church by the Patriarchate of Constantinople in early 2019.[28] This development caused heated reactions from the Moscow Patriarchate, which saw in this step a curtailing of its ecclesiastical rights in the region and which subsequently broke off its communion with Constantinople. There were mixed reactions on the part of the other Orthodox Churches to this radical development, a fact signifying that the issue will bother the Orthodox world in the years to come. From our perspective, the ways this conflict is being carried out using modern media channels and attempts to influence political institutions in one's own favour clearly show how

---

26 Kristina Stoeckl, "The Russian Orthodox Church as Moral Norm Entrepreneur", *Religion, State & Society* 44 (2016) 132–151; Alexander Agadjanian, "Tradition, Morality and Community: Elaborating Orthodox Identity in Putin's Russia", *Religion State & Society* 45 (2017) 1–22; Kristina Stoeckl/Kseniya Medvedeva, "Double Bind at the UN: Western Actors, Russia, and the Traditionalist Agenda", *Global Constitutionalism* 7 (2018) 383–421.

27 Vasilios N. Makrides, "Le concile panorthodoxe de 2016. Quelques réflexions sur les défis auxquels le monde orthodoxe doit faire face", *Istina* 62 (2017) 5–26 ; Emmanuel Clapsis, "The Great and Holy Council and the Orthodox Churches in the Public Sphere", in Giuseppe Giordan/Siniša Zrinščak (eds), *Global Eastern Orthodoxy: Politics, Religion, and Human Rights*, Cham 2020, 77–99. See also Vasilios N. Makrides/Sebastian Rimestad (eds), *The Pan-Orthodox Council – A New Era for the Orthodox Church? Interdisciplinary Perspectives*, Berlin 2020.

28 Alexander Ponomariov, *Theopolitics on the Grand Chessboard: Ukraine between the Church Canons and the Canons of War* (University of Zurich, Center for Eastern European Studies, Working Paper 2), September 2019, URL: https://www.cees.uzh.ch/de/Publikationen/workingpapers.html [30.05.2020]. Regina Elsner/Nadezhda Beljakova, "Geopolitik, Macht und kirchliche Identität: Der Konflikt um die orthodoxe Kirche in der Ukraine", *Ukraine-Analysen* 221 (2019) 5–8.

the Orthodox Church has become part of the modern world. Needless to say, there are similar ongoing conflicts in the wider Orthodox world, some of which are treated in the present volume as well.[29]

Furthermore, the situation in the Orthodox Christian diasporic communities in Western settings around the globe is quite interesting in our context. It reveals the unexpected and complex dynamics that these communities often unleash towards enabling novel adaptations and reformulations of tradition according to the specifics of each local context. Tradition is thus not a fixed element beyond space and time, but is constantly negotiated in numerous creative ways by various categories of believers including converts to Orthodoxy.[30] The cases of the Orthodox communities in Western Europe[31] and the USA[32] are quite telling in this respect. The concept of religious agency is very important here,[33] as it is about individual believers that are eager to creatively adapt the Orthodox tradition to their particular life circumstances. As the first two chapters by Kostarelos and Karpathakis in the volume show, this process may follow either a traditionalist direction or a more innovative path.

Bearing all this in mind, the contributions in this volume attempt not only to revise the outdated view that Orthodox Christianity is an immobile and fixed religious system, but also to show the multiplicity of developmental strands within Orthodox Christianity, which exhibit quite various facets and trajectories. We should bear in mind, though, that it is not possible to put all these changes strictly and exclusively under a common denominator and describe the course of Orthodox Christianity in a single, pre-arranged direction. In fact, the options remain open and flexible, and Orthodox institutions or individual actors take decisions, depending on the circumstances, that are far from uniform. In other words, the Orthodox dynamics that unfold in specific contexts may take various directions, not an *a priori* defined and prescribed one. This situation has been aptly summarised in the subtitle of the present volume as an oscillation between "tradition, innovation, and *Realpolitik*".

This means, first, that one option always turns towards the past and the inherited tradition, no matter how these may be concretely interpreted and

29 Aside from the contribution of Oleg Kyselov on Ukraine, see especially the contributions by Sebastian Rimestad, Nenad Živković and Emil Hilton Saggau.

30 Amy Slagle, *The Eastern Church in the Spiritual Marketplace: American Conversions to Orthodox Christianity*, DeKalb/IL 2011; Oliver Herbel, *Turning to Tradition: Converts and the Making of an American Orthodox Church*, Oxford 2013.

31 Maria Hämmerli/Jean-François Mayer (eds), *Orthodox Identites in Western Europe: Migration, Settlement and Innovation*, Farnham 2014.

32 Lydia Bringerud, *Whose Tradition? Adapting Orthodox Christianity in North America,* Ph.D. Dissetration, Department of Folklore, Memorial University of Newfoundland, May 2019

33 Laura M. Leming, "Sociological Explorations: What Is Religious Agency?", *The Sociological Quarterly* 48 (2007) 73–92.

employed today. Such a re-traditionalisation in our context should not occasion any surprise since Orthodox Christianity can be considered as the most tradition-bound Christian Church compared to Protestantism and even to Roman Catholicism. Cases of re-traditionalisation and even of traditionalism are thus not out of the ordinary here, and it is in this direction that current changes are still taking place today. The phenomenon of Orthodox rigorism/fundamentalism, which experiences a growth in many Orthodox contexts, attests to this.[34] A second option relates to innovation attempts, even if the term "innovation" often has a negative connotation among Orthodox thinkers, who see it as being connected with Western Latin deviations. Yet, in actual fact, a whole array of novelties is what characterises the Orthodox scene in modern times up to our times, even if these novelties are often covered under the protective veil of tradition and are subsequently portrayed as "traditional".[35] Orthodox ecclesiastical nationalism was such a sweeping innovation in the Orthodox Church structure, a change that radically altered the traditional face of the Orthodox Church worldwide. This notwithstanding, for a number of reasons this nationalisation of the Orthodox world is paradoxically often portrayed today as being fully in conformity with traditional Orthodox practice.[36] Finally, the aspect of *Realpolitik* points to the very fact that changes often take place in realistic terms and pragmatic ways according to specific factors, parameters, power struggles, and constellations. In other words, Orthodox institutions or actors are forced to make *ad hoc* compromises underscored by reasonable considerations rather than absolute ideals and premises. Especially the terrain of ecclesiastical politics is full of such cases showing how the Orthodox Churches pursue their goals or allow for realistic concessions. But, *mutatis mutandis*, the same holds true at the level of individual Orthodox religiosity in the wake of growing reflexivity, which is a core dynamic of modern personal religious experience.[37] Hence, the above outline intends to show that changes in the context of Orthodox Christianity do not strictly follow a one-way road, but exhibit significant diversity and allow Orthodox dynamics to operate in numerous different ways. In turn, this speaks once more, yet from another angle, against perceptions about Orthodox Christianity as a basically static, past-oriented, arid, and motionless religious system.

---

34 Vasilios N. Makrides, "Orthodox Christian Rigorism: Attempting to Delineate a Multifaceted Phenomenon", *Interdisciplinary Journal for Religion and Transformation in Contemporary Society* 3 (2016) 216–252.

35 Vasilios N. Makrides, "Orthodox Christianity, Change, Innovation: Contradictions in Terms?", in Trine Stauning Willert/Lina Molokotos-Liederman (eds), *Innovation in the Orthodox Christian Tradition? The Question of Change in Greek Orthodox Thought and Practice*, Farnham 2012, 19–50.

36 Vasilios N. Makrides, "Why Are Orthodox Churches Particularly Prone to Nationalization and Even to Nationalism?", *St Vladimir's Theological Quarterly* 57 (2013) 325–352.

37 Gerardo Martí, "Religious Reflexivity: The Effect of Continual Novelty and Diversity on Individual Religiosity", *Sociology of Religion* 76 (2015) 1–13.

Undoubtedly, there are plenty of cases to be examined from the above perspective, yet the present volume focuses on three major clusters, namely issues of identity construction, relations to politics, and jurisdictional conflicts. All of them illustrate the encounter of Orthodox Christianity with modernity at different levels. Thus, the first part of the volume touches on issues of Orthodox identity and what it means to be Orthodox in different settings. First, Frances Kostarelos focuses on the Greek Orthodox Archdiocese of America (GOARCH) and is concerned with developments within this church structure related to the influence of the Athonite monk Ephraim, who has considerably changed the Orthodox Christian landscape in the country through the spread of Athonite monasticism and the founding of numerous monasteries. The Orthodox worldview promoted by Elder Ephraim and his adherents cannot be characterised as modernity-friendly (in the conventional meaning of the term), yet it became particularly attractive to many Orthodox in the USA, including also to numerous converts to Orthodoxy. It focuses on processes of re-traditionalisation and at times radicalisation oriented towards an Orthodox heritage that claims to be more authentic than various allegedly secularised versions of Orthodoxy that have been established in the USA. Such a genuine Orthodox tradition was lost within the pluralist, liberal, and syncretistic American religious melting pot. This specific case demonstrates that full adherence to an open and liberal modernity is not always the most attractive option for a religion today and that more traditional or conservative worldviews have good chances of becoming very influential and effective. The recent intensification of Orthodox rigorism/fundamentalism in various contexts is a case in point, a phenomenon that also relates to the movement initiated by Elder Ephraim. Given that the GOARCH is overall firmly rooted in modern culture, Elder Ephraim's influence among clergy, monastics, and ordinary believers created serious cleavages within Orthodoxy in the USA between long-established conformist and conventional trends and new traditionalist ones, with the latter claiming absolute truth and fidelity to the Orthodox tradition and castigating the former. Kostarelos has done empirical research in several Orthodox parishes documenting the internal rifts among Orthodox believers along the question as to what constitutes the genuinely Orthodox identity. This development has also been a serious test for long-standing parish members as far as their loyalty to the Orthodox Church was concerned. Interestingly, Elder Ephraim's teachings resonate in many respects with the overall rise of conservative worldviews and outlooks within American society at large, a phenomenon with far-reaching repercussions. In addition, Ephraim's growing influence is hardly openly opposed or constrained by the GOARCH leadership that keeps a rather diplomatic and mediating stance on the matter, a fact that in Kostarelos' view complicates the overall situation and does not resolve tensions and conflicts. It remains thus to be seen how all these fermentations will affect the articulation of Orthodox identities in the USA in the future, especially after the death of Elder Ephraim in 2019.

Anna Karpathakis also focuses on the GOARCH, but with a slightly different emphasis. Based on her extensive fieldwork among Greek Orthodox immigrants in the USA and on numerous conducted interviews, her focus is on gender and especially on Orthodox women. She focuses on women that at some point felt that their Orthodox parish was not able to provide them with the spiritual home they were looking for in the modern world, as it was mostly male-oriented and utterly ignored the women's special needs and problems. Consequently, by initiating their "silent revolt", many women started drifting away from everyday parish life, although some of them decided, few decades later, to return to an active community role out of different considerations (e.g., the strong interconnection between Orthodoxy, Greek history, and identity). This reveals, first, the strong individualisation urges among such women, who were also influenced by feminist ideas and intended to find their own particular way to the Orthodox faith; for instance, by distinguishing their belief in God from the church institutions and the priests. This was mainly a result of growing reflexivity on their part, which lead to the ability to cognitively disembed themselves from institutional ties and to construct new ways of legitimising their religious ideas, worldviews, practices, and in the end, their Orthodox identities. Second, it shows the existing ambivalence in their course of action, which did not provide a final or permanent solution to their problems. Third, it discloses the women's openness towards other Christian traditions, such as when they admired Protestant communities for their intense social consciousness and work. Karpathakis traces all these ambiguities, namely the journey of these women away from the parish and back again, showing that for many interviewees the important thing was not whether the local parish had fully arrived to modernity, but rather how modernity could be integrated in the everyday parish life. This quest included both conservative and traditional as well as more flexible and liberal positions.

The third chapter in this part tells the story of evolving Ukrainian Orthodox identities during demonstrations and civil unrest between November 2013 and February 2014 on the *Independence Square* (Maidan Nezalezhnosti) in Kiev (also called "Euromaidan" in this context). This was a significant turning point in the political history of independent Ukraine in post-communist times. As is well known, the later history of Ukrainian Orthodoxy became even more complex and conflictual due to the mounting ecclesiastical problems with Russia and finally the declaration of the Ukrainian Church autocephaly by the Patriarchate of Constantinople in 2019, which led the Moscow Patriarchate to break off its communion with Constantinople. This rift and the processes connected to it have completely changed the current face of Ukrainian Orthodoxy. Oleg Kyselov's chapter on Maidan Orthodoxy sheds light on the period prior to church autocephaly, which is a quite important one for understanding the momentous changes within Ukrainian Orthodoxy, even though some of the church structures that he describes no longer exist. The chapter, thus, offers a useful view and assessment of the politicisation of Orthodox identities and their opposition to the government in this specific context. This is quite an important point, given that the Orthodox Churches did not usually challenge political authority in the past and have a strong tradition of subservience to the state. The situation during the communist was a case in point. As Kyselov mentions, there were also some Protestant participants on Maidan, however their opposition activities do not surprise, as Protestants have always had a long and influential tradition of anti-regime opposition. Such demonstrations were quite unusual for the Ukrainian Orthodox, who thereby showed a quite different face than in the past. Here again we observe a considerable change, which in turn calls in question the alleged immutability of the Orthodox religious system and its supposed overwhelming fixation to the past tradition.

The four chapters in the second part on politics cover the multi-layered relationship between the political institutions of modernity and various structures of the Orthodox Church at different levels. First, Daniel Jianu's chapter on blasphemy in the current Greek Orthodox Church sets the scene against the background of the *longue durée* of church-state relations in Byzantium and under Ottoman rule. He thereby attempts to show that the modern concept of the rule of law does not fully resonate with the Orthodox tradition of *symphonia*, where the religious and the political sphere harmonise and provide the legitimacy for each other. The separation between church and state in West European modernity does not apply fully to the Orthodox contexts, in which there is a mixture of traditional and modern elements. This phenomenon can be aptly described as "symphonic secularism", which shows the still existing ambivalence between the religious and the secular in the Orthodox context. Drawing on cases of perceived blasphemies against Greek Orthodoxy that were raised during the recent severe economic crisis in the country, Jianu argues that these blasphemy cases are quite telling. Initially raised at the political level by a newly emerged extreme right-wing political party and not by the official church, they tend to upset the ideally sought harmonious link between church and state by challenging the foundations and the ideological parameters of a presumed state secularity.

The chapter by Georgios E. Trantas concerns the political culture in Greece and the role of the Orthodox Church in the context of the European Union (EU) by comparing the political role of the two most recent Archbishops of Athens and All Greece – Christodoulos (1998-2008) and Hieronymos II (since 2008). This is a quite fruitful comparison, since these two church primates were fairly, if not radically, different in their approach to the political involvement of the church, especially in relation to the EU. On the one hand, Christodoulos was very extrovert and assertive and pushed for a direct and active interventional role of the Greek Orthodox Church in EU politics. On the other hand, his successor, Hieronymos II, has showed a much more compromising approach, leaving the international scene and foreign policy to the elected politicians and focusing much more on the fruitful cooperation with the state, on social welfare, and on the spiritual mission of the church. In other words, he was more respectful to the established delineation between the spheres of church and state in modern times, which resonates better with the overall logic of modernity. Trantas' contribution underlines the role of agency by making clear that a lot depends on the specific Orthodox actors that undertake important functions within a given set of socio-historical parameters. In turn, this also means that such cases are always contingent and relative, thus they should never be generalised as reflecting the very "essence" of the Orthodox stance in such matters.

Such a differentiated approach to the political involvement of the church is also evident in Dragan Šljivić's chapter, which traces the development of democracy in Serbia and Bulgaria in post-communist times and especially in the period between 2007 and 2012. For Šljivić, the concept of "symphonic democracy" concisely delineates the functioning of these two polities, of church and state. A closer look at both countries reveals an alliance between church and state that may appear peculiar to a Western political scientist. Šljivić shows how these countries must be looked at in a nuanced way and with a flexible agenda in mind, one that challenges the discussions in the early post-communist years about the incompatibility between liberal democracy and Orthodox Christianity. This is because the apparently failing democratic institutional structures in these countries surprisingly hide democratising forces and a related potential, which even include the Orthodox Church as a significant actor. This underlines once more the necessity of looking at Orthodox cultures in a differentiated manner, looking at the agents involved in specific processes and without pre-conceived ideas and stereotypes.

The final chapter in this second part provides a transition to the last part of the volume, namely to jurisdictional issues. Nicolas Kazarian takes the difficult relationship between the Patriarchates of Constantinople and Moscow into consideration, putting it on a broader geopolitical canvas, thus showing the great geopolitical relevance of Orthodox Christianity in the present global age, which has been underlined in various civilisational theories including the notorious "Clash of Civilisations" of Samuel Huntington. This is because both Patriarchates are highly interested in representing global Orthodoxy, albeit with very different approaches, agendas, and available means. This role was traditionally undertaken by the Patriarchate of Constantinople, which as the sole Orthodox Church also bears the name "Ecumenical", and still is. However, the gradual rise and the strengthening of the Moscow Patriarchate has marked a serious challenge to Constantinople's authority, a phenomenon that appeared anew in post-communist times. It is thus interesting to observe how the Patriarchate of Constantinople adapted its policies and changed its resources of power in order to counterbalance the growing Moscow influence. The developments in Ukrainian Orthodoxy since the end of 2018, which are not treated in this chapter, also justify the above image.

Hence, the conclusions of this chapter remain valid, also in relation to the situation of Orthodox Christians in France, which Kazarian succinctly analyses.

The third part of the volume is concerned with jurisdiction, namely with the clashes between different Orthodox Churches on the basis of canon law arguments, administrative concerns, politically motivated ambitions, and concomitant territorial claims. Frankly speaking, the idea that the worldwide Orthodox Church is one and indivisible is starkly contrasted by the actual geopolitical struggles that take place on the boundaries between various administratively independent church structures. Most of these struggles exhibit strong national connotations, thus they are closely related to the nationalisation process that swept through the Orthodox world in modern times, a serious innovation in sharp contrast to the Orthodox past. The first chapter in this part by Sebastian Rimestad analyses the role of historiography in these conflicts. Usually, the two competing church sides display widely divergent versions of "historical truth" and related claims, deployed to serve the purpose of justifying one side or the other and usually projecting modern aims into the distant and often nebulous past, a process that, in any event, is not in a position to provide clear and unambiguous answers. Rimestad identifies three types of such church conflicts involving coexistence, secession, and protection. In the end, it seems that no church party involved can fully implement its own version of history due to various constraints. Thus, a (temporary) solution of the conflicts usually entails a necessary and pragmatic compromise amidst various existing and suggested options.

The two chapters that close the book off provide more in-depth and highly interesting analyses of such conflicts with regard to the Orthodox Church in former Yugoslavia and in the states that emerged after its dissolution. Nenad Živković unravels the complex Macedonian Church schism, whereas Emil Hilton Saggau presents and analyses the fabricated historiography underlying the attempts to create and legitimise an independent Orthodox Church of Montenegro. Both these cases clearly show the consequences of the still virulent nationalism within Orthodox Christianity and involve secession attempts from the Serbian Orthodox Church, which reacts against the violation of its "canonical territory". Although these two church organisations, the Macedonian and the Montenegrin, are rather different in scope and size, the manner in which they try to legitimate their own independent existence is largely similar. In the Macedonian case, the connection with the historical past is more clear and persuasive, whereas in the Montenegrin case the use of the historical depth contains many arbitrary interpretations from a contemporary perspective (e.g., through the use of visual means and a "sacralisation" of past events). In both cases, however, the aspired independent church structures receive strong political backing, whereas external influential church structures (e.g., the Moscow Patriarchate, the Bulgarian Orthodox Church) are also involved, not the least out of their own interests in these areas. Here we have clear cases of a connection between tradition and innovation in conceiving and promulgating one's own church history and past. At the same time, it seems plausible that both these disputed church structures, as well as their opponent, the Serbian Orthodox Church, will be forced in the end to make pragmatic compromises and eventually resolve the related conflicts. This transition to *Realpolitik* is a realistic scenario, considering the previous history of conflictual inter- and intra-Orthodox relations during the last centuries.

To sum up: All the contributions to the current volume attempt to highlight different aspects and facets of an evolving Orthodox Christianity at the beginning of the twenty-first century. This takes place after this historical and important Christian Church came into contact with modernity and was forced to deal with its multiple challenges, even if not in a thorough and comprehensive way. There is no doubt that such a close analysis of the Orthodox responses to the modern world remains a multi-layered and complex yet rewarding endeavour.

The present volume shows that coping with change was never an easy task for Orthodox institutions and actors, yet modernity forced them to deal with challenges in different ways, either accommodating or reactionary. Ulrich Beck's judgement that with increasing modernisation, religions do not disappear, but change their appearance,[38] holds true for Orthodox Christianity as well. The question is, however, what such processes lead to. The contributions to this volume show that it is never a one-way path that involves either returning to past tradition or endorsing innovative developments. Instead, both these options remain valid as Orthodox Christianity has to address – not necessarily comply with – the many challenges of the current global era, which threaten to alter its overall profile. In any event, the dilemmas and the ambivalences between past, present, and future are overcome inasmuch Orthodox institutions and actors often resort to *Realpolitik* to resolve tensions and problems, namely to reasonable decisions and pragmatic compromises that entail both traditional and innovative elements. Even so, the Orthodox dynamics that transpire through all these processes make evident that this Christian Church is far away from a monolithic and petrified religious system. On the contrary, it fosters pertinent strategies that deal with ongoing changes and enable various ingenious adaptations, both traditional and innovative. The Orthodox Christian case is thus a prime testing ground for various hypotheses about how religious dynamics operate, evolve, and exert wider influences. Among other things, this applies to adaptations and transformations, both at the personal level and in the public sphere; re-inventions of tradition and formulations of related discourses; processes of individualisation

38 Ulrich Beck, *A God of One's Own: Religion's Capacity for Peace and Potential for Violence*, Cambridge/Malden 2010, 39.

by diverse agents; and strategies of historicisation, representation, and narration, accommodating both continuity and change with pragmatic goals.[39]

39 See Christoph Bochinger/Jörg Rüpke, "Introduction", in iidem (eds), *Dynamics of Religion: Past and Present. Proceedings of the XXI World Congress of the International Association for the History of Religions, Erfurt, August 23-29, 2015*, Berlin/Boston 2017, 1–8.

IDENTITY

Elder Ephraim and Contested Identities in the Greek Orthodox Archdiocese of America

Frances Kostarelos

In this chapter, I discuss the influence of Elder Ephraim (1927-2019) and the monasteries he established in the United States on members and parishes of the Greek Orthodox Archdiocese of America (GOARCH). In this account of Elder Ephraim's teaching and institutions, I draw on wider ethnographic research I am conducting concerned with challenges GOARCH institutions face as they adapt to a plural American cultural and religious landscape.[1] The ethnography focuses on social and cultural forces transforming the lived experiences of Greek Orthodox Christians, parishes, and GOARCH institutions in twenty-first century America. The wider ethnographic account points to complex forces rooted in changing American social, cultural, and religious beliefs, values, and institutions reshaping personal and collective social and moral beliefs, practices, and identities. Laity within American religious bodies, including Greek Orthodox Christians, are challenging church leaders to address religious beliefs and practices in the light of changing social norms and values that centre on individualism, freedom, and the pursuit of happiness unencumbered by tradition. In response to challenges from the laity, religious authorities and institutions are examining and modifying positions on laity roles in directing church affairs, the roles of women in church leadership and ministry, the gender equality and sexual diversity in church life and leadership.[2] Within the GOARCH, the challenge to reform the church is largely coming from first generation Greek Americans and their descendants who identify with mainstream American perspectives on human freedom and individual choice in private matters including religious life. They are upwardly mobile and largely work and live in urban and suburban neighbourhoods. They seek post-secondary education and professional training in large numbers. They are integrated into American society and positioned to take advantage of economic, social, and political opportunities leading to upward mobility. For these individuals, the Greek ethno-national identity constructed by Greek settlers who founded parishes in the early twentieth century and asserted

---

1 For discussion of religious pluralism in America, see Diane Eck, *A New Religious America: How a "Christian Country" has Become the World's Most Religiously Diverse Nation*, San Francisco/CA 2001. See also "The Pluralism Project" at http://pluralism.org [19.02.2019] for updated research projects and reports on the religious pluralism in North America.

2 For a discussion of unencumbered individualism and the separation of private and public spheres in American religious life, see Robert Bellah *et al.*, *Habits of the Heart: Individualism and Commitment in American Life*, Berkeley/CA 1985, 219–249.

by Elder Ephraim and his following have outlived its purpose of holding a community together.[3]

In 2009 while preparing a manuscript addressing cultural and social changes and contested discourses shaping Orthodox Christian identity, parishes, and institutions in the early years of the twenty-first century in the United States, a lay parish leader contacted me to discuss Elder Ephraim's teachings and monasteries. He explained that in his and other Midwestern parishes Elder Ephraim's teachings introduced by parish priests were giving way to disruptions in parish community routines and broken relationships. I had noted several Greek Orthodox monasteries cropping up in the United States established by Elder Ephraim. Parishes established by Greek Orthodox Christians in urban settings are the primary locus of my research, and I had not considered monasteries relevant in parish life. I wrongly assumed that Elder Ephraim and his monasteries did not matter in an account of Greek Orthodox parishes with a focus on the lived experiences of parishioners shaping their identities in a plural socio-cultural and religious landscape.

Since 1990, Elder Ephraim has established a total of 17 monasteries in North America under the Greek Orthodox Archdiocese of America. He has planted his monasteries across the United States and the eight GOARCH Metropolises.[4] Saint Anthony's Monastery in the ecologically diverse and fragile Sonoran Desert near the town of Florence, Arizona, was founded by Elder Ephraim in 1995 and served as his residence base. This is also where he passed away on 7 December 2019. The monastery grounds include multiple buildings and chapels, fountains, gazebos, palm trees, citrus trees, a vineyard, and an olive tree grove. The facility is operated by state-of-the art technology that taps solar energy. Saint Anthony has accommodations for overnight guests who are welcome to stay for a few days in exchange for a free will donation. Men, women, families, and church groups from across the United States and Orthodox lands travel to Saint Anthony seeking spiritual direction and a blessing from Elder Ephraim and his disciples. Monks who live at Saint Anthony along with volunteers provide labour to sustain daily routines. His followers have told me that the monastery grounds are an oasis and miracle made possible by Elder Ephraim. Observers estimate that the cost of the Saint Anthony project is approximately 30 million dollars. There is no information on the sources that fund the project and operating expenses. The

---

3 For a discussion of the place of the church in contemporary Greek American life, see Peter Moskos, *Greek Americans Struggle and Success*, New Brunswick/NJ 2014. This updated edition first written by Charles Moskos includes discussion of church organisation and parish practices as they have adapted to the American context (Ibid., 87–108).

4 For the locations of Elder Ephraim's monasteries in the United States, see URL: http://www.stanthonysmonastery.org/map.php [19.02.2019]. For a description of the monasteries founded by Elder Ephraim, see Alexei Krindatch, *Atlas of American Orthodox Christian Monasteries*, Brookline/MA 2016.

founding story of Elder Ephraim's monasteries centres on his spiritual formation and supernatural qualities cultivated on Mount Athos under the care of his spiritual father, Elder Joseph the hesychast – discussed further below. Saint Anthony's Monastery houses a press that publishes books about the Elder's teachings, books on the lives and teachings of spiritual elders, children's books, and a calendar noting Orthodox saints and feast days sold at the monastery and available on the online bookstore along with other items.

In a few short years, Elder Ephraim had established a culture of monasticism and spiritual elders that was missing in the Orthodox experience in the United States. The Elder attracted cradle and convert Orthodox Christians seeking his spiritual advice and direction. However, many Orthodox Christians find his spiritual claims and beliefs unacceptable and harmful. In the following account, we will see that Elder Ephraim was a pivotal and controversial religious leader among Orthodox Christians in the United States. We will see that his beliefs have given way to sweeping changes in parish routines that many have accepted while others have rejected them.

In this chapter, I first discuss the fieldwork and theoretical approaches informing the analysis. I next consider Elder Ephraim's teachings, worldview, and spiritual practices. I then turn to a discussion of conflicts in parish life and parish fragmentation resulting from Elder Ephraim's teaching carried to parishes by clergy and laity who follow him. I also consider challenges from the laity aimed at GOARCH leaders at institutions who are not responding to reports of individual harm, broken relationships, and parish fragmentation and decline resulting from contact with Elder Ephraim and his disciples. Clergy and laity who oppose Elder Ephraim seek to hold church leaders accountable to the *General Regulations of the Establishment and Operations of Holy Monasteries in the Greek Orthodox Archdiocese of America*, signed by Patriarch Bartholomew of Constantinople and Archbishop Demetrios of America along with several other Synodical Metropolitans.[5] Reports of misconduct at monasteries and violations pursuant to the *General Regulations of the Establishment and Operations of Holy Monasteries in the Greek Orthodox Archdiocese of America*, reported by clergy and laity, are openly disregarded by GOARCH bishops, and this is a growing source of friction and mistrust.

5 The *General Regulations of the Establishment and Operations of Holy Monasteries in the Greek Orthodox Archdiocese of America*, New York 2005, URL: https://www.goarch.org/documents/32058/3058354/2005-monasteryregulations.pdf/3d5f18fa-997a-424a-8f27-103bf68e8918 [19.02.2019].

Theoretical Approaches and Fieldwork

In the account that follows, I rely on symbolic anthropology and the sociology of religion to guide my research and analysis. Following Geertz and Douglas, I direct attention to collective symbols as they shape systems of personal and collective meaning and social action.[6] I follow Weber on the problem of meaning and charismatic religious leaders in my discussion of Elder Ephraim's calling and worldview.[7] Drawing on theories of collective consciousness, religious imagination, and collective memory,[8] used by anthropologists to study religious life, I seek to explain symbols, meanings, and routine practices shaping the Greek Orthodox Christian understanding of personal and collective moral and social identity. As in my earlier work on evangelical African American storefront churches,[9] the approach in the current study looks to historical contingencies and human agency to account for changes and continuity in Greek Orthodox Christian life in the America. Drawing on symbolic anthropology, the focus is on an insider understanding of religious life, practices, and parish community aims in this period of heightened conflict embedded in contested beliefs and practices vying for control over Orthodox identity and institutional development.

Several Orthodox clergy and laity interviewed for this study use the term "fundamentalism" to describe Elder Ephraim's teachings and practices. However, Makrides has noted analytic shortcomings of applying the term "fundamentalism" to the study of Orthodox Christianity.[10] In this account, I still apply the term "fundamentalism", as it is used by insiders interviewed for this study, to describe their views on Elder Ephraim's teachings and practices. The *Fundamentalist Project*, held at the University of Chicago under Martin Marty and R. Scott Appleby in the 1990s, did not include the Orthodox Church. I have found the analytic frames from the *Fundamentalism Project* presented by Almond *et al.*[11] useful in my work and have used them in public presentations on the matter of

---

6 Clifford Geertz, "Religion as a Cultural System", in Michael Banton (ed.), *Anthropological Approaches to the Study of Religion*, London 1968, 1–46; Mary Douglas, *Implicit Meanings: Selected Essays in Anthropology*, London 1999.

7 Max Weber, *Economy and Society*, Berkeley/CA 1978.

8 Maurice Halbwachs, *On Collective Memory*, Chicago/IL 1992.

9 Frances Kostarelos, *Feeling the Spirit: Faith and Hope in an Evangelical Black Storefront Church*, Columbia/SC 1995.

10 Vasilios N. Makrides, "Orthodox Christian Rigorism: Attempting to Delineate a Multifaceted Phenomenon", *Interdisciplinary Journal for Religion and Transformation in Contemporary Society* 3 (2016) 216–252.

11 See Gabriel A. Almond/R. Scott Appleby/Emmanuel Sivan, *Strong Religion: The Rise of Fundamentalisms Around the World*, Chicago/IL 2003.

Elder Ephraim.[12] In recent years, scholars from multiple academic disciplines have turned their attention to fundamentalism in the Orthodox Church.[13]

This analysis of the influence of Elder Ephraim's teachings on GOARCH parishes and the lived experience of Greek Orthodox Christians draws on fieldwork conducted in Greek Orthodox parishes in Midwestern urban, suburban, and rural settings. It is informed by open-ended and semi-structured interviews conducted since 2009 when I first heard of Elder Ephraim's teachings and influence in the lives of Greek Orthodox Christians and parishes. Individuals interviewed for this study include laity and clergy, college educated young adults, professional men and women, entrepreneurs, singles, married couples, skilled and semi-skilled workers, retirees, "cradle" Orthodox Christians, and "converts" who have come to the Orthodox Church as adults. I interviewed men and women active in Orthodox parishes and a wide range of GOARCH institutions. Some of these interviewees insist on the primacy of Greek identity in practicing their faith and in forming parish practices while others are working towards Pan-Orthodox unity. Men and women who adhere to the Elder's teachings and those who reject his beliefs and claims were interviewed. This study includes interviews among the parents who have adult children living in one of Elder Ephraim's monastic communities. These parents and families have lost contact with their offspring altogether or have minimal contact.[14]

This study extensively draws on materials and field observations collected in parishes located in the Greek Orthodox Metropolis of Chicago. Several parishes in the Metropolis are under the direction of clergy followers of Elder Ephraim. Parish fragmentation and significant decline have resulted as the priests introduced Elder Ephraim's teachings and carried out the Elder's practices in their

---

12 Frances Kostarelos, *Religious Pluralism, Fundamentalism, and Contested Identities in North American Orthodox Religious Life: The Case of the Greek Orthodox Church in North America* (Orthodox Christian Laity. Occasional Paper Series 8), West Palm Beach/FL 2018.

13 In 2016, the Orthodox Christian Studies Center at Fordham University in New York sponsored a conference focused on tradition and fundamentalism in the Roman Catholic and Orthodox Church. See Aristotle Papanikolaou/George E. Demacopoulos (eds), *Fundamentalism or Tradition: Christianity after Secularism*, New York 2020. In 2018, the Volos Academy for Theological Studies (Greece), along with several other Orthodox institutes and academies, sponsored a conference on fundamentalism in the Orthodox Church in Belgrade (Serbia). A publication of selected papers from this conference is forthcoming.

14 I am thankful to many individuals interviewed for this study. I have learned a great deal about the meaningful place of beliefs and practices enlivened in parishes across the Midwest. From these discussions, I have gained insights concerning the place of parish life and the Orthodox faith in shaping personal and collective identities in a religious heritage cherished by many interviewed for this study. I am solely responsible for findings and interpretation in this account.

parish communities. The analysis below also draws on websites hosted by groups who promote Elder Ephraim and those who oppose him.

As a follow up to interviews and parish fieldwork, I visited a female monastery in the Midwest founded by Elder Ephraim and discussed by several interviewees. Over two-hundred and fifty people were in attendance on the Sunday morning I visited the monastery. Families with small children, middle-age couples, young adults, and seniors participated in the service that morning. Women and men separated as they entered. The liturgy was entirely in Greek. Several individuals, including children, took communion. Five families held memorial services that morning. After the liturgy, the crowd headed to the dining hall for fellowship. An imposing black and white portrait of Elder Ephraim was mounted on a wall leading to the dining hall and adjacent bookstore. In the dining hall, they served coffee, pastries, and distributed the koliva, a dish prepared with boiled wheat and other ingredients,[15] used in Eastern Orthodox liturgies commemorating the dead. While koliva were distributed that morning, I sat next to a woman who held her husband's memorial at the monastery. She, along with her adult children, explained that the family preferred attending the monastery. In her experience, the local parish she attends is run by economic and social groups who look down on working class Greek immigrants like herself.[16] According to her, the nuns make her feel welcome and make it easy to hold memorial services at the monastery. She explained that one has simply to place a phone call to the monastery to request a memorial service. The nuns take care of the details related to the memorial service and social gathering following the liturgy, a custom that is an established practice in parish communities. She explained that the nuns accept a donation to the monastery for hosting the memorial service. The donation is a private matter and handed to a nun at the end of the fellowship. She explained that her family finds the memorial service at the monastery meaningful and comforting as the nuns have a blessing from Elder Ephraim. Her adult children were present as she explained their preference to have the memorial service at the monastery. They praised the nuns and spoke highly of their experiences at the monastery.

After the morning service, several individuals went to the "Quick Hear Chapel" to meet with the abbess. This building includes a small gift shop, a chapel and private waiting rooms. I saw a room that matched descriptions given by interviewees as the place where they waited for several hours with the hope of

---

15 For a discussion of koliva recipes and related prayers, Scripture readings, and meanings encoded in the enactment of memorial services, see URL: https://www.goarch.org/-/koliva [20.10.2018].

16 For a discussion of social class identity distinctions and boundaries in Greek American religious institutions, see Victor Roudometof/Anna Karpathakis, "Greek Americans and Transnationalism", in Paul Kennedy/Victor Roudometof (eds), *Communities across Borders: New Immigrants and Transnational Cultures*, London 2002, 41–54.

seeing their daughter, relative, former girlfriend, or friend who had joined the monastery. In the gift shop, nuns sold breads, eggs, egg noodles, spinach pies, and pastries. Incense, censors, candles, and icons used in homes for personal devotion were also available for purchase. Elder Ephraim's books were available for purchase along with biographies of Orthodox spiritual fathers and mothers.

The expansive monastery grounds were well maintained and included a paved parking lot that can accommodate over two hundred cars. Behind the main chapel, there were several small cabins. As I approached the cabins, dogs tied down with chains appeared making it clear that visitors were not allowed in this area. I noted security cameras throughout the property, including inside the "Quick Hear Chapel" and hallways leading to the waiting room. As I left the monastery that morning, the nuns and the priest who offered the liturgy were with a family in the cemetery holding a graveside prayer service. Clergy and laity interviewed for this study disagree with the enactments of sacraments – baptisms, confessions, holy unctions, and funerals – conducted routinely in Elder Ephraim's monasteries. Conducting the sacraments at the monastery – so the argument – undermines the ministry of local priests, diminishes the place of local parish communities, and limits laity roles in parish life and leadership. Several interviewees indicated that enacting sacraments on monastery grounds is a breach of the *General Regulations of the Establishment and Operations of Holy Monasteries in the Greek Orthodox Archdiocese of America*.

Elder Ephraim's Calling and Teachings

Biographical information on Elder Ephraim is scant and found in various sources.[17] Elder Ephraim was born in Volos, Greece, in 1927. His Greek Orthodox mother, described as God-fearing and pious, raised him in the Orthodox tradition. His yearning to pursue a spiritual calling began when he was fourteen years old. At the age of nineteen, he joined Mount Athos. The path to living an Orthodox Christian monastic calling requires leaving worldly desires, family, and friends behind. It requires the support of a monastic community and the supervision of a spiritually gifted elder. It calls for obedience and subservience to the spiritual elder and a way of life regulated by austere routines and rules defined by the elder and the monastic community. Elder Ephraim's calling and extraordinary abilities were discerned and developed by his spiritual father, Elder Joseph the hesychast on Mount Athos. Elder Joseph first recognised Elder Ephraim's special spiritual

17 For biographical information on Elder Ephraim, see Ephraim, *My Elder, Joseph the Hesychast*, Florence/AZ 2013; Ephraim, *Counsels from the Holy Mountain: Selected from the Letters and Homilies of Elder Ephraim*, Florence/AZ 1999; Krindatch, *Atlas* (as n. 4). See also "Elder Ephraim of Philotheou, Arizona Turns 91 (+VIDEO)", *OrthoChristian.Com*, 03.07.2018, URL: http://orthochristian.com/114115.html [20.08.2018].

qualities in his dreams. Elder Joseph and the Mount Athos monastic communities shaped Elder Ephraim's temperament and worldview. Elder Joseph's teachings and life on Mount Athos required seclusion and tempering the body and mind by fasting, all-night vigils, and incessant recitation of the Jesus Prayer: *Lord Jesus Christ, Son of God, have mercy on me a sinner.* Elder Ephraim proved gifted in his prayer life and capacity to embrace the strict rules that denied the body and disciplined the mind to obey God's will. He became the Abbott of Philotheou, one of the twenty monastic communities on Mount Athos. Elder Ephraim's formal education ended at the elementary school he attended in Greece. His authority and legitimacy to function as a spiritual guide are rooted entirely in his claim to God-given gifts discerned and fostered by Elder Joseph and the monastic communities of Mount Athos.

The social roles of spiritual elders and spiritual children are long-standing in the Orthodox Church across cultures and regions.[18] Elders are believed to have superior spiritual abilities that allow them to discern the will of God and the devil in human and worldly affairs by virtue of their God-given charisma and commitment to an ascetic life tempered by renouncing worldly concerns, fasting, unending prayer, and hesychia. Elder Ephraim claimed that he had spiritual children throughout Greece and the Greek diaspora. In the 1980s, he became ill and was supported by his Greek Canadian spiritual children to seek medical care in Canada. During his stay in Canada and travels to the United States, he began to despair over errant beliefs and practices he observed in Greek Orthodox Church life. He viewed the illness that brought him to North America, his recovery, and his contact with a wayward Orthodox Church as God's call to establish monasteries to bring the Orthodox Church in North America back on the right path.

Elder Ephraim's worldview and teachings are presented in two texts published by the Fathers of Saint Anthony's Monastery: *The Counsels from the Holy Mountain* and *The Departure of the Soul*.[19] The "Holy Mountain" in the title refers to Mount Athos, conceived as a sacred Orthodox territory by Elder Ephraim and his followers. Both texts are comprised of collections of Elder Ephraim's letters and homilies addressed to his spiritual children. Elder Ephraim boldly proclaims that those who fail to follow his instructions will lose their souls to the devil and suffer eternity in hell. According to Elder Ephraim, hesychia is the path to *theosis* or unity with God:

---

18 For a discussion of the history and culture of charismatic spiritual elders in the Orthodox experience in Russian and wider Orthodox contexts, see Irina Paert, *Spiritual Elders: Charisma and Tradition in Russian Orthodoxy*, DeKalb/IL 2010.

19 Ephraim, *Counsels* (as n. 17); Nikolaos S. Hatzinikolaou, *The Departure of the Soul according to the Teaching of the Orthodox Church: A Patristic Anthology*, Florence/AZ 2017.

> Hesychia is the ascetical practice of noetic stillness linked to watchfulness and deepened by the unceasing Jesus prayer. Hesychia is an undisturbed nous and a heart with peace, freed from thoughts, passions, and from the influences of the environment. It is dwelling in God. The only way for man to achieve theosis is through hesychia. External stillness can help one achieve hesychia. Hesychia can also mean noetic stillness itself.[20]

His teachings, beliefs, austere bodily practices, and instructions to purge the mind of impure thoughts by confessing to a spiritual father are "spiritual tools" a person must use in hope of salvation. Elder Ephraim paints a picture of evil emanating from the devil's hold over persons. The devil is ever-present and waging spiritual warfare. The devil's aim is to capture the human soul and commit it to hell for eternity. An impure mind and body are afflictions imposed by the devil to ruin a person. Purity is achieved by living a chaste and humble life in fear and obedience to God. Sexual relations are limited to married couples and only for the purpose of having children. Prayer, vigils, confession to a spiritual father, and repentance are spiritual practices required of persons seeking to save their soul. Spiritual fathers assign punishment for disobeying God: one case included whipping oneself with a cord for "dirty" thoughts. As is to be expected, Elder Ephraim condemns homosexuality.

The soul, according to his teachings, is judged on its way to heaven in hope of unification (theosis) with God. When a person dies, the soul is judged as it ascends towards heaven. On death and the soul's journey Elder Ephraim states:

> At the extremely difficult and exceedingly grievous hour of death, there is no one to help a person except his works. In fact, no one except God. If we serve Him, we shall have an almighty helper and protector at the fearful and deadly separation of our soul and body. What a struggle the soul has as it is separated from the body! Keep this struggle constantly in mind: think and note that we also have to pass the aerial *toll-houses* which impede souls from ascending as they present the deeds of our life in order to obstruct our souls' ascent and drag them down into Hades. Then we must bear in mind that we also have to face a tribunal. And alas, what a tribunal! Saying, "I have sinned" and "forgive me, the sinner," is not effective then, for every mouth shall be silenced with no excuse.[21]

To meet the harsh judgment that awaits the soul, humans must confess their sins to a spiritual father/mother, preferably a monk or nun. Elder Ephraim and confessors under his direction ask questions about sexual relations and habits during confession. The confessors are direct and want explicit details about the person's sexual activities. The inquiry into sexual behaviour during confession is unexpected, judgemental, unforgiving, and disarming. Elder Ephraim's worldview and teachings embody a formula for salvation that requires strict adherence to spiritual practices, renouncing worldly concerns, shunning fellow

---

20 Ephraim, *Counsels* (as n. 17), 426.
21 Ephraim, *Counsels* (as n. 17), 71.

parishioners, friends, parents, siblings, and spouses who do not follow the Orthodox spiritual formulations framed by him.

In the *Call from the Holy Mountain*, he is critical of the Ecumenical Patriarch and ecumenical dialogue. His clergy followers in parish settings speak against Protestants, Catholics, and Muslims from the pulpit. Greek Orthodox priests who adhere to Elder Ephraim's beliefs are critical and dismissive of Greek Orthodox Christians who resist the Elder's teachings and practices.

Believers argue that elders who have spiritual qualities rooted in the spiritual undertaking of hesychia are superior to priests and bishops. According to believers, gifted elders are extraordinary, rare, and have superior abilities while priests, bishops, and patriarchs are limited in their spiritual development, as they must wrestle with worldly matters. In Elder Ephraim's cultural schema, formal theological schooling has no bearing on spiritual development, salvation, and theosis. Elders, monks, and nuns are ideal types who embody otherworldly qualities and serve as exemplars for ordinary Orthodox Christians seeking spiritual development with the ultimate aim of theosis or unification with God.

Elder Ephraim's monasteries attract cradle and convert Orthodox Christians from across the globe.[22] He attracts young urban professionals, adult and young adult converts from varied Christian denominations, wealthy entrepreneurs, skilled and semi-skilled workers, stay at home mothers, retirees, and seminarians. His followers refer to him as a saint who has a gift from God to work miracles, heal the sick, and provide instruction to guard the soul. His spiritual abilities include prophetic insight into the devil's agency in claiming human souls. Elder Ephraim and the monks and nuns working in his institutions are viewed within his group as men and women who have extraordinary spiritual powers to extricate the devil from a person's mind and body by prescribing spiritual techniques that require bodily disciplines that deny the body and control the mind. There is a settlement near Saint Anthony's established by Orthodox Christians and the monastery serves as their spiritual home. These individuals and families express a desire to live closely under the spiritual care of Elder Ephraim.

At first appearance, Ephraim's monasteries were welcomed and viewed as institutions that would enrich the spiritual lives of Orthodox Christians in North America. In the eyes of his followers, the monasteries filled a spiritual void in North American Orthodox life. Believers seek Elder Ephraim for confession, intercessory prayer, and spiritual blessings. They look to him to cure disease and mend broken relationships. In the eyes of his followers, Elder Ephraim embodies supernatural abilities resulting from his spiritual formation on Mount Athos and the instruction and blessing he received from Elder Joseph. Elder Ephraim's reach

22 For a discussion of Orthodox Christian convert spiritual beliefs and practices, see Amy Slagle, *The Eastern Church in the Spiritual Marketplace: American Conversions to Orthodox Christianity*, DeKalb/IL 2012; Phillip LeMasters, *The Forgotten Faith: Ancient Insights for Contemporary Believers from Eastern Christianity*, Eugene/OR 2014.

into parish life has given way to questions about his legitimacy and actions on the part of the laity to remove him and bring the monasteries' operations in line with acceptable standards that do not encroach on parishes and private individual matters and relations.

Elder Ephraim is a pivotal and polarising figure. His teachings have been unevenly received among GOARCH laity and clergy. According to some, his practices are excessive and inappropriate for ordinary Orthodox Christians. Some call him a saint and spiritual healer of soul and body. Others call him a dangerous cult figure, an impostor, and religious fundamentalist. In some GOARCH parishes, his teachings are welcomed as safeguards against encroaching pluralism undermining true beliefs and practices that define the Orthodox tradition. Other parishes reject his teachings and authority. In the section that follows, I discuss the disruptive impact on parish life and lived experiences of Orthodox Christians resulting from Elder Ephraim's teachings. In the concluding section, I discuss the lay groups who oppose him and the concomitant transformations in laity dispositions towards challenging GOARCH leaders who have failed to discredit Elder Ephraim and his following.

Elder Ephraim and Changing Parish Culture

The introduction of Elder Ephraim's beliefs and practices in parish institutions have resulted in fragmentation and significant parish decline. Greek Orthodox Christians in North America primarily engage and practice their faith in parish communities. There are about five hundred GOARCH parishes in North America concentrated in global hubs including Chicago, Los Angeles, Boston, New York, Atlanta, San Francisco, and Detroit and widely spread throughout the Unites States. Orthodox parishes in the Unites States are voluntary associations. Parish routines and community life depend on the interests, abilities, and financial support provided by members. For Greek Orthodox Christians the parish has served as a spiritual home and a prized community centre. Most parishes include halls for community events and meetings. Some parishes have classrooms for Sunday school and Greek language and culture classes.

For this study, I have focused on three GOARCH parishes that have experienced changes in liturgical and community life under the direction of GOARCH priests who have carried Elder Ephraim's teachings into the parish community.[23] Greek immigrant settlers founded two of these parishes in urban and suburban settings in the 1900s. The two urban parishes experienced

23 While the focus for participant observation research was primarily conducted in three parishes, interviews have been conducted among GOARCH parishioners across the US and Canada for this study. Interviewees observed clergy behavioural patterns and related changes in the three parishes, which I discuss in this account of GOARCH parish culture.

significant decline in the 1970s resulting from race discrimination and white flight.[24] In the 1990s, both parishes supported by American-born, middle-class members improved and expanded the church buildings to add capacity for community programming. The neighbourhoods surrounding these parishes were undergoing gentrification and the parish leaders envisioned changes that would serve urban young professionals and their families settling in the area. The vision included expanding Greek educational and cultural programming that would attract young adults and families with small children. One of the urban parishes added a community centre. The other refurbished a hall, expanded the kitchen, and remodelled the church office. Both parishes served approximately 350 members by 2000. The suburban church was expansive from the beginning to accommodate the large numbers of Greek immigrants who were moving from the city to the suburbs; the sanctuary included a large choir loft, fellowship hall, kitchen, gym, and ample parking spaces for what developed into a vibrant parish of nearly 800 members.

All three parishes experienced fragmentation and significant memberships decline under the direction of priests who introduced beliefs and practices informed by Elder Ephraim's teachings. Many individuals who left were active on church committees and boards. Several taught Sunday school, sang in the choir, and participated in fund-raising campaigns. Several individuals were intergenerational parish members with no thought of ever leaving their parish community. One interviewed woman in her seventies was married in the suburban parish. Her three children and two grandchildren were baptised in this parish. She sang in the choir, attended weekly events and Sunday liturgy with her husband, who served on the parish council, but then left the parish. Her family along with several others from her generation also left the parish when the choir was disbanded, and homilies and practices informed by Elder Ephraim's teachings became the new norm in the parish. At the time of the interview, she and her husband were visiting other Orthodox Churches like "a pair of lost souls", as she put it, looking for a new spiritual home and parish community.

The priests in these parishes used the altar, the pulpit, confession, funerals, and memorial services to impart Elder Ephraim's worldview. Their message, informed by the teachings of Elder Ephraim, transformed religious practices and redefined parish community activities, diminishing the role and voices of the laity in operating church affairs. Priests disciplined altar servers and their assistant priest who did not adhere to Elder Ephraim's teachings during services. These priests have no misgivings about openly humiliating parishioners who do not

24 I have discussed the impact and lasting influence of race discrimination and white flight in the development of GOARCH parish culture in Frances Kostarelos, "Eastern Orthodox Christian Churches in North America: Continuity and Change in the Twenty-First Century", in Douglas A. Sweeney/Charles Hambrick-Stowe (eds), *Holding on to the Faith: Confessional Traditions and American Christianity*, Lanham/MD 2008, 172–186.

comply with changes required to meet Elder Ephraim's worldview and vision for personal conduct during the liturgy. The priests used the homily to impart Elder Ephraim's message of death, judgment, aerial tollhouses, punishment, and good works as instructed by a spiritual elder. The priests in these three parishes insisted on confession to a spiritual father or mother at the local monastery or with them. Individuals who had not participated in confession were denied communion. Confession was used to shame, humiliate, and subordinate individuals in the hands of the spiritual fathers, spiritual mothers or priests approved by the parish priest. These priests articulated intolerance towards those who did not follow the new rules for parish worship. Messages from the pulpit include prejudice towards non-Orthodox Christians, Jews and Muslims. Parish members who did not comply with the new rules were scorned and shunned. Inter-faith couples married in the parish and seeking to raise their children in the parish community were made to feel uncomfortable and often shunned. After all, approximately sixty percent of GOARCH marriages are interfaith, thus challenging clergy to minister to couples and families that encompass cultural and religious beliefs and practices.[25]

Life-long Orthodox Christian LGBTQ active in these parishes were targeted and rejected. In one case, two men who were active in parish life on boards and committees were denied communion and shunned. Non-Orthodox Christians were allowed to observe church services, but rules varied on where they could stand and what they could do during the service. Rules for venerating icons for non-Orthodox Christians vary in these parishes and were made known as the service unfolded by ushers who have been instructed by the priest. Non-Orthodox Christians were instructed to contact the parish priest to learn about the Orthodox faith. From the pulpit, women were reminded of their subordinate role in family and church life. Women were told to be obedient to their husbands, brothers, spiritual fathers or mothers, and to the parish priest. During confession, men and women were questioned about their sexual practices and guided to end sexual relations if they were beyond their childbearing years. Changes in parish life included disbanding established choirs and thus silencing the voices of women during liturgy. One priest took over the Sunday school programme and purged elements of popular culture from classroom activities. The parish priest dismissed teachers who challenged removing popular cultural elements from the programme. The majority of Sunday school teachers in these parishes were female. Two women who had taught Sunday school in the parish for twenty years had to comfort children who were yelled at by the parish priest for drawings that included figures featuring public television children programmes. In these parishes, Valentine's Day, Halloween parties, and other long-standing parish community events that included popular cultural themes were discontinued.

---

25 For GOARCH perspectives and approaches to interfaith marriage, see URL: http://www.goarch.org/archdiocese/departments/marriage/interfaith [19.02.2019].

In all three parishes, dress codes and rules for conduct during liturgical services also changed. Women and girls were no longer allowed to wear slacks. Women and girls were asked to wear long skirts or dresses, flat shoes, shirts that cover the neck and arms, and scarves. While not all women adhered to the new dress code, an atmosphere of judgment prevailed, and the clergy used the homily to frame the preferred female dress codes pleasing to God. Men and boys were required to wear long-sleeved shirts and slacks. They were not allowed to grow long hair or beards, the bodily markers of male novices exploring a monastic calling, monks, and ordained clergy. Bodily practices and veneration of icons also changed to include prostrations expressed by touching the floor with the right hand three times before kissing the icon. Between 2010 and 2013 all three parishes lost over half of the members. One of the three parishes was left with 85 members and struggled to sustain operations. By 2006, Orthodox Christians who had come into contact with Elder Ephraim's teachings questioned his otherworldly claims, miracle-working abilities, and intolerance. Alarmed by homilies that spoke of aerial tollhouses, the virtues of dying from cancer, an unforgiving God with no love or mercy for the disobedient, contempt and condemnation of non-Orthodox people, shunning Orthodox Christians who do not follow Elder Ephraim's beliefs and practices, attacks on Patriarch Bartholomew and his embrace of Pope Francis and wider work on behalf of ecumenical dialogue, the obsession with sexual behaviour during confession, demanding that married couples live like brother and sister after the children are born, refusing to offer communion to individuals who had not gone to confession, and denying LGBTQ Orthodox Christians communion resulted in countless individuals and families leaving these parishes. People who left include members of the parish council, parish council presidents, Sunday school teachers, and choir directors. Many of these individuals served on church national boards and offices. These individuals had long-standing parish commitments, friendships, and memories forged over several generations. They expected to live as members of the parish community until they died. Leaving their parish homes was a difficult and emotionally painful decision. After leaving the parish, many were without a church, some sought a new parish in the GOARCH or another Orthodox jurisdiction.

Laity and Church Leader Responses to Elder Ephraim

Challenges to Elder Ephraim's teachings and institutions have come from college educated men and women with advanced degrees in law, education, or medicine. Among those who oppose Elder Ephraim are successful entrepreneurs and local politicians. Leaders in the effort to address Elder Ephraim's encroachments into parish life and the lived experiences of Orthodox Christians are long standing members of parish communities. They have served on parish councils and in leadership positions in national GOARCH organisations. They have been members of the choir and served as Sunday school teachers. They are proud of their Greek heritage and invested in Greek institutions, including the Greek Orthodox Church in the United States. They are also fully integrated in American society, professionally successful, and upwardly mobile. As a group, their aim is to see the Orthodox Church maintain its Greek heritage and rich liturgical and community life in a plural society. They seek to build a church that allows for unity and dialogue among Orthodox jurisdictions and meaningful engagement with other people from across the American plural religious landscape. They reject the religious enclave mentality imposed by priests following Elder Ephraim in their parish communities. They also reject what they view as arcane practices that subvert individual choice and free will. They cannot accept religious intolerance in their parish community.

As a first step, parish leaders contacted their local bishop to address beliefs about aerial tollhouses, the practice of using confession to judge and demean people, the public humiliation of altar servers and assistant priests, as well as the shunning and bullying that was unfurling in the parish resulting from the parish priest's divisive messages and practices. These church leaders expected that the bishop would agree that the beliefs and behaviours the priests were spreading in the parish from the altar and pulpit were unacceptable and would intervene on behalf of people who were harmed. They expected the bishop to discipline and/or remove the priest. However, the local bishop did not see a problem, dismissed the claims, and ended the meeting with no acknowledgment of wrongdoing on the part of the priest. In each of the three parishes, the local bishop allowed priests to revise liturgical and sacramental practices, religious education, and community events in light of Elder Ephraim's teachings.

As reports of spiritual abuses and parish fragmentations under the direction of clergy carriers of Elder Ephraim's teachings spread, concerned laity in 2010 persuaded Archbishop Demetrios to authorise a Monastery Review Committee (MRC) to investigate Elder Ephraim's monasteries. The MRC conducted interviews among individuals and families who had been impacted by Elder Ephraim's teachings and institutions. The investigation was national in scope and included interviews with over 100 individuals. The MRC group completed the investigation and submitted a report to the Archbishop in 2011. The report findings have not been disseminated as promised to the families who participated in the study, and the Archbishop did not address the findings collected by the team he commissioned. In this contentious climate, GOARCH leaders continued to endorse Elder Ephraim and his monasteries. Links to his monasteries are thus listed on the GOARCH website[26] along with an article that explains the place of

26 For a list of monasteries with links that provide information for visitors, see URL: https://www.goarch.org/archdiocese/monasteries [19.02.2019].

monasteries in Orthodox Christians life.[27] Several individuals interviewed for this study travelled to Istanbul to meet with Patriarch Bartholomew to discuss the harm to individuals, the break-up of families, and the fragmentation of parish communities resulting from Elder Ephraim's teachings in parish communities. Patriarch Bartholomew was sympathetic to their concerns but placed the burden on GOARCH bishops to address the problem.

Lay leaders approached the faculty at Hellenic College and Holy Cross Greek Orthodox Seminary (HCHC) located in Brookline, Massachusetts, to discuss Elder Ephraim and to ask the faculty to address the spiritual claims and beliefs articulated by Elder Ephraim and his disciples. HCHC faculty did not respond to the allegations of spiritual abuse or challenge the spiritual authority and claims made by the Elder and his disciples in their exchanges with the laity who travelled to the seminary. The matter of Elder Ephraim was a subject for an HCHC campus-wide debate organised by seminary students and faculty. Seminary students participating in the debate and interviewed for this study reported a large turnout among students and faculty for this campus debate. At the end of the debate, the seminary President announced that both sides had made plausible arguments concerning Elder Ephraim's spiritual authority and claims.

Lay groups have launched websites to educate Orthodox Christians about Elder Ephraim, his teachings, and the damaging impact on unsuspecting individuals and parishes. Two web sites directly address the matter of Elder Ephraim: *Go Truth Reform*, and *We Are Orthodox*. The mission of *Go Truth Reform* is as follows:

> We Greek Orthodox Christians of the Metropolis of Chicago will no longer accept the conditions that have spread and caused irreparable harm to our Faith. We are of the opinion that our current Hierarchs of the Metropolis of Chicago are complicit in allowing a cancerous cult to permeate the theology of our church. Therefore, we will focus the efforts and attention of our members to expose inappropriate teachings, practices and customs as they concern our Faith.[28]

We Are Orthodox frames their purpose, vision of problem, and church leadership as follows:

---

27 For a discussion of the place of monasticism in Orthodox history and spiritual formation, see URL: https://www.goarch.org/ourfaith/monasticism [19.02.2019].

28 For a discussion of the activities that this group has undertaken to challenge Elder Ephraim and his following, see URL: http://gotruthreform.org [19.02.2019]. Several interviewees indicated that articles posted on "Go Truth Reform" proved invaluable in helping them understand changes taking place in their parish communities under the leadership of priests who were transforming their parish routines in the light of Ephraim's teachings. Many contacted the "Go Truth Reform" editors to tell their stories and share concerns for the future of their parish communities.

> We are Orthodox Christians. We have concerns. We are not going away.
>
> We love our Church. We are proud and grateful to the Lord for His holy Church. We affirm every line of the Nicaean-Constantinopolitan Creed. We promote our Church's beliefs: sacraments, scripture, holy tradition, canons, parish life, monastic life. We respect, love, and support our leaders: our beloved Patriarch, Metropolitans, Bishops, Priests, and Monastics. And we also try to have a sense of self respect for the gift of who we are as well: respectable laypeople of the Body of Christ.
>
> We do not expect our leaders to be perfect. We realize that we are not perfect either. The lessons we glean from Saint Peter and Saint Paul are important. In spite of their differences, they were able to build the Body of Christ. Peter insisted on emphasizing certain things that Paul proved to be a stumbling block for bringing people to the fold. We look up to these saints and ask for their guidance, together with the prayers of the Holy Virgin Mother, that we may build the Church of Christ, together. We have logic and reason at our disposal too. These are God given attributes that we believe God wants us to utilize in a respectable manner. We will do that.
>
> There is a growing fundamentalist movement in the Greek Orthodox Archdiocese that we vehemently object to. This has nothing to do with any of our ethnic backgrounds. But it has everything to do with a type of monasticism that is spreading extreme fundamentalism which is affecting clergy and laity alike. In many reported cases, it is *militant*. This is also affecting other Orthodox jurisdictions. We are not monastics. We have nothing against monasticism. But the fact of the matter is that mimicking a monk is not a litmus test for how sincere our commitment to our Faith is.
>
> The problem is that there are those in the Church who insist on promoting the idea that holiness only resides within monastic circles. This undercuts the very nature of the Church and her sacramental life. We honour and respect monasticism as *another* way of life, but *it* is not the Church. We all are. *Together. There is no exclusivity.* We are not aristocratic elitists.[29]

Both groups seek to educate Orthodox Christians about Elder Ephraim's impact on families, individuals, clergy, and parishes. Many interviewees for this study identified these sites as useful resources for grappling with changes they have witnessed in their parish communities and among family and friends who have become followers of Elder Ephraim's teachings.

Conclusion

Elder Ephraim succeeded in planting a culture of spiritual eldership and monastic communities that enjoy wide appeal and support from Orthodox Christians across jurisdictions in the United States. Challenges from clergy and laity to expose Elder Ephraim's impact on individuals, families, and institutions have revealed

29 For further discussion of the challenge framed by this group, see URL: http://weareorthodox.com [19.02.2019].

weaknesses in GOARCH structures. Customary prohibitions against criticising GOARCH institutions and leaders no longer hold. Discussions about the quality of the education seminarians received at HCHC abound as most of the clergy carriers of Elder Ephraim's teachings, including the three I researched extensively, are graduates of HCHC. Incumbent bishops who have dismissed laity concerns and allowed the spread of Ephraim's teachings and his monasteries have lost the confidence of laity. In this account, we have seen that there are contested voices and strands seeking to define GOARCH parish and institutional purpose and identity in a plural American society. Attention has been directed to Elder Ephraim who along with his following in a few short years spread a system of beliefs and practices that some embrace and others find unacceptable.

GOARCH leaders can no longer count on ethnocentrism, ethnically separated neighbourhoods, endogamy, and a shared understanding of Greek tradition to control parishes and parishioner lived experiences. Elder Ephraim's teachings and institutions hinder discussion of expanding the roles of women in the church, silence and cast out LGBTQ Orthodox Christians,[30] and discourage inter-faith couples. There is a great deal of bitterness, frustration, and disbelief in the body of Orthodox Christians who have been displaced from the parish communities with the spread of Elder Ephraim's teachings. There are no signs that the testimony of hundreds who have shared their stories of abuse and misconduct from Elder Ephraim and his disciples, as well as reported violations of the GOARCH regulations are resulting in systematic examination from church leaders. While Elder Ephraim was widely esteemed, many Orthodox Christians challenge his authority as they raise questions about paternalism, sexism, and homophobia in the Orthodox Church. Elder Ephraim's opponents, following the example of inclusive Christian bodies in the United States and beyond, seek an Orthodox Church that will expand roles for women in the church, welcome LGBTQ Christians, and include people from all races and nations. GOARCH clergy leaders respond by asserting the primacy of males in clergy and leadership roles in church tradition and history. The response is acceptable for some but not all women. LGBTQ Orthodox Christians are seeking an open and inclusive place in the Orthodox Church as social norms have changed and the legal system protects the civil rights of gay, lesbian, and transgender individuals. The Assembly of Canonical Orthodox Bishops of the United States of America (formerly SCOBA) was quick to disagree with the landmark United States Supreme Court decision on 26 June 2015 Obergefell v. Hodges making same-sex marriage legal in all 50 States. In the July/August 2015 issue of *The Orthodox Observer*, the Assembly of Canonical Orthodox Bishops called the decision,

30 For a discussion of Orthodox Christian LGBTQ community perspectives on inclusion in the church, see the following websites: www.axios.org, www.orthodoxandgay.com, and www.inclusiveorthodoxy.org.

sustained by the Fourteenth Amendment of the Constitution by the Supreme Court, an "invented" constitutional right.

In sum, there are multiple and contested socio-cultural strands, voices, and discourses shaping the future of GOARCH with no easy answers for church leaders and laity seeking to define the Orthodox Christian identity and purpose in plural America. All this is also indicative of the major changes that are taking place within American society and culture and of the challenges that American Orthodoxy is currently facing under the influence of growing liberalism, pluralism, and individualism. Elder Ephraim and his adherents have tried to cope with such challenges through a systematic re-traditionalisation of the Orthodox way of life, a development that has caused serious deep cleavages in several Orthodox communities across the US. It remains to be seen how the movement initiated by Elder Ephraim will operate in the future and how the vacuum left by his death in 2019 will be filled. Needless to say, his charisma, calibre, and appeal are not easy to replace, and this may have a catalytic influence upon the future course of the entire movement.

The Spirituality of Greek Orthodox Women in America: "You have to question…, but you also have to find answers that bring you peace with God and with yourself"

Anna Karpathakis

> "Just keep in mind that there are very few true Greek atheists. Many Greek men and women may be angry with the church and many may not go to church except the holidays, but they still believe in God and call on God. Greeks talk with God every day."
> Eleni, 68

> "Greeks may not show up in church often, but they always look for God beside them."
> Grace, 35

Greek immigrants' and Greek Americans' relations with their community's institutions have been in flux over the past twenty years I have been interviewing members of this community. While Greek society and politics and the perceived roles that the Church of Greece and the Greek Orthodox Archdiocese were the background against which the immigrants and their American-born children saw and evaluated the church through the decades of the 1970s-1990s, the changing American political and spiritual landscapes, as well as the immigrant and ethnic community themselves are acquiring greater significance regarding how immigrants and their American-born children and grandchildren now see and evaluate the Greek Orthodox Church in America. This is a reflection of the fact that the community is no longer a community of freshly arrived immigrants. Greek immigration to the U.S. in the post-1965 period peaked in the mid-1970s, which means that the majority of the once recent immigrants have now been living in the U.S. for nearly forty years and their Greek or American-born children are adults with children of their own. The frames of reference for these latter is no longer Greek, but rather American society.

In addition to this, the descendants of the immigrants of the earlier decades of the twentieth century are now third or fourth generation American born with little, if any, connections and contact with Greece. Overall, immigrants and the American-born faithful are increasingly looking to American politics, culture and spiritual trends/phenomena in addition to those of the ethnic community in orienting and evaluating their relations with the Greek Orthodox Church in America. While at one time the Greek Orthodox Church in the U.S. was evaluated against the backdrop of Greek society, politics and history, the current trend is that the Greek Orthodox Church in the U.S. and the faithful's relations to the church are evaluated against the backdrop of the politics and events of the American Greek ethnic and religious community. On an even more micro-social level of the individual, the faithful are evaluating their relations to the Greek Orthodox Church and even their own religious participation against the backdrop of parish politics, culture and events.[1]

This chapter analyses interviews that were carried out as part of a larger project on Greek immigrant and Greek American relations to the home society and Greek immigrant organisations and community institutions. My interests were on how community, national and global politics impact the immigrants' and their American- born children's and grandchildren's relations with the home society institutions, as well as their relations with immigrant and ethnic community institutions and the Greek Orthodox Archdiocese of America (GOARCH) in the United States.

On the one hand, the secular home society region-based associations immigrants formed upon their arrival are no longer as active, but have rather been replaced by national level organisations, whose officers are overwhelmingly among the well-educated American-born children and, to a lesser extent, grandchildren of the immigrants. These are, in a sense, becoming professional ethnic associations connecting the local with the national and the international. The new local is the church parish. As the community's institutions are changing, the church is acquiring a more multi-faceted role in the community. On the one hand, the local parishes are replacing the immigrant hometown associations in terms of support for both the immigrants, the parishioners, as well as the home society during crises.[2] As the secular hometown associations lose membership and decrease their activities in the community, the local parish increases its social activities by creating a variety of men's, women's, youth and children's groups. It is on the local parish level that the faithful learn of the history of Greek Orthodoxy and by extension the history and culture of Greece and Greeks. As both men and women I interviewed over the years have expressed, to be Greek is to be Orthodox, the two identities are enmeshed in one.

This chapter analyses the interviews of one specific group of respondents: Greek Orthodox women that had left the church as young adults, only to return to active involvement in the church after several years outside. The analysis proceeds in three steps. First, I provide a glimpse into the interview situations, before a theoretical look at the American spiritual landscape places them in context. The third and by far most extensive step is the interview analysis, which covers three main aspects. These are, first, the way the women interviewed situate

1 While the current political and ecclesiological crisis in the Ukraine has in some ways led to those already active in the GOARCH parishes to strengthen their commitment to the Archdiocese and the Ecumenical Patriarchate, the Ukrainian Church crisis does not appear to have an impact on the faithful who are not as active in the church's daily life.

2 During the last few years, for example, first during Greece's financial crisis, the refugee crisis and fires in the Attica region, numerous parishes and the National Philoptochos Society (Friends of the Poor) have raised funds as well as other donations for Greece.

themselves in relation to the GOARCH. Second, there are the reasons they cite for feeling uneasy with the church, before the third part analyses their narrative in relation to their "return".

The Women

Early on in my interviews, a sub-group of women emerged: women who at a younger age had made a deliberate and conscious decision to "leave" the church and had now returned. This small group of women spoke about their disappointment with the church and the reasons they walked away from the church but were now returning to the same pews they had walked away from in their younger years.

As I read over the interviews with immigrant and American-born men and women of the past twenty plus years and remembered the "mood", it became clear that no other single issue brought forth tears and laughter, expressions of disappointment, anger and hope as issues of their relations to the church and their spiritual struggles and journeys. It is for this reason that I will allow the women to tell their stories with a minimal analysis.

Looking back at the interviews, I also realised that some of the women who were older than I was at the time and had "found [their, A.K.] way back to those pews" were "advising" me and through me other Greek and Greek American younger women about the importance of returning to the church. As one woman said, "there are very few Greek and Greek American women who don't question our church", or, "questioning is part of the journey. Greek and Greek American women are in a tough place. We have to remember that priests are only human and what is important is God". In one of the 2007 interviews, Stefania, fifteen years older than myself and a self-described "spiritual seeker", said that she had read my essay on my reflections of being a Greek Orthodox woman in a patriarchal institution: "You have to question. It is who we are. God made us each different. But you also have to find answers that bring you peace with God and with yourself."

Georgia, a 68-year-old retired social worker had just returned from her visit with a 90-year-old Greek Orthodox woman at the local hospital. She had accompanied the priest who gave Holy Communion to the woman, but Georgia visited for another two hours.

> Most Greek Orthodox women I meet have seeds of doubt, disappointment and even anger. Thomas questioned and Jesus reassured him. It's important for Greek Orthodox women to know that it's ok to question, it's better if we deal with questions and doubts, work through these and come to peace with God, because we need Him. Too many of us walk away and we shouldn't. Our church is special, the Orthodox faith is a jewel that is discovered only after scrubbing off all those layers of politics, of nasty people we meet at the pews… by politics we mean not just government, but also the

> politics in the parishes, the politics between parishioners, the clergy, the personal stuff that push us from the church and from God because there is a cry inside us that says, "no, it should not be this way". I wish all Greek Orthodox women to come to peace with God and realise that God is not who people in those pews claim He is. If only I could stand up where the priest is, look out at the women and tell them, don't walk away, work through it, just stay where you are.

Even though the women themselves use the term "leave" or "left" to describe the process of distancing themselves from the church, they also point out that this is a misnomer. Short of conversion, a Greek Orthodox cannot "leave" the church or her religious tradition. As the immigrants and American born I interviewed pointed out, to be Greek or Greek American is to be Christian Orthodox and to be Christian Orthodox (in their case) is to be Greek or Greek American; the reason they give for this is that the worship in the Greek Orthodox Church is Greek Byzantine. Greek Orthodoxy was brought to the United States by the immigrants themselves and while the majority of the local churches now celebrate the Liturgy and other worship services and sacraments (e.g., wedding, baptism) in English, there are elements of the Greek language still used in prayers and hymns.

Greek Orthodoxy is an ethno-confessional identity – one is born into both an ethnic and a religious group and is baptised while still an infant. Baptism and Chrismation signify the person's entry into the church, the body of Christ. Indeed, the way that the women describe their experiences, this is a very important lynchpin for them: No human can undo baptism, and second, historically, the Greek Orthodox Church does not excommunicate even if someone is an outspoken critic of the church's politics and policies. This enables the women to begin their personal journey of politics and spirituality in their younger years with the knowledge and faith that "God knows my heart". This indeed is a foundational assumption for the women who "left" the church either for political or ideological reasons or simply because of time constraints and pressures. These women did not interpret their "leaving" the church as "leaving" God behind them.

This chapter focuses on Greek immigrant and Greek American women; it does not consider the issues presented here within the Greek context.[3] While the majority of the interviews were done with Greek and American-born Greek Orthodox women in New York City, some were also done with women living in or growing up in different parts of the country, including Nebraska, Illinois, California, Texas, Ohio, Florida and other Eastern coast states. The ages of the women whose interviews are used for this paper range from eighteen to seventy-two. The education levels ranged from less than a high school education to PhD's

---

3 For an overview of gender relations, politics and identity issues in the Church of Greece, see Eleni Sotiriu, "'The Traditional Modern': Rethinking the Position of Women in Greek Orthodoxy", in Victor Roudometof/Vasilios N. Makrides (eds), *Orthodox Christianity in 21st Century Greece: The Role of Religion in Culture, Ethnicity and Politics*, Farnham 2010, 131–153.

and other professional degrees. Occupations varied from domestic workers and food servers to women with careers in a variety of professions.

Framing the Processes of "Distancing" and Returning: The American Spiritual Landscape

The Patriarch Athenagoras Orthodox Institute of The Graduate Theological Union at Berkeley surveyed Greek and Russian Orthodox in the U.S. and found a conservative body of faithful in relation to church life. Only four percent of those polled described themselves as "liberal" regarding their approaches to church life, approximately a quarter as "moderates", and the remaining as "conservative" or "traditional". On the question of women's ordination, only 14 percent of the Greek Orthodox laity said they would welcome such a change.[4] It should be noted that this is a survey of the affiliated and dues paying Christian Orthodox parishioners rather than the ethnic community at large, so that it does not capture precisely those women (and men) who leave the church in their teens or early twenties and do not return to it in some cases for a couple of decades. Also, the survey did not poll on politics and social justice issues so that we do not see the often deep divide accompanying the belief system of the Greek Orthodox.

Feminist epistemologies and critiques of religion question the universality and truth value of androcentric ideas and beliefs,[5] or kyriarchy/kyriocentrism.[6] For example, Kinsley points out that feminist critiques of religion often reveal two different religions in one, namely, one for men and one for women.[7] Radford Ruether argues that misogyny in religion is articulated in two assertions, namely that, women are subordinate to men in the creation of things and intended this way by God, and that humanity entered sin through woman.[8] From these basic assertions, a feminist hermeneutics of religion has arisen in which women's roles

4 Alexei Krindatch, *The Orthodox Church Today: A National Study of Parishioners and the Realities of Orthodox Parish Life in the USA*, Berkeley/CA 2008, URL: http://hartfordinstitute.org/research/OrthChurchFullReport.pdf [19.02.2019].

5 Mary Ann Stenger, "Feminist Philosophy of Religion", in Arvind Sharma (ed.), *Methodology in Religious Studies: The Interface with Women's Studies*, Albany/NY 2002, 147–178.

6 Elisabeth Schüssler Fiorenza, "Method in Women's Studies in Religion: A Critical Feminist Hermeneutics", in Arvind Sharma (ed.), *Methodology in Religious Studies: The Interface with Women's Studies*, Albany/NY 2002, 207–242.

7 David Kinsley, "Women's Studies and the History of Religions", in Arvind Sharma (ed.), *Methodology in Religious Studies: The Interface with Women's Studies*, Albany/NY 2002, 1–16.

8 Rosemary Radford Ruether, *Sexism and God-talk: Toward a Feminist Theology*, Boston 1983; eadem, "Methodologies in Women's Studies and Feminist Theology", in Arvind Sharma (ed.), *Methodology in Religious Studies: The Interface with Women's Studies*, Albany/NY 2002, 179–206.

in holy texts are re-examined from a "feminist" perspective.[9] In this endeavour, a number of research studies have been published examining the ways in which gender ideologies are integrated into the theological understandings and presentations. Kelly and Kelly, for example, found that Catholic devotions to St Philomena and our Lady of Perpetual Help in Pittsburgh in the 1930s have been interpreted by later generations as being imbued with gender ideologies that represented women in passive and secondary roles.[10]

Winter, Lummis and Strokes use the term "defect in place" to describe the Catholic and Protestant women's responses to male centred perspectives, theologies and ecclesiologies in their respective churches.[11] There are Greek Orthodox women who also "defect in place" and do not leave the church. However, unlike the Catholic and Protestant women, Greek Orthodox women do not create smaller worship and support groups with other Greek Orthodox women; rather, they either stay in the church and continue their work with the numerous volunteer groups or decide to stop attending church worship services. This chapter focuses on the women who leave the church and return to it at a later time.

The processes of Greek Orthodox women distancing themselves from the church and later returning to it is more like a "silent revolt"; the women leave the Church for a number of years, and their exit is "silent" – they simply stop attending weekly worship services. The reasons the women give for this exit are numerous, ranging from "lack of time" to more political issues arising in the church and its related groups. Greek Orthodox women do not discuss their decision to stop attending worship services with anyone, whether clergy or other women. Theirs is a silent revolt because the women do not speak about their concerns, they do not engage the clergy in a dialogue. The reason the women give is that the priests and other clergy, all men, do not understand the uniqueness of women's lives and spiritual challenges. As a result, while the clergy realise that not all the girls who attended church services and took part in the various programmes for children and teenagers, will be sitting in the pews as they grow into young adulthood, they do not understand the reasons. Often enough, as one of the women in the group said, "the priests see this as these women rejecting God. They cannot imagine that women have real concerns which are not addressed." And yet, while the women "leave" the physical structure and building

---

9 Elisabeth Schüssler Fiorenza, "We are Church – a Kindom of Priests", Keynote Speech delivered in Ottawa 22.07.2006, URL: http://www.womenpriests.org/wow/fiorenza.asp [19.02.2019]; Mara Kelly-Zukowski, "The Subversiveness of the Marginalized Women of Scripture: Models of Faith and Action for Twenty-first Century Women", *Gender Issues* 22/4 (2005) 29–42; eadem, "The Catholic Church's Restrictions on Female Participation and some Biblical Responses", *Gender Issues* 22/4 (2005) 43–55.

10 Timothy Kelly/Joseph Kelly, "Our Lady of Perpetual Help, Gender Roles and the Decline of Devotional Catholicism", *Journal of Social History* 32/1 (1998) 5–26.

11 Miriam T. Winter/Adair Lummis/Allison Stokes (eds), *Defecting in Place: Women Claiming Responsibility for their own Spiritual Lives*, New York 1995.

of the church and weekly worship services, they do not abandon or leave behind them the love and need for God and the church. Despite their years away from the pews, the women said they did not stop considering themselves Greek Orthodox, did not stop considering the Greek Orthodox Church as their church.

The Greek Orthodox women's exit as a silent revolt is reinforced even upon their return to the church. When the women do return, their concerns of years earlier have not been dealt with in the church. Rather, these concerns then become the women's own individual concerns and problems that they must spiritually work through on their own. Whether in their youth when the women decided to leave the church or in later years after their return, there is a silence, a chasm, between these women and the priests.

The women's return is much more informed theologically, spiritually, politically, and in terms of values than their exit of years earlier. It is not that the women have changed on the political spectrum; they have not become politically or socially conservative. On the contrary, some of the ideologies and values that pushed them away from the church in their earlier years have deepened with experience, wisdom, and even greater compassion, as well as theological and spiritual understanding.

Literature on women's spirituality shows a diversity of methods women faithful have used to integrate themselves into the church's or synagogues' structures and work towards more responsive and open institutional structures.[12] Research by Perl, on the other hand, found that there is a visible trend among some of the Protestant denominations with women ministers to have an overrepresentation of women who converted from Catholicism.[13] With regard to Greek Orthodox women, there is no organised or massive movement for women's ordination in the Greek Orthodox Church or Orthodox Christianity in general. A number of conferences have been held to study the role of women and especially of the deaconesses in the church, but these have also not resulted in any concrete changes. Second, while the Greek Orthodox women in the sample did speak about visiting and knowing of others who temporarily switched over to more liberal Protestant denominations, there was no indication of Greek Orthodox women converting and becoming ordained. It must be noted, however, that there is little research on Greek Orthodox women's spirituality and religious experiences in general, so that we cannot *de facto* exclude this possibility

---

12 See, for example, Elaine H. Ecklund, "Organizational Culture and Women's Leadership: A Study of Six Catholic Parishes", *Sociology of Religion* 67/1 (2006) 81–98; Katie G. Cannon, "The Positionality of Women in the African American Church Community", in Miriam T. Winter/Adair Lummis/Allison Stokes (eds), *Defecting in Place: Women Claiming Responsibility for their Own Spiritual Lives*, New York 1995, 210–216.

13 Paul Perl, "Are Former Catholic Women Over-represented among Protestant Clergy?", *Sociology of Religion* 66/4 (2005) 359–379.

Unlike their Catholic counterparts, the Greek Orthodox women do not directly confront the patriarchal structures of their church.[14] They do not gather in groups to break bread and take Holy Communion, nor has there been an organised effort for the ordination of women. The Orthodox Christian Laity's (OCL) call in the 1990s for the church to re-evaluate women's roles in the church was received with suspicion in the midst of the group's Americanisation politics.[15] Despite the call by Miriam Therese Winter (1989) for "Women Church" to become an inclusive movement of women of diverse church traditions, Greek Orthodox women do not join the movement for two reasons. First, the movement emerged out of the Catholic Church, and as a result, Greek Orthodox women feel that they cannot contribute to the movement.[16]

More than this, however, the call of "Women Church" to include women from a variety of church traditions was interpreted with great unease by the Greek Orthodox women in the sample. Elsie, 68, repeated herself excitedly: "We know what Winter called for. We also know what and who showed up and still shows up at their meetings. For Winter, it was supposed to be only Christian women, church women. Go and see for yourself how loosely defined church is. Women Church is not an option for Orthodox women." While "Women Church" was/is a Christian movement, the women in the sample who were familiar with the movement rejected the movement because of the spiritual diversity of the women attending. As Elsie continued, "Christians don't do goddess worship… some of the women there have confused issues with how an all-male clergy do not respond to women's social and spiritual needs with goddess worship… it's no place for Orthodox women".

Whether the women's understanding/interpretation of the Women Church Movement is accurate or not is not a subject matter of this chapter. The movement, from their perspective, has attracted nominal Christian women who incorporate

14 For a discussion of Catholic women, see Christel J. Manning, "Women in a Divided Church: Liberal and Conservative Catholic Women Negotiate Changing Gender Roles", *Sociology of Religion* 58/4 (1997) 375–390.

15 See for example Anna Karpathakis, "The Greek Orthodox Church and Identity Politics", in Tony Carnes/Anna Karpathakis (eds), *New York Glory: Race, Religion and Ethnicity*, New York 2001, 374–387.

16 Approximately 1,400 women gathered for the "Woman Church Speaks" Conference in Chicago in November 1983. In 1989, Miriam Therese Winter, a Catholic medical Mission Sister, called for a "Women Church", a movement of and by women who are spiritually unfulfilled in their home church. The Women Church movement does not have clear goals and guidelines other than it to be an opportunity for women to provide spiritual support for one another. The movement failed to attract women from the Orthodox and Protestant traditions. Diann L. Neu, "Women-Church on the Road to Change", in Miriam T. Winter/Adair Lummis/Allison Stokes (eds), *Defecting in Place: Women Claiming Responsibility for their own Spiritual Lives*, New York 1995, 241–247; Schüssler Fiorenza, "We are Church" (as n. 9).

non-Christian forms of worship in their spiritual lives, including goddess worship. The Greek Orthodox women in the sample reject and disagree with the assessment that neo-pagan goddess worship is truly and ultimately feminist in nature.[17] The women's perceptions of the diverse landscape of "feminist" or feminine spirituality and their refusal to distinguish between the various strands of feminist spirituality are indicative of their rejection of diverse spiritualities in their own cultural history

A small pagan polytheistic movement in Greece has been widely criticised by both the religious and secular press in Greece and the Greek American community. The ancient Greek religion and myths are still very much a part of the Greek and Greek American cultural stock and consciousness. The women are familiar with the gods and goddesses of the ancients but reject them as an undesirable form of spirituality. For, as one woman during a book club meeting said: "God freed us from the lower spirits of vengeance. Why would we want to go back to that? Why would you want to return to a place of sacrificing each time you asked for guidance or help in your life? Let's not forget Iphigenia."[18]

Greek Orthodox women have taken a somewhat different trajectory from the Catholic and Protestant women in male centred church hierarchies. While there are some commonalities between them and their other Christian and Jewish counterparts, their experiences are unique in some important respects. Like Catholic women, Greek Orthodox women do not and cannot separate themselves from the church and establish independent parishes because of the ecclesiology; each parish must have a validly ordained priest.

Greek Orthodox women have an additional disincentive to breaking away and joining other denominations, namely, their identity. The Greek Orthodox are an ethno-confessional group. Their identity is both a religious and a secular identity. Breaking away and either joining or creating another religious institution would entail a negation of this enmeshed identity, and it is not clear that, at this stage of assimilation into American society and identity formation, they are willing to do this (at least the women in the sample). Krindatch, for example, also found that ethnic heritage and identity were still important for the Greek Orthodox faithful surveyed.[19]

The women also did not join other Christian Orthodox Churches precisely because of their ethnic identity. Two of the women who relocated for work did

---

17 This argument is put forth by Rebecca Gordon, "Earthstar Magic: A Feminist Theoretical Perspective on the Way of the Witches and the Path to the Goddess", *Social Alternatives* 14/4 (1995) 9–11; Jon P. Bloch, "Countercultural Spiritualists' Perceptions of the Goddess", *Sociology of Religion* 58/2 (1997) 181–190.

18 In Greek mythology, Iphigenia was sacrificed by her father, King Agamemnon, prior to setting sail for Troy. In some versions of the myth, Iphigenia was sacrificed at Aulis, in other versions, she was rescued by Artemis.

19 Krindatch, *The Orthodox Church* (as n. 4).

attend parishes of other jurisdictions, as these were available. However, they travelled back to their home Greek Orthodox parish for the sacraments of marriage and the children's baptism. The American Orthodox Christian Churches were originally founded by immigrants arriving from a variety of countries in collaboration with the church back home; the (Russian) Orthodox Church in America attracts more converts from other Christian denominations than other jurisdictions of the Christian Orthodox in the United States.[20] The women in the sample were too aware of the politics of the numerous Christian Orthodox Churches and as an American-born woman in the sample said, "why would I want to get Russian politics involved in my spiritual life? American politics is bad enough. It's like going from the frying pan into the fire." The Greek or Greek American identity is still too important for the women in the sample, and they perceived their attendance in another Christian tradition or church as denying their cultural heritage and identity.

During my interview with Georgia at her home, her niece Effie, 23-years-old and studying for her master's degree in non-organic Chemistry, came by for a visit.

> Georgia asks Effie: "Effie, you're a feminist. We were talking about Iphigenia? Did you know that in one version Agamemnon was ordered by Artemis to sacrifice Iphigenia because he angered the goddess? In another version, she was saved by Artemis. Which do you believe is the true story?"
> Effie: "Both. Agamemnon angered Artemis who demanded the virgin's sacrifice, and then God intervened and ordered Artemis to save the girl."
> Georgia: (*laughing*) "And there you have the Greek Orthodox feminist."

The ancient Greek pagan traditions and mythology play a very important role in the women's development of their spirituality and their evaluations of the American spiritual landscape. A temperamental feminine divinity demanded the sacrifice of a virgin girl. The lesson for these women is that there is nothing inherently good or holy in the feminine divine simply because a spirit is feminine. A spirit is not worthy of worship simply because it is feminine; rather, a deity is worthy of worship because it is Holy. The Greek Orthodox women in the sample found affirmation for the value of the feminine in Christianity. The Greek Orthodox ethno-confessional identity incorporates historical memories of the Ancient Greek religion, which in effect acted as a stopgap for the women to explore or participate in the worship of the goddess.

As was often repeated in sections on identity in the interviews, "we are Orthodox of Greek descent", or, "we are Greek Orthodox and the two go together". In another case, "this is our history, I can't join a Protestant Church and

---

20 See, for example, Alexei Krindatch (ed.), *Atlas of American Orthodox Christian Churches*, Brookline/MA 2011.

not lose both the spiritual sensitivities or featherings (sic) in my heart and my Greek heritage. The two go together."

It is precisely because of this ethno-confessional identity that the women who left for political reasons found themselves without a spiritual home for a few years or in four cases, for as long as three decades. Furthermore, none of the women in the sample throughout the years they maintained their distance from the Greek Orthodox Church stopped seeing the Greek Orthodox Church as "their church".

An additional element that needs further exploration is the perceived differences in the interpretations of the role of the feminine in the Divine between the Greek Orthodox and other Christian traditions—not the differences themselves, but rather, perceived differences in the interpretations. I am not here making a historical or sociological argument that there is "less" sexism or misogyny in the Christian Orthodox tradition. Rather, I am pointing to different interpretations and understandings of how the feminine is integrated into the theology of the Divine, at least for the Greek Orthodox.

Catholic and Protestant women's experiences and interpretations of religious institutions should not become the standard against which Greek Orthodox (or other Christian Orthodox) women's spiritual experiences are measured and understood. On the one hand, to do so would entail abstracting women from particular historical and social contexts and creating the abstract concept of "woman", which is both an a-historical and a trans-historical concept. The concept of "woman" fails to capture the diversity of social and political structures within which women, as social agents, interpret and act. Women interpret the Divine and the political within specific historical contexts, so that the forms that feminist inquiry and critiques take vary.

For the Greek Orthodox women, the Divine is not limited to the males. Frederica Mathewes-Green, a convert from Roman Catholicism to Orthodox Christianity via the Episcopal Church, argues that if one can see beyond the gender of the clergy issue, one will find that women are in effect very active and integral agents in Orthodox Christianity.[21] Women saints are venerated in the same manner as men saints, they are teachers, go on spiritual journeys and pilgrimages, and all of these are both acknowledged and encouraged in Orthodoxy. Women in the sample were in many ways echoing Mathewes-Green. For example, based on the interviews, the women do not see female saints and the Theotokos (Holy Mary, Mother of God, or as is more commonly referred to by the Greek Orthodox, Panayia: The Holiest of the Holy) as either passive or occupying secondary positions/roles in relation to the male saints. On the contrary, while God is the Father and Jesus is the Son, the Theotokos, the God Bearer, the one through whom the Logos was Incarnate, is a woman. In numerous group discussions, the women often reminded one another of one of the Orthodox

21 Frederica Mathewes-Green, *Gender: Men, Women, Sex, Feminism*, Ben Lomond/CA 2002.

hymns to the Theotokos, "more glorious than the Cherubim… we magnify thee".[22]

While Eva Catafygiotu Topping's publication of the *Holy Mothers of Orthodoxy*[23] was critical in its assessment of how the church's institutional structures do not reflect God's revelations to humanity also through women, the book also strengthened that which the women in the sample already knew: God does not distinguish between men and women, and in fact, as one woman in the sample said, "That's when it clicked. God is a feminist. God gives both love and power to both men and women. God doesn't care about this stuff. He looks at the heart. Same in the Catholic tradition, so I don't know what the fuss is about. Men care about gender ideologies, not God." In some ways, the active spiritual seekers in the sample are like the Catholic Sisters in the Hartford Seminary study of women's spirituality. Namely, they are the most feminist of all the women in the sample.[24]

For the women in the sample, the feminine is neither invisible nor lost in the Greek Orthodox tradition; the women were not critical of the theology itself, rather, they find ample evidence of women having important roles in the ways in which the Divine reveals itself to humanity, and the women acknowledge that women are integral in the theology of the church. The issue for the women in the sample is rather that the institution of the church has men in important positions of authority. However, this becomes important not as an end in itself, but rather, for the consequences it entails. From the women's perspective, the male clergy often do not see the subtle or not so subtle differences in men's and women's experiences, as well as the experiences of marginalised groups and their spiritual and other needs in a hierarchical society. Some of the women in the sample argued that the problem is a disconnect between the theology and this-worldly politics and cultural ways in the daily running of the institution that contribute to the further marginalisation of vulnerable groups. This becomes especially troubling in a church whose goal is to nurture and enable the faithful to achieve theosis, i.e., to have eternal life in God.[25]

In sum, the American spiritual landscape did not provide the Greek Orthodox women in the sample who "exited" the church with viable alternative spiritual

---

22 The Akathist Hymn to the Theotokos praises the Mother of God: "It is truly meet to bless you, O Theotokos, ever-blessed and most pure, and the Mother of our God. More honourable than the Cherubim, and more glorious beyond compare than the Seraphim, without defilement you gave birth to God the Word. True Theotokos we magnify thee!"

23 Eva Catafygiotu Topping, *Holy Mothers of Orthodoxy: Women and the Church*, Minneapolis/MN 1987.

24 Winter/Lummis/Stokes, *Defecting in Place* (as n. 11).

25 A clear and concise definition of theosis is that the faithful are to become more Christ-like in the way they live their lives, so that they may unite with God rather than be absorbed in God in a pantheistic manner. See Demetrios J. Constantelos, *Understanding the Greek Orthodox Church* (Fourth edition), Brookline/MA 2005.

homes. It appears that for these women, changes regarding the nurturance of women's and members of marginalised groups' spirituality must come from within their own church. The women want the church to fulfil its historical mission of ministering to the weak and vulnerable. Those who left for a few years or for many years, whether they "hungered" for God or were too busy to think about God or whether they experimented with other traditions, upon their return want to see their church change its daily workings in ministering to the vulnerable, in bringing back the young they lose. The religious virtuosi or active spiritual seekers who did venture out to other Christian traditions or New Age movements/groups, speak with urgency about the church's responsibility, namely, to "help gather God's people" because the spiritual landscape is changing in "ways that few understand".

We can begin understanding what Greek Orthodox women do through this distancing-return dynamic as an exercise of their religious agency. The concept of religious agency "provides a window on how individuals, by their choices and actions, give shape and form to the structures of society, including religious institutions, even as they participate in their ongoing, gradual transformation".[26] Greek Orthodox women "exit" the church, from their perspective, letting it be known that there are problems "in the pews".[27] However, it is not clear that the clergy are in fact aware of the precise "problems in the pews". Georgia, 68, often expressed: "The women do not talk about these things, they don't say a word of what they think or feel. They're acting alone in a vacuum."

Some of the women, who "exited" in their earlier years and return to the church in their later years, still lack a voice. Upon their return, the women are already mothers and oftentimes "seasoned" in daily politics of dealing with patriarchal institutions. Despite this, the women still do not approach the clergy about the "problems in the pews". They do not confront the church hierarchy directly. Instead, some become active in the church and focus their energy in supporting and transforming the church-related lay groups, especially those for children.[28] As the interviews revealed, the women had an important expectation from the interviews for this particular research project and the possible publication; they exercised their "religious agency". They wanted their voices to be heard because, from their perspective, their demands were not unreasonable. Their demands were quite simple: to create a church which nurtures the

26 Laura M. Leming, "Sociological Explorations: What is Religious Agency?", *The Sociological Quarterly* 48/1 (2007) 73–92, here 74.

27 Albert O. Hirschman, *Exit, Voice and Loyalty: Responses to Decline in Firms, Organizations and States*, Cambridge/MA 1970.

28 See, for example, Anna Karpathakis, "Priests are only Human, what is Important is God", in Victoria L. Erickson/Susan A. Farrell (eds), *Still Believing: Jewish, Christian and Muslim Women Affirm their Faith*, Maryknoll/NY 2005.

spirituality of women and members of other marginal groups just as it nurtures men's spirituality and to bring in the youth it loses with each new generation.

The Women Situating Themselves Politically and Theologically

The reasons that women left or distanced themselves from the church varied from simple time constraints to clearly defined political, ideological and other social/ psychological issues. The sample of seventy-four showed that the single largest group (forty-four) is comprised by women who stopped attending church because they reached an age with responsibilities such as college or work that conflicted with church events and services. There was a smaller group of women (thirty in all) who spoke about making a conscious and deliberate decision to distance themselves from the church because of politics and ideologies. The passion for social justice issues for some of these women bespeak of a group of young people critical of inequalities within and outside the community and see the church as not adequately addressing these issues; whether justified or not, a smaller number of these women, during their younger years, saw the church as a bastion of conservatism and ideological supporter of hierarchies and inequalities both within the church and in society at large.

The level of religiosity among the women in the sample varied greatly, and the greatest variation was among the women who distanced themselves from the church because of time constraints. It should be noted that five of the women I interviewed are highly active spiritual seekers or persons "for whom spiritual and metaphysical concerns are a driving force".[29] Still other women who did not describe themselves as active spiritual seekers, did talk about having a "yearning" or "hunger inside that would not go away" or "feeling a gaping hole or emptiness" that "followed [them, A.K.] around for years".

When the women in the sample were asked if they consider themselves feminists, their answers varied, and a few of the women I interviewed said they did not understand feminism and so they could not answer.

Unlike Jewish women who return to Orthodox Judaism partly as a rejection of postmodernity, none of the women in the interviews saw themselves as returning to the church because of a rejection of the world or the cultural transformations causing shifts in gender roles. The Greek immigrant and Greek American women returning to the church were quite comfortable in a world where gender roles and relations were becoming increasingly balanced. Even women who did not consider themselves ideologically feminists spoke of how men and women are ontologically equal. It is interesting to note that the majority of women

29 Wade C. Roof, *A Generation of Seekers: The Spiritual Journeys of the Baby Boom Generation*, New York 1993.

framed this ontological "equality" within theological rather than political ideas and values.

The reasons the women returned to the church varied. Those who "left" for time constraints in their earlier years, discovered chunks and days of free time when the children were grown, married and had moved on with their own lives. Others returned for the sacraments of marriage and the children's baptism, and later again for the children to attend Greek afternoon or weekend classes, for the children to "grow up in the church" or have the opportunities of growing up in a community as they did. A smaller group of women returned after a personal or family crisis; none of the women interviewed sought a spiritual mentor or advisor during this crisis, but rather they simply began attending services again for prayer and spiritual strength. The women who described a "hunger" or "yearning inside" often returned to the church through no major events or crises, but rather simply to "light a candle and pray". The five active spiritual seekers, all of whom distanced themselves from the church for political reasons, returned after experimenting with other religious and spiritual traditions and found these ineffective in meeting their spiritual needs. More importantly, they found serious spiritual problems in the New Age movements and they see the church as having a responsibility in "righting the world", in "bringing God into the world to protect his people because the spiritual landscape is going crazy".

So, in effect, Greek immigrant and Greek American women who leave or distance themselves from the church at a younger age, come to rediscover the church years later. The women talked about discovering or "rediscovering [their, A.K.] spirituality", raising children and grandchildren in the church, reconciling feminism with Orthodoxy, discovering a "feminist God" or a God "who values women as much as He values men", and rediscovering a spiritual tradition within a diverse and changing religious landscape.

The women who said that time constraints caused them to stop attending church services hold diverse political beliefs. They are evenly split between self-described conservative or liberal. Twelve of the women in the sample said that they were not "political" and/or did not "understand politics" and took no positions on political issues. The overwhelming majority of the women in the sample who said that they exited the church for reasons other than time constraints described themselves as politically liberal or on the left. It is important to note that many of the women who described themselves as liberal or on the left used the Bible as the source of inspiration for their politics. Cain's question, "Am I my brother's keeper" and Jesus' social teachings of forgiveness, feeding and clothing the poor and shepherding the lost, were the background against which many of these women said they articulated their politics. In short, the women's faith informed their politics rather than their politics informing their faith. This particular study cannot estimate the demographics of Greek Orthodox women by political party affiliation. However, it becomes clear through the interviews that this group of women are women of deep faith and deeply committed to social justice and ministering to the poor, marginalised and suffering. The women discuss their volunteer work using words of faith.

Some of the women spoke about how the Orthodox Church did not fulfil its mission of ministering to the most vulnerable of the population. They compare the outreach and missionary work of the Greek Orthodox Church with the work that Protestant Churches, and more specifically, the non-denominational (Low Church) Protestants do with the poor and marginalised groups and find the Orthodox lacking. Rena is a 59-year-old mother of three, with a master's degree in clinical social work.

> Our church does not do a good job of shepherding the lost. Protestants do a much better job… there are pastors in the streets talking with the homeless and the sex workers and the substance abuse victims. We don't do this. A week after I stopped going to church a friend asked me to volunteer with her in a soup kitchen…. I still volunteer in two soup kitchens. One of the Protestant Churches has a programme for the teenagers after church… they come down to the soup kitchen and serve lunch to the poor and homeless. Some of the kids start showing up with their friends on Saturdays and you see Jesus working through them… I am the only Orthodox volunteer in both. This is how it was thirty years ago, and it's still the same now. We're [the Orthodox, A.K.] good at collecting cans of food and clothes, but we're not good at giving of our time and our heart… We give money and food and clothes because the priest tells us to. And that is one of the problems in the pews. We're not pounding the pavement to shepherd the lost, to comfort the suffering.… I cried the first day I volunteered… this is what the church is supposed to be doing.

Georgia, a 68-year-old grandmother with a graduate degree in medical anthropology, also spoke about her younger years:

> I would watch TV and see those pastors going to take food to the homeless… we did not do that. We did not cook and invite the poor and homeless in our church lunchroom the way my friend's Protestant Church did. I volunteer at hospitals and with children at risk… I do this with a friend through her church… a Protestant Church. We don't have any such programmes in the Orthodox Church. We have other programmes but nothing to take the faithful into the community on a regular basis… well, the poor and homeless are in a daily crisis… Jesus said the poor will be with us always… I don't vote. I have not voted for over twenty years. It makes no difference whether the Republicans or Democrats are in office. The poor and homeless are still there, and the only thing we can do is bring some comfort to the suffering.

The idea, expectation and need for the Greek Orthodox Church to take a daily proactive role in ministering to the poor and suffering in the community, even towards those who do not share the faith, was repeated numerous times by the women in the sample. As a number of them said, this was one of the background issues, which contributed to their exiting the church and looking to do some of this work through other churches, even if they themselves did not join those other churches. Both Diane and Georgia, for example, found their volunteer positions through friends who did volunteer work. Another woman, Mara, 47, with a commercial truck driver's license, was approached by a Protestant woman at work to volunteer one weekend to drive donations and a couple of volunteers to an out of state soup kitchen. Mara said that she has been doing this for almost twenty years. She said that her friend's church works with two churches in one of the poorest areas of Appalachia, and they deliver supplies to them every two months. "Why isn't the church [Greek Orthodox, A.K.] doing things like this? Regularly. People say that we're a small church and we're overtapped in our resources. I say we have a lot more resources in our hearts that we have not tapped into."

While a number of the women did find a venue or opportunity to, as Diane said, "put Jesus' teachings into action" through other churches, the majority did not, and a few of these women spoke with great misgivings about their own failures to do so. Peggy, 29, said, "I see my friends volunteering through their church. Some days I think that I should join them, but somehow feel that if I join them in the volunteer work, I will have to join their church and I can't do that… maybe something will come up in church through the kids' groups now that my son is in Sunday school, maybe someone will organise something… this is what we're supposed to be doing, isn't it? I don't do too well in this area unfortunately."

Two of the spiritual seekers have master's degrees in theology. Three offered interpretations of Jesus' teachings and the Church Fathers' writings, which they believed were different from what they experienced in the pews. These women repeated St John Chrysostom's teaching that the church is a hospital, a place of healing for souls, not a courtroom. Georgia was

> strongly opposed to the way that this is interpreted by many in the church... They bring in St Nektarios' teachings about the kind of medicine the church is to dispense to heal us of our sins and the medicine hurts… My response to that is that it depends on the medicine being dispensed. The only medicine we are to dispense is forgiveness. We are to forgive. Forgiveness does not hurt. When we see someone who is harmed, whether they are aware of it or not, we are to forgive. This is part of the unspoken… The Spirit is in the church. How can you talk about the Spirit? Some think they know God's will and that God punishes a woman for sinning or a homosexual man… Men punish. Jesus healed. Many see punishment as the medicine. Did Jesus punish any of the sinners? Jesus bound no one. He forgave all for whatever they did. The sin is punishment enough. People in the church know what people know, not what God knows. Jesus told us what is expected of us. How do you say this to people in the pews? How do you say this to priests? I could not. Short of calling them Pharisees and hypocrites, saying one thing and doing something else… I left. I don't want to sound like a zealot, but Jesus' words and deeds were clear on this. There was no other choice for me.

For the majority of the women in the sample, distancing themselves from the church was not a deliberate decision, but was rather a result of new responsibilities, which required time and effort. Whether living in big cities or smaller towns, young adults who begin college find that Sunday mornings or weekday evenings that were at one time reserved for church attendance or other church-related events are now scheduled for studying and working.

More than fifty percent of Greek American women enrol in college at some point. Melissa V. perhaps expressed the issue of time constraints the clearest for this group of women. She started college at the age of seventeen and entered law school at the age of twenty. By the age of thirty, she became a partner in a medium sized law firm in Chicago:

> There was no time for anything but work and study... Even Christmas I worked a couple of years. Easter was the only Sunday I took off because of my mother... And then law school and that was oh my God. Class and study. You couldn't do anything else. There is no such thing as Sunday. Christmas is reduced to the day of Christmas just for the family supper… Easter is reduced to Saturday night at the Anastasi [Resurrection service, A.K.] and then Easter supper. When I started working… Sunday was my only day off… I did my preps… on Sundays… I stopped going to church and everything in the community not because I was angry or disappointed and I know a lot of people like that. I just had no time… I enjoyed doing all those things as a kid. I enjoyed Sunday school; I enjoyed the dance group... I enjoyed the Christmas chorus. I missed all of that. I have very fond memories of growing up in the community. Even now there are times I just find time difficult to find (*laughs*).

Another reason the women gave for why they stopped attending church was related to the husband. Five of the women in the sample said they had grown up attending church services regularly. Upon marriage, their husbands did not consider religion important, so the young wives in effect followed suit. Sunday mornings were now spent doing "other things". It is these women, however, who insisted that the couple attend "at least Easter services" and four of these five women talked about a "hunger inside that wouldn't go away".

> It's part of being a good girl I suppose. You're young, in love, you just got married, your husband wants you beside him on Sunday morning, you stay. It's the only time we really had to be alone together.

> He doesn't go – you don't go. Or if he asks, "you're going to church again?" and it's Wednesday evening and the kids are acting out, you end up not going. It's a small thing, nothing that is pre-planned or deliberate. You just, I don't know, you just stop going and you do other stuff.

The women who stopped attending church because of time constraints are a very diverse group in terms of their reported levels of religiosity and belief. Two women, for example, used the expression "religion does not click". Another woman said: "Religion doesn't make sense to me", or "it's not that I don't believe, I don't know if I believe". As Claire, 44, and mother of two, said:

> I'm not sure I believed then or I believe anymore now. I went through Sunday school and all that. It didn't make sense to me then and it still doesn't make sense to me. I have no troubles with it, I know a lot of people believe but it just… doesn't add up in my mind.

Some of the women who say that they stopped attending church because of time constraints, have quite complicated relations with faith and with God. Behind the "I don't have time to go" or "I'm too busy with work", there are stories and experiences which are deeply spiritual in nature, and lack of attending church worship services is in fact an expression of the women's spiritual struggles. Laura, a 39-year-old emergency room doctor and trauma specialist, expressed a quite nuanced approach and belief in God despite the fact that she stopped attending church services and despite her statement that "church never made sense" to her. Laura was an intern at the emergency room/trauma unit the days following 9/11. Laura began the interview in a self-described "cool manner"; and yet, within half an hour, I reached over for the box of tissues for both of us.

> Max [the chief surgeon, A.K.] prays sometimes… He's Jewish Orthodox, and I'm Greek Orthodox. We make an interesting pair of doctors in the [operating room, A.K.] (*She laughs*). When I see him closing his eyes for that one moment in silence, I know we're in trouble. I know the guy on that [stretcher, A.K.] is in trouble. I just want to get in, do what needs to be done to save the patient's life… I was always like this. It didn't matter that my mother was upset that I didn't go to church because I was studying… I preferred to stay home and study biology (*laughs*)… Church never made sense to me. It's a different way of understanding things… Yes, I do feel like we're on our own and I'm ok with it. I think I was always ok with it. I mean if there is a God, I hope he's ok with me because I do live a good life. Live a life you won't be ashamed to talk about with your children and grandchildren. I think that if there is a God, this is what he looks at anyway… Do I believe? I can't say that I disbelieve. I think that if I ever meet God, I have a few questions to ask him… but look, there is Thomas and he questioned, so I'm in good hands because ultimately I believe that if God does exist, there must be a goodness in him that we are not capable of even imagining… why? Because nothing else could hold this world together (*wiping tears from her eyes*).

Based on the interviews with women who had stopped attending church worship services because of "time constraints", it would be unwise to say that these women lack faith or have such little faith that they choose to busy themselves with other things on Sunday mornings. The women who talked about time constraints did not use the terms having "left" or "walked out" of the church. Rather, they used the words "stopped attending church services" or "I didn't have time to go", or, "I worked" or "I studied" Sunday mornings. These women did not see themselves as "leaving" the church, even if they did not attend Sunday worship services for a number of years.

Some of the women have learned that explaining their absence from the pews because of lack of time is easier than explaining the reasons they choose not to attend. This issue arose during the interviews with two nurses. Mena is a gynaecology nurse in the operating room. Early on in the interview, Mena said that she did not attend church services for a few years because she was working weekends.

> Half an hour ago, I told you that I didn't go to church for years because I worked weekends. I used to tell people that two weekends out of the month were the only full days I had to spend with my husband… The last time I was there the priest gave a sermon on abortion… I am pro-life, anti-abortion… A few months before I was one of the operating nurses for what turned out to be an abortion… A woman went through chemotherapy and … got pregnant… It was an exploratory procedure… the doctor found a dying baby… some pregnancy tests do come back negative, but it's still a statistical near improbability with all those tests in her case... What do you say and to whom do you say anything to when women are condemned in these situations? It was one of those one in a million situations that comes your way as an [obstetrics gynaecology, A.K.] nurse with lots of [operating room, A.K.] hours and you look up and ask, 'God, why? Why don't you hear her prayers?' … I had heard that type of sermon dozens of times before, but this time it was different. It was not an exceptional sermon, just more of the same. But I had seen something that the priest did not see… I talked about it with my husband and the other nurses at the unit… I would not even know how to approach this with the priest… I don't know if my faith was shaken… maybe… probably… I just saw something in the sermon that day that stayed with me for a long time. All the way until my own son was born and I thought… my miracle baby, God gave him to us in our late thirties, unexpected gift… I don't care what the priest says because God touched us those days in that hospital, and honestly, that's all I had to go by. God was there even if priests and pastors were not there and would never even know about this girl.

There is a smaller group of women (30 in a sample of 74) who made a conscious and deliberate choice to "leave" the church. These are women who tend to be politically on the left in terms of social justice issues. They tend to be anti-racialist, feminist, and demand a society that is respectful of socially marginalised groups. Justified or not, in their younger years they saw the church as a bastion of conservative politics. At the same time, the majority of the women in this group described themselves as "believers".

Diane, one of the spiritual seekers who "left" the church and "returned", said the following:

> These are precisely the young people who believe in Jesus' teachings of love and compassion. A living God. But they don't understand this because they're young and haven't read theology. And these are precisely the young people that the church wants in those pews and in its groups ministering to the poor, the marginalised, the sick. These are precisely the young people the church should be nurturing because they have the heart… if they only knew how to approach and nurture the spirituality of the young with love in their hearts. Instead their politics chases these young people out of the church and at least the clergy that I know are not aware of why these young people are leaving. Bigger parishes see many young people in the pews and they think that they are doing a good job of keeping the young. They're keeping the politically conservative or the young who have no interest in politics and that's not good enough… politics should not affect our place in the church… But they [the clergy, A.K.] don't see that there are even more out there who are not in those pews.

Reasons for Unease with the Orthodox Church

Sexual Politics

While the church teachings distinguish between the "sin" and the "sinner", i.e., homosexuality and a homosexual person, the young often fail to see this distinction and conflate the two. For the young, the idea that homosexuality is a sin implies that a homosexual person is spiritually condemned. All of the women who raised the issue of sexual politics as contributing to their distancing from the church, knew a homosexual man or woman in their youth and were distraught at the thought of this person's rejection by God. To the extent that young homosexuals are experiencing a host of identity, emotional and other social difficulties in their relations with peers, family, and even simple acquaintances and strangers, the church becomes one additional institution that adds to their troubles. Indeed, for those who believe in God or whose spirituality has been awakened, the church's positions have a tremendously negative impact on these young people's spirituality and emotions.

The women often distinguished between occasional same-gender sex and homosexuality and commented that homosexuality is not a lifestyle choice. A number of the women also mentioned that they knew of at least one gay or lesbian Greek Orthodox person who "went elsewhere for spiritual guidance."

Marilyn, 57, a highly active spiritual seeker and a member of a "liberal" group of interfaith women who met monthly for prayer and discussion, said:

> I used to hear the priest and I would freak out. Homosexuality as sin. I knew a lot of people who were gay... I couldn't bear the thought of these people going to hell because of their sexuality. They were good people. [The priests did not say the homosexual person would go to hell, A.K.], of course not. But when you're 18 or 20, in your mind this is what follows... If homosexuality is a sin, then gays will go to hell. Now I know [that they are no more likely to go to hell than straight people are, A.K.] and I think priests know it also. People who need God more than most people because life is tough for them leave the church.

A few of the women spoke about how the spiritual needs of sexual minority group members are unique, and in many ways this population has greater need of spiritual support because of their sexuality than heterosexuals but leave the church precisely because of their sexuality. Nellie, from a small Midwestern town moved to NYC at the age of 22 and felt

> relief that I didn't have to deal with the church anymore. I go for Holy Week, light my candle, say a prayer, and that is it… I go because it's Easter. Anastasi [Resurrection, A.K.]. I don't think the priests have managed to kill that in me. In other people, I know yes, but I still love God. I know a lot of gay people who are so angry with God because of the priests... It's sad… Let me explain the process of why homosexuals leave the church... Imagine being gay, needing God and being told that God disapproves of homosexuality and gay people. Would you go to church?... It's

> difficult for a person who believes in God to be gay and it's difficult for a gay person to believe in God because of the way that God is presented in the church… why would anyone want to believe and love a God when they're told that this God condemns who they are?

Helen, 54, said that she accepted the fact that she was lesbian in her late teens; by the age of twenty-one she decided to no longer attend church services.

> I was made to feel that God had rejected me. I was in eternal condemnation. You can't listen to this. It's hard when you're young. So you leave to maintain your sanity and you lose your spirituality. Not a good choice gay people have to make.

Race

Race in USA is a multi-faceted and multi-tiered continuum, often leaving ethnic minorities in ambiguous in-between positions between the two ends of the spectrum of "White" and "Black".[30] The young with liberal, progressive or left-leaning politics also find issues of race important on the parish level. While the Greek Orthodox Archdiocese has consistently taken anti-racist positions, the young still find the ideological racism of the occasional priest extremely troubling. At the same time, the Greek Orthodox young growing up in areas of the country with a predominantly white population may themselves become the receivers of racism. Race thus played a double role in the lives of the women interviewed. In both cases, the young were confronted with community institutions lacking cultural knowledge and resources to discuss issues of race. As one community activist I interviewed (for a different research project) said,

> this is the US – the home of the [Ku Klux, A.K.] Klan. It is beyond my comprehension that the most important institution in our community is not addressing issues of race on the parish level. Sociologists and psychologists tell us that race is complex, that it's not an either/or thing, it's everywhere, affects our everything, our psyches, our emotions, everything, and they just ignore it on the parish level.

Athena was 26 when she moved to New York City for work. She grew up in a large Southern city with ethnic and racial diversity. Athena said that it was "stifling" to

> go to a church with a priest who was racist. I now know that most Greek Orthodox priests are not, but ours was. I couldn't just sit there and listen to a racist talk about God. The parishioners were just as racist. Being racist and being a Christian… My friend's brother married a Black woman and the community divided. No kidding. Those who were against, those who were for, and those who didn't care one way or the other… I met two racist priests living in this part of the country. It's part of the

30 Anna Karpathakis, "Greek Immigrants: Simply a Reflection of America's Contradictions", in John P. Myers (ed.), *Minority Voices: Linking Personal Ethnic History and the Sociological Imagination*, New York 2004.

> southern tradition. You can't be a good southerner and not be racist, and when you're young, *two priests feels like they're all the same* [i.e., the two priests are representative of all priests, A.K.]. Now I know, it's not that way, but when you're a teenager the world just seems to, I don't know, it's just different. I don't know, it still boggles my mind to think that someone who says he loves God is a racist. Two years later, I was doing a paper in college and I came across a picture of Archbishop Iakovos walking along side Martin Luther King Jr. in Selma, and I was so relieved, and then years later I saw the same picture hanging on the walls of the [Hellenic, A.K.] Cultural Center in Astoria.... I wanted to cry from joy when I saw that picture. I was so happy when they decided to move that bishop to the South. So happy. I saw this and say this as an adult after having gone through almost fifteen years of being out of the church.

Upon graduating college, Marlene moved from Mississippi to the east coast with her fiancé. She befriended a Greek Orthodox woman from Texas:

> My friend and I compared the priests we had growing up. Ours was a good man... Hers was a racist. The parishioners in both churches, not all, I can't say all, but a lot were racist and again I keep saying this, but when you're young, you don't make fine distinctions. Now I pray for racists. Back then, I ran from them and the church. College came and I was working on the weekends and I just stopped going... It turned me off... My mother ... would tell me not to pay attention to what others think or feel because God had done right with me and just to keep my eyes on God. Now I think I understand, but I didn't back then... There was one young man. A few years younger than me. He had the same problems I did. But he stayed in the church. Years later... he told me that the new priest ... called him a few times and they met and talked... I had already left for college by the time the new priest arrived. This is what they need to do, and it's easy to do this in smaller communities.

Those in small towns with a majority white population and few if any other racial minorities may have been targets of racism and found no support system in the community. It was almost a cliché for women (and men in interviews with them) who grew up in overwhelmingly white towns to point to their skin and say "my skin isn't pink" or "we weren't like the four Black families or the Vietnamese, but we weren't white either. It was weird. White to the Blacks or Vietnamese, not white to the whites."

Mary, 48, grew up in a mid-western town with five other Greek American families.

> I remember feeling so overwhelmed every time someone asked my religion, where I got my black eyes from...My skin isn't pink... We weren't white... and Holy Friday and then Anastasi... I dreaded it... This was the Bible Belt... I think the whole community tried keeping a low profile and celebrated everything with understated dignity. I was too embarrassed to talk about it... Greeks still don't talk about race. The only Greeks who talk about race are the racist Greeks. The rest avoid it like the plague. They do their hardest to blend in thinking that if they don't notice it won't be there... I probably sound more bitter than I am, but really I wish someone at Sunday school or the priest talked about these issues because our parents were clueless... I don't think it's different now. When I visit I see it repeating with the only three Greek

> American teens in the town, and they don't understand like I didn't… I was Mary the Greek. Stupid people. Anglo name with the Greek tag added on… I got to Chicago after college and met Greeks who were racist. Went to church and [first day there, A.K.] ran into the most racist guy in the parish. I was so ashamed… self-conscious. It's growing up and being seen as weird. Less than. And to see your people do to others what was done to you because you are who you are… I guess I just needed time off from all that and I took off from everything Greek until I met my very Greek husband who was even more liberal than me, but very religious.

Patriarchy

The women's understanding of feminism is informed by their faith. During a group interview with four women who describe themselves as spiritual seekers, Fena says that God created both men and women in His image and both men and women partake of the Divine, we just have to

> work through all that muck inside us and let the Holy Spirit strengthen in us… Women are socialised to reflect on every little thing we feel, think, say and do. When the priest looks out at me and sees all these doubts, I often wonder if he understands the source of these doubts because my whole day and week and year and life come tumbling at me and I'm so self-evaluative, I really don't think he understands. One of the important spiritual differences between men and women.
> Georgia, 68: Yes, but in God there is neither Jew nor Gentile, slave nor free, male nor female.
> Fena: Neither Jew nor Gentile, slave nor free, male nor female, but our lives are different, and there are important differences in our spiritualities, and the all-male clergy do not understand this.

Many of the women I interviewed spoke about how they first learned of feminist ideas through the liberal feminist framework of Betty Friedan and Gloria Steinem with its emphasis on individual freedoms and achievements.[31] One of the basic

31 Betty Friedan launched the second feminist movement in the United States with the publication of *The Feminine Mystique* and Gloria Steinem was an activist and spokeswoman for the feminist movement in the 1960s. In 1972, Steinem founded *Ms. Magazine*, the publication for the feminist movement in the United States. One of the criticisms racial minority and working-class women made of the women's movement in the 1970s was that it assumed that all women's experiences modelled those of white middle and upper middle class. The women's movement, headed by Friedan and Steinem, advocated for the woman's right to work outside the home and called for equal opportunities for women in the professional field. By the late 1970s, a number of racial minority and working-class women, who demanded that class and racial injustices also be incorporated into the feminist movement's political platform, left the national feminist movement and created their own organisations. Another major point of contention between the national women's movement and African American feminists were reproductive politics; white women were vulnerable to unwanted pregnancies and had clandestinely performed abortions, often resulting in negative consequences to the women's health; African American women, on the other hand, had a history of forced sterilisation

demands of this framework is the breakdown of gender boundaries in institutions, including religious ones. The political demands are quite simple and straightforward: To change society from a patriarchal to a more gender equal society, women need to enter institutions on all levels, and on the one hand represent women's interests in the decision-making processes and also incorporate women's perspectives into the institutions' daily workings. From this perspective, the Greek Orthodox Church is a bastion of patriarchy. Not only are clergy strictly male, but one of the most important and holy places for Greek Orthodoxy, Mount Athos, is restricted to male pilgrims.

Catherine, a 61-year-old architect and grandmother of fourteen, describes herself as a feminist who believes in and loves God's word:

> Ever since, I was a young girl. Somewhere along the way, politics became important the way it usually does for young people. For me it was feminism… Some rough men in my family. I saw them as overbearing sexists. They were that too, but more importantly they were nasty people. I read Betty Friedan when I was fifteen... None of what she wrote described my experiences… but still it affected me… My father pushed me and my sister into college at a time when American women got married after high school… I wanted to see a woman priest and there were none … My questions were why no women priests and why can't I receive Holy Communion when I'm menstruating? This is important for young women. What do both of these mean for women in relation to God? No one could answer me of course because I don't think they mean anything.

Bessie, a 55-year-old teacher, added to Catherine's comment:

> I did lent for a whole week and I couldn't receive [Holy Communion, A.K.] because I menstruated. I was furious. My brother would never have to deal with something like this, but I would for the rest of my life… I couldn't go into the altar because I was a girl. All these things we couldn't do because we're girls. No way. I rebelled and I rebelled big time. I rebelled alongside my Catholic and Jewish girlfriends, and we all said "no" (*laughs*).

In addition to issues of women's roles in the church, the women also pointed to more general issues of gender relations, and in a few cases how local priests at times responded to cases of domestic violence or marital problems and conflicts.

Maria, a 54-year-old social worker, had worked with Greek and Greek American women in two cities with large Greek and Greek American communities; a number of her clients were victims of domestic violence:

> There were so many days I wanted to call especially that one priest and let him have a piece of my mind. More than once, he told women to be patient and try to change the husband's ways. I can't see that. I can't see an institution telling a battered woman to be patient. I can't see God telling the woman be patient, take the beatings because

---

procedures, beginning in the 1920s during the eugenics movement. Angela Davis wrote and spoke widely about how African American women's reproductive rights were not incorporated into the women's movement's reproductive issues platform.

> you're supposed to turn the other cheek, so you can go to heaven by being a martyr to some… They say they don't do that anymore, but only because women don't go to the priests for help and advice anymore. And why don't they have social workers in the parishes? Have one for two or three or even four parishes… Have social workers travel to the parishes. Give them space to do their work. Why are priests doing what social workers should be doing? They are men who are clueless about women's lives.

Reproductive Politics

Some of the young women also rebelled against the church's position on issues of reproduction. Young women familiar with American politics of reproduction often resented what one woman termed the "politicisation". of sermons at the end of the service. Abortion is the issue that joins politics and spirituality together. In the words of one woman, abortion is like

> a ball of cat yarn. You don't know where it begins and where it ends. You can't unravel it, and the women are stuck with the job of undoing the ball without on the one hand losing control of the little they can control of their lives after a disaster, and on the other hand losing their spirituality. It's not a good place for women to be at.

Grace, 35 at the time of the interview, decided to stop attending church services when the priest would

> too often talk about abortion and women. It was the early 90s. Same everywhere all over the country. Reproductive politics everywhere. I flipped… A girl I knew had an abortion. Strange how a child's heart and mind work. She had no other choice. She did something stupid and she paid the price *(sighs)*. I don't know. It's hard for young women, I think. There was nothing in the church for us. It felt like the only thing there was, was condemnation. Please don't get me wrong, but when you're young you sometimes feel overwhelmed and you have nowhere to go to, and when the priest becomes somebody else to avoid, you just don't go to church anymore.

Maria, 45, talked about her own reflections on how reproductive politics had entered the priest's sermons.

> Yes, abortion is wrong. No feminist will celebrate abortion… Even at a young age, I was thinking you priests cannot do this to us. You have no idea what is going on in a woman's life… my aunt had an abortion for health reasons... These aren't easy choices women make. Priests sometimes think that women use abortions as birth control. An abortion is something that stays with the woman for the rest of her life. A priest is someone the woman should be able to go to for something like this and not have to run away from. I see it with the younger women today. Even those who are not sexually active. They cringe every time the priest says something about abortion. There is a fear in their eyes… what if something happens to them or someone they know, and they have to do this? Will God condemn them? Will they go to hell?... I was twenty-one when this stuff started coming down in my parish. I remember screaming inside my head: "God you can't condemn my aunt for making this decision... You have to help her. She's been living in hell ever since."

Some of the women, troubled by the presentation of women's issues in the church, delved into educating themselves and reflecting upon a "near impossible position to be in", as Cathy, a 48-year-old American-born mother of three, freelance writer with a graduate degree in anthropology, expressed. Women's roles in Greek Orthodoxy are "byzantine":

> I don't mean just old and outdated, I mean byzantine as in… too many layers, too many complexities, and we see and are in the services presented with the most simplistic views. The woman is responsible for her family's spirituality in more ways than … the men are too busy working, providing, it's the women who are close to the home, the husband, the children. There is a long history of Greek men, of men in general, being less religious and spiritual than women... It's neither sexist nor anti-feminist to say this. It's the women who prepare the family to receive communion, to bring Jesus into the home, teach the children the prayers and the importance of staying connected with God. It would be a mistake to overlook it… if spirituality is important, then we have to look at the woman's role in her family's spirituality, and she is definitely more important than the men. Who shows up in church on Sundays? It's the women. The priests need to see this and act accordingly to invite more women in, bring and keep the young girls in. They lost two to three generations of women from the 70s to the 80s, and I would say even later when Bush and the crazy reproduction politics were brought into the church… They're head on a self-defeating course… Education is the answer to this. Don't just impose. Educate, discuss, create a space for young people to discuss these things because they need this.

During another interview, Cathy said the following:

> I think that the priests think that we are stupid. I don't think they know that we understand that reality is much more complex, and they present things in such simplistically absolute terms. They dumbify everything when they're talking to us. They need to understand that most of us now are college educated… we read the Scriptures, we read the Fathers and the saints… The women also study them, but they still talk to us like we're our grandmothers with less than elementary school education.

Politics in the Parish

Parish politics are prominent in some of the women's discussions of their becoming alienated from the church in their youth. Since the laity in the Greek Orthodox Church are important in parish affairs, the emergent politics of the parishes are reflective of the personal politics between individual council board members. Many of the women interviewed, who were familiar with the parish level politics, spoke with misgivings about these. Parishes with either a laity with strong personalities or a priest with poor people skills were especially prominent in the women's discussions. One woman described the frequent clashes between personalities in the parish – "it all left a bitter taste in my mouth".

Similarly, while the Orthodox Christian Laity (OCL) was much more active and vocal in local parish affairs until a few years ago,[32] the women remember the impact that the group's often negative politics had on the parish level and contributed to the youth's distancing themselves from church-related groups and activities. In the 1990s, the group had embarked on the campaign for the Americanisation of the church, and their activities in parishes often created conflicts in parishioners' personal lives.

Paula said she grew up in a "world of a couple of hundred Greek American families in the church" across three towns. She was referring to the parish that her grandfather, a young immigrant from a village on mainland Greece and with less than a high school education, helped establish. When her grandfather was accused of wrongdoings but was denied the opportunity to fight these allegations in a court of law because official charges would not be pressed, Paula said that she and her cousins left.

> We went away to college so we wouldn't have to deal with it… it took me years to set foot in church again… there was that fear. Maybe I was over-reacting, but when you're a teenager and you see your family thrown in disarray over politics, you just run... I know I wasn't the only one… most of the teenagers at the time dreaded going to anything in the church because the adult stuff would eventually trickle down to what we were doing… You can't have politics in the church. Once politics enters, it's game over… The priest couldn't control them. You couldn't control them. He tried and I know this for a fact, but these people were just too determined.

Paula and the eight other women who talked about the Americanisation politics of the OCL emphasised that "things have changed". Kathy: "The same people are still there, but they're not nasty anymore… One is still on the council, but he's quiet… Maybe the priest finally told them to change their tune? I don't know why, but things have calmed down, and there's finally peace with these people."

In smaller parishes, family histories and biographies are well known, especially since immigrants often settled near family members and others from the same village or region of Greece. As a few women said, parishes are often "like an extended family". Just as success and achievements by some family member become occasions for celebrations in the parish, so do family conflicts and crises become part of the communal information networks, i.e., gossip, which often negatively affects the children, i.e., the most vulnerable. The women talked about how the negative dynamics of this aspect of community lead to the marginalisation of the children among their peers and the psychological need and urge to "flee". Fotini was nineteen when she decided "not to go back":

> I remember very clearly why I left the church. There was a girl… Her brother came out… he was gay. Well, things didn't go well... He stopped showing up at church on Sundays. Less than a year after that the parents separated. The girl was sad, she was

32 Karpathakis, "The Greek Orthodox Church" (as n. 15).

> ashamed. The kids ostracised her… you know, they never called her anymore to do things. She and her mother stopped coming... My mother called the woman often and checked up on her. I know my mother did what she could, but we weren't rich either. One day my mother said they were moving to New Jersey to be with her family, and that was the last I heard of them… I think we and my aunt were the only family that reached out to them… Just when the family needed support, the rug was pulled from underneath their feet. Not only was there no support, it's like people were just mean to them, people were mean to the kids. It's one of those moments when you want to scream out, "God, what are you doing? Why are you allowing this to happen?" It wasn't right… I don't know if the priest knew what was going on with them. It was one priest with all those parishioners – no secretary to bring the gossip in to him (*laughs*). I mean now I can see how he probably had no idea about the emotional trauma that these things involve, but at the time I didn't see it that way… I saw it as the priest not caring, that it was all part of a big lie somehow.

Aliki, a 49-year-old accountant and mother of three:

> My mother would take me [to church, A.K.] every Sunday when I was little… I was always an outsider. I didn't find out how or why until I was older (*laughs*). You know, I didn't learn of the family secret until the age of eighteen. Then it all made sense. One Sunday when I saw this one very mean woman turn her face from me the way she always did, I got up, walked out of church and didn't go back… I felt like God had abandoned me. He made his proclamations through people. I was not wanted in his house… No, no one from the church called to see where or how I was.

The issue of the parish priest being aware of the young people's troubles and the importance of support given by the parish priest is most poignant in the following case. Susie grew up in a mid-sized town in the southwest. At the age of seventeen, Susie was raped and two months later her best friend drove her three hours to a nearby clinic for an abortion.

Susie was 41 at the time of interview. She said that the parish priest called repeatedly.

> He kept calling, coming by the house looking for me… I was too ashamed to talk to him… I felt like God had abandoned me, I had done something wrong, and I deserved it... It was the only decision I could make… I knew then and still know I couldn't do otherwise, and no woman can make any other decision. I was seventeen... It took another twelve years for me to walk into church again… to make preparations for my wedding. And it was [the same priest, A.K.] and he stood there, he was in the altar, he came out, staring at me. I saw he was beginning to look frail. When he recognised me, he opened his arms to me and I ran into his arms. Literally ran into his arms. He wrapped his arms around me and said, "welcome back home, Susie". At that point, I started balling [crying, A.K.] so hard and so loud, it all came out, all those years of secrecy, of emotional torture, no one but the doctor and my best friend and later on my husband knowing what happened… (Wiping tears from her eyes)… We went to his office and we talked for over two hours… He was crying with me and he told me that God understood my decision… I should have talked to him when I was seventeen and not waited till thirty. God rest his soul; God keep him because he gave me back my life that afternoon.

When asked if the priest was aware of the particular issue or problem, the women who grew up away from cities often responded with "just one priest with all those parishioners", or, "too many people, too many things, how can one person keep up with all that is going on?". Lena grew up in a small mid-western city with one Greek Orthodox Church within a hundred-mile radius:

> People coming from over a hundred miles away. How can he visit people a hundred miles away and keep in touch with parishioners? You need young men with energy to dedicate themselves to keep up with the one hundred families living a hundred miles away from the church in all directions. The number of people is small, but the distances are great and that was and still is a problem in the parishes in the South, Mid-West and the West… It's a problem in all parishes outside the cities.

Women in cities with large parishes, however, also talked about the shortage of priests. Annie, a 52-year-old mother of three teens, is a team leader for one of the elementary-school girls' sports teams in her local parish.

> There are hundreds of families and two priests. And these are the regulars. There are hundreds more who don't come regularly and have problems, and the kids have problems and they come a few times and leave… I still see it with my daughter's groups. I see the kids that come and go. The kids who need this the most are the ones who leave… They need help in the parishes.

Sense of Betrayal

The women often used the words "anger", "hurt", and "betrayal" to describe their emotional responses to an institution they perceived as lacking a connection with the "realities of their lives". As many of the older women reflected on their reasons for leaving the church in their earlier years, they often remarked that in their younger years they were too angry to distinguish between God and the institution. Quite often the older immigrant women I interviewed made a point of distinguishing between God and priests or God and the institution of the church, especially an institution in which the laity play important roles in the daily workings of the church, but which laity often lacked sensitivity to others' experiences. As was often a mantra, "priests are only human", or "God is God, but priests are only human and women should not forget this", or "down South they say to keep your eyes on God, not the people in the church", or "now I can distinguish between God, the priest, and the laity on the boards".

Eleni was reflecting upon the day she decided she would not go to the Sunday service and told her mother:

> She asked why. I said I feel betrayed. It just came out I wasn't aware of it. I stopped and thought about it for a moment. I didn't understand. I was seventeen at the time. This was the 70s. Women's movement on the one hand, and priests telling us to be

> good girls on the other. It was about the ERA.[33] The priest said something about women's equality. That God made us different, and women should see this and not go chasing after men's work or something like that. I wanted to raise my hand and tell him that different does not mean unequal. An apple and an orange are different, but they are both fruit. One is not better or more than another… priests have no right to say things that hurt people. My parents worked hard to put all three of us through college. Who was this guy to stand there and speak in that disrespectful way about women? I know that our church is quite liberal in these issues now, but back then when I was a teenager, things were different and a lot of women of my generation left.

Syny, 61, was 24 years old in 1982, and

> that Sunday was my birthday, and on my birthday, I got up and walked out of the church.
>
> I felt confused because this twenty-year-old girl and her family were betrayed. The priest heard what happened and he decided to preach about the topic that Sunday… how would this affect an already vulnerable twenty-year-old girl if she found out that her problem was the topic of the sermon for the week. I wanted to scream. It all depends on whether we're willing to pray for forgiveness for everyone, regardless. Instead I got up and walked out… Two young women got up and walked out that Sunday. Silently… No… No one knew what was going on in my head or my heart. I walked out without saying a word to anyone. Just to Panayia… I asked her for her forgiveness for everyone.

The women who exited the church took with them these feelings of anger, hurt and betrayal, "carrying them around like a sack of rotting potatoes", as one woman said. Cally, who described herself as an "ultra-believer and lover of God", a feminist and politically on the left, expressed the following:

> The stuff stays in you, it's there. I would go just for Anastasi and stand outside and be very cynical of the priest. I grew up in the 80s. A very different time for women in the church. I would be looking for the wrong things – he would say – and I always found something. It took me years to say in my head [about the priest, A.K.] "enough, you're in the wrong with your judgements, I'm in the right, I have as much right to be here as you who keeps messing up with people". I was angry. I'm still angry. I feel that I was robbed of my spirituality all those years. What was I supposed to be doing? Where was I supposed to be? Where was I supposed to go? I believe that God has a plan for each of us and I feel like I missed the road all those years. And I was stupid for doing this. Maybe I just needed to mature, to be more certain of these convictions of right and wrong, of justice, before I found my way back to church and be strong enough to not let some things affect me… The church has changed a lot in these last thirty years… No. It's not the church. It's the priests…

---

33 ERA is the Equal Rights Amendment to the U.S. Constitution and was first introduced to the United States Congress in 1923; the ERA calls for legal equality for men and women. The Bill passed the Senate and the House of Representatives in 1972 and was sent to the states for ratification. As of 2018, 37 out of the required 38 states have ratified the Bill.

Why Women Return to the Church

The reasons women gave for “returning” to the church vary. Some “returned” for the sacraments of marriage and later baptism for the children and to enrol the children in Greek afternoon or weekend classes, others returned during a personal crisis, others because there was still a “yearning inside” that could “not be filled no matter what”; and still the smaller group of active spiritual seekers returned because their experimentations with other spiritual traditions left them unfulfilled and concerned with the church’s responsibilities in a changing spiritual landscape.

Spiritual Responsibilities to Children

While women may return to the church for the sacrament of marriage and baptism of the children, this does not mean that they return to the pews on a regular basis nor that they become active in church-related groups and activities. It is rather the arrival of the children, which is the most important and frequent reason women give for “returning” to the church. Women talk about how they “started going to church again” when the children came of school age, and they enrolled the children in Sunday school and/or Greek afternoon school.

The women who grew distant from the church because of practicalities or time constraints say that time constraints are even more prominent now. In particular, when working mothers of school-aged children describe the decisions they make regarding the family’s participation in community life, they invariably talk about the stress associated with this.

Katherine, 45, expressed the following:

> I stopped going to church and all those organisations because I didn’t have time. Time is still limited. When you have two kids and a demanding job and you have a house and husband and so many things to take care of, you start prioritising. Sunday school and Greek afternoon school. I take them to Sunday school; my mother drives them to Greek school. If there is anything in the community, they go with their grandmother… You can’t do everything… When the kids are in Sunday school, I’m in church… I’m finally sitting in church again and I find peace. My days are stressful; I need those two hours on Sunday morning. My cousin would tell me these were the most peaceful two hours of her week and I would laugh. Now I see it. Go, sit and be at peace. Wow! I must be getting old (*laughs*).

Many of the women remember engaging their mothers in important and open discussions about gender issues and they themselves now try to keep this open channel of communication with their own children. The women talked about how they learn and re-evaluate their own experiences through their discussions with their children who grow up at a time when an ontological equality between the genders is simply assumed.

Martina, a high school science teacher, stated:

> One day I was so angry… about Holy Communion and menstruation. How can I be dirty if God made me as I am? How and why would God make all these millions of women dirty? Why couldn't he find an easier way for us to reproduce without making us dirty and keeping us away from him a week each month (*laughs*)? My mother got so frustrated that she yelled right back at me: "I don't know why. Go ask God if this is the case and why this would be the case. Sit, read, think, pray. I'm not God. I'm only your mother and I don't know what God is thinking."… I try to do the same for my kids... Just talk about everything… My daughter isn't tortured by all these questions. She gave herself the answers I couldn't give myself. God does not make us dirty. This stuff is men's interpretations. It's a different type of feminism for these kids. It's "don't give me bullshit, God made us equal and that's all there is to it"…. Our generation, we felt powerless and we left…. I'm learning from my kids… My son is the same way… They learned from me to keep your eyes on the prize and the prize is God, not men… God is God. God doesn't change, but our receiving of God changes. That one is my daughter's lessons to me (*laughs*).

Several women who had described themselves as not certain in their faith or "not very religious" also returned to the church for the marriage and baptismal sacraments and later to enrol the children in the Greek language programmes and Sunday school. These women spoke about parents' spiritual responsibilities. Claire, a math teacher, expressed the issue of spiritual responsibilities parents have to the children, even when the parents themselves are not clear regarding their own belief system and faith:

> I don't know what I believe. But I'm not an active atheist. I don't think there are many Greeks or Greek Americans who take vows of atheism (*laughs*)… I baptised all my children… I can't take that away from my children... The two older are in Sunday school. They need to know what religion is before they can make the decision to dump it or accept it. If God does exist, I don't want the responsibility of not teaching my children about God... It's not fear. It's responsibility. I will do what my mother did… she took us to church, put us in Sunday school… just because it doesn't click for me, it doesn't mean it won't click for them. I see it with my brothers and sister. My brother is funny… He's very political on the left and doesn't like the church or priests… his wife takes the kids to church… I think if anything he would be bothered if there was a Sunday the kids didn't go to church (*laughs*)… Why? Because there is a difference between being an atheist and not liking church politics… What I see in my family are these different approaches to religion… So I need to give my kids the option of believing in God. Of having a religion. My mother and sister call it faith. I don't understand, but it's my responsibility to give them the opportunities to understand or not understand… (*laughs*)… The point is they have to know and if there is a God, he will take care of the rest and it will be ok.

Personal Crisis

Still some women referred to a personal crisis later in life that led them back to church and prayer. During the personal crises, the women described the process of "literally walk(ing) into a church for a moment of prayer and guidance", or as Gloria said, even "a heart to heart hollering match with God":

> I had just gotten the pregnancy results. I got home, prepared a candlelight dinner for my husband and waited. He never showed up. I was going crazy. My brothers were out looking for him. Looking for his car, taking all the possible ways home looking for the car. We called the police; my brothers and uncle went to all the emergency rooms of all the hospitals in Manhattan and Queens. Nothing. Finally, at nine the next morning he called and said he wasn't coming home and he wanted a divorce… I told him I was pregnant, and he said he knew and he didn't want the baby and I should take care of it… abortion... I called my brothers to tell them to stop the search… It was all so unreal… I got dressed and walked to St Markella church. I hadn't been to church since I got married. I sat there, and at one point, I started yelling at God... Yeah well, I'm not sure how God takes it when we yell at him (*laughs*). Demanding he tell me what was happening. Why? What did I do? What was I supposed to do? I was yelling for a couple of hours… crying, yelling… inside my head... At some point, I was crying and said, "God, can you please watch over this baby because I'm not gonna abort, and I don't know how to raise a child on my own. I need your help God. This child needs you God. You have to promise me that you're gonna watch over this baby." Or something like that (*wipes tears from her eyes*). I just felt a calm and peace come over me. It was going to be ok. And everything turned out ok.

Eleni said she had not been in church since her four-year-old had been baptised. She and her family would attend Good Friday and Resurrection services, but always from outside the church building because they would always arrive late, and there would be no room inside. She lost loved ones during the 9/11 attacks of the Twin Towers. Like so many "survivors" that day, Eleni was tormented because as she said,

> the only reason I'm still here is because I was late… everything was late… I woke up late, the school bus was late, I was late dropping off the little ones at day care. Just late. God didn't want me to go anywhere that day.
> It took me a few weeks to get out of bed. One day I got up, put on my sweats and went to church. It was a weekday. I sat there and cried. I just cried. I wanted to talk to God, but I couldn't. I didn't know what to say. I cried… my cousin dead. Five of my co-workers dead… What was I to say? There is nothing to say. I cried. For weeks, I would go in and just sit there and cry. It took me a few months to say a prayer… I asked God to watch over my family and to give me strength because I have three little children and elderly parents who depend on me… I still find peace in the church… I registered my kids in Sunday school and I go every week… The priest knows what happened… there are three of us [in the parish, A.K.] who survived that day… one man was… lost… He [the priest, A.K.] still prays for us and those who were lost.

Tania is 51. She said that she knew she was lesbian since she was a teenager, and it left her confused and frightened. She left the church in her early twenties

> because I didn't know what else to do… 9/11 did it for me… I needed to be in God's house. I know God is with us wherever we are, but it's different. Now I do go to

> Church. I go, but I don't receive Holy Communion. I don't believe that others there are any less sinners than I am, just different sins. The fact that someone sees me as just a sinner, while they tell themselves they are following God's ways, is the way of the Pharisee. So I just look at me and know that I still have a lot of work to do with God, but I have to do it without the priests, because the first thing priests want to do when you tell them that you're gay or lesbian, is to condemn you. I don't believe God condemns people just because they're gay or lesbian. I believe that when Jesus comes during the Final Judgement to judge the world, more prostitutes, more gay and lesbians and more criminals will be rising up with Jesus than sexual prudes and straight and law abiding citizens… because otherwise it doesn't make sense that God would leave behind all those people who love him and want to be with him. There are times I want to scream at Jesus and ask him why he gave men the power of condemnation… loosening and binding, salvation or condemnation… we're not theologians, right? And our words don't mean anything to those who proclaim they know God. So I just go and sit there and say my prayers and keep quiet.

"There was a yearning, a hunger inside that just wouldn't go away"

Some of the women talked about a "yearning" and "hunger" that they "had inside that just wouldn't go away", or, as Hope said,

> I knew something was missing. Nothing would fill me. There was a void inside me that no one and nothing could fill. Even music didn't fill it… it was there from the day I walked out of the church until the day I went back almost fifteen years later.

One would expect this "hunger" and "yearning" to be characteristic of the spiritual seekers; however, even women who described themselves as simply believers or uncertain of their faith also talked about experiencing this "hunger", "emptiness", "thirst", or "gaping hole inside".

Kathy, a nurse, stopped attending church services because as she said,

> there was no time. And I didn't like priests (*laughs*). So, it was convenient that I worked on weekends, nights, days, nurses have crazy hours and the two Sundays a month I was off I needed to sleep… There was this thing inside me that just would not fill. An emptiness. I was always hungry no matter what and how much I ate. For years this went on… no, I never prayed, I just didn't know what it was. Until one day I was walking past St Irene, went in, lit a candle and sat there… there was no service. I just sat there. Quiet. Then I talked to God. I said and I didn't even know what I was saying, "thank you God for bringing me here. I needed you all these years and I didn't know what it was. Thank you. You filled me". And that was it. And now twice a month when I'm not working on Sundays, I go… No, I'm not hungry anymore.

Alina, a 46-year-old financial analyst, said,

> I didn't know I was what some call spiritual. When I decided "no more", I had put all this behind me… There was just an emptiness. There came a time when my work was still enjoyable, but there was something that was missing inside… a need to connect, this tunnel that kept telling me, "you're not travelling with me".

The spiritual seekers in the sample differ from the other women as to the processes and reasons for returning to the church as well as their participation in church life. All five of the spiritual seekers in the sample returned to the church, said Janine, with "great deliberation"; Diane added, "and urgency".

Janine and Diane became friends while in college; each had in her own time and for her own reasons "walked out of the church". The two women spent a few years exploring New Age groups. They soon met three other Greek Orthodox women who also exited the church and were "without a spiritual home"; the five became close friends for the next few decades. As Janine said: "Five Greek Orthodox women who walked out of church in our late teens or early twenties but did not leave God behind. Instead, we went looking for God elsewhere. For whatever reason, God had put all five of us in the same room, and He was watching us (*laughs*)."

I asked Diane and the other spiritual seekers why they returned to the church: "Oh… one of us was invited to a Wiccan retreat… and all five of us went to church (*laughs*)."

Upon their return, the women took on active roles as volunteers in church as well as other community organisations, working with children, elderly, sick and the poor. Despite their participation in church-related groups and missionary work, the women's return to the church is still characterised by "silence". While the women discussed with clergy (specifically their priest and spiritual fathers) the reasons for their return, they did not discuss the problems that drove them away.

> It's part of the confession. So, the priest can help. Wicca and Buddhism are no joke. I worked with Wiccans for decades and I did not even know… I told my priest one of the things that pushed me away, and he started arguing with me to prove how that priest was right… I just stopped talking. There was no dialogue… I guess we're very careful with our words and our battles. We focus on the work. … There's a silence. Nothing is verbalised, but there's a lot going on… Some priests and laity… hold the mantle of judgement with pride… Georgia says they pounce the gavel of judgement quite powerfully… And that's why we don't think women as clergy would change anything… They need a re-orientation of hearts and minds… both the men and the women in those pews, it's not just the clergy... Jesus changed everything. He changed the game rules… The young know this, they are weaned on Jesus' words. And they grow up and they see what's going on and they leave. There are real reasons that so many women and young people lose themselves in the New Age groups, but they [the clergy, A.K.] don't want to hear anything about this. I wish God would bring us another St Paisios for these young people.[34]

34 St Paisios the Athonite (1924-1994) was canonised by the Holy and Great Synod of the Ecumenical Patriarchate of Constantinople in January 2015. St Paisios lived through the twentieth century and is remembered by his kindness to those who sought his advice. While St Paisios did not write his teachings, these have been gathered from those who knew him, visited him and/or wrote to him for guidance.

Conclusion

Roof estimates that two thirds of baby boomers left their religious institution during their teens or early twenties.[35] His study of the general American population found that only 25 percent of those who made a conscious decision to leave their religious institution were "returnees". There are no numbers or statistical trends for the Greek Orthodox. In fact, there is a dearth of sociological and anthropological research on Greek Orthodox spirituality and religious practices in the United States. This paper did not examine rates of distancing and returning to the Greek Orthodox Church. Rather, it looked at the processes and reasons women gave for distancing themselves from the church and their return to the church. While there are men and women in my larger sample of interviews who have not returned to the church, their interviews were not analysed for this paper because that entailed a very different research question than the one I was interested in exploring.

Greek Orthodox women, like other women in the Abrahamic traditions, leave their original spiritual home and years later some return to it. During their years "away" from the church, these women considered the Greek Orthodox Church as "their" church. While the majority of the Greek Orthodox women in this study talked about exiting the church for time constraints, a smaller but significant group left the church in their younger years for political reasons. These women defined themselves as feminists and/or on the left who found the church's structure and politics stifling and not nurturing of their spirituality. After spending a number of years away from the church, the women returned. Neither their politics nor their values have changed. These women are still feminists, still on the left, and their commitment to social justice is even stronger than it was in their youth. The women's politics are informed by their faith, specifically, they rely on Jesus' social teachings.

The women often offered what they understood to be different interpretations of non-dogmatic teachings of the Greek Orthodox tradition, as regards issues of the church's responsibilities in relation to sinners. Some of the women said that they left the church because they found that their own understanding of the "healing medicine" the church is to offer differed from what they actually saw in the pews. Warning against sounding like zealots, the women spoke about Jesus' teachings of non-judgement and of forgiveness as the premise of healing, not punishment or suffering; for the women, the sin itself was/is the punishment. The women were careful to point out that these are non-dogmatic issues, but very important in determining whether the faithful stay or leave the Church.

The issue of women reconciling their politics and values with a patriarchal institution upon their return does not lend itself to a simple answer. While one may be tempted to say that these women decided to "overlook" some of the

35 Roof, *A Generation of Seekers* (as n. 29).

political ideologies still existent in the church, it would nevertheless be an erroneous assessment. The women do not overlook the hierarchical structures of the institution, but also do not directly challenge the institutional hierarchies. The reasons for this are complex. The women distinguish between the theology and prayer in Greek Orthodoxy on the one hand, and the institutional structures on the other hand. To the extent that the women returned for sacraments or for the children or for the theology and spiritual nurturance, they orient their evaluations/assessments precisely towards these issues in the church. The women do not interpret the theology of Greek Orthodoxy as male-centred, but rather, find ample evidence for the importance of women in the church's historical and theological traditions; both men and women saints are venerated, respected and honoured for their contributions to the church and their work in bringing the Divine into this world.

To the extent that Greek Orthodoxy is an ethno-confessional identity and a religious tradition that carries with it two thousand years of cultural history, the women on the one hand felt unfulfilled in other churches or traditions, and some even found that it was precisely this duality of the theology and the social history of the group that contributed to their feminism and spirituality. All of the women in the sample used the group's social history, including the Ancient Greek pagan traditions as a prism through which to situate themselves and relate to the larger American changing religious landscape. In particular, this history has in some cases acted as a stopgap for women to explore New Age groups or to venture out into the more popular or more esoteric forms of worshipping the feminine or Goddess worship.

The religious virtuosi or active spiritual seekers pointed out that many of the young begin exploring New Age healing groups and arts, which are spiritually at odds with the Abrahamic traditions. These women ask the church to take a pro-active position and educate (not dictate) on the differences between the Abrahamic and New Age spiritual and healing traditions.[36]

All of the women in the sample acknowledged that the church has changed some of its politics towards women in the last few decades but are still burdened by the fact that the church is still not welcoming of homosexual individuals. For the active spiritual seekers or the religious virtuosi, this is especially troubling given the changing spiritual landscape of the U.S. From the perspective of this small group of women, it is imperative that the church begin nurturing the spirituality of both men and women, heterosexuals and homosexuals, as well as other marginalised groups equally and to take proactive steps to welcome, bring in and bring back the young it loses with each new cohort.

When they were young, the women said they felt powerless and they left the church. They did not speak to others in the church about the issues they were

36 The research I had done for this part of the story could unfortunately not be included in this article due to space restraints.

concerned about. The women spoke about a disconnect or "gap" between themselves and the clergy. They feared that they could not approach the clergy with their concerns. This was the case even when the women experienced a crisis of faith, whether the crisis was brought on because of the politics presented as theology or other events. Their exit was silent – they simply walked out. Their return is also "silent". While the women do approach the priest and talk about the reasons for their return as part of their confession, they do not talk about why they had left years earlier. Some of the women, on the one hand, expressed that they now see that the church is responsive to the needs of the faithful, at least those who remain in the pews. On the other hand, the women still have misgivings about "things that are not verbalised"; about personal relations based on issues of the church's responsibility for forgiveness and charity of the heart.

The women who left the church in their earlier years for political reasons spoke about how they "struggled" with their spirituality. Some of these women said that they became avid readers of Scriptures and saints' writings as they began finding their way back to the pews. The women set their discussions within theological frameworks – they are well versed in the teachings of the Greek Orthodox tradition. The women are not outsiders to the church, their misgivings and disappointments are those of "insiders" who want to improve the church's mission. Many expressed regrets that they did not receive spiritual guidance in their earlier years or even after their return. They spoke about the "gap" between them and clergy, often using words like "felt/feel isolated", "alone", or "spiritually struggling",

Many of the women in the sample were using the interviews as part of their religious agency to affect change in the church. From their perspective, the Greek Orthodox Archdiocese of America is a relatively small church, and it does have a spiritual commitment to the faithful and an interest in hearing what the faithful have to say. Despite the women having left the church for as long as two or three decades, all of the women in the sample considered the Greek Orthodox Church as "their" church, and invariably the women would remind me that "they read everything", precisely because of the fact that it is a small church in a changing spiritual landscape. And so, the women expressed great hope that "their" church would be responsive to the changing needs of the faithful and re-evaluate the role of politics and ideologies in the church presented as dogma.

The women did offer practical advice to the clergy of the Greek Orthodox Archdiocese: reconsider the issue of young girls as altar girls, the reinstitution of the office of the deaconess with training to work with different vulnerable populations, hiring or recruiting volunteer social workers in the parishes with training in family counselling, the formation of weekly or monthly group meetings lead by women volunteers and men volunteers to discuss issues important to young women and men, and extending spiritual educational programmes for the young in the parishes.

Religion on Maidan: The Case of Orthodox Christians in Ukraine

Oleg Kyselov

Religion takes up different positions in society. It could be private or public, in the core of social structure or marginal. It also can be the guardian of the old social order or effect various social changes. Each religion can take up any of these positions, which depend on external factors. If there is a prospect that a marginal religion can take up a better position in society, this religion will probably support social changes. By contrast, if there is a prospect for a religion to lose financial support from the state or any other privilege, then this religion will probably be on the side of the old social order and turn against any social changes. From the perspective of the Rational Choice Theory, which considers the interactions among religious organisations in terms of their competition,[1] a religious organisation will support those social changes, which can lead it to a new niche in the religious market, and it would be against social changes if they lead to the loss of customers. The main goal of this chapter is to highlight the reasons why the various Orthodox Churches in Ukraine held divergent positions during the *Revolution of Dignity*.

The notion *Revolution of Dignity* stands for the mass civil and political protests against the Ukrainian president Victor Yanukovych and his government over the course of 2013. The protest's primary cause was the unwillingness of the president to sign the European Union Association Agreement, but subsequently the protest grew into a movement for human rights and against police brutality towards students. Considering that the crucial events happened on the main square of the Ukrainian capital city *Maidan Nezalezhnosti* [Independence Square], the protests originally were called *Euromaidan*, and then *Revolution of Dignity* or simply *Maidan*. It must be mentioned that the protests took place not only in Kyiv, but also in Lviv, Ternopil, Odessa and other cities. All of these protests were collectively called *Maidan*, but this chapter will focus solely on Kyiv's Maidan. Ukrainian social scholars as well as public intellectuals are inclined to believe that the *Revolution of Dignity* is a sort of a Rubicon, which marks a turning point in the modern stage of Ukraine's history. Considering that the war with Russia started immediately after the revolution, this point of view is seldom criticised.

To understand the place of the Orthodox Churches on Maidan, a brief digression into the history of local Orthodoxy and its peculiarities in the structure

1 Rodney Stark/Roger Finke, *Acts of Faith: Explaining the Human Side of Religion*, Berkeley/CA 2000.

of the Ukrainian religious landscape is needed.[2] The Soviet Union celebrated the millennium of the Baptism of Kievan Rus' in 1988. This took place during *Perestroika* times, meaning the liberalisation of state-church relations and the formation of a more tolerant attitude towards religious believers. In this context, the Ukrainian Autocephalous Orthodox Church (UAOC) and the Ukrainian Greek Catholic (Uniate) Church were officially registered by the authorities.[3] The UAOC claimed to be the revival of the UAOC that had been established in 1919 as a national church using the Ukrainian language in worship, which re-appeared in the 1940s during the Nazi occupation of Ukraine's territories. The relations between the UAOC and the Ukrainian Orthodox Church (UOC) – an Exarchate of the Russian Orthodox Church (ROC), i.e. of the Moscow Patriarchate (MP), until 1990 – were rather conflictual. This was due to the fact that the UAOC (similar to the Greek Catholic Church) developed its structure by taking over entire UOC parishes with their church buildings, as well as by enticing individual believers. After Ukraine gained its independence in 1991, the UOC also raised the question about achieving autocephaly, that is full ecclesiastical independence. This would help it to become competitive within the demanding Ukrainian religious market. When the Moscow Patriarchate rejected this idea, a part of the UOC with its head Metropolitan Filaret (Denysenko) proceeded to a union with the UAOC and the creation of an autocephalous Ukrainian Orthodox Church of the Kyiv Patriarchate (UOC-KP) in 1992, which, however, did not enjoy a Pan-Orthodox canonical status.[4] In addition, as a result of the inner struggle for power within the UOC-KP a group of clerics re-established the UAOC in 1995. From then onwards, there were three main Orthodox Churches in Ukraine: the UAOC, the UOC, and the UOC-KP.

The Orthodox Churches in the Structure of the Ukrainian Religious Landscape

The official statistics of the Ministry of Culture of Ukraine show that in the beginning of 2013, there were 36,995 religious organisations and 52 percent of them (or 19,107) were Orthodox. 12,895 religious organisations were associated with the UOC, 4,702 with the UOC-KP, 1,247 with the UAOC, and 253 with other

2 This chapter was written before the declaration of the autocephaly of the Ukrainian Orthodox Church in 2019 by the Ecumenical Patriarchate of Constantinople, which decisively changed Ukraine's religious landscape and subsequently led to a schism between Constantinople and Moscow.

3 See Zenon V. Wasyliw, "Orthodox Churches in Ukraine", in Lucian N. Leustean (ed.), *Eastern Christianity and Politics in the Twenty-First Century*, London 2014, 312–333, here 312–313.

4 Ibid., 314–315.

Orthodox communities, such as the Russian True Orthodox Church and the Russian Orthodox Church Abroad (see Figure 1).

Figure 1. The Number of Religious Organisations among Ukraine's Orthodox Churches (2013)

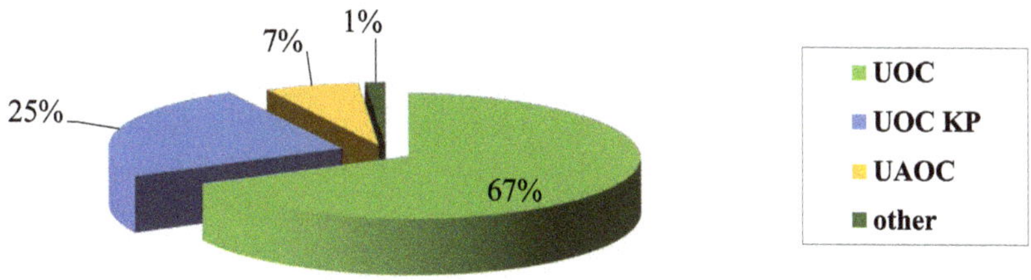

Data of the Ministry of Culture of Ukraine as of 01.01.2013.[5]

The second aspect, which characterises the situation of the Orthodox population in Ukraine, is the self-identification of Ukrainian citizens with a certain church jurisdiction. According to the data of various sociological surveys, 68-77 percent of Ukrainians identify themselves as Orthodox Christians. The data of the Institute of Sociology of the Ukrainian National Academy of Sciences show a distinctive geographical repartition of Orthodox Christians: In most of the regions (24 out of 27), the majority of citizens followed the UOC and the UOC-KP and in seven of them their joint percentage was higher than 90 percent. Concretely, more than 40 percent of the UOC adherents were located in 13 regions and they exceeded 60 percent in three of them (Sevastopol', Lugansk and Dnipropetrovsk). Similarly, more than 40 percent of the people identifying with UOC-KP were located in 14 regions, and the number of adherents of UOC-KP exceeded 60 percent in five regions. At the same time, there was no region in which there was more than 10 percent of UAOC adherents and 70 percent of all its parishes were located in Western Ukraine.[6]

5 *ЗВІТ про мережу церков і релігійних організацій в Україністаном на 1 січня 2013 року (Форма No 1)* [Report on Church and Religious Organisations Network Ukraine on 01.01.2013 (Form 1)], URL: http://risu.org.ua/php_uploads/files/articles/ArticleFiles_51768_Forma1_2013.pdf [22.06.2016]. A similar picture persists in 2018. There is a total of 36,184 religious organisations, and almost 54 percent of them (19,453) are Orthodox. 12,675 religious organisations are associated with the UOC, 5,319 with the UOC-KP, 1,211 with the UAOC, and 248 with other Orthodox communities. See *ЗВІТ про мережу церков і релігійних організацій в Україністаном на 1 січня 2018 року* [Report on Church and Religious Organisations Network Ukraine on 01.01.2018], URL: https://risu.org.ua/php_uploads/files/articles/ArticleFiles_70440_FORMA_I_-_2018.xls [10.05.2018].

6 Oleg Kozlovskiy, "Рівень релігійності та конфесійна структура областей України (соціологійний вимір)" [The Level of Religiosity and the Confessional Structure of Ukraine (A Sociological Perspective)], in V. Vorona/M. Shulga (eds), *Українське*

Furthermore, the sociological surveys of the Razumkov Centre demonstrated that Ukrainians preferred the UOC-KP until 2010. Scholars traditionally explain this fact with reference to psychology: Ukrainians, most of them indifferent to jurisdictional church issues, simply chose that questionnaire answer which was closer to them, more familiar, and associated with something more local (Kyiv), rather than that which was remote, unknown, and associated with something foreign (Moscow). In this context, it should be noted that in December 1991, 92 percent of Ukrainians voted for the independence of Ukraine from the USSR (conceived as independence from Russia and Moscow). Besides, the survey of the Razumkov Centre demonstrated the domination of UOC followers in 2010. The increase in the number of believers who sympathised with the UOC (from 14 percent in 2000 to 34.5 percent in 2010)[7] happened on account of the "ordinary Orthodox Christians" (see Table 1), namely those "believers" who simply considered themselves as Orthodox Christians by cultural identification, but did not know or care about the church affiliation of their specific parish.

Table 1. Citizens' identification with Orthodox Churches (Data of the Razumkov Centre).[8]

	UOC	UOC-KP	UAOC	Ordinary Orthodox	Don't know
2000	9.2	12.1	1.3	38.6	4.6
2010	23.6	15.1	0.9	25.9	1.6
2013	19.6	18.3	0.8	28.8	2.5
2014	17.4	22.4	0.7	28.1	1.4
2016	15.0	25.0	1.8	21.2	2.0
2017	12.0	26.5	1.1	24.3	0.8
2018	12.8	28.7	0.3	23.4	1.9

суспільство 1992-2010. Соціологічний моніторинг [Ukrainian Society, 1992-2010. Sociological Monitoring], Kyiv 2010, 441–448.

7 It must be mentioned that after the *Revolution of Dignity*, a contrary trend is observed: The number of UOC-KP "adherents" has increased and from 2014 citizens show their support to UOC-KP. See Table 1.

8 *Особливості релігійного і церковно-релігійного самовизначення українських громадян: тендеції 2010-2018 рр.* [The Pecularitites of Religious and Church-confessional Self-identification of Ukrainian Citizens: Tendencies between 2010 and 2018], Kyiv 2018, 16.

This shift in the believer's attitudes can be correlated with the personality of the new Moscow Patriarch Kirill (in office since February 2009), who systematically visited Ukraine between 2009 and 2012. His close contacts with the Ukrainian flock promoted the spread and the strengthening of the loyalty to the ROC.

The 2013 data of the Razumkov Centre demonstrated an almost equal number of adherents between the UOC and the UOC-KP: 19.6 percent and 18.3 percent respectively. The decreasing number of UOC adherents can also be connected to the visits of Patriarch Kirill, which were transformed in the meantime from something exclusive to commonplace events. Even the Patriarch himself was transformed from a long-awaited person to an ordinary VIP, who was surrounded by public scandals.

The first scandal was connected to the Patriarch's visit to Kharkiv in May 2011. The organisers expected that his liturgy on the Square of Freedom would be attended by approximately 100,000 people. However, there were only 40,000 according to the ROC and 5,000 according to the journalists. One of the official sites of the UOC tried to overcome this gap by photoshopping the pictures, doubling the quantity of the believers shown. Yet, the lie was exposed as soon as the original photo was also published.

The second scandal happened in April 2012. Journalists noticed that the Patriarch had a Swiss-made luxury watch Breguet, whose value was estimated to approximately 30,000 Euros. This was extremely contradicting the status of the Patriarch, who in fact is a monk and should not possess any property. It was also contradicting his official rhetoric, in which he condemned the modern consumerist culture and recommended his flock to live modestly. The Patriarch himself claimed that his photos with the Breguet watch were photoshopped. At the same time, his press office heightened the scandal – it erased the watch on all the photos where it could be seen. However, a blogger located a photo on the official site of the ROC, where there was no sight of the watch on the Patriarch's hand, but the watch's reflection on the lacquered surface of the table was still visible. These scandals negatively affected the enthusiasm and the inspiration among "new adherents"[9] of Russian Orthodoxy in Ukraine.

Before the *Revolution of Dignity* in 2013, therefore, the UOC dominated in the number of parishes (religious organisations) as well as in the number of adherents. But the UOC-KP permanently kept increasing its number of parishes and believers on the national and local levels. We can also presume that the overall marginal status of the UAOC can be explained by its insignificant influence on the state and regional levels and the small number of its adherents.

---

9 This expression does not refer to real converts and believers who consciously practice religion. In this context, it refers to people who sympathised with the ROC and its affiliation in Ukraine, the UOC, but were not deeply religious.

The Religious Factor in the *Revolution of Dignity*

It must be pointed out from the outset that I do not consider religion as a defining factor on Maidan,[10] as it is quite possible to tell the story of the three months of Ukrainian protests without ever mentioning religion. Such an interpretation "without religion" is presented in the book of Ukrainian journalist Sonya Koshkina: *Maidan. Nerozkazana istoriya* [Maidan. The Untold Story].[11] There are just a few episodes in which the book mentions religion: the rescue of students from police persecution in Saint Michael's Monastery during the night between 29 and 30 November 2013;[12] the peace-making pleas made by priests to police and protesters during the second assault on Maidan on 10 and 11 December 2013;[13] the participation of Ukrainian President Victor Yanukovych in the public prayer on the Day of Ukrainian Unity on 22 January 2014;[14] the meeting of Victor Yanukovych with churchmen on 24 January 2014;[15] the clergymen protecting the protesters who were taken to custody by the police on 18 February 2014;[16] the evacuation of the field hospital from the House of Trade Unions to Saint Michael's Monastery;[17] and the burial service for deceased protesters.[18] Several other episodes on Maidan in which religion was involved (e.g., the priests standing between the protesters and the police on Grushevsky street, the letter of the Ukrainian Ministry of Culture to the Ukrainian Greek Catholic Church, the addresses of the All-Ukrainian Council of Churches and Religious Organisations) are not covered in this book. However, the last photo in the second block of

---

10 This is also the position of Tetiana Kalenychenko, who wrote: "The religious factor does not play a central role in the current social and political conflict in Ukraine" (Tetiana Kalenychenko, *Релігійна складова суспільно-політичного конфлікту кінця 2013-2017 рр. в Україні* [The Religious Component of Social and Political Conflict between 2013 and 2017 in Ukraine], Kyiv 2018, 34). It should be mentioned that Kalenychenko not only refers to the *Revolution of Dignity*, but also to the war in Donbas. Indeed, there are several articles and collective volumes, which have focused on the religious dimension of these developments. See, for example, Catherine Wanner (ed.), "Religion and Political Crisis in Ukraine", *Euxeinos* 17 (2015); Rob van der Laarse/Mykhailo N. Cherenkov/Vitaly V. Proshak/Tetiana Mykhalchuk (eds), *Religion, State, Society, and Identity in Transition Ukraine*, Tilburg 2015; Cyril Hovorun, "Churches in the Ukrainian Public Square", *Toronto Journal of Theology* 31/1 (2015) 3–14; Andrii Krawchuk/Thomas Bremer (eds), *Churches in the Ukrainian Crisis*, London 2017.

11 Sonja Koshkina, *Майдан. Нерозказана історія* [Maidan. The Untold History], Kyiv 2015.

12 Ibid., 65.

13 Ibid., 133.

14 Ibid., 180.

15 Ibid., 184.

16 Ibid., 253.

17 Ibid., 257.

18 Ibid., 274, 302.

pictures (between pages 208 and 209) shows the silhouette of a priest with a cross and has the following caption: "During all three months, the priests of all confessions were standing on the barricades, often forming a live shield between the protesters and the police."[19]

Nevertheless, different religions were present on Maidan, and two books have dealt specifically with this issue: *Maidan i Tserkva* [Maidan and the Church] edited by Lyudmila Fylypovych and Oksana Gorkusha, and *Tserkov' na Maidane* [The Church on Maidan] by Alexei Gordeev. In general, there is enough data about the place of religion in the Maidan events to write several books. Even if we consider religion as having little effect on the protests against government or on the rally activity, it still affected the everyday life of rally participants in many ways.

There is no doubt that religion was a part of Maidan's life both on an official level (e.g., clergymen present on the Maidan stage praying with and supporting protesters) and on an informal level (e.g., clergymen conducting prayers in the prayer tent and distributing copies of the Gospels). The letter of the Ministry of Culture of Ukraine to the Ukrainian Greek Catholic Church proved that the participation of Churches in Maidan's life was so evident that the authorities tried to limit it.[20] The actions of the Orthodox clergy, the Greek Catholic priests, and the Protestant missionaries supported the moral and psychological state of the rally participants. This was the most important outcome of the presence of religion on Maidan.

It is worth mentioning that most rally participants initially had only elementary religious knowledge. According to the author's observations in December 2013, the people on Maidan were generally indifferent to the priests on the stage, as well as to the politicians or civil activists. This is why we cannot argue that religion was a very important factor for rally participants. The following data confirm this assumption: Nearly half of the protesters participated in the prayer *Our Father* (because it is the most known prayer), but only about one fourth prayed the *Hail Mary*. The crowd on Kyiv's Maidan chanted *Glory to the Heroes!* after *Glory to Ukraine!*[21] more clearly and confidently than *Forever!*

---

19 One of the chapters in Koshkina's book bears the title "Political Orthodoxy serving Victor Yanukovych". It does not deal with the reaction of the Orthodox Churches to the Maidan events, but with the usage of Orthodoxy as an instrument in the policy of Yanukovych and his party. Under the term "political Orthodoxy", we should understand the politicisation of the Orthodox Church, as well the political activity of non-governmental organisations, which identify themselves with the Orthodox Church using its religious symbols and rhetoric.

20 In this letter, the Ministry warned against religious services in public places (Maidan) without prior coordination with the authorities. The Ministry even threatened the Ukrainian Greek Catholic Church with removing its official registration.

21 "Glory to Ukraine! Glory to the Heroes!" ("Слава Україні! Героям слава!") is a Ukrainian nationalistic greeting and slogan. It was so widespread during Maidan that even

Amen after *Glory to Jesus Christ*. A possible interpretation is that in the perception of Ukrainians the political slogans are more easily memorised than the religious ones. Some observers noted that religious indifference was typical only for the first weeks of the *Revolution of Dignity*, but with time, religious slogans became an integral part of the Maidan space.[22]

For some of the rally participants, though, the Christian motivation absolutely dominated the political one. In Gordeev's book the interviewees (all of them Protestants) use Biblical argumentation to explain the functioning of Maidan and their direct participation therein.[23] Moreover, all of them underlined the peaceful nature of the rally and most of them clearly claimed that they were not ready to use violence. The majority of Protestant activists considered Maidan as a place for evangelism. On the one hand, the number of copies of the Gospels[24] handed out was impressive, but, on the other hand, this proves our observation that the rally participants were indifferent to religion, at least at the beginning of the *Revolution of Dignity*.[25]

Tetiana Kalenychenko reckons that we should distinguish several different roles of religion in the conflicts of 2013-14. She marks out four stages of the *Maidan* and shows that the role of religion varied: At the beginning, there was no religion at all, then the churches publicly confirmed their condemnation of violent conflict. When the violence between rally participants and police began, the churches became a noticeable part of Maidan, and at the last stage, there were religious rites for the dead Maidan activists.[26]

---

the liberals used it. On 4 October 2018, it also became the official greeting of the Ukrainian army and police.

22 Gennadiy Tselkovskiy, "Релігія вплетена в ландшафт Майдану так, як і в усе українське суспільство" [Religion is Interwoven with the Maidan Landscape in the Same Way as it is with the Entire Ukrainian Society], in Ludmila Fylypovych/Oksana Gorkusha (eds), *Майдан і Церква. Хроніка подій та експертна оцінка* [Maidan and the Church. A Chronicle of Events and an Expert Evaluation], Kyiv 2014, 90–92.

23 Aleksei Gordeev, *Церковь* на *Майдане* [Church on Maidan], Kyiv 2015.

24 An activist from a Protestant prayer tent claimed that during the three months of the *Revolution of Dignity* the Protestants handed out nearly 50,000 New Testaments (Ibid., 204).

25 Alla Kyrydon, "Церква як складова громадянського суспільства (2013-2014)" [The Church as Part of Civil Society, 2013-2014], in O. Kyrychuk/M. Omelchuk/I. Orlevyk (eds), *Історія релігій в Україні: науковий щорічник – Книга 1* [History of Religions in Ukraine: Scientific Yearbook, Volume 1], Lviv 2015, 576–585, here 580.

26 Kalenychenko, *Релігійна складова* (as n. 10), 75–79.

The Orthodox Churches in Relation to Maidan

Two Orthodox Churches, the UOC and the UOC-KP, had a legal status in Ukraine at that time, but they took up different positions within the international Orthodox world: The UOC was recognised and was a part of the ROC, whereas the UOC-KP was still unrecognised either by the Moscow Patriarchate or by any other Orthodox Church.

Generally, when the churches tried to establish friendly relations with Ukrainian politicians, they usually hoped to get some benefits (e.g., land for the construction of church buildings, restitution of church property). Besides the pragmatic, there was also an ideological dimension to this policy: The churches and their adherents usually focused on political forces whose ideology and foreign policy vector corresponded to the ecclesiastical orientations. In our specific context, the overall scene appeared as follows: The adherents of the UOC-KP tended to support right, right-of-centre, national democratic, and pro-Western political parties and blocks. At the same time, the adherents of the UOC preferred to give their votes to left, left-of-centre, and pro-Russian political forces. The churches in Ukraine have always addressed their believers concerning future elections, often hinting at or agitating for a particular candidate.

Furthermore, both these churches participated in the All-Ukrainian Council of Churches and Religious Organisations (AUCCRO). This inter-confessional and inter-religious organisation exists since 1996 and includes Orthodox, Catholic, and Protestant Churches, as well as Jews and Muslims. It was created by the Ukrainian government with the purpose of minimising the potential for inter-Orthodox and Orthodox-Catholic conflicts. After the Orange Revolution of 2004, however, the AUCCRO refused to be controlled by the government and became an independent institution. Since then, it has promulgated numerous addresses to the President, the Parliament, and the Ukrainian people on up-to-date issues of social and political life.

As already stated, the main goal of the protests at the end of 2013 was to support the stronger connection of Ukraine to the European Union. In this context, it must be mentioned that on 30 November 2013 a part of the members of the AUCCRO published the document *Звернення Церков і релігійних організацій до українського народу* [An Appeal of the Churches and Religious Organisations to the Ukrainian People], in which religious leaders advocated in favour of the governmental policy of European integration: "Our historical roots naturally determine Ukraine's future – to be an independent state in the sphere of free European nations."[27] The appeal appeared on the eve of the visit of Ukrainian religious representatives to the European Parliament in Strasbourg and the

27 *Heads of Churches and Religious Organizations Express their European Integration Position*, 30.09.2013, URL: http://risu.org.ua/en/index/all_news/ukraine_and_world/international_relations/53846 [19.02.2019].

European Council in Brussels. Nevertheless, the document was not ratified by all AUCCRO members, although it reflected the dominant trend in the council. Many of the critical voices came from the UOC community, asking the UOC head, Metropolitan Volodymyr (Sabodan), not to sign it and expressing scepticism towards European integration.

Between December 2013 and February 2014, the AUCCRO reacted to all the unfolding events on Maidan and promulgated seven related official addresses, declarations and communiqués. In all these documents, the support for protest rallies and the condemnation of all forms of violence can be witnessed. There was not even a hint of support for the president or the government. There was also a critical attitude towards foreign affairs (e.g., the unsigned association with the European Union) and domestic issues (e.g., the undemocratic engagements between state authorities and the participants in protest rallies).

The Ukrainian Orthodox Church of the Kyiv Patriarchate and Maidan

The UOC-KP entered the Maidan with Maidan entering the church. On the night of 30 November 2013, the police brutally broke up a peaceful student demonstration, beating the students with batons and chasing them in the city centre. The students found shelter in the Saint Michael's Monastery, affiliated with the UOC-KP. The Kyiv Orthodox Theological Academy is also located in this monastery, which makes it the most important centre of the Kyiv Patriarchate. Because the monastery is only a ten-minute walk from Maidan Nezalezhnosti, it became an essential part of Maidan's infrastructure during the following three months of protest actions. In the monastery, there was also a first-aid post, and in February 2014, it became the place where the bodies of the killed protesters were brought together.

The participation of clergymen of the UOC-KP in Maidan was blessed by Patriarch Filaret of Kyiv, the head of this church. Its priests, as well as the priests of other churches, morally supported the rally participants and performed various religious rites (e.g., confession, Eucharist), spiritual talks, and public prayers *in situ*. Public prayers were the most widespread practice, because they were initiated from the Maidan stage and planned for all the rally participants. Thus, the UOC-KP explicitly supported protest actions. One of the reasons for such an active position was the fact that President Viktor Yanukovych had planned to dissolve this church in the first year of his presidency. In addition, this church had for a long time maintained relations with national and democratic forces, which also participated in Maidan events. In his interviews in December 2013 and January 2014 Patriarch Filaret stated that Maidan's main goal was to support the

European integration of Ukraine, although this goal was not the top priority for rally participants.[28]

Denis Shestopalets has conducted a discourse analysis of Patriarch Filaret's speeches and interviews[29] and identified several rhetorical topoi: a) the church supported the Ukrainian people; b) the church was not an agent in the conflict; and c) the church was above politics. These discourses were intimately connected with each other. What Shestopalets particularly focused on was that all these positions were a part of the overall church ideology rather than a reflection of current affairs. First, sociological surveys show that only 40 to 60 percent of Ukrainians supported the *Revolution of Dignity*. Hence, when the church stood on the rally's side, it supported just one part of the Ukrainian people. Second, a large number of Filaret's statements legitimated Maidan and its demands, while none supported the government, the president or the police. Third, in spite of the fact that Filaret often claimed that the church principally was above politics, more common for his church was the position that an independent state (in this case: Ukraine) must also have an independent church. Solely under this condition can a state be truly independent. Therefore, according to Shestopalets, Filaret's position rendered the UOC-KP a public religion on state level.[30]

The Position of the Ukrainian Orthodox Church on Maidan

The situation regarding Maidan is more complex and interesting with regard to the UOC. On the official level, the UOC did not support and did not bless the participation of its clergymen in the Maidan events. Hence, officially it was not present on Maidan and tried to keep itself away from the political process as much as possible. The UOC followed the thesis of the church being above politics much more consistently. Certainly, this does not mean that its clergy and adherents were indifferent to the Maidan events. All the UOC official addresses at the end of 2013 and the beginning of 2014, however, were aimed not at supporting the people on

28 Ukrainian sociologists maintain that in early December 2013 the main reasons for rally participation were: the brutal beating of students on 30 November 2013 (70 percent), the refusal of President Yanukovich to sign the European Union Association Agreement (53.5 percent), and the aspiration for a better life (50 percent). See: *Майдан-2013: хто стоїть, чому і за що*? [Maidan-2013: Who stands by, why, and what for?], 10.11.2013, URL: https://dif.org.ua/article/ maydan-2013-khto-stoit-chomu-i-za-shcho [19.02.2019].

29 Denys Shestopalets, "Публічні релігії в Україні: дискурсивний аспект участі церков у Євромайдані" [Public Religions in Ukraine: Discursive Aspects of the Involvement of Churches in Euromaidan], Paper presented at the Congress of Young Scholars of Religion "Religion in Modern Culture", Kyiv, 24 October 2014.

30 See José Casanova, "What is Public Religion?", in Hugh Heclo/Wilfred M. McClay (eds), *Religion Returns to the Public Sphere: Faith and Policy in America*, Washington/DC 2003, 111–139.

Maidan or the authorities, but at condemning the violence on both sides. The UOC's position was the following: The church is above politics, its clergymen and laity hold different political positions, and therefore the church in general cannot support solely and exclusively one political party.

Nevertheless, various clergymen and laity from the UOC were still present on Maidan. Their activities differed from those of the other churches/confessions, because they did not have their own prayer tent and did not conduct any religious rites. The spokesman of the church, Father Georgiy (Kovalenko),[31] provided an explanation for not having a separate prayer tent: Kyiv had a sufficient number of churches and other religious buildings, which could perfectly satisfy the religious needs of Kyiv residents and guests.[32] Furthermore, the clergymen and laity publicly expressed different and sometimes even opposing positions and views concerning Maidan. No doubt, one can identify some major trends in the related UOC stance. Ukrainian society had noticed that the UOC was critical to the Maidan demands and many UOC churchmen held a negative attitude towards Maidan. For example, the head of the main Orthodox sanctuary of Ukraine, Kyiv Pechersky Lavra, Bishop Pavel (Lebed), publicly condemned Maidan and spoke harshly of rally participants. There was also a similar negative appraisal on the part of some famous Kyiv priests, such as the head of the Mission department of the UOC Kyiv eparchy, Andrej Tkachov. In his sermons, he outspokenly and severely condemned Maidan and the rally participants and called on his parish not to take part in these activities. His sermons became widely shared on the Internet in December 2013 and then in January 2014. Tkachov also mentioned that he prayed for the participants of protest rallies to fall ill, a point that caused many reactions. He was even rebuked by Bishop Antoniy (Pakanych), who was the Chief Executive Officer of the UOC, for his anti-Maidan sermons in February 2016. As a result, Tkachov admitted his mistake and after Maidan he moved to Moscow. Kirill Frolov, known as one of the ideologists of the *Russkiy mir*, as well as Tkachov himself, presented this move as a political flight,[33] although it is more

---

31 He was the spokesman of the Church and led the Synodal department of information and educational activity.

32 Georgiy Kovalenko, "Почему нашых священников нет на Евромайдане?" [Why are our Priests not on Euromaidan?], in Ludmila Fylypovych/Oksana Gorkusha (eds), *Майдан і Церква. Хроніка подій та експертна оцінка* [Maidan and the Church. A Chronicle of Events and an Expert Evaluation], Kyiv 2014, 241.

33 Kirill Frolov, "Хунта устроила репрессии против сторонников московского патриархата. Список пострадавших" [Junta Persecutes the Supporters of Moscow Patriarchate. A List of Sufferers], *Релігія в Україні*, 08.07.2015, URL: http://www.religion.in.ua/zmi/foreign_zmi/29975-xunta-ustroila-repressii-protiv-storonnikov-moskovskogo-patriarxata-spisok-postradavshix.html [19.02.2019].

probable that he was invited to Moscow for a better position within the church and a perspective for developing his activities further.[34]

Aside from this, the UOC also made several statements in support of Maidan. For example, on 10 December 2013, 25 UOC priests issued a statement, in which they acknowledged the integration with Europe and its values, which were considered as Christian in their basis. The churchmen called on the Ukrainians to unite, despite their regional differences, and formulated concrete commandments for peaceful resistance: "Observe laws and respect the freedom of everybody", "Do not be afraid!", "Do not fall for provocations", "Smile to passers-by", "Help your fellow humans in what you can", and "Reduce aggression. The police and the *titushki*[35] are also your fellow men".[36]

The UOC official position was influenced by the fact that the authorities usually identified themselves with this church. The majority of its believers from Central and Eastern Ukraine not only voted for the *Partiya Regioniv* [Party of Regions] – the party in power at that time –, but they also supported Ukraine's integration with Russia and Belarus, not with Europe. And if we consider that President Yanukovych, who was the leader of *Partiya Regioniv* and a member of the UOC, had pro-Russian political views, then it should be clear why Ukrainian society associated the UOC with Yanukovych's regime.

Despite everything, the peace-promoting action of UOC monks, who stood between the police and the protesters throughout the night of 21 January 2014 remains remarkable. The monks prayed for 23 hours, also joined by Protestant clergy and laity. While they were praying, there was no violent confrontation. But as soon as the monks stopped this "prayer marathon", the clashes resumed. It is interesting that there were people who considered these monks as being on the side of the police. This was because their prayer was regarded as a subterfuge to give *Bercut*[37] more time to regroup and to plan special techniques.[38] This shows

34 Denis Targonskii, "Падение звезды. По следам недавних выступлений о. Андрея Ткачева" [The Fall of a Star. Following Recent Speeches by Father Andrei Tkachov], *Релігія в Україні*, 15.01.2016, URL: http://www.religion.in.ua/main/31538-padenie-zvezdy-po-sledam-poslednix-vystuplenij-o-andreya-tkacheva.html [19.02.2019].

35 This was a generic term to characterise the aggressive young people with athletic appearance, who exerted violence against the rally participants. The term stems from the surname of Vadim Titushko, who took part in such actions in the spring of 2013 against the political opposition to Victor Yanukovych. He was subsequently sentenced to two years on probation. See Gordeev, *Церковь* (as n. 23), 18; Koshkina, *Майдан* (as n. 11), 40.

36 *Побеждай зло добром – обращение священнослужителей* [Fight Evil with Good – An Appeal of the Clergy], 10.12.2013, URL: http://www.kiev-orthodox.org/site/events/4963 [19.02.2019].

37 A notorious special operations unit of the Ukrainian police, which was blamed for violent actions during Maidan. It has been disbanded since then.

38 Olga Nedavnya, "Церковно-релігійний фактор Євромайдану в оцінкаї його учасників та прихильників" [Ecclesio-religious Factors of Euromaidan in the Evaluation of its

once more that the UOC was not perceived as an essential part of Maidan. At some point, there was also a rumour that the participants of Anti-Maidan[39] and the *titushki* spent the night in Kyiv Pechersky Lavra. Yurij Chernomorets in an interview opined that there were no real facts behind this rumour.[40] In any case, this incident reflected the general mood of Maidan vis-à-vis the UOC as "the Moscow Church", which did not support Maidan officially in contrast to the UOC-KP and the Ukrainian Greek Catholic Church.

It is also interesting how the position of the UOC influenced Vitali Klitschko, one of three oppositional politicians who represented Maidan in the negotiations with President Yanukovych. Here is how Anatoliy Kaluzhny, an active participant in Maidan, the chairman of the Council of Independent Churches, and pastor of the Pentecostal Church *Nove Zhyttya* [New Life] described these negotiations:

> Klitschko was fixated with being an adherent of the Orthodox Church of the Moscow Patriarchate. The activists of this church "anathematised" him for his activity on Maidan and demanded that he stops it. He did not understand the diversity of churches and thought that the UOC was the only church. Thus, he suffered from internal antagonism: On the one hand, he understood that he ought to be on Maidan, but on the other hand, he was not blessed by his church to do it.[41]

The death of several people was the result of the clashes on Grushevsky Street in Kyiv on 21 January 2014. Everybody understood then that this was a major step towards a wholesale civil war in Ukraine. All religious organisations declared the need to find a peaceful way of resolving the conflict. Several UOC churchmen authored a statement that was also signed by adherents of other Orthodox and Protestant Churches:

> In spite of the calls of the heads of the Ukrainian Churches and Blessed Metropolitan Volodymyr of Kyiv and all Ukraine, the authorities did not make a step to settle the conflict, stop violence, and establish a real dialogue. The situation became heated to the highest degree, when the opposition seemed unable to control the mood of the protesters. "To disband Maidan" in this situation is impossible, and a violent dispersal

Participants and Supporters], in Ludmila Fylypovych/Oksana Gorkusha (eds), *Майдан і Церква. Хроніка подій та експертна оцінка* [Maidan and the Church. A Chronicle of Events and an Expert Evaluation], Kyiv 2014, 168–185, here 177.

39 This term stands for protest actions against Maidan. They were organised by the government, whereas the people participating in these actions were allegedly motivated more by financial gains than by political ideas and convictions. See Olena Zvarych, "Мій милий 'тітушка'" [My beloved "titushka"], *Українська правда*, 13.12.2013, URL: https://www. pravda.com.ua/columns/2013/12/13/7006654/ [19.02.2019].

40 Yuriy Chernomorets, "Із цих подій Україна вийде оновленою (інтерв'ю Є. Білоножка, 28.12.2013)" [Ukraine will Emerge Renewed from these Events (interview with E. Bilonozhko, 28.12.2013)], in Ludmila Fylypovych/Oksana Gorkusha (eds), *Майдан і Церква. Хроніка подій та експертна оцінка* [Maidan and the Church. A Chronicle of Events and an Expert Evaluation], Kyiv 2014, 85–90, here 87.

41 Gordeev, *Церковь* (as n. 23), 166.

> will entail the beginning of a civil war, in which there will be no winner and no heroes.[42]

All these statements and views have been mentioned because it is important to understand that, aside from the UOC's official position, there were also other perspectives within it. The official position was formulated in such a way as not to come into conflict with any of the other existing and especially different perspectives. There were many other facets, which could be used to illustrate the position of the UOC on Maidan. For example, there was also a petition from several Orthodox Christians to the UOC leadership to excommunicate and anathematise Victor Yanukovych.[43]

Conclusions

Orthodox Christians were active participants in the *Revolution of Dignity*, but their positions were not always connected to the official positions of their churches. In general, the adherents of the UOC-KP were in a better position because this church officially supported Maidan. However, many Orthodox believers of the UOC were confused, because this church abstained from condemning the authorities and especially Viktor Yanukovych. The respective links to the Yanukovych regime were the main reason for the different strategies of the churches during the anti-governmental protests. In other words, the positions of the Orthodox Churches towards Maidan heavily depended on their divergent attitudes to the government.

On the one hand, the UOC-KP position was due to Yanukovych's attempts to ban it, hence it occasions no surprise that Patriarch Filaret blessed the rally participants. If Maidan had lost in the confrontation and Yanukovych had resumed his presidency, the UOC-KP activity would have been restricted. During the last year of Yanukovych's presidency, he was clearly supporting solely the UOC, which is a part of the ROC. This is in many ways similar to Vladimir Putin's desire and policy to make the ROC dominant in the Russian religious market and even beyond that. Bearing this in mind, the UOC-KP had credible reasons to expect new attempts to ban it on the part of government.

On the other hand, the UOC position was mainly due to its support and promotion by the state authorities and the Yanukovych regime, which counted as

---

42 *Звернення священнослужителів і мирян з приводу кризової ситуації в Україні* [An Address of Clergy and Laity on the Crisis in Ukraine], 24.01.2014, URL: http://www.kiev-orthodox.org/site/events/5048 [19.02.2019].

43 *УПЦ (МП) закликають відлучити від Церкви Януковича і піддати його анафемі* [UOC (MP) is Urged to Excommunicate Yanukovych and to Anathematise him], 19.02.2014, URL: https://risu.org.ua/ua/index/all_news/state/church_state_relations/55387/ [19.02.2019].

its members. Truth be told, a part of the laity and many clergymen of the UOC were also active on Maidan. In this particular constellation, the UOC had to follow a careful and neutral strategy navigating through the diverging loyalties of its members. Naturally, Maidan and the pro-Maidan part of the society, which also claimed to represent the "civil society" in Ukraine, wanted all the civil and religious organisations to condemn the governmental abuse of human rights and the attempt to change Ukrainian foreign policy from a pro-European to a pro-Russian direction. All in all, for the UOC the pro-Russian position (exactly as for Yanukovych) was more appropriate and that was another reason as to why it did not officially support Maidan, which had been initially triggered by the contentious issue of Ukraine's European integration.

To sum up: We can observe two different positions of the Orthodox Churches towards the *Revolution of Dignity*: active support and neutrality. Both of them could be explained as specific tactics in the religious market. The UOC, as the biggest church on the parish level, as well on the level of the number of believers, opted for neutrality because it did not intend to lose either governmental support or any of its believers who were still supporting Maidan. In the case that Maidan had not succeeded, this church would have reached some kind of a monopoly in the religious field afterwards. The UOC-KP, as a major competitor to the UOC, chose instead to actively support Maidan. Thereby it expected to earn the favour of the civil society and consequently to achieve more fruitful circumstances for its own future development. The success of Maidan meant the overthrowing the Yanukovych regime, organising democratic presidential and parliamentary elections, and making nationalistic discourse dominant in the public sphere. The idea of creating a Local Ukrainian Orthodox Church that would eventually gain a canonical status from a Pan-Orthodox perspective, promoted by Patriarch Filaret and the UOC-KP, became one of the key aims in this context.[44]

These two positions of the Orthodox Churches continued to exist after Maidan in the context of the hybrid war with Russia. For the UOC adherents it was a challenge, given that some of its believers eventually changed their affiliation to another Orthodox Church. In 2014-2015, there were more than 100 attempts of Orthodox parishes to change their jurisdiction. Almost half of them were successful, but some of them became the cause of conflicts. In general, the UOC-KP has profited from this development and gradually became more influential. Furthermore, the UOC connection with the ROC, as well as the refusal to blame

44 The question of securing a *Tomos* of autocephaly for the Ukrainian Orthodox Church from the Ecumenical Patriarchate of Constantinople appeared to be the logical continuation of this discourse. This is what finally happened in 2019. The President, the government, and the Parliament considered the full independence of the Ukrainian Orthodox Church from the Moscow Patriarchate and its canonical recognition as an issue of utmost importance regarding national sovereignty and security. See also the contribution by Sebastian Rimestad in this volume.

Russia for the annexation of Crimea and the hybrid war in Donbas have shaken the Ukrainian society's faith in it. Not the least, this was reflected in the decreasing number of people identifying themselves with this church. In addition, the UOC enjoys unique privileges in the Donbas territories, which are not controlled by Ukraine, as well as in the annexed Crimea and is one of the few religious organisations that can still exist legally and operate freely there. In this case, one may talk about a "religious monopoly" enjoying full state support within a state-regulated religious field.

Maidan was just one episode in the current history of Ukraine, and the religious factor was certainly not the dominant one in it. In spite of this, Maidan did affect deeply various spheres and sectors of Ukrainian society, including the religious one. It made an impact on the alignment of forces in the political and economic spheres, as well as in the religious one. The churches in Ukraine, even if they did not fully realise these changes in political or economic terms or their long-term significance, were still important players in these transformation processes according to their own specific agendas and existing loyalties. Their main strategic aim, regardless if always realistic or not, consisted of keeping their societal privileges and state support, as well as becoming more powerful and influential organisations in every respect.

POLITICS

The Greek Orthodox Church and Symphonic Secularism: Church-State Relations Seen through the Prism of Blasphemy

Daniel Jianu

This chapter examines the implications of "symphonic secularism" in the behaviour of the Orthodox Church during the recent economic crisis in Greece. It focuses on the developments of church-state relations during the crisis and the attempts of the Greek Orthodox Church (GOC) to maintain its political and social legitimacy in light of the long background of church-state engagements in Eastern Orthodox Christianity. The chapter further analyses the political links between the GOC and the newly empowered extreme right-wing political movements through the prism of the political and legal concept of blasphemy.

Secularism and Orthodoxy in Greece

Secularism as a political ideology and as a form of political authority has never really assumed the same importance in managing social, political, cultural, and economic relations in Orthodox Greece as it did in the Western Christian cultural sphere. The construction of modern secular political and social arrangements in Greece is based on religious scaffolding. This is why, in this country, we still find interesting cases of hybrid forms between the religious and the secular.

For a long time, the modern consensus was that the social order is based on human rationality, not on religion. Hence, modern societies were perceived to be secular at their core with religion placed firmly in the private sphere. This modernisation pattern, prevalent in Western Europe (i.e., in Roman Catholic and Protestant societies that have experienced modernity), implied a substantial decline of religion and religious beliefs both in the political arena, as well as at the individual level. The modern social and political arrangements in Western societies had this understanding of religion (as a set of private beliefs and a personal faith) as their foundational core for a long time. The decline in religious beliefs in Western Europe also led to hopes on the part of some political actors, scholars, and policymakers alike that at some point this dynamic would utterly relegate religion to the trash bins of history. Nonetheless, this ideology of secularism that was underlying much of modern science and Western modernity for centuries is today considered more problematic and fragile than assumed.

For example, recent scholarship argues that Europe's future is not progressively moving only towards secularisation, but also in different directions due to various factors, such as the "multiple" and "locally adapted" modernities,[1] the increased presence of Islam in its midst, and last but not least, the historical differences between Catholic and Protestant Christianity on the one hand, and the Eastern Orthodox Christianity on the other.[2] Because of all these factors, the current European experience of secularisation is being challenged on many fronts by many individuals and institutions. Before we go deeper into this discussion, we should start with how religion can be conceptualised and analysed in relation to secularism.

There is a threshold that separates the pre-modern from the modern view of the social and political arrangements of states and nations. This threshold manifests itself in the discontinuity between early conventions of religion and politics where religion is all-encompassing and determinative, and the seventeenth century attempt to redefine this role, culminating in the Westphalian "invention" of religion.[3] The related conceptual framework has shifted from a public engagement to a private significance of religion in domestic and international fields. During pre-modern times, the social order of the day was a web of interlocking relationships sanctified by religion and where social solidarity and a sense of community were prevalent.[4] In many ways, this communitarian concept of religion is still very much alive and meaningful in predominantly Orthodox countries such as Greece, where modernity and society have a tortuous and complex relationship at best. This is because modernity was not a natural product of the Orthodox historical tradition. The anti-modern attitudes of institutional Orthodoxy and a significant part of the general population may be understood if we take into account the desire to preserve the Orthodox symbolic traditional power within the nation's cultural and public space.[5]

During the modern phase of the conceptualisation of "religion", this sense of belonging to a community or tradition was lost as religion had started to be identified with specific practices and rituals separated from local social

---

1 Peter J. Katzenstein, "Multiple Modernities as Limits to Secular Europeanization?", in Timothy A. Byrnes/Peter J. Katzenstein (eds), *Religion in an Expanding Europe*, Cambridge 2006, 1–33, here 9–10.

2 Sabrina P. Ramet, "The way we were – and should be again? European Orthodox Churches and the 'Idyllic Past'", in Timothy A. Byrnes/Peter J. Katzenstein (eds), *Religion in an Expanding Europe*, Cambridge 2006, 148–175.

3 Scott M. Thomas, "The Revenge of God? The Twentieth Century as the Last Modern Century", in idem (ed.), *The Global Resurgence of Religion and the Transformation of International Relations*, New York 2005, 21–45.

4 Daniel Payne, "The Challenge of Western Globalization to Orthodox Christianity", in Jonathan Sutton/Wil van den Bercken (eds), *Orthodox Christianity and Contemporary Europe*, Leuven 2003, 133–144, here 135–138.

5 Ion Cordoneanu/Marius Velica, "Religion and Modernity in the Romanian Public Space (In Search of an Explanatory Theoretical Model)", Paper Presented at the Conference *Secularism and Beyond – Comparative Perspectives,* Copenhagen 2007.

communities.[6] The modern invention of religion assumed that the privatisation and differentiation processes more or less successfully marginalised faith-based political structures and that religion had left the scene of political and social relations. This privatisation has indeed been prevalent in many European societies,[7] but in many non-Western societies, such as in the Greek case, this transition was not complete, as it faced strong opposition from the historical symphonic relationship between state and church. In the Orthodox Christian world generally, the churches are institutionally and symbolically often inseparable from the political establishment and have long been instrumental in defining the boundaries of the national collective identities.[8] In Greece, religion is conceptualised as a core constitutive element of national and ethnic identity; it is a vessel for community description with a strong public and institutionalised character.

Theoretically, the Greek state can be considered and accordingly conceptualised as a state that manifests and promotes an "established religion". Here, Eastern Orthodox Christianity is granted official and legal recognition by the state, and both church and state mutually benefit from a formal alliance. This political and social alliance does not preclude the existence of separate and independent institutions belonging to church and state respectively. Distinct functions are performed by the staff of each such institution. Yet, there is an important connection between the two: they share a "common end" largely defined by religion. Moreover, there is a connection, albeit contested, between church and state at the level of policy and law. In Orthodox countries, the institutional disconnection between church and state often goes hand in hand with a connection at the level of policies and law. Basically, a fully secular state means a full disconnection at all three levels, whereas a theocratic state implies a full connection at all three levels. Hence, Eastern Orthodox countries such as Greece find themselves in a hybrid mode of secularism. They are not fully secular, but not fully religious states either. They represent an interesting and idiosyncratic form of what we may call "symphonic secularism".[9]

---

6 Jack Snyder, "Introduction", in idem (ed.), *Religion and International Relations Theory*, New York 2011, 1–23, here 11–12.

7 Ibid., 11.

8 Slavica Jakelic, *Collectivistic Religions: Religion, Choice, and Identity in Late Modernity*, Farnham 2010, 2–4.

9 See also the chapter by Dragan Šljivić in this volume.

Symphonic Secularism: Its Historical Background and Modern Articulation

The term "symphonic secularism", coined by social anthropologist Kristen Ghodsee as an Orthodox type of church-state relations,[10] is a two-prong structure based on two determinative concepts that have evolved during the long history of Orthodox Christianity: *symphonia* and *millet*.

In order to understand the re-emergence of the issue of blasphemy in contemporary Greek society, we would need to take a look at the peculiarities of the historical relationship between church and state in a predominantly Eastern Orthodox country such as Greece. The historical trajectory of the concept of *symphonia* can shed light on the common traditional aspects of church-state relations and their different dogmatic offshoots with regard to politics, culture, and society. The legacy of *symphonia* still survives in Greece, even though the modern political and cultural system of the country has largely undergone the process of secularisation. The symphonic harmony between the religious and the secular in Greece is reflected in the numerous privileged and hegemonic partnerships between church and state and in the ways public administration has developed and established itself.

The Concept and the Theology of Symphonia in the Early Christian Church

At the beginning, Christians represented a new and distinct community of believers, a sacred one distinct from the natural world. But by the fourth century, starting with Emperor Constantine I (r. 306-337), this community began to encompass all of Roman society and became indistinguishable from the larger civil community. At the same time, the doctrine of the church required a distinction between the realm of the natural world and the sacred one. The two communities started to clash in different dimensions, yet this situation posed the question of their integration into the dominant monotheistic discourse, supported by both church and state. According to the new worldview, Christians belonged both to the world and to the church, and both of them merged together. But because this was a Christian world, it had two claims to authority: the imperial and the priestly. Consequently, the problem of church and state concerned the relations between two authorities, the secular and the spiritual, within the state itself. This was exactly the problem that Emperor Justinian I (r. 527-565) tried to solve with his legislation on church-state *symphonia*.

The emperor and the patriarch held different offices, but physically lived and worked in the same place and hence were forced to work together in a symphonic

10 Kristen Ghodsee, "Symphonic Secularism: Eastern Orthodoxy, Ethnic Identity and Religious Freedoms in Contemporary Bulgaria", *Anthropology of East Europe Review* 27/2 (2009) 227–252, here 228.

relationship between the two institutions, between the two spheres of power and legitimacy. There were certainly many cases where their political "co-habitation" led to conflicts and made it difficult to assess where the balance of power resided and to what extent the emperor had managed to exercise control over the church. At the beginning, the idea of *symphonia* was an ideal and not a fully elaborated political theory. Yet, this does not mean that it was not the subject of a considerable amount of thought and debate in the early Byzantine period.[11] Gregory of Nyssa (ca. 335-ca. 395), one of the Cappadocian Church Fathers, expressed the classical understanding of *symphonia* in the belief that if the emperor followed the will of God and the people had faith in God as well, then God would bless the affairs of the empire and keep its subjects safe. Such a *symphonia* of earth and heaven would result in the protection of the Christian empire from its enemies. Basically, this reflects the belief in the Biblical idea of God protecting his covenant people.[12]

John Chrysostom (349-407), Archbishop of Constantinople, also tried to define *symphonia* by clearly demarcating the proper role of the church from that of the state. To this purpose, he used the example of the King Ozias, who was punished with leprosy because of his impertinence to offer priestly incense to God. He thus succinctly describes the jurisdictions of these two domains as follows:

> Therefore, stay within your proper domain. The government and the priesthood each have their own boundaries, even though the priesthood is the greater of the two. A king should not be judged merely on the appearance, or valued merely from the gold and jewels in his costume. His domain is the administration of earthly affairs, whereas the jurisdiction of the priesthood is a power derived from above [...] Bodies are under the care of the king, souls under the care of the priest. The king remits earthly debts, the priest remits the debts of guilt. One uses earthly weapons, the other uses spiritual weapons, and it is the latter which bears greater power. This is why the king bends his head to the hand of the priest, and why, in the Old Testament, kings were always anointed by priests.[13]

Hence, both the king and the priest had to support and reinforce each other and to collaborate in symphony to please God. This concept had clearly been expressed by the Sixth Novella of Emperor Justinian, issued in March 535. Justinian described exactly the same principle in his letter convoking the Second Ecumenical Council of Constantinople in 553: "It is the duty of the priests to

---

11 Iuliana Conovici, "Concepts of Church-State Relations in Romania: Beyond Symphonia and the 'Privileged Orthodox Church'", Oxford/OH 2015, URL: https://www.yumpu.com/en/document/view/15872830/concepts-of-church-state-relations-in-romania-unitsmuohioedu [19.02.2019].

12 John A. McGuckin, "The Legacy of the 13th Apostle: Origins of the East Christian Conceptions of Church and State Relation", *St Vladimir's Theological Quarterly* 47/3-4 (2003) 251–288.

13 Cited in McGuckin, "The Legacy" (as n. 12), 279.

define the faith, and the task of the emperors to carry out the conciliar decrees."[14] In the preface to the Sixth Novella, Justinian delineated the relations of the respective spheres of the *imperium* and the *sacerdotium* as follows:

> The greatest gifts that God's heavenly philanthropy gave to men are the *sacerdotium* and the *basileia,* of which the former serves divine affairs, and the latter presides and watches over human affairs, and both proceed from one and the same principle and regulate human life. So, nothing should be so much the care of the emperor as the saintliness of the priests since these constantly pray to God on his behalf. If the *sacerdotium* is in all ways blameless and acceptable to God, and the *basileia* rules justly and properly over the state entrusted to it, good harmony will result, which will bestow all that is beneficial on the human race.[15]

Justinian went even further in the theory of the *symphonia* between the two powers:

> The priesthood and the imperium do not differ very greatly. Nor are sacred things so very different from those of public and common interest.[16]

According to McGuckin, this text is not a text where Justinian imposes or tries to impose a new theology, but on the contrary, it is a learned Biblical allusion to Psalm 131 (v. 8-12) to define the Christian understanding of political *symphonia*. The king is blessed by God, he ensures the holiness of the priests who in turn pray for the welfare of the kingdom, so that his throne shall endure. In other words, *symphonia* represents the Biblical doctrine of the conditional blessing from God based on covenant fidelity.[17] This Justinian interpretation of the *symphonia* needs to be put in perspective. It was only a part of Justinian's efforts to sacralise the entire Byzantine society, both through his major building project in the capital of the empire, which culminated in the restoration and rebuilding of Hagia Sophia, and his attempt to codify hundreds of years of imperial legislation. These "rebranding" efforts of the previous legislations were Justinian's way of reshaping the law in a Christian form and expression. It is within this context that we need to place and understand the meaning of the Sixth Novella and the concept of *symphonia*. Justinian was the first Christian Roman ruler to unite empire and church in such an intrinsic way. Justinian's codification had influenced Roman society in both East and West and remained the foundation of the imperial legal system for as long as the East Roman (Byzantine) Empire lasted while it also became a basis for the Western legal system.

According to Dunn, *symphonia* is not just a political doctrine, but a broader religious ethos deriving from the eschatological hope of the church. Both early resistance to the empire and the church's later acceptance of it were informed and

---

14 Cited in McGuckin, "The Legacy" (as n. 12), 282.
15 Cited in McGuckin, "The Legacy" (as n. 12), 283.
16 Cited in McGuckin, "The Legacy" (as n. 12), 283.
17 McGuckin, "The Legacy" (as n. 12), 283.

motivated by eschatology. Prior to Emperor Constantine, the church had seen the world as a light version of the kingdom of God, as a "foretaste" of the kingdom to come. The church tried to be in the present what God would one day make it in the future. The increase of the influence of the church after Constantine did not alter this goal; it only expanded its scope, and *symphonia* was the name given to this eschatological mission. The harmony sought between the affairs of the church and the state was proof that both were properly working together to make contemporary social and political life a more perfect icon of the kingdom of God to come.[18]

In the West, however, Pope Gelasius I (492-496) supported a more separatist vision of the spheres of church and state in contrast to the developments in the East. Having been called to account by Emperor Anastasius I (r. 491-518) for not informing the Byzantine court of his election in the time of the Acacian Schism (484-519), Pope Gelasius answered by elaborating on the idea of a distinction between the imperial *potestas* and the church *auctoritas*:

> There are two things, August Emperor, by which this world is ruled: the sacred authority of the pontiffs and the royal power. Of these two the priests carry the heavier weight, as they must render an account to the Lord's judgment seat even for kings. Most merciful son, you know well enough that you surpass all mankind in your dignity, yet even so you must bend your head in submission to the ministers of divine things, and from them receive the pledge of your salvation. In receiving the heavenly sacraments, which it is their office to dispense, you must depend on their judgment and not desire to submit them to your will. In matters concerning public life, the ministers of religions understand that the imperial power has been given to you from above and they themselves will obey your laws.[19]

This back and forth between Anastasius and Gelasius reflected the pressure of ongoing claims of successive emperors to control ecclesiastical affairs. Gelasius' arguments against these requests were his subtle examination of the two forces that ruled the world, the sacred sovereignty of the priesthood and the executive power of the prince. Both were blessed by God, and while the priestly authority was greater as it guided the emperor as a son of the church, yet the priesthood obeyed the emperor in matters of secular interest. With the passing of time, these arguments had become the foundation of strong authority, power and influence of the Papal See in Rome, which in its turn emphasised the autonomy and independence of the church from the state. This was the beginning of a period of

18 David J. Dunn, "Symphonia in the Secular or how to be Orthodox when you lose your Empire", in Fevronia K. Soumakis (ed.), *Power and Authority in the Eastern Christian Experience*, New York 2011, 209–218.

19 Cited in McGuckin, "The Legacy" (as n. 12), 285.

intense debates and conflicts between popes and political leaders in the Middle Ages (cf. the investiture controversy) over authority and supremacy.[20]

Regarding church-state relations in Byzantium, Geanakoplos identified a threefold division of areas of contention: first, the secular falling entirely under the control of the emperor; second, issues pertaining to the organisation and administration of the church; and third, the doctrine of the church, in which the emperor repeatedly interfered, although it ought to belong to the clergy alone.[21] In fact, these three spheres of conflict are derived from the attempts of the preamble of Justinian's Sixth Novella to regulate church-state relations. In Meyendorff's view, we cannot understand the full significance of this text if we do not take into account that this text is only a preamble to a longer constitution on church discipline where Justinian defines what he means by the "dignity of the priesthood". Meyendorff argues that the "harmony" itself mentioned in the text is not a harmony between two powers, or between two distinct societies, the church and the state, but rather it is meant to represent the internal cohesion of one single human society for whose orderly welfare on earth the emperor alone is responsible. He sees the empire and the church as one single body of the faithful, administered by a twofold and God-given hierarchy, namely the *imperium* and the *sacerdotium* that are to be found in a balanced duality.[22]

Another way to interpret Justinian's Sixth Novella is that the law governs the entire society and only the emperor can issue laws. Hence, the ecclesiastical traditions and conciliar decisions can be turned into laws by imperial decree, but they have no legal and binding existence by themselves. Between the legal structure of the empire under the absolute rule of the emperor and the nature of the Christian religion itself, there remained a gap, which texts like the Sixth Novella were unable to completely fill. While this can be seen as the emperor having the upper hand and the political initiative in the affairs of the church, there are many cases where the opposite was true. Specifically, there are many examples where the church successfully filled the political void left open by state actors. For example, Patriarch Nicholas Mystikos (852-925) was regent of the young Byzantine Emperor Constantine VII Porphyrogenitus. The same tradition survived in the broader Orthodox world, even until today. Thus, Metropolitan Alexii of Moscow (1353-1389) ruled the Principality of Muscovy during the childhood of Grand Prince Dmitry II Donskoy. Another interesting case relates to

20 Vasilios N. Makrides, "Eastern Orthodox and Western Latin Churches under Communism: Differences and Parallels", in Thede Kahl/Johannes Kramer/Elton Prifti (eds), *Romanica et Balcanica. Wolfgang Dahmen zum 65. Geburtstag*, München 2015, 703–724, here 707–708.

21 Deno J. Geanakoplos, "Church and State in the Byzantine Empire: A Reconsideration of the Problem of Caesaropapism", *Church History* 34/4 (1965) 381–403.

22 John Meyendorff, "Justinian, the Empire and the Church", *Dumbarton Oaks Papers* 22 (1968) 43–60, here 49.

the Principality of Zeta in 1516 when the heir to the throne, Prince Georgi Chernoevich, transferred the government of the state to the metropolitan of the local Orthodox Church. In fact, Montenegro was ruled by its metropolitans until 1851. In another case, in 1866, Metropolitan Kliment of Tarnovo became Prime Minister of Bulgaria, while Archbishop Makarios III combined his duties as church head with those of the President of Cyprus between 1960 and 1977.[23]

The Millet System of the Ottoman Times

The concept of *symphonia* also found expression in the *millet* system of the Ottoman times, which srengthened the symphonic relationship between church and state in a particular way. This happened because under the provisions of the *millet* system, the Patriarch of Constantinople became the legitimate spiritual, and in some ways political, leader of all Orthodox subjects in the Ottoman Empire. This system recognised only one type of community, namely a religious community, and consequently reinforced the church's role as guardian of ethnic identity and as bearer of *de facto* statehood. More importantly, the *millet* system allowed the Orthodox Church at times to step in and become politically active, especially in circumstances in which the secular authority did not exist or could not function properly. The church then became a provisional government until the restoration of secular authority.[24] This historical experience turned the Orthodox Churches into peculiar "reserve governments" standing by to assume functions of political leaderships in times of crisis. These "reserve governments" had "departments for foreign affairs" and conducted active policies regarding relations with other states and churches.[25]

Nicolae Iorga in his essay "Byzance après Byzance" argued that Byzantium survived as a political and cultural entity throughout many of the Ottoman territories.[26] The political, social and economic traditions of Byzantium continued to flourish during the Ottoman times and informed many of its legal and administrative practices. The *millet* system embraced these Byzantine cultural and political paradigms and parameters and built around them the necessary framework within which the Ottoman Empire ruled its non-Muslim subjects and specifically the Orthodox Christian minority. The Ottoman governmental bureaucracy dealt with the religious minorities under their control not as

23 Daniela Kalkandjieva, "Eastern Orthodox Christianity and Democracy: Foes or Allies in a Globalizing World", Paper presented at the Italian Political Science Association (SISP) Annual Conference, Venice, 16–18 September 2010 (Panel on "Religion and Democracy").

24 Vjekoslav Perica, "The Politics of Ambivalence: Europeanization and the Serbian Orthodox Church", in Timothy A. Byrnes/Peter J. Katzenstein (eds), *Religion in an Expanding Europe*, Cambridge 2006, 176–203.

25 Kalkandjieva, "Eastern Orthodox Christianity and Democracy" (as n. 23).

26 Nicola Iorga, *Byzantium after Byzantium*, [1935], translated by L. Teptow, Oxford 2000.

individuals with specific religious beliefs and social mores, but as members of a larger community legitimised by one person or office as the head of this community. This clearly made the efforts of the Ottomans to manage these communities infinitely easier than having to implement and coordinate integration and acculturation strategies for the religious minorities of the empire.

Fortuitously, the Ottoman administrators found preciously invaluable intellectual and political support in the concept and the tradition of the Byzantine *symphonia*. This allowed the empire to mobilise its resources in defining each religious community based on its individual essential characteristics, namely its religious identity. A complete merge between the community and their religious belonging ushered a long-term transformation and political legitimisation of the earlier symphonic experience. Thus, we cannot fully comprehend the function of the *millet* systems without its deep connections to the state-church arrangements that had evolved before the Ottoman Empire. Braude has written eloquently about the foundational myths of the *millet* system and argued that this system has been more of a vague general approach than a fully developed Ottoman institution.[27] This peculiarity of the *millet* system also allowed the Orthodox Church to help instil and preserve a sense of belonging and common identity among the Orthodox population of varied ethnic provenance that even after the collapse of the empire continued to entangle the spiritual and temporal authorities in the context of church-state relations.

Symphonic Secularism in Contemporary Greece

These two pillars, *symphonia* and *millet*, have jointly contributed to the development of symphonic secularism that in countries such as Greece includes a constitutionally enshrined traditional church, as well as governmental regulation of all religious activities. This means that the government has the power to dissolve churches considered as a threat not only to public order and national security, but also to the legitimacy and national unity of the state. In this context, the official acceptance of Orthodox Christianity is a public declaration of affiliation with a historically, culturally, and linguistically constituted religious group. Within this political and social arrangement between state and church, Orthodoxy plays a dominant role through its openly public manifestations and hence by defining the boundaries of its historical ethno-national community.

In general, the elements of symphonic secularism have considerable influence, both open and latent, upon contemporary society. Many of the Greek economic, political, and cultural institutions are preconditioned by the historical legacies of *symphonia* and *millet*. This means that the institutional formation of

27 Benjamin Braude, "Foundation Myths of the Millet System", in Benjamin Braude/Bernard Lewis (eds), *Christians and Jews in the Ottoman Empire: The Function of a Plural Society*, Vol. 2, New York 1982, 69–88.

governmental agencies, if not in their constitutional foundation, at least in the procedural and functional capacities, are much indebted to the historically close relationship between church and state.[28] Many public choices made in Greek society and the way institutional and cultural reforms are accepted or rejected seem to be fundamentally driven by an ideological *substratum* created over the long history of the Greek nation, to which Orthodoxy also belongs.

Religious and national identity are two faces of the same coin within Greek society. The link between them relates to strong historical claims going back to Ottoman times when religion was the most important mark of group identity. This historical legacy continues to underscore and strengthen the significance of Orthodox Christianity to modern Greek identity. Prime Minister Constantinos Karamanlis had formulated this connection back in 1981 as follows: "The nation and Orthodoxy [...] have become in the Greek conscience virtually synonymous concepts, which together constitute our Helleno-Christian civilisation."[29] As the late Chief Prelate of the GOC, Archbishop Christodoulos, repeatedly said, "Greece means Orthodoxy."[30] As a result, the GOC has considerable institutional power, derived partly from the country's Constitution, which favours the Orthodox colouring of the state, and partly from the GOC's long historical connection with the Greek nation, which it supposedly "saved" from extinction during Ottoman rule.[31]

The GOC and its Relations with the State through the Prism of Blasphemy

In legal and practical terms, the institutional choices that determine state-church relations in Greece are in large part derived from the 1975 Constitution, which begins with a reference to God in its preamble. It continues with Article 3, which indicates that Greek Orthodoxy is the "prevailing religion" in the country. The legal concept of a "prevailing religion" is grounded in Section II of the Constitution "On the Relations of Church and State", where it is stipulated that

28 Richard Potz, "State and Church in the European Countries with an Orthodox Tradition", *Derecho y Religión* 3 (2008) 33–54.

29 Quoted by Kallistos Ware, "The Church: A Time for Transition", in Richard Clogg (ed.), *Greece in the 1980s*, Basingstoke 1983, 208–227, here 208.

30 Victor Roudometof, "Orthodoxy as Public Religion in Post 1989 Greece", in Victor Roudometof/Alexander Agadjanian/Jerry Pankhurst (eds), *Eastern Orthodoxy in a Global Age: Tradition Faces the Twenty-first Century*, Walnut Creek/CA 2005, 84–109, here 88.

31 Nikos Chrysoloras, "Why Orthodoxy? Religion and Nationalism in Greek Political Culture", *Studies in Ethnicity and Nationalism* 4 (2004) 40–61.

"the prevailing religion in Greece is that of the Eastern Orthodox Church of Christ".[32]

This "prevailing religion" has come to mean different things over time and is interpreted in different ways. It is a statement of fact reflecting that Eastern Orthodox Christianity represents approximately 97 percent of the population in Greece. This descriptive meaning of the concept of "prevailing religion" is the predominant view among legal experts and scholars in Greece. However, there are other Greeks who argue that the term should reflect the historical legacy of the church in Greek society and allow it in practice to be treated as if it were the official and pre-eminent one, granting the GOC a privileged status over other religious groups in the country. The GOC is also organised as a legal entity of public law, which allows it a number of prerogatives, such as the right to determine public holidays in accordance with its own tradition.[33] As a result, the GOC enjoys certain government benefits such as:

- Financial support that is not extended to other religions.
- Mandatory instruction in the Orthodox Christian tradition in all public schools, except for students declaring adherence to other religions.
- Freedom from the administrative obstacles that other religions face, for instance when seeking permits for maintenance or construction of religious buildings.

Blasphemy in the Greek Legal System

This close and intertwined relation between church and state in Greece often takes specific political and cultural shapes when concrete actions and behaviours make themselves felt in the daily life of Greek society. For example, in October 2012 a Greek theatre company prepared to stage the premiere of Terence McNally's play "Corpus Christi" at a small theatre in central Athens. "Corpus Christi" is a play that tells the story of Jesus Christ and the Apostles portraying them as homosexuals. As was to be expected, the plan resulted in intense controversy and public outcry, even physical violence. It is worth noting that the opposition came not only from clerics of the GOC, but also from extremist circles and ordinary Greek citizens.[34] The extremist side inciting to violence were members of or generally supported the Greek Golden Dawn Party – an ultranationalist, racist and

32 Effie Fokas, "Pluralism and Religious Freedom in Majority Orthodox Contexts", *ELIAMEP Working Paper* 49 (2014), URL: https://www.eliamep.gr/wpcontent/uploads/2014/06/49_2014_-WORKING-PAPER-_Effie-Fokasfinal.pdf [19.02.2019].

33 Ibid.

34 Daphne Halikiopoulou/Sofia Vasilopoulou, "Political Instability and the Persistence of Religion in Greece: The Policy Implications of the Cultural Defence Paradigm", *RECODE Working Paper* 18 (2013), URL: http://www.recode.info/wp-content/uploads/2013/02/Fin_RECODE-18-Halikiopoulou-Vasilopoulou-2013_Final.pdf [19.02.2019].

neo-Nazi political party, which has gained representation in the Greek Parliament for the first time in May 2012. The deep economic crisis affecting Greece at that time had operated as a catalyst, among other things bringing far-right extremism to the foreground. In the rerun June 2012 parliamentary elections, the party obtained the support of over 400,000 Greek citizens, thus consolidating its representation to 18 parliamentary seats. The most violent protests against the aforementioned theatrical play stemmed from such Golden Dawn activists and Members of the Parliament, who also issued threats to the actors and their families. They objected to the play as being blasphemous and a religious insult to the public decency of the overwhelming majority of the Greek people. As a result, the premiere was cancelled, and the play was eventually withdrawn. Although it was the far-right party that radicalised the protests against "Corpus Christi", all the protests stemmed from a religious objection and with the support of various Orthodox actors and the tacit approval of the GOC.[35] In actual fact, the Golden Dawn Party was far from pro-Orthodox, and its ideology included numerous pagan elements. Yet, it also attracted various Orthodox supporters and sympathisers because of its intense nationalism and conservative moral orientation, which are also shared to a large degree by the overall Greek Orthodox culture. At the official level, the GOC generally tried to keep its distance from this party and its various activities, but in popular perception the potential link between Orthodoxy and the extreme right-wing political spectrum remained alive.

Another example of this link is the case of 27-year-old Philippos Loizos, who in September 2012 was arrested for "malicious blasphemy" and "religious offence".[36] His "crime" and the alleged act of blasphemy had taken place on a satirical Facebook page, where Loizos depicted a popular Greek Orthodox monk, Elder Paisios the Athonite (1924-1994), in an unflattering manner by ironically renaming him "Elder Pastitsios" (a play on words, with "pastitsio" being a popular Greek pasta dish). The profile featured photoshopped images of the monk with pasta on his face. Besides the picture, the site also contained satirical posts criticising the GOC and its obsession with the popular and widespread eschatological prophecies of Elder Paisios.[37] In fact, Paisios was canonised by the Ecumenical Patriarchate of Constantinople in January 2015 and is today venerated as a saint.

The arrest took place a few days after Golden Dawn MP Christos Pappas made a motion in the Greek Parliament. These complaints from Golden Dawn need to be understood from the perspective of the economic and financial crisis ravaging Greece in the years before and the unprecedented ascendancy of the far-right political party. Loizos had also taunted and made fun of the far-right

35 Ibid.

36 Erasmus blog, "Sainthood and Stoicism", *The Economist*, 19.01.2015, URL: https://www.economist.com/erasmus/2015/01/19/sainthood-and-stoicism [19.02.2019].

37 Ibid.

nationalists by inventing a miracle story performed by Elder Paisios, which was widely published in the far-right media outlets. In most past cases related to blasphemy, the first-instance criminal court has tended to decide against the accused and to impose an appropriate penalty. But, after a few months, the appeal court has tended to acquit the accused in the name of freedom of speech or freedom of art. In this instance, the appeal court's verdict in January 2014 was to convict Loizos to a suspended ten-month prison sentence, whereas in a retrial in 2017 the case was finally dismissed.

The above cases show a tendency in the GOC to take advantage of the newly emboldened extremist rhetoric of the Golden Dawn Party and to pursue blasphemy charges as a means of hegemonic influence in contemporary Greek society. It is important to remember that blasphemy is an offence also in a number of other European/EU states, such as Austria, Denmark, Finland, Italy, Liechtenstein, the Netherlands, and San Marino, though trials related to this offence seem to take place more frequently in Greece than in other countries. The most famous among them have concerned public spectacles, works of art, films, and books that generally address the divine or the Orthodox tradition in a humiliating way in order to provoke the public's sacred beliefs. Of particular importance is that all cases of blasphemy in Greece deal only with acts against the GOC and not with inappropriate behaviour against any of the so-called "known", "tolerable", and "recognised" religions. The Greek state has not used its blasphemy laws to protect any religion other than Eastern Orthodox Christianity. The crime of blasphemy represents an example of how the law reflects Orthodox Christian morality and the close relationship between state and church in Greece.[38]

According to a survey by the Council of Europe's Venice Commission, "the solid historical links between the Eastern Orthodox Christianity and the emergence of the Greek nation, are used in order to justify a high level of interference of the church in the state affairs, in all different levels."[39] The prosecutions for blasphemy under Penal Code Articles 198 and 199 in recent years can be attributed to the influence of the Orthodox Church. In Greek case law, blasphemy is defined as any public manifestation whatsoever (oral, in writing, by way of images, symbols and/or gestures) involving mockery, affront, offensive or vulgar expressions against God as the Supreme Being of monotheistic religions or against the divine, including anything that is considered sacred by a recognised

38 Michael Tsapogas, "Blasphemy and Justice in a Greek Orthodox Context", in Venice Commission (ed.), *Blasphemy, Insult and Hatred: Finding Answers in a Democratic Society* (Venice Commission's Science and Technique of Democracy Collection, 47), Strasbourg: Council of Europe Publishing, 2010, 113–119.

39 European Commission for Democracy Through Law (Venice Commission), "Annexe II: Analysis of the Domestic Law Concerning Blasphemy, Religious Insults and Inciting Religious Hatred", *Study* 406 (2006) 46, URL: https://www.venice.coe.int/webforms/documents/?pdf=CDL(2008)090add2-e [19.02.2019].

religion.[40] The concept of blasphemy shows up in the Greek Constitution in Article 14:

> Seizure by order of the public prosecutor shall be allowed exceptionally after circulation and in case of:
> a. an offence against the Christian or any other known religion.
> b. an insult against the person of the President of the Republic.
> c. a publication which discloses information on the composition, equipment and set-up of the armed forces or the fortifications of the country, or which aims at the violent overthrow of the regime or is directed against the territorial integrity of the State.
> d. an obscene publication which is obviously offensive to public decency, in the cases stipulated by law.[41]

Articles 198, 199, and 201 of Chapter 7 of the Greek Penal Code create offences, which involve blasphemy as well.[42] Article 198 "Malicious Blasphemy" provides:

1. One who publicly and maliciously and by any means blasphemes God shall be punished by imprisonment for not more than two years.
2. Except for cases under paragraph 1, one who by blasphemy publicly manifests a lack of respect for the divinity shall be punished by imprisonment for not more than three months.

Article 199 "Blasphemy Concerning Religions" states: "One who publicly and maliciously and by any means blasphemes the Greek Orthodox Church or any other religion tolerable in Greece shall be punished by imprisonment for not more than two years."

Article 201 provides: "One who willfully removes a corpse, parts of a corpse or the ashes of the dead from those who have lawful custody thereof or one who commits an offense with respect to a corpse or acts blasphemously and improperly towards a grave, shall be punished by imprisonment for not more than two years."[43]

The Article 14 of the Constitution and the Chapter 7 of the Greek Penal Code are indications that the Greek criminal order is based on a religious foundation as a result of the particular position of the GOC within the state. The very existence of Chapter 7 of the Greek Penal Law can be regarded as solid evidence of the integration of Orthodox Christianity into the penal machinery through the concept

---

40 Dimitris Sarafianos, "Blasphemy in the Greek Orthodox Legal Tradition", in *Blasphemy, Insult and Hatred: Finding Answers in a Democratic Society* (Venice Commission's Science and Technique of Democracy Collection, 47), Strasbourg: Council of Europe Publishing, 2010, 105–111, here 105.

41 Venice Commission (ed.), *Blasphemy, Insult and Hatred: Finding Answers in a Democratic Society* (Venice Commission's Science and Technique of Democracy Collection, 47), Strasbourg: Council of Europe Publishing, 2010, 176.

42 European Commission, "Annexe II" (as n. 39).

43 Ibid.

of blasphemy.[44] It is also evidence of how the evolution of the legal history and the identity of modernity itself are closely bound with the evolution of religious beliefs. Blasphemy prosecutions such as the ones in modern Greece remind us that the secular culture in Greek society still has to negotiate a viable relationship with the strong and influential religious sphere.

The Historical Evolution of Blasphemy in Greece

Historically speaking, blasphemy was essentially and fundamentally instrumentalised in forging the secular. It was the composite tool of disrespect and creative destruction needed for the secular to emerge from the sacred and religious establishment.[45] Hence, it has a reserved place of honour between the secular and the sacred, between state and church. It also needs to be seen as fully enmeshed and historically linked to the relationship between state and church in the Eastern Orthodox Christian realm. On the other hand, we must not forget the fact that blasphemy can be also connected with the foundation of Christianity given that Jesus Christ was accused by his opponents of performing acts of blasphemy on at least two separate occasions. French historian Cabantous once noted that when Jesus claimed for himself a divine nature, his claim was condemned as blasphemy. That blasphemy led to his death, and the death was followed by resurrection. "In this one respect", Cabantous writes, "blasphemy founded Christianity".[46] In the aforementioned Greek case, it was the Golden Dawn Party that introduced the issue of blasphemy into the public discussion, not the GOC. In the last few years, Greek society has experienced a significant political vacuum due to the deep financial crisis, a vacuum that in Orthodox countries has often been filled by the church. In this case, a political party (Golden Dawn) occupied both the political and religious institutional spaces left unattended and hence determined the course of Philippos Loizos' penal case.

Historically, blasphemy has established religious and political norms. In Ancient Greece, blasphemy meant speaking ill of the gods, disturbing the peace and dishonouring principles of government. Prohibition of blasphemy was a divine ordinance supposedly revealed to Moses for the governance of the Israelites, shortly after the appearance of the Ten Commandments. Exodus 22:28 states: "You shall not revile God, nor curse a ruler of your people." In early Christianity, blasphemy began to acquire various and complex meanings. It soon

---

44 Dimitris Christopoulos, "Καταληκτικά για την λογοκρισία στην Ελλάδα" [Concluding Remarks on Censorship in Greece], in Giannis Ziogas/Leonidas Karabinis/Giannis Stavrakakis/Dimitris Christopoulos (eds), *Όψεις λογοκρισίας στην Ελλάδα* [Aspects of Censorship in Greece], Athens 2008, 67–86.

45 David Nash, *Blasphemy in the Christian World: A History*, Oxford 2007.

46 Alain Cabantous, *Blasphemy: Impious Speech in the West from the Seventeenth to the Nineteenth Century*, New York 2002, 5.

commenced to signify the breaking of the unity of Christendom and its true faith. Any utterance that deviated from the established and assumed "true faith" was deemed to be heretical and blasphemous. In the Byzantine Empire, Emperor Justinian I sponsored the massive codification of the laws – the *Corpus Juris Civilis* – with its statute on blasphemy, dating from 529 CE, alleging that "famine, earthquake and pestilence" recurred because of a failure to punish blasphemy, which "provoked God's wrath".[47]

The mingling of state and church in modern Greece becomes clear in the blasphemy cases and prosecutions, which remind us that secular culture here has still not negotiated a viable relationship with the religious domain. As already mentioned, blasphemy has a reserved place of honour between state and church in Eastern Orthodox Christianity generally. Blasphemy is also entangled with the question of political toleration and the formation of the modern secular state. It is both a regulator of the structural dimensions of faith as belonging, as well as an instrument of social and political control over the social community. Thus, through this prism we need to understand blasphemy as a political concept. The church tradition of regulating norms in society and its deep foundational role played in the birth of the modern Greek state has been supplanted to some extent by the rise of the far-right political movement. The latter has co-opted the historical legitimacy of the church so as to challenge the political, economic, and social contemporary meaning of Greek national identity.

In the last few years, the deep economic crisis has affected Greece as a whole including the GOC in many ways. However, even before the recent crisis the GOC had faced several problems involving corruption, sex, financial dealings, and last but not least, its overall relationship with the state. The period of Archbishop Christodoulos (1998-2008) with his controversial policies is a case in point.[48] However, the period of his successor, Archbishop Hieronymos II, has so far been evaluated more positively, as he has followed another agenda vis-à-vis the state and society.[49] In all probability, it is against this background that the GOC could not institutionally bring forward the complaint of blasphemy in the above two cases for fear of backlash. Thus, it was in a way happy to let the Golden Dawn Party take the initiative and complain of the blasphemous behaviours, not only regarding the Facebook case, but also the theatrical play depicting Jesus and the Apostles as homosexuals. Historically, when there were cases of the state allowing for a political vacuum, the church usually stepped in and fulfilled secular duties, in a way forming a temporary government. During the economic crisis, the

47 Tsapogas, "Blasphemy" (as n. 38), 117.

48 See Vasilios N. Makrides, "Scandals, Secret Agents and Corruption: The Orthodox Church of Greece during the 2005 Crisis – Its Relation to the State and Modernization", in Victor Roudometof/Vasilios N. Makrides (eds), *Orthodox Christianity in 21st Century Greece: The Role of Religion in Culture, Ethnicity and Politics*, Farnham 2010, 61–88.

49 See also the chapter by Georgios E. Trantas in this volume.

Greek state found itself many times incapacitated and unable to function properly. But this time, the GOC did not step in and thus allowed the Golden Dawn Party to fill this vacuum.

Due to these political and economic upheavals, the GOC has technically withdrawn quite a bit from the public sphere. The space for secularism in contemporary Greek society has increased somehow, as the GOC found itself under increased pressure to give up some of its benefits, such as free tax status, some of its land holdings, and even to make Orthodox education in schools more optional. In any event, the GOC is far from a monolith in its relations with state authorities and political parties including the Golden Dawn. Some local bishops appeared to support Golden Dawn positions and enhance their legitimacy, but at the same time, many other bishops have been vocal in rejecting and denouncing the party's ideology and actions.[50] Be that as it may, it should also be mentioned that the Golden Dawn Party failed to enter the Greek Parliament in the 2019 parliamentary elections, whereas since 2015 there has also been a still pending legal process against its leader and several of its MPs on suspicion to have formed a criminal organisation.

Conclusion

The connections between church and state in Greece are the result of many historical legacies from Byzantine and Ottoman times, legacies that somehow managed to be renewed over and over again in modern times including during the recent economic crisis. This crisis has presented the GOC with a few blessings in disguise, as it managed to maintain its influence (e.g., through philanthropy) in a crisis-stricken Greek society much less open to its overtures than in the past. In our context, the relationship between church and state is basically characterised by the system of co-reciprocity, a doctrine which was initially developed in Byzantium. As Meyendorff states, "the great dream of Byzantine civilization was a universal Christian society, administered by the emperor and spiritually guided by the Church".[51] As an ideal, "both the Church and the state should collaborate towards achieving a sublime destiny of the people under their jurisdiction and there is no conflict between the means employed by the church or the state in promoting the welfare of their subjects".[52] In the modern context, a formal separation between the secular character of the state and the religious status of the

50 See Stavros Zoumboulakis, *Χρυσή Αυγή και Εκκλησία* [Golden Dawn and the Church], Athens 2013; idem (ed.), *Νεοναζιστικός παγανισμός και Ορθόδοξη Εκκλησία* [Neo-Nazi Paganism and the Orthodox Church], Athens 2013.

51 Meyendorff, "Justinian" (as n. 22), 58.

52 Lucian N. Leustean, "The Concept of Symphonia in Contemporary European Orthodoxy", *International Journal for the Study of the Christian Church* 11 (2011) 188–202, here 189.

church undoubtedly remains. But co-reciprocity, adjusted to the modern exigencies, is thought to promote equality and an intimate relationship between these institutions while they retain their different priorities and methods of operating. In a way, this particular situation is aptly described by the aforementioned concept of symphonic secularism, which points to the combination of pre-modern traditional with modern elements and ideals in shaping contemporary church-state relations.

The analysis of the use and/or misuse of blasphemy penalisation in Greece is a prime example of this situation, where the boundaries between the religious and the secular have not yet been clearly demarcated and fully outlined. Through these cases of blasphemy and even through its informal alliance with the Golden Dawn Party, the GOC further pursued the legitimisation of Orthodoxy within Greek society, emphasising tradition, group identity, and group boundaries. As a sentient commingling of religion and secular politics, symphonic secularism in Greece – and *mutatis mutandis* in other predominantly Orthodox countries in Eastern and South Eastern Europe – could thus develop into a fresh language of politics that could challenge absolute Western secularist assumptions.

Shifting the Centre of Gravity of Greek Orthodox EU Policies: A Matter of Leadership?

Georgios E. Trantas

Concerning the attitude of the Greek Orthodox Church (hereafter GOC) towards the European Union (EU) since 1998, one ought to distinguish two different periods on the basis of fundamentally dissimilar strategic, essentially political, approaches. The eras of Archbishops Christodoulos and Hieronymos II diverged markedly, considering the differences in personality but also of the tasks at hand, as those were co-dictated by the circumstances of the time. As regards Christodoulos, it has been well established that interventionism in extra-ecclesiastical, predominantly political affairs was part of his agenda and polity.[1] This was variably supported by the Holy Synod of the GOC, at times reluctantly or otherwise wholeheartedly. In fact, it would not be out of order to maintain that this attitude exceeded national boundaries; particularly as regards the intra-European fermentations in dealing with the formulation of an EU Constitutional Treaty under construction and all that it ought to articulate, what its group-personhood[2] – if any – stands for, what it represents, and what its essence is, including its religio-cultural identity. It is worth mentioning a few examples along those lines, by focusing on the relationship of the GOC with the EU and its institutions, in order to better capture the context and broader political conditions of the time. If anything, they are indicative of an attitude, ultimately an agenda that took shape in practice. However, it is pertinent to also take into account the relationship of the modern Greek state with the EU, in order to better appreciate the political context and culture within which the GOC operates.

---

1 Vasilios N. Makrides, "Scandals, Secret Agents and Corruption: The Orthodox Church of Greece during the 2005 Crisis – Its Relation to the State and Modernization", in Victor Roudometof/Vasilios N. Makrides (eds), *Orthodox Christianity in 21st Century Greece: The Role of Religion in Culture, Ethnicity and Politics*, Farnham 2010, 61–88, here 83.

2 Edward Hallet Carr, *The Twenty Years' Crisis, 1919-1939*, Basingstoke 2001. Carr was the first to contemplate the possibility of applying the principle of "state personification" to a society of states, which in the present case applies to the EU, within the theoretical context of the English School of International Relations. See also Georgios E. Trantas, *Being and Belonging: A Comparative Examination of the Greek and Cypriot Orthodox Churches' Attitudes to 'Europeanisation' in Early 21st Century*, Frankfurt am Main 2018.

The State as Context

The delicate relationship with the EU is multifaceted and nested within a broadly defined social framework, where politics and culture – always under construction – ferment their own anti-Western contributions to the state of affairs. Parallel to those processes one comes across the opposite, positively inclined tendencies towards the EU and – perhaps not as frequently – the West. Moreover, this applies to theological circles as well.[3] Therefore, one should steer clear of sweeping generalisations, while acknowledging, however, uneasiness with the West, together with the sociocultural dimensions that make up a predominant political culture, which inevitably spills over into the church's frame of mind. For, if one concedes that "No institution – and that means also no Church – can be understood outside its historical context"[4], then it follows that the ecosystem within which an institution (a church) emerges and develops is formative of the latter. This framework is telling of the volatility of approaches and policies, even of an organisation that is saturated with its own diachronic, deep-seated character that more or less co-determines its course of action. In addition, the GOC is among other things person-dependent, given that leadership is not neutral, nor does it occur in a vacuum. In that sense, archbishops too are subject to the influences of their environment and ultimately to the conditions that contribute to one's conduct and leadership traits, beyond the entrenched policy guidelines that permeate the church as an organisation.[5]

The uneasiness with the West, however, in conjunction with memorable historical markers, spills over into the general relationship of Eastern Orthodoxy with history, mostly as regards modernity and its fruits, contrary to its comfortable relationship with its own traditions and its own "Idyllic Past".[6] This is part of a broader discussion, however. Certainly, the GOC, when it comes to the EU, has had its own uneasiness to deal with, either latent or obvious. History's burden of old enmities and unsettled scores finds its way through the cracks of time and still

---

3 Vasilios N. Makrides, "Orthodox Anti-Westernism Today: A Hindrance to European Integration?", *International Journal for the Study of the Christian Church* 9/3 (2009) 209 –224.

4 Sabrina Ramet, "The Way We Were – and Should be Again? European Orthodox Churches and the 'Idyllic Past'", in Timothy A. Byrnes/Peter J. Katzenstein (eds), *Religion in an Expanding Europe*, Cambridge 2006, 148–175, here 149.

5 It must be made clear though that this is by no means an attempt towards endorsing or appropriating Behaviouralism and its supposed value-neutrality. See Robert A. Dahl, "The Behavioural Approach in Political Science: Epitaph for a Monument to a Successful Protest", *The American Political Science Review* 55/4 (1961) 763–772; David Easton, "The New Revolution in Political Science", *The American Political Science Review* 63/4 (1969) 1051–1061. Eaton advocated this approach as revolutionary.

6 Ramet, "The Way We Were" (as n. 4), 327. See also Savvas Agourides, *Οράματα και Πράγματα* [Visions and Facts], Athens 1991.

affects perceptions of the other. The first sacking of Constantinople by the Crusaders (1204), for example, which is such a trauma, tends to be re-animated and becomes a constituent of the contemporary view of the West, contributing to the perpetuation of its estrangement. This applies to the broader Eastern Orthodox Balkan region too, in various ways.[7]

It should be pointed out that the GOC's relationship with the EU is not much different than that of the Greek state with the European bloc actor. In that sense, one should avoid the pitfall of attributing to the church more than its share. It would be best to bear in mind the environment within which this institution functions, when looking into its conduct. After all, there is an array of historical developments that never took place in the East, regardless of the church and certainly outside its control, influence, or responsibility, which undeniably contributed to the formation of a distinct political culture. For instance, a major shift occurred in the West during the nineteenth century, which included urbanisation, its effects on social life and the restructuring of a whole class system, the means of production, commercialisation, the emergence of real estate, finance, and by extension of a whole range of socioeconomic types; not to mention the association between the notions of urbanity and modernity, with the latter connoting the former and vice versa. In any case, urbanisation gave rise to a new form of social organisation.[8] In contrast, at the same time in the newly founded state of Greece, the process of state-building, modelled after the Western bureaucratic paradigm, stumbled over sociocultural obstacles. This was due for the most part to the absolute lack of administrative infrastructure and to a cultural negative predisposition towards such "imports". Suffice it to mention that within the bounds of Greece's nineteenth-century Europeanisation – the first experiment of that kind[9] – immense difficulties surfaced, one of which was selecting a proper state capital, for, only Nauplion was fitting in an urban sense, contrary to the bazaar towns of an Ottoman feel, like Tripolitsa, Thebes, and Lamia (known as Zeitoun(ion) back then, Gr.: *Ζητούνιον*).[10] It is also worth mentioning that the Greek state grew and solidified itself as an entity while maintaining a special relationship with the church, a relationship of co-optation and interdependence, which in turn co-shaped the personhood of the state. This pattern is not easy to break when it marks a political culture.[11]

7 Vasilios N. Makrides/Dirk Uffelmann, "Studying Eastern Orthodox Anti-Westernism: The Need for a Comparative Research Agenda", in Jonathan Sutton/Wil van den Bercken (eds), *Orthodox Christianity and Contemporary Europe*, Leuven 2003, 87–120, here 91, 106.

8 Jürgen Osterhammel, *Die Verwandlung der Welt: Eine Geschichte des 19.Jahrhunderts*, (Sixth edition), München 2011, 360–366.

9 Michael W. Weithmann, *Griechenland: Vom Frühmittelalter bis zur Gegenwart*, Regensburg 1994, 184–186.

10 Ibid.

11 Pedro Ramet, "Autocephaly and National Identity in Church-State Relations in Eastern Christianity: An Introduction," in idem (ed.), *Eastern Christianity and Politics in the*

In addition to this, to briefly juxtapose the above mentioned impression of Europeanisation with the one from 1981 onward (i.e., the actual period of Greece's formal Europeanisation), Greece's behaviour as an EU Member State attracted a lot of negative attention; it was heavily criticised on a number of occasions, which in turn is indicative of the unruly Greek perception of the EU as a necessary evil. Not unlike the early years of the Greek state, the twentieth century was one of external patronage. Namely, from the end of World War II and the Civil War (1946-1949), Greece was successively under British and American protection. This was disrupted by joining the European Economic Community (EEC) in 1981, which was mostly due to Greece's deep disappointment with its traditional allies and the little benefits that the NATO membership had yielded, following the invasion of Cyprus in 1974 and the Greek-Turkish disputes in the Aegean. Therefore, the turn to Europe was seen as an alternative alliance and alignment towards serving the national interests. It was not a genuine Europeanist impetus but the need for national security that dictated this political decision that stemmed from utilitarian calculation – to be sure, legitimate from a realist point of view –, but of little, if any social relevance, let alone popular demand. Concerning the latter, suffice it only to mention how widely held was the anti-Western rhetoric of Prime Minister Andreas Papandreou (1981-1989 and 1993-1996) and his turn to the Third World.[12] Fluctuations notwithstanding, such tendencies have been exacerbated at times when expectations from the European partners could not have been met, for example when the "Macedonian Question" tested their solidarity to Greece in the 1990s; not to mention the diametrically opposite attitudes between Greece and its Western allies concerning the treatment of Orthodox Serbia after the dismantling of Yugoslavia.[13]

Further, on a number of occasions, Greece has proven to be a problematic partner by opposing the implementation of common policies within the framework of the European political cooperation. Examples of that sort are numerous: Greece prevented criticism of the Libyan intervention in Chad (1981), refused to support sanctions against the Soviet Union after it imposed martial law in Poland (1982), prevented the unanimous condemnation of the Soviet Union for shooting down a civilian Korean aircraft (1983), and proclaimed unwavering support to the Arabs against Israel, which was recognised by the Government of

---

Twentieth Century, Baltimore/MD 1988, 3–19, here 18. See also Andreas M. Wittig, *Die Orthodoxe Kirche in Griechenland: Ihre Beziehung zum Staat gemäß der Theorie und der Entwicklung von 1821-1977*, Würzburg 1987.

12 Heinz-Jürgen Axt, "Financial Transfers and Security: Why Greece Favoured the Maastricht Treaty on European Union", in idem (ed.), *Greece and the European Union: Stranger among Partners?*, Baden-Baden 1997, 99–134, here 122–124.

13 Ibid., 129–130.

Prime Minister Konstantinos Mitsotakis (1990-1993) as late as 1990.[14] This is not too different from the picture that Samuel P. Huntington painted when he went as far as to maintain that Greece is "an anomaly, the Orthodox outsider in Western organisations",[15] adding that it had a poor record in keeping up with the economic EU standards, as well as with the norms and principles of the EU and the North Atlantic Treaty Organisation (NATO), being essentially at odds with its partners and allies.[16] It is also worth mentioning that the Greek state grew and solidified itself as an entity while maintaining a special relationship with the church, a relationship of co-optation and interdependence, which in turn co-shaped the personhood of the state. As already mentioned, this pattern is not easy to break when it marks a political culture.[17]

The Politically Assertive Era of Christodoulos

Already in December 2000 the GOC Synod did not leave the Nice Summit unchecked, which was held under the French Presidency of Jacques Chirac (1995-2007) and was intended to prepare the EU institutions for the impending enlargement and reform of the European Commission and the Council of Ministers. What impelled the Synod to react was the suggestion of the French Presidency to remove from the European Charter of Human Rights any reference to Christian tradition and heritage as a factor that co-shaped a common European consciousness, shared by the citizens of the EU. The reaction was entirely political, and the GOC made sure to inform via an official letter a number of officials and institutions of how displeased it was. Namely, some of the recipients were: President Jacques Chirac, the European Commission, the Members of European Parliament (MEPs), the heads of Member States, Greek President Kostis Stephanopoulos (1995-2005), heads of Christian Churches in Europe, the Council of European Churches, the Commission of the Catholic Bishops' Conferences, as well as the Ecumenical Patriarch of Constantinople Bartholomew (in office since 1991).[18] If anything, this was a political way of protesting and expressing one's positions, in line with diplomatic practices, not least conducted by an actor, who perceived his own role as political among others.

---

14 Heinz-Jürgen Axt, "National Interests on Top of the Agenda – Greece's Role in Common Foreign and Security Policy", in idem (ed.), *Greece and the European Union: Stranger among Partners?*, Baden-Baden 1997, 153–197, here 157–159.

15 Samuel P. Huntington, *The Clash of Civilizations and the Remaking of World Order*, London 2002, 162.

16 Ibid., 163.

17 Ramet, "Autocephaly and National Identity" (as n. 11), 18. See also Wittig, *Die Orthodoxe Kirche* (as n. 11).

18 Holy Synod of the Church of Greece, "Δελτίον Τύπου της 19ης Δεκεμβρίου 2000" [Press Release of 19.12.2000], *Ekklesia* 78/1 (2001) 43–44.

Another example of the same spirit would be the Encyclical No. 2740, issued by the Synod of the GOC in order to put forward its own views and recommendations on the European Constitution, then under construction. It is worth mentioning, in brief, that those suggestions were legislative. Among other things, they touched on the banning of proselytism while explicitly consolidating religious freedom; the safeguarding of the Christian spiritual heritage and consciousness that the European peoples share in common; and a church-state relations opt-out from the subsequent European Treaties, thus leaving their regulating framework to each state's national legislation, in accordance with Article 11 of the Treaty of Amsterdam.[19] This was intended to convey the positions of the GOC to the public domestically. However, the then interventionist practices were not one-dimensional, meaning that the content of the broadcasted material was expected to enter the public discourse, reproduce and exert political pressure, either directly or indirectly. In the case of the aforementioned encyclical, the suggestions contained therein were intended to delineate the future of the twenty-first century personhood of the EU, as this would ultimately host the Greek Orthodox peoples and their own future.

Examples such as these indicate what was typical of that period, that is, European affairs being dealt with as a high priority by Archbishop Christodoulos, amidst other issues of an already political agenda. The end goal was pursued via "ecclesiastical diplomacy", in which the GOC was neither alone nor chasing Chimaeras in its own view, as one effortlessly detects in the attempted coordination with the Vatican. Even though much stood between the two churches from a historical perspective, realism dictated cooperation in light of a shared goal. This was overtly demonstrated when the most notable visit of Pope John Paul II to Athens took place on 4 May 2001, the first in almost a millennium, where the pontiff attempted to alleviate the grievances of the past by apologising for the Crusaders' responsibility as regards the first sacking of Constantinople in 1204 and all that ensued thereafter. The Greek Archbishop did not shy away from making the common goals of the GOC and the Vatican known, as he described their cooperation as a means to keep the EU Christian, maintain its identity, and prevent it from becoming equivalent to an *état laïque*.[20] In turn, when the GOC reciprocated the visit one year later, the cooperation of the two ecclesiastical institutions mainly focused on the major EU issues. The fermentations and exchange of ideas that ensued there steered clear of theological topics, as they rather revolved round the optimal ways in which they could work towards co-

19 Holy Synod of the Church of Greece, "Εγκύκλιος 2740 – Θέμα: Το Μέλλον της Ευρώπης και η Εκκλησία της Ελλάδος" [Encyclical 2740 – Topic: The Future of Europe and the Church of Greece], *Ekklesia* 79/7 (2002) 467–470.

20 "Η Προσκυνηματική Επίσκεψη του Ρωμαίου Ποντίφικος στην Ελλάδα" [The Pilgrimage Visit of the Roman Pontiff to Greece], *Ekklesia* 78/5 (2001) 377–394, here 383.

formulating the European reality under construction from which a Constitution was due to germinate.[21]

To that end, the GOC and Christodoulos personally sought to utilise other, domestic means as well, in order to influence the European decision-making centres, directly or otherwise. For instance, in February 2002 he held a luncheon where Anna Diamantopoulou, the Greek Commissioner to the EU (1999-2004), as well as the Greek MEPs were hosted. He explained his positions by emphasising an ideal type of EU, where special importance ought to be attached to its Christian foundations and respective national traditions, which could contribute to dealing with Europe's social problems, instead of merely focusing on its mundane, practical aspects. Here, the Orthodox Church – so Christodoulos – has a role and a contribution to make too.[22]

Likewise, the GOC lobbied then Mayor of Athens Dora Bakoyannis (2003-2006), who, having been invited to take part in a workgroup under the President of the European Commission Romano Prodi (1999-2004), was deemed influential. The content of that letter was in line with the legislative suggestions that had already been communicated via the Encyclical No. 2740, while referring to inherent identity traits as those emanating from the European Christian tradition and heritage, as well as to the threat of church marginalisation, in contrast to fundamental European values. But most importantly, Bakoyannis' exertion of influence was solicited, in order to effectively shift the weight to Greece's benefit.[23]

The same pattern is detectable in the communication with the Greek MEPs. Once again, the GOC wrote to them in order to inform them of its positions concerning the potential European Constitutional Treaty. This letter, however, was more than a framework of principles; rather, it was a set of legislative suggestions. Thereby, the European identity ideal type as perceived by the GOC was outlined on the basis of its foundations, that is, Christian religion, Hellenic education (*paideia*, Gr.: *παιδεία*), and Roman legal tradition. Hence, it was suggested that these ought to be mentioned in the preamble of the Constitutional Treaty, as former French President Valéry Giscard D'Estaing, who presided over the "Convention on the Future of Europe" that drafted the above Treaty, had also proposed. Moreover, other recommendations were outlined, with reference to most aspects of public life and administration: among other things, education,

21 Holy Synod of the Church of Greece, "Η Επίσημη Επίσκεψη της Εκκλησίας της Ελλάδος στο Βατικανό – Δελτίο Τύπου της 10ης Μαρτίου 2002" [The Official Visit of the Church of Greece to the Vatican – Press Release of 10.03.2002], *Ekklesia* 79/3 (2002) 170–174, here 170.

22 Holy Synod of the Church of Greece, "Δελτίον Τύπου της 12ης Φεβρουαρίου 2002" [Press Release of 12.02.2002], *Ekklesia* 79/3 (2002) 194.

23 Theologos Apostolidis, "Επιστολή της Ιεράς Συνόδου προς την Δήμαρχον Αθηναίων" [Letter of the Holy Synod to the Mayor of Athens], *Ekklesia* 80/3 (2003) 209.

social care, ethical code of business conduct, cultural promotion, but also preservation of the churches' legal *status quo*, ban of proselytism, and national/religious holidays, while closing with wishes for swift European unification.[24]

However, what the strategies of several actors – political, religious, and economic – across the board aimed at was eventually annulled in one stroke by the referenda that rejected the suggested Constitutional Treaty; namely, those in France and the Netherlands in 2005. Elsewhere in Europe, ratification was either accomplished via the parliamentary route or put on hold. Be that as it may, the GOC did neither lose sight of the European project nor did it withdraw it from its agenda. Non-ratification may have been an important impediment, but not decisively detrimental to the European unification process. This is because the aim of an "Ever Closer Union" is still enshrined in the EU Treaties, as this resolve has been explicitly confirmed in the Lisbon Treaty of 2007, which is essentially an amendment of the 1992 EU Treaty (also known as the Maastricht Treaty) and the Treaty on the Functioning of the EU (else known as the 1957 Treaty of Rome). Therefore, the issue of an overarching type of European identity and all that this entails remained still at large. Looking to the future then, pressure did not cease to be exerted in order to co-formulate the official European personhood. An outstanding example of that sort would be the 27 February 2007 letter of the GOC Synod to Prime Minister Kostas Karamanlis (2004-2009), where the unabated concern for international and European affairs was expressed. What is more, a particular type of content regarding the "Berlin Declaration"[25] was recommended, as was the case with six other Member States' churches: namely, that Europe's Christian values and principles ought to be explicitly stated in the document.[26] This request was not satisfied, displeasing not only the GOC, but also the Vatican, as Pope Benedict XVI (2005-2013) protested that the European peoples' identities were thus being ignored.[27]

---

24 Archbishop Christodoulos and Theologos Apostolidis, "Επιστολή της Ιεράς Συνόδου προς τους Έλληνες Ευρωβουλευτές" [Letter of the Holy Synod to the Greek MEPs], *Ekklesia* 80/4 (2003) 282-83.

25 The "Berlin Declaration" was the 50th anniversary since the monumental Treaty of Rome. Thereby a non-binding document was to be produced, following the failure to ratify the EU Constitutional Treaty; it could potentially signify the future course of action nonetheless, hence the attention to it on behalf of the churches.

26 Holy Synod of the Church of Greece, "Προς τον Πρωθυπουργόν κ. Κωνσταντίνον Καραμανλήν περί των Χριστιανικών Ριζών της Ευρώπης" [To Prime Minister Mr Konstantinos Karamanlis about the Christian Roots of Europe], *Ekklesia* 84/3 (2007) 183.

27 Ian Traynor, "As the EU Turns 50, Pope Says it's on Path to Oblivion", *The Guardian*, 26 March 2007, URL: http://www.theguardian.com/world/2007/mar/26/eu.catholicism [14.01.2015].

One could carry on *ad infinitum* with examples of political involvement, lobbying, and soft power[28] exertion with an eye on the EU and the European affairs, either via the international or the domestic route. But in any case, the intent to appropriate and keep officials with a say in Brussels and elsewhere in check is established by evidence throughout Christodoulos' period in office. It appears that within the context of the "Reverse Westphalia", where the nation-state and the constituents of its sovereignty are under review and re-theorisation[29] – as is the case with the EU, where powers are shifted upwards to Brussels within a context of an "Ever Closer Union", not to mention the currents of globalisation –, the GOC realised that apart from challenges, this emergent *status quo* also had opportunities in store. This was in fact articulated explicitly by Christodoulos, when he mentioned the need for a new "geopolitical pastoral consciousness", in tune with the challenges and requirements of the times.[30] He particularly raised the question of a broader episcopal responsibility within the shrinking world and by extension the EU, which was now rendered as the playing field where Greek Orthodoxy could demonstrate an extrovert strategy and essentially function as an independent actor.[31]

This explicitly articulated attitude and intent was backed by actions that sought to produce tangible results and not merely maintain the GOC and its Archbishop active in the public discourse. Soft power was not an end in itself, but rather a means to an end. By establishing the Christian heritage and culture as a common European denominator and unifying principle of identity, it was expected that pressure to Brussels and, what is more, in tune with the Vatican, would bear fruits. Thereby the GOC and the Roman Catholic Church would ultimately shadow-legislate, which, in terms of outcomes, meant: a) the *de facto* acknowledgement of the churches as political actors; and subsequently b) the *de jure* establishment of a model of "constitutional de-secularisation". The churches had every reason to pursue their chances to influence such development.[32] However, hints and traces of the GOC investing time and effort in order to be upgraded to a co-opted soft power within the bounds of the permissiveness that the EU membership indirectly provided are to be found beyond *ad hoc* diplomatic gestures, meetings, visits, and correspondence, utilised in order to co-shape an EU ideal type via its utmost institutional, legislative, and founding act, namely the Constitutional Treaty.

---

28 Joseph S. Nye Jr., *Soft Power: The Means to Success in World Politics*, New York 2004.

29 Kimon Valaskakis, "Westphalia II: The Real Millennium Challenge", *The Paris Center for New Learning*, December 2000, URL: http://www.paricenter.com/library/papers/valaskakis01.php [08.05.2015].

30 Archbishop Christodoulos, "Προσφώνησις ενώπιον της Ι.Σ." [Address before the Holy Synod], *Ekklesia* 81/9 (2004) 750–753, here 751.

31 Ibid.

32 Trantas, *Being and Belonging* (as n. 2), 95–96.

The Archbishop valued the permanent form of representation greatly, namely, the office of Representation of the Church of Greece to the European Union (hereafter RCGEU), which is an example of permanent ecclesiastical diplomatic presence in Brussels and a communication means with the EU institutions. The fact is that the RCGEU was first and foremost Christodoulos' own aspiration and project.[33] The same applies to the Special Synodical Committee for the Monitoring of European Affairs, which was intended to function as a home institution in coordination with the office in Brussels under the supervision of Christodoulos. These two would establish a fully functional foundation, which would enable the systematic dealing with the EU in a specialised and dedicated fashion. This, in the long run, would help get the GOC actively involved in the European project, by providing the means to better fathom its constituent institutions and processes, as well as the EU as a bloc actor and international organisation, given the direct linkage of the RCGEU to the EU structure and institutions and its immediate understanding of the political culture in Brussels.[34]

More to the point, the RCGEU, in light of the non-unitary and somewhat vague domestic perception and understanding of the EU – due by and large to parochialism, a by-product of bishopric decentralisation into eparchies/localities, which are prioritised by their bishops – had to introduce to the hierarchy an accurate and clear-cut appreciation of the EU, which emanated from its proximity to the institutions and decision-making processes. Thereby, the Greek metropolitans were to be exposed to an inclusive mindset of European citizenship as part of a broader level of belonging and identity. Not to mention that in this way, they would be in a position to better fathom the linkage of decisions made in Brussels to their own eparchies, and understand by what mentalities those are developed to become directives, affecting them directly or indirectly.[35] Hence, a number of hierarchs visited the seat of the European Commission, being hosted and guided by the director of the RCGEU since 2000, titular Metropolitan Athanasios of Achaia, who has been very active, particularly during the Greek Presidency of the Council of the EU in 2003.[36] But apart from the office's activities and engagement with international, both political and religious, organisations, influential figures, as well as its function as a linkage between Athens and Brussels, its existence itself was valued highly by Christodoulos. It constituted essentially a permanent ecclesiastical diplomatic mission and secured a presence amongst influential political entities at the highest level of the EU structure, in a period when the GOC was the sole autocephalous church being

33 C. T., Interview with author on 29.10.2013 (Brussels).
34 Ibid.
35 Ibid.
36 G. E., Interview with author on 27.11.2013 (Brussels).

represented there.[37] This was part and parcel of the geopolitical pastoral consciousness that the Greek Archbishop asserted, as mentioned earlier.

Yet, another sign of Christodoulos' sustained extrovert policies with the EU as a point of reference involved the consolidation of Eastern Orthodoxy as a soft power contender therein. For, the impending European Enlargement, given its geo-cultural dimension, emerged as an opportunity to consolidate Eastern Orthodoxy as a considerable cultural-political actor – ideally a unitary one. Already the EU membership of Greece, together with those of Bulgaria, Romania and Cyprus, constituted a considerable homogeneous religio-cultural bloc in the eyes of the Archbishop.[38] All it lacked was the drive, which could be provided by the realisation that this could potentially be a source of power in its own right, amplified by an internationally acknowledged leading actor of matching qualities, namely Russia.[39] The fact that the latter was not an EU member, though, stood in the way of radically co-shaping the European personhood, and hence Christodoulos openly advocated Russia's accession, so that ultimately a bloc of homodox states would counterbalance the overwhelmingly dominant Western influence, cultural, religious, and otherwise. Thereby, the balance of power within the EU's governing institutions would shift in Eastern Orthodoxy's favour.

This inclination towards the Russian EU membership was consistently demonstrated, both on bilateral and multilateral occasions, albeit expressed as wishful thinking for the most part rather than as a realistically planned outline. Further, this suggestion lacked a concise reference to any EU costs/benefits, or any clear articulation of how this would serve the European interests. For example, when Christodoulos visited Russia in 2001, he maintained that bringing the country into the EU, together with the rest of the homodox Eastern European candidates – the EU enlargement had not yet taken place – would serve as a hindrance to the expansion of globalisation and Western proselytism that threatened Orthodoxy.[40] It should be pointed out, however, that this statement should be taken with some reservation, as, apart from getting his message across, the Greek Archbishop was also seeking to win over his audience, even if that entailed the use of emotionally charged utterances. In contrast, via his message to the international conference *Cristianesimo e Democrazia nel Futuro dell'Europa* (13-14 July 2002), which was attended, among others, by both the President of the European Commission Romano Prodi (1999-2004) and the President of the

37 C. T., Interview (as n. 33).

38 Konstantinos Cholevas, "Η διεύρυνση της Ευρώπης" [The Enlargement of Europe], *Ekklesia* 80/5 (2003) 376–377.

39 Savvas Agourides, *Θεολογία και Κοινωνία σε Διάλογο* [Theology and Society in Dialogue], Athens 1991, 21–22.

40 Agathangelos Charamantidis, "Η Ειρηνική Επίσκεψις του Μακαριωτάτου Αρχιεπισκόπου Αθηνών και πάσης Ελλάδος Χριστόδουλου εις την Εκκλησίαν της Ρωσίας" [The Irenic Visit of His Beatitude the Archbishop of Athens and All Greece Christodoulos to the Church of Russia], *Ekklesia* 78/6 (2001) 455–492, here 462–463.

European Parliament Pat Cox (2002-2004), the tone was different. Christodoulos unravelled his vision, rather, his ideal type of the EU, while adding to it an extended geographical dimension, including Russia.[41] In addition, *Ekklesia*, the official monthly bulletin of the GOC, did not cease to sporadically remind its readership of this ambitious aspiration, that is to reinforce the Christian Orthodox presence in the EU and, by extension, its institutions; to continue where Cyril and Methodius left off, and ideally, install and establish within Europe the Orthodox civilisational heritage, reminiscent of Dmitry Obolensky's "Byzantine Commonwealth".[42] The strategic objective of the "Orthodox Christian Easternisation of the EU" can be described as,

> the policies and processes that aspire to instil the EU with elements of the Eastern Orthodox value system and embed its corresponding priorities into the institutional organisation and principles of the EU and its founding treaties.[43]

It was indeed an overly ambitious aspiration. Be that as it may, it does demonstrate a deep-seated interest in European affairs, not to mention, a keen eye for the matters that touch on a broader geopolitical and cultural scale. In that sense, despite the ambivalence that evidently springs out of the Euroscepticism that accompanied this sustained extrovert stance, it remained a distinctive mark of Christodoulos' era.

At least just as strategic an objective was the accession of Cyprus to the EU as far as the Greek Archbishop was concerned. It may not have been deemed a source of power as such, that is, one which would have a significant effect on Brussels, but the EU was considered vital in the promotion of national interests of Greece and Cyprus combined. Joint forces, with the corresponding national churches included, was a *sine qua non* in Christodoulos' view: in unison spiritually and nationally, towards achieving maximum gains.[44] On several occasions Christodoulos had contacts with both the Cypriot political establishment as well as with the Orthodox Church of Cyprus (OCC), making sure to promote his view of a singular, unitary national, and geo-cultural entity; hence

---

41 Archbishop Christodoulos, "Προς το Συνέδριο *'Cristianesimo e Democrazia nel Futuro dell'Europa'*" [To the Congress "*Christianity and Democracy in the Future of Europe*"], *Ekklesia* 79/8-9 (2002) 569–570.

42 Cholevas, "Η διεύρυνση της Ευρώπης" (as n. 38), 376–377. See also Dimitri Obolensky, *The Byzantine Commonwealth: Eastern Europe, 500–1453*, New York 1971; Agourides, *Θεολογία και Κοινωνία* (as n. 39), 22.

43 Trantas, *Being and Belonging* (as n. 2), 97–98.

44 Press Office of the Holy Synod of the GOC, "Συνάντηση του Μακαριωτάτου με τον Πρόεδρο του Κινήματος Σοσιαλδημοκρατών κ. Βάσο Λυσσαρίδη" [Meeting of His Beatitude with the President of the Movement for Social Democracy Mr Vasos Lyssaridis], *Ekklesia* 78/4 (2001) 357. See also Press Office of the Holy Synod of the GOC, "Συνάντηση του Μακαριωτάτου με τον Πρόεδρο της Κυπριακής Δημοκρατίας" [Meeting of His Beatitude with the President of the Republic of Cyprus], *Ekklesia* 78/5 (2001) 441.

the above mentioned strategic goal of Cyprus' EU accession, which was thought of as an indirect means to that end.[45] Not to mention that, functioning in coordination within the EU, the OCC and the GOC would be stronger together in the pursuit of the co-shaping of its personhood via trying to institutionally instil into it references to its Christian heritage, or at least help promote Christian values, despite its secular foundations and direction. What is more, the national interests of the Cypriot state and by extension of Hellenism would be best served within the EU, thought Christodoulos, who valued its potential towards the improvement of future political conditions.[46]

The Politically Revisionist Era of Hieronymos II

This overall assertiveness, however, was detrimental to the already tense relationship of the GOC with the Ecumenical Patriarchate of Constantinople due to the jurisdictional claims of the latter within Greece. For, the Greek Church intervened in the international arena as an actor of respective rights and entitlement, by and large owed to Christodoulos' revisionist geopolitical pastoral consciousness, even though the Orthodox ecclesiastical equivalent of geopolitics is traditionally thought of and reserved as the exclusive domain of the Patriarchate. Christodoulos believed that any retreat inwards, away from the international affairs, which the EU's Post-Westphalian conditions facilitated, would constitute institutional marginalisation, restriction of independence, and episcopal responsibility, not to mention observation of stagnant, outdated practices, irrelevant to the exigencies of the times.[47] Yet, this discord was one of the first issues to be dealt with – together with many others – as soon as Hieronymos II succeeded Christodoulos in 2008. But meanwhile, it took direct political intervention by the government of the New Democracy Party (Gr.: Νέα Δημοκρατία) in 2004 to appease both counterparts and defuse the situation, which could well spill over diplomatic affairs and injure Greece's long-standing interests, should further escalation ensue.[48]

---

45 Archbishop Christodoulos and Bishop Theologos of Salona, "Επιστολή της Ι.Σ. προς τον Πρόεδρον της Ελληνικής Κυβερνήσεως επι τη Εντάξει της Κύπρου εις την Ευρωπαϊκήν Ένωσιν" [Letter of the Holy Synod to the President of the Greek Government on the Accession of Cyprus to the European Union], *Ekklesia* 80/4 (2003) 254.

46 Archimandrite Epifanios Oikonomou, "Χρονικόν Επισήμου Ειρηνικής Επισκέψεως του Μακαριωτάτου Αρχιεπισκόπου Αθηνών και Πάσης Ελλάδος κ. Χριστόδουλου στην Ορθόδοξη Αυτοκέφαλη Εκκλησία της Κύπρου (Β΄ ΜΕΡΟΣ)" [Chronicle of the Irenic Visit of His Beatitude the Archbishop of Athens and All Greece Mr Christodoulos to the Orthodox Autocephalous Church of Cyprus (Part B)], *Ekklesia* 84/6 (2007) 436–479, here 439.

47 Christodoulos, "Προσφώνησις" (as n. 30), 751.

48 G. E., Interview (as n. 36).

With Hieronymos II at the GOC's helm, things changed. Christodoulos' successor has an immensely different public image, one that matches his shift in policies, orientation and objectives. He had already been clear on how he envisaged the church as Metropolitan of Thebes and Levadeia (1981-2008). He maintained that the GOC had experienced an identity crisis under Christodoulos' guidance, as it resembled rather a political party than a spiritual, ecclesiastical institution, something that could spread from the top of the hierarchy to the grass roots level of clergymen, thus eroding the character of the church.[49] And, remaining true to his personal views and vision for the GOC, he made sure to communicate them publicly via his enthronement speech, which took place on 16 February 2008. The occasion could not be more appropriate for setting the new order of things and making sure it would reach the broadest possible audiences. Hieronymos made sure to underline that it was not his intention to make any particular agenda announcements on future policies, let alone, refer to a programme as such. He rather suggested a general framework or philosophy, which implied the upcoming *modus operandi*. First and foremost, emphasis was put on the spiritual and otherworldly dimension that the GOC should be preoccupied with as a priority, not the mundane, and most importantly the involvement with it in an equally mundane manner. If some kind of intervention were to be called for, it should occur appropriately, along the lines of the church's role; that is, with consideration of its historical and social institutional role and its obligation to the people, but always strictly within these bounds. And certainly, he stressed that it should steer clear of any partisan or ideological inclinations, as this would be detrimental to the church itself and cause confusion, given that the state has its own institutions and mechanisms, which should not be undermined. In that way he showed a preference for the distinction of the roles of church and state, and by extension of institutional missions and tasks – but to be clear, not that their formal separation was implied.[50]

That said, he did not dismiss his predecessor's positions altogether, he simply opted for a different approach that emanated from a divergence of philosophies. He too was uneasy with the works, effects, and end-goals of globalisation for example, with cultural deterioration, identity erosion, or consumerism at the expense of spirituality. But, instead of intervening in political affairs, he emphasised the philanthropic duties of the GOC to tackle such contemporary

49 Metropolitan Hieronymos of Thebes and Levadeia, "Αποσπάσματα από την Εισήγησιν του Σεβασμιωτάτου Μητροπολίτου Θηβών και Λεβαδείας κ. Ιερώνυμου περί του Διαλόγου Εκκλησίας και Κοινωνίας" [Excerpts from the Speech of His Eminence the Metropolitan of Thebes and Levadeia Mr Hieronymos on the Dialogue of Church and Society], *Ekklesia* 83/9 (2006) 742–743.

50 Archbishop Hieronymos II, "Ενθρονιστήριος Λόγος του Μακαριωτάτου Αρχιεπισκόπου Αθηνών και Πάσης Ελλάδος κ. Ιερώνυμου" [Enthronement Speech of His Beatitude the Archbishop of Athens and All Greece Mr Heronymos], *Ekklesia* 85/3 (2008) 196–202.

challenges.[51] Concerning the causal linkage of personality traits with policies, a year later in an interview to journalist Stephanos Kasimatis, he elaborated on the differences between him and his predecessor, clarifying how they spilled over into extra-ecclesiastical affairs and inevitably affected corresponding institutions, directly or indirectly. Most notably, he described Christodoulos' church ideal type as one that had a messianic mission, metaphorically speaking, which involved state affairs and national interests. By extension, this entailed the risk of unwillingly undermining the state institutions, which had been appointed corresponding roles and tasks, if anything, due to confusion caused by polyphony. In contrast, he clarified that he had no interventionist intention. Hieronymos II maintained that moderation and self-restraint were the optimal attitude, rather than passionate fervour with the safeguarding of national identity and interests in the face of globalisation and other such perceived threats, for fervour clouds one's judgement.[52] Therefore, undoubtedly and publicly, he articulated the shift in terms of rhetoric and conduct, so it would not be out of order to consider his positions a departure point towards a paradigm shift.

As attested by other instances as well, he made sure not to leave room for doubt concerning the direction to which he wanted to steer the GOC. Depoliticisation was clearly a priority as he sought to eradicate the standing political and ideological inclinations, which oftentimes reached the public.[53] Namely, referring to this matter in the Extraordinary Convocation of Bishops on 24 June 2008, he told the hierarchy that having taken the contemporary challenges – ranging from religious to sociocultural and beyond, including international ones – into account, he had a full appreciation of the situation and the duties of the GOC. In a few words, he signalled the abandonment of previous policies, especially those which fell within the framework of Christodoulos' geopolitical pastoral consciousness, and suggested a change of attitude and, accordingly, of the publicly projected image of the church. In so doing, he discouraged taking liberties individually towards pursuing personal interventions, calling for a synodical strategy instead, based on sober contemplation in line with theologically valid principles; if not for any other reason, to preserve the integrity and interests of the church from further injury.[54] Apart from this reason though,

---

51 Ibid., 199.

52 Stephanos Kasimatis, "Συνέντευξη του Μακαριωτάτου Αρχιεπισκόπου Αθηνών και Πάσης Ελλάδος κ. Ιερώνυμου στο Βήμα της Κυριακής, 8 Φεβρουαρίου 2009" [Interview of His Beatitude the Archbishop of Athens and All Greece Mr Hieronymos to the Newspaper 'To Vima tis Kyriakis', 08.02.2009], *Ekklesia* 86/2 (2009) 122-126.

53 A. N., Interview with author on 04.12.2013 (Athens).

54 Archbishop Hieronymos II, "Εισήγηση του Μακαριωτάτου Αρχιεπισκόπου Αθηνών και Πάσης Ελλάδος κ. Ιερώνυμου στην Έκτακτη Σύγκληση της Ιεραρχίας" [Speech of His Beatitude the Archbishop of Athens and All Greece Hieronymos in the Extraordinary Convocation of the Church Hierarchy], *Ekklesia* 85/7 (2008) 489–492.

the depoliticisation of the GOC was in line with his own lack of interest in international politics as well.[55]

Further, as regards the narrowly perceived domain of European politics, Hieronymos II, out of idiosyncrasy alone, was not at ease with pursuing any agendas, shadow-legislate or lobby for what constitutes, by definition, political involvement. Even though he did not doubt the church's social role, he was careful not to cross boundaries and thus signify interventionist intent on behalf of the GOC anew. Keeping politics at bay also applied to EU politics, while being permissive to low-level exchanges, when those were filtered through the institutions of the state and provided that they did not entail harmful concessions to the detriment of faith and culture. This included, for example, EU's available means and economic resources to particular ends.[56] It should be clarified at this point that this does not constitute Euroscepticism, but rather the perpetuation of an invariable advice for caution, regardless of who is at the head of the GOC, and for fear of cultural erosion and social fragmentation due to globalisation.[57] This cautious attitude, a rather instrumentalist position, indicates that a shift in policies does not necessitate an analogous one in principles and values regarding entrenched views.

At the same time, there are strong indications that the RCGEU was informally and silently demoted, for, with the radical changes in the management of foreign, therefore European affairs as well, Athens reclaimed its control of activities and initiatives, via the Special Synodical Committee for the Monitoring of European Affairs.[58] This noticeable change was communicated in public, as a particular reference was made to the Committee and to the outline of its duties on 2 June 2009, during the works of a conference on intercultural dialogue in Veroia. Namely, its purposes and functions involved, in brief: a) to communicate with the EU institutions (EU Parliament and Commission representations in Athens) and intervene when that is deemed necessary; b) to take part in EU funded programmes towards educating the clerics and laity who work for the GOC; c) to secure funding for the restoration of churches, monasteries and the construction of buildings of public interest (e.g., museums etc.); d) to take part in conferences and events organised by the representations of the EU Parliament and Commission in Athens, as well as organise equivalent events; e) to cooperate with the MEPs towards securing their invitations for Metropolitans and church staff to

55 M. D., Interview with author on 17.12.2013 (Athens).

56 Archbishop Hieronymos II, 'Μήνυμα στην Γ΄ Ημερίδα της Ειδικής Συνοδικής Επιτροπής Παρακολουθήσεως των Ευρωπαϊκών Θεμάτων στο Διορθόδοξο Κέντρο της Εκκλησίας της Ελλάδος στην Ιερά Μονή Πεντέλης" [Message to the Third Meeting of the Special Synodical Committee for the Monitoring of European Affairs at the Inter-Orthodox Centre of the Church of Greece at the Holy Monastery of Penteli], *Ekklesia* 86/4 (2009) 231–232.

57 Hieronymos II, "Ενθρονιστήριος Λόγος" (as n. 50), 200.

58 C.T., Interview (as n. 33).

Brussels; f) to cooperate with the EU Member States' embassies in Athens; and g) to cooperate with the office of RCGEU in Brussels.[59] However, it must be pointed out that the role of the RCGEU was not clarified; neither the specific functions delegated to it, nor the type and degree of administrative cooperation with its counterparts in Athens were explained. Rather, it left the impression that that the so-called lions' share of duties concerning the EU, therefore control over actions and contacts, was essentially shifted to Athens, as direct communication with the key EU institutions' representations in Athens (Parliament and Commission) was emphasised, even though the RCGEU is a permanent representation in Brussels and can better access the administrative headquarters of the EU. This constitutes a departure from the previous *status quo*.

As regards the relationship with the Ecumenical Patriarchate of Constantinople, which was affected by the initiatives of Christodoulos within the permissiveness of the EU's "Reverse Westphalia",[60] Hieronymos II made sure to mend the collateral damage done by his predecessor and moved on to a – much desired by the Greek political establishment – rapprochement with Bartholomew; one of his priorities early on as Archbishop. Notably, the two hierarchs agreed that it would be optimal for Orthodoxy to express itself unanimously in Europe, which entailed an institutional reconfiguration.[61] During his visit to the Patriarchate (9-11 May 2008), it was evident that there was a mutual agreement to turn the page and re-establish the relationship on the basis of common identity and homogeneity; but also, it was understood that in light of future challenges, it would be best to stand together.[62] And later, on 8 January 2014, in Athens, on the occasion of the ceremony for the commencement of the Greek Presidency of the

---

59 Hieronymos Karmas, "Ο Ρόλος του Γραφείου της Ειδικής Συνοδικής Επιτροπής στη Διαμόρφωση του Ευρωπαϊκού Γίγνεσθαι" [The Role of the Office of the Special Synodical Committee in the Formation of the European State of Affairs], *Ekklesia* 86/9 (2009) 542–543.

60 Valaskakis, "Westphalia II" (as n. 29).

61 Elpidoforos Lampriniadis/Kyrillos Misiakoulis, "Πρακτικόν Συμφωνίας κατά τας Διμερείς Συνομιλίας εις τα Πλαίσια της Ειρηνικής Επισκέψεως εις το Οικουμενικόν Πατριαρχείον του Μακαριωτάτου Αρχιεπισκόπου Αθηνών και πάσης Ελλάδος κ. Ιερωνύμου" [Transcript of Agreement during the Bilateral Talks in the Framework of the Official Visit of His Beatitude the Archbishop of Athens and All Greece Mr Hieronymos to the Ecumenical Patriarchate], *Ekklesia* 85/5 (2008) 361–362.

62 Patriarch Bartholomew, "Προσφώνησις της Α.Θ.Π. του Οικουμενικού Πατριάρχου κ. Βαρθολομαίου κατά την Επίσημον Υποδοχήν του Μακαριωτάτου Αρχιεπισκόπου Αθηνών και Πάσης Ελλάδος κ. Ιερωνύμου εν τη Αιθούση του Θρόνου" [Address by His Holiness the Ecumenical Patriarch Mr Bartholomew during the Official Reception of His Beatitude the Archbishop of Athens and All Greece Mr Hieronymos in the Throne Chamber], *Ekklesia* 85/5 (2008) 329–332. See also Archbishop Hieronymos II, "Αντιφώνησις του Μακαριωτάτου Αρχιεπισκόπου Αθηνών κατά την Επίσημον Υποδοχήν εν τη Αιθούση του Θρόνου" [Replying Speech by His Beatitude the Archbishop of Athens during the Official Reception in the Throne Chamber], *Ekklesia* 85/5 (2008) 333–335.

European Commission, their common public appearance helped convey the message of unity, harmony, and solidarity.[63]

Regarding a broader geopolitical perspective, but with the European "Reverse Westphalia" as starting point, and in conjunction with the aforementioned rapprochement with the Ecumenical Patriarchate, Hieronymos II did not follow up on Christodoulos' engagement with the Russian political establishment and the church there, nor did he enter the geopolitical domain by pursuing the holistic doctrine of Greece and Cyprus as one geo-cultural unit. The former had already contributed to the friction with the Patriarchate, whereas the latter could entail severe complications and the disturbance of very delicate balances, beyond the possible control and capacity of the GOC. Further, the domestic and international conditions had changes in store, thus bringing with them new priorities; for instance, by the time Hieronymos II was elected Archbishop, the European Constitutional Treaty was already a dead letter and its ratification was put indefinitely on hold, only to be re-introduced as the Lisbon Treaty. Yet, the content and details of the latter were not subject to review and change by non-political institutions outside the decision-making centres in Brussels anyway. In fact, because of that, it was no object for Christodoulos already since 2005, although it had been the major issue at the top of his agenda. By the same token, it was off the table for Hieronymos II too, as other priorities emerged in the meantime, with the Greek debt crisis outbreak as the most significant one.

It appears that conditions and capacities determine agendas and the way they are pursued, together with the personality of the leading figures who are responsible for their share of decision-making. Indeed, personal visions and perceived threats to church and society have by and large distinguished the conduct of the two archbishops in focus. Christodoulos considered the church an actor that is entitled to intervene in political issues, and himself a citizen who ought to exercise his right to express his views in the public sphere, including the international affairs of the state, as if he were the head of a church party. Hieronymos II thus far demonstrated the opposite characteristics; by considering postmodernity and its constituent uncertainties and adjustments – social openness, multiculturalism, globality – a fact of life rather than a threat. In that sense, he did not deem church interventionism necessary. What is more, this spills over into the overall role of the church and its relations with the state.[64] In a nutshell, worldviews and personal predispositions co-determined the differences addressed earlier in the text.

63 G. A., Interview with author on 25.01.2014 (Bonn).

64 Vasilios N. Makrides, "Die Orthodoxe Kirche Griechenlands und der lange Weg zur Modernisierung", *Glaube in der 2. Welt* 10/38 (2010) 18–21.

Conclusion

It has been within the context of Greece's relations with the EU that the GOC is required to operate, and it is not immune to them. The state itself has often been considered a problematic EU member and cooperation has not been flawless and easy. In that respect, it would be erroneous to attribute the fluctuations of the relationship between the GOC and the EU Institutions only to Orthodox anti-Westernism. The volatility that is endemic in the domestic political culture when it comes to dealing with the EU, coupled with the timidity and suspiciousness to engage the bloc-actor, is not an exclusive trait of the church, as it is rather representative of the broader Greek socio-political culture. And it has been within this context that the GOC endeavoured to contemplate its role in the post-secular era and retrace its steps.

To be sure, it is not out of place to take initiatives as such, given that, for an organisation, adaptation to change guarantees its survival. Nor is it extraordinary to identify false strategies and redraw them. Yet, as regards the GOC, the shift is radical from one archbishop to another, and it did not emanate out of a major change in the relationship of the state and the EU. There is a correlation between the environment and the actor's conduct, in the sense of government checks and balances concerning the conduct of the church, but no evidence of causality as such appears to have played a role in this deep change. In addition, the pervading church personhood and the patterns of its behaviour remained unaltered on an institutional level.

As for the international environment, the major EU issues that Christodoulos sought to influence ceased to be debatable and the possibility of contributing to the Constitutional Treaty of the EU was thereafter obsolete. What remained was the will to play an international role, but among others, he was lacking the means and the international partners, which meant end-game for his geopolitical pastoral role. Hieronymos II did not inherit a specific European agenda, and from that perspective change ought to be expected. Yet, his overall attitude and his programme of depoliticisation involved the EU as well. He genuinely wished to steer clear of political initiatives and plans, but at the same time he appeared to be undoing some of the progress that Christodoulos had accomplished by withdrawing from the playing field altogether. The international absence signified a contraction to the domestic – admittedly pressing – affairs, yet at the same time, the EU remains open across the board for all kinds of actors and exchanges of ideas, and in that sense one can identify a soft power vacuum in dealing with the affairs of the EU. After all, emergent issues that leave room for interventionism did not cease to exist, if one were inclined to get actively involved. Still, Hieronymos II could not be held accountable for keeping away from affairs that by and large exceed the church's object and competence, particularly within a domain of specialists. If anything, this signified a return to realism and a departure from questionable, ambitious aspirations, such as that of Europe's "Christian Orthodoxisation", or shadow legislation. Not to mention that the developments in Greece, presented new, major domestic challenges that had to be prioritised.

Be that as it may, personal leadership decisions are evident throughout; for it appears that the persons who led the GOC during the period of interest have left a very visible mark on the record of this church's conduct. And, when all is said and done, while taking the broader environment into account as co-determinant, the decisive role that leadership has played has heavily affected the attitude and place of the GOC in the EU. In that respect, assumptions that the GOC can be led by the inertia of its own policies, i.e., that it functions automatically and despite the personality of its leadership, are far from true.

Symphonic Democracy: Is there a Form of Modern Democracy Suitable for Orthodox Countries?

Dragan Šljivić

Not that long ago, one of the leading scholars in the field of democratisation, Samuel P. Huntington, expressed his lack of optimism regarding democracy's future in predominantly Orthodox societies.[1] Some quarter of a century later, his prognosis might look too pessimistic. Its frequently criticised generosity notwithstanding, the 2017 report of the Freedom House "Freedom in the World" depicted the situation in twelve predominantly Orthodox countries as a little better than the global average. Five Orthodox countries were labelled as "free", another five as "partly free" (some on the very threshold of being "free"), with Russia and Belarus described as autocracies.[2] Interestingly, the last two countries also represent some of the least religious traditionally Orthodox societies in Europe. When in 2009 Gallup asked, "how important is religion in your life?", the Russians and the Belarusians were among those Europeans least likely to say that it mattered to them.[3]

The very debate on whether Orthodox countries can sustain democracies seems quite outdated in the second decade of the twenty-first century. Greece appears to be a case in point. Among the three Southern European "third-wave" democracies – Portugal, Spain and Greece –, ten years into democratic transition, the Orthodox had the highest approval of both their church and their democracy.[4]

---

1 The Orthodox, in his view, "seem much less likely to develop stable democratic political systems. The Velvet Curtain of culture has replaced the Iron Curtain of Ideology". Samuel P. Huntington, *The Clash of Civilizations and the Remaking of World Order*, New York 1996, 29–30.

2 The Freedom House in January 2017 listed five predominantly Orthodox countries as free: Bulgaria, Cyprus, Greece, Romania, Serbia. Another five were listed as partly free: Georgia, Macedonia, Moldova, Montenegro and Ukraine. Belarus, Russia, and disputed territories with significant Russian security presence in the former USSR were designated as not free. URL: https://freedomhouse.org/sites/default/files/FH_FIW_2017_Report_Final.pdf [10.04.2018].

3 Steve Crabtree, "Religiosity Highest in World's Poorest Nations", *Gallup*, 31.08.2010, URL: http://news.gallup.com/poll/142727/religiosity-highest-world-poorest-nations.aspx [10.04.2018].

4 After ten years of democratisation, 87 percent of Greeks, 70 percent of Spaniards, and 61 percent of Portuguese believed that democracy is better than any other form of government. The consensus on democratic values was so high that there were no real anti-system political parties. See Wolfgang Merkel, *Systemtransformation: Eine Einführung in die Theorie und Empirie der Transformationsforschung*, Wiesbaden 2010, 182–204; Juan J.

More recently, Greece also suffered a significant social shock, which less than a hundred years ago would knock most democracies into the iron-fist rule. Although its party system might have been changed, the basic rules and procedures of the democratic Hellenic Republic appear to be institutionally stable.

The predominantly Orthodox democracies are not without their specific issues. Greece is also a record holder in the number of sentences by the European Court of Human Rights (ECHR) regarding breaches of the Article 9 of the European Convention on Human Rights. This article deals specifically with the freedom of religion[5]. Between 1959 and 2016 Greece was sentenced 13 times – one in five verdicts related to this article were against this country. Greece was followed by eleven verdicts against Turkey, nine verdicts against Russia, and seven against Bulgaria. In 2016, the Orthodox countries (without Oriental Christian Armenia) accounted for 38 out of 56 of the Article 9 breaches established by the ECHR (58 percent).[6]

Although there are areas within which the Orthodox democracies have constantly improved their performance (according not only to Freedom House, but also to Bertelsmann Transformation Index pundits),[7] many developments within the sphere of church-state relations appear puzzling to outside observers, to say the least. No new predominantly Orthodox democracy, regardless of its constitutional provisions, opted for a neutral relationship towards its local Orthodox Church's hierarchy, and no local Orthodox Church opted for strict separation of church and state either.

It appears that within the Orthodox democracies the political elites tend to exhibit something one might label as a *symphonic reflex*, that is, a tendency to mimic the cooperative church-state relationship of the pre-modern Orthodox past. As the comparison of the two post-communist democratisations in Serbia and Bulgaria might demonstrate, this does not have to emerge as a result of a

---

Linz/Alfred Stepan, *Problems of Democratic Transition and Consolidation: Southern Europe, South America, and Post-Communist Europe*, Baltimore/MD 1996, 132–133.

5 *European Convention on Human Rights*, Article 9: Freedom of thought, conscience and religion:
1) Everyone has the right to freedom of thought, conscience and religion; this right includes freedom to change his religion or belief and freedom, either alone or in community with others and in public or private, to manifest his religion or belief, in worship, teaching, practice and observance.
2) Freedom to manifest one's religion or beliefs shall be subject only to such limitations as are prescribed by law and are necessary in a democratic society in the interests of public safety, for the protection of public order, health or morals, or for the protection of the rights and freedoms of others.

6 European Court of Human Rights, "Violations by Article and by State 1959-2016", URL: http://www.echr.coe.int/Documents/Stats_violation_1959_2016_ENG.pdf [10.04.2018].

7 Bertelsmann Foundation country reports available at URL: https://www.bti-project.org/en/country-reports/ [10.04.2018].

conscious design, but rather as an outcome of a series of negotiations between church and state, which tend to end up in an equilibrium here named *symphonic democracy*.

Symphonic democracy exhibits some degree of secularism, but it is also characterised by a tendency to insist on a cooperative church-state relationship, to let church officials participate in many state ceremonies, to emphasise the people/nation-church-state nexus, and depending on the available possibilities, the Orthodox sacralisation and legitimation of the new democratic order. There is a trade-off similar to that of the pre-modern monarchies. On the one hand, the state demonstrates its resolve to protect the church, especially in matters of canonical jurisdiction. On the other hand, the church tends to stay out of the active and organised engagement in daily politics and reacts only in situations deemed as "national emergencies". The "symphonic" here appears as a modifier of democracy, often taking precedence over fidelity to the liberal (and Western) democratic blueprint.

The name of the concept was borrowed from Kristen Ghodsee's *symphonic secularism*, a coexistence of modern secular with traditional religious elements of the Orthodox past in the church-state-nation relationships. In her view, *symphonic secularism* is a product of certain historical developments, including religion's role within the Ottoman Empire. These developments impacted the way certain freedoms are perceived today. *Symphonic secularism* according to Ghodsee also represents a frame of reference for all the other religious communities within the state. Such an arrangement occurs in societies strongly marked by overlapping ethnic and religious identities, where the religion of the titular nation is also perceived as the foundation of state sovereignty. On the other hand, religious and ethnic minorities tend to accept the basic rules, as set by the majority (titular) nation.[8] The foundations of this arrangement are secular – church and state are formally separated from one another. But it is a cooperative and coordinated separation of – in the ideal case – two representatives of the same nation, which cherish mutual respect and have benevolent attitude to one another. This particular relationship affects many other features of democracy as well.

8 Kristen Ghodsee, "Symphonic Secularism: Eastern Orthodoxy, Ethnic Identity and Religious Freedoms in Contemporary Bulgaria", *Anthropology of East Europe Review*, 27/2 (2009) 227–252, here 234, 241–243. See also the chapter by Daniel Jianu in the present volume.

Symphonia in Theory, History, and Changing Realities

The word *symphonia* or simply symphony (meanings of which may include accordance, agreement, and compliance)[9] often figures in discussions on Orthodox political theologies. In brief, Orthodox thinkers often advocate a close level of cooperation between the spiritual and the secular powers, mimicking the one of the Eastern Roman Empire. This somewhat romanticised idea has profoundly marked Orthodox political thinking, some recent re-evaluations notwithstanding. According to Stamatios Gerogiorgakis, this principle requires restraint in the mutual relationship between the state, which has to express its political will to take care of the interests of the church, and the church, which in return seldom expresses views regarding daily political life.[10] When engaging in politics, the church may only act as the moral force, the *conscience* of the state, but is not expected to challenge the government's supreme authority in political affairs, let alone engage in fine-tuning the broader institutional framework.

Symphonia emerged as a direct consequence of the Roman Empire's transition from a pagan into a Christian state when a new hybrid of Christian ideas and Roman institutional traditions was created.[11] Ever since the times of Constantine the Great, radical state intervention in religious dogma was usually met with vigorous resistance in the Christian East. The church, the second party to this political transaction, had to refrain from teaching the believers how to fulfil their obligations towards their state. Church and state existed as two separate entities, which cooperated and institutionally intermingled as long as the other side respected its part of the bargain. Therefore, Huntington's claim that in Orthodoxy "God is Caesar's junior partner"[12] has very little to do with the historical reality of *symphonia.* It is more applicable to the Petrine and post-Petrine Russian Empire, within which the autonomy of the Orthodox Church, which characterised the previous symphonic arrangements, was severely limited.

It is important to stress that in the Orthodox East a doctrine of complete separation between church and state never achieved the strictness which emerged after long centuries of turmoil in the West. John Chrysostom in the fourth century believed that the ideal political society had to be a Christian one, headed by a Christian ruler, embodying Christian virtue, who would govern in cooperation

---

9 Stamatios Gerogiorgakis, "Symphonie für große Trommeln und kleines Triangel: Staat und Orthodoxes Christentum", in Jürgen Nautz/Kristina Stöckl/Roman Siebenrock (eds), *Öffentliche Religionen in Österreich*, Innsbruck 2013, 175–186.

10 Ibid., 175–176.

11 Zoran Krstić, *Pravoslavlje i modernost* [Orthodoxy and Modernity], Belgrade 2012, 38–39.

12 Huntington, *The Clash of Civilizations* (as n. 1), 70: "In Islam, God is Caesar; in China and Japan, Caesar is God; in Orthodoxy, God is Caesar's junior partner."

with the church and its bishops.[13] The state was a necessity – its law enforcement was needed to preserve good order and assist in implementing the church's verdicts. Its military was indispensable for maintaining a peaceful environment for the Christians. The most important purpose of the state was to create favourable conditions for human communion with God. Realising this task was the business of the church alone, and the state was to act more as a vessel, which protected the church from an unfavourable environment. The ideological unity between church and state was desired, if *symphonia* was to work. Yet, the institutional and functional separation between church and state was never substantially questioned. Both church and state maintained their separate identities.

Paradoxically, it was Westernisation that frequently led to attempts to decrease the autonomy of the Orthodox Church. In Petrine Russia, the priests, who became public servants, had to pledge an oath of defending all the powers, rights and prerogatives of the Tsar, to report any incriminating information obtained in confession, to cooperate with the police and to denounce political dissent[14]. Tsar Peter I in effect ended *symphonia* in Russia – not only by removing the figure of the Orthodox Patriarch from the equation, but also by introducing a civilian oversight of ecclesiastic affairs. However, none of the new independent Orthodox countries in the Balkans during the nineteenth century opted for the Petrine model. Despite the obvious tendency of the new states to exert visible control over their churches' affairs, none went as far as Tsar Peter I did.

The Petrine crackdown on the autonomy of the Orthodox Church was harsh even if measured by the standards of the Ottoman Empire. Ottoman society was organised on the principle of autonomy of distinct confessional communities (*millet*). The Orthodox were treated as the Roman *millet (millet-i Rûm)*. The Patriarch of Constantinople was its highest religious and political leader, who was directly responsible to the Sultan. In cases when no Muslim was involved, the church assumed a judiciary role. It oversaw collecting taxes for its own sake and on the Sultan's behalf. The limited educational possibilities that were available to Orthodox subjects of the Empire were for a long time almost exclusively provided by the clergy-run schools or monasteries. As religion rather than ethnic origin played a decisive role in assigning legal status to the Ottoman subject, it became a strong marker of personal identity. Christian uprisings were often led by the Orthodox clergy members, as they were among the few leaders with sufficient social capital to organise collective actions. The Orthodox Church also assumed a representative role before the non-Orthodox authorities in Habsburg lands after 1690. Both the representative and the leadership role of the Orthodox clergy

13 Aristotle Papanikolaou, *The Mystical as Political: Democracy and Non-radical Orthodoxy*, Notre Dame/IN 2012, 23–26.

14 Ibid., 32.

contributed to the church-nation bond, which was then easily translated into the modern context of nationalism.

According to Vasilios N. Makrides, "nationalism could be expressed in both secular and religious ways, whose relations can be either complementary, neutral, or opposite."[15] Language, and secular nationalism with it, prevailed over religion in Albania. In neighbouring Yugoslavia, language failed miserably as the cohesive factor. More than once in the twentieth century, Serbo-Croatian speakers chose religion over language as their primary identity and political marker. Orthodoxy arguably developed a strong, organic connection between religion and nationalism, faith and ethnicity.[16] National orientation, visible within many local Orthodox Churches of our time, could be regarded as a relatively recent phenomenon, which emerged in encounter with nationalism's Western prototype.[17] After all, the Eastern Roman Empire's understanding of Christianity was the universalistic one, aimed at overcoming divisions among the peoples (cf. Romans 10:12; Galatians 3:28). Yet, the pre-modern Orthodox orientations were not difficult to readjust to fit nationalism's modern frame. As this did not appear to contradict the Orthodox past, the entire process was accepted as something natural. According to Makrides, the role of the Orthodox Church in the ethnogenesis, indigenisation, and vernacularisation of the Christian faith, the historical closeness between church and state and the resulting interconnection between the concepts of church, people and homeland could be regarded as the decisive events.[18] To modern nationalism, it did not suffice that the ruler and the supreme bishop (or the bishops' assembly) jointly run the affairs of the state. By means of nationalism, the people, who in pre-modern times were ruled by a sovereign, gradually emerged as a political subject and primary possessor of sovereignty.

Nationalism became a convenient vehicle, which brought the nation-state and the national church together. Within this paradigm, both church and political authority represented the reflection of similar, if not identical collectives. Consequently, the church could assert its position as the legitimate representative of the people, capable of criticising and even challenging the officials of the state. In times of crisis, it could bolster or undermine the political agenda of the state, which to some extent made church-state relations in Orthodox countries a politically sensitive issue, even under communism.

---

15 Vasilios N. Makrides, "Why Are Orthodox Churches Particularly Prone to Nationalization and Even to Nationalism?", *St Vladimir's Theological Quarterly* 57/3-4 (2013) 325–352, here 329.

16 Silviu E. Rogobete, "Morality and Tradition in Postcommunist Orthodox Lands: On the Universality of Human Rights, with Special Reference to Romania", *Religion, State & Society* 32/3 (2004) 275–297, here 287.

17 Alexander Schmemann, *The Historical Road of Eastern Orthodoxy*, Crestwood/NY 1992, 289.

18 Makrides, "Why Are Orthodox Churches" (as n. 15), 329–349.

The communist takeover in Orthodox countries was usually coupled with a relative rapid secularisation and atheisation of society. The Orthodox Church usually ended up as a "patriotic servant" to the state, expected to assist in its societal euthanasia.[19] Without mechanisms to extensively disseminate its teachings, the church under communism had to accept a reduction of its complex doctrines to the level of rituals, traditions, and folklore. Regarding religion, the communist era resulted in secularised intellectual and political elites, the representatives of which were either hostile to religion, indifferent, or simply ignorant. Religion was frequently conflated with the ideas of "traditional" or "national", and the church became an open-air museum to many, where one could have a look at the cultural, artistic and spiritual achievements of the national past. Paradoxically, at least in the Balkans, in terms of identity, communism strengthened the church-nation connection. In Yugoslavia, the national emancipation of the Macedonian Socialist Republic (today's North Macedonia) and the declaration of the Macedonian Orthodox Church autocephaly were both supported by the communist establishment.[20]

As the communist regime was approaching its end, another paradoxical phenomenon became visible. Direct and outright repression mostly gave way to subtler, bureaucratic means of state control. The upper hierarchy of the Orthodox Churches developed a certain amount of specific social capital, both within the establishment (on which it depended for most bureaucratic approvals) and within the emerging opposition groups (especially in Serbia).[21] The hierarchs in Bulgaria were disproportionately frequent collaborators with the Bulgarian equivalent of

19 Daniel Philpott, "Explaining the Political Ambivalence of Religion", *American Political Science Review* 101/3 (2007) 505–525, here 507; James L. Hopkins, *Църква, народ и държава: Опит за социоисторически анализ на отношенията в България* [The Church, the People, and the State: An Attempt of a Sociological Analysis of their Relations in Bulgaria], Sofia 2008, 307–329. The English original from the same year bears the title *The Bulgarian Orthodox Church: A Socio-historical Analysis of the Evolving Relationship between Church, Nation and State in Bulgaria*, but the Bulgarian edition includes more material.

20 Pedro Ramet, "The Serbian Orthodox Church", in idem (ed.), *Eastern Christianity and Politics in the Twentieth Century: Christianity under Stress*, Vol. 1, Durham/NC 1988, 232–250, here 238–239, 242–244. See also Nenad Živković's contribution in this volume.

21 For Serbia: Ljubomir Ranković, *Sveti vladika Nikolaj: život i delo* [Saint Bishop Nikolaj: Life and Work], Šabac 2013, 198–199. Since there is only sketchy evidence at hand, one could tentatively conclude that the levels of collaboration of the Serbian bishops with the Yugoslav secret service were below those in Bulgaria or other communist countries: Ivan Bešlić, *Čuvari Jugoslavije: Suradnici Udbe u Bosni i Hercegovini* [Guardians of Yugoslavia: The Associates of Udba in Bosnia and Herzegovina], Vol. 4, Posušje 2003, 9–11, 45–47, 522–523.

the KGB (11 out of 15 serving in 2012),[22] which in turn created connections with the underpinning structures of the later Bulgarian Socialist Party.

The post-communist period has only partly been marked by a "return to Europe,"[23] as returning to pre-WWII national traditions often took precedence. Eventually, not only the anti-communists, but the former communists as well, supported some kind of inclusion of the Orthodox Church into the new, democratic political order. Thus, the church could benefit from the restoration of certain pre-communist policies. Many post-communist Orthodox states had an interest in international democratic legitimation, which meant adopting secular, liberal and democratic norms. For this order to become rooted in society, it had to be reconciled with the perceived national traditions. The result was a cooperative church-state relationship, reminiscent of *symphonia.*

Symphonic Democracy in Bulgaria and Serbia

In Bulgaria and Serbia, countries of comparable size and comparable democratisation trajectories, the renamed communists (socialists) won the first multi-party elections.[24] Both countries began their proper democratisation after the internationally supported "electoral revolutions", facilitated by international "democracy assistance".[25] While their democratisation paths have been similar, many issues related to ecclesiastical matters were not. The Serbian Orthodox Church (SOC) played a much more active role in Serbian politics, while the Bulgarian Orthodox Church (BOC) could hardly assert its own autonomy from the political structures (especially on issues related to its long internal schism). In terms of power relations between church and state, Serbia could be described as a country with a more visible, stronger and more influential church. Also, according to European Values Study data from 2008, the SOC was trusted by 60.2 percent of the respondents, compared to 40.6 percent in the case of the BOC.

---

22 Marco Arndt, "Проблеми и предизвикателства на Българската православна църква" [Problems and Challenges Facing the Bulgarian Orthodox Church], 08.04.2012, URL: http://www.pravoslavie.bg/анализи/проблеми-и-предизвикателства-пред-бъ/ [24.02.2018]. Truth be said, the motives and pressures faced by every single bishop were different, which resulted in different levels of understanding for their actions: See Diana Petrova, "Църквата загуби от мълчанието за сътрудничество с държавна сигурност" [The Church Lost by its Silence on Cooperation with the State Security], *Bogoslovska Mislăl* 3–4 (2011) 128–132, here 129, 132.

23 Mary Kaldor/Ivan Vejvoda, "Democratization in Central and East European Countries", *International Affairs* 73/1 (1997) 59–82, here 60.

24 The Bulgarian Socialist Party (BSP) and The Socialist Party of Serbia (SPS).

25 Valerie Bunce and Sharon Wolchik, "Favorable Conditions and Electoral Revolutions", *Journal of Democracy* 17/4 (2006) 5–17.

Furthermore, religion was important to 73.8 percent of the Serbian and to 55.4 percent of the Bulgarian respondents.[26]

When explaining the political ambivalence of religion, Daniel Philpott introduced the concept of differentiation, i.e., "the degree of mutual autonomy between religious bodies and state institutions in their foundational legal authority" or the "extent of each entity's autonomy over the other's basic prerogatives to hold offices, choose its officials, set its distinctive policies, carry out its activities, in short, to govern itself".[27] The societies with a high degree of differentiation can be called "differentiated", and the ones with a low degree "integrationist." Differentiation should not be confused with the influence that religion and state exercise on one another's policies through persuasion, ideological influence or electoral power. On the other hand, higher differentiation means no constitutional status of any single religion (no established religion), less promotion of religion through legislation and judicial powers (including religious education), less restrictions of freedom of religion (including proselytism), and less prerogatives, standing titles, offices and legal privileges in appointing state officials. It also means fewer possibilities of religious actors to veto government decisions. It is important to stress that in terms of quality, differentiation can either be consensual (mutually accepted) or conflictual (with one party challenging the arrangement).[28] Table 1 illustrates the four possibilities this theory accounts for, including examples of states that Philpott placed in each category.

Table 1: Types of Church-State Relationships[29]

Degree↓ Kind →	Consensual	Conflictual
Integrationist	USA, India	Chile under Pinochet, Kemalist Turkey
Differentiated	Iran, Saudi Arabia	Soviet Union, Postcolonial Arab nationalist regimes

Differentiation can change over time. In Serbia, on the eve of the first multi-party elections, differentiation was relatively high and conflictual. In Bulgaria, differentiation was low, as hardly any action could be undertaken without prior consent issued by the authorities, but conflictual, as it was imposed against the BOC's will.[30] The 1990s could be described as a time of frequent church-state

26 Data available at URL: http://zacat.gesis.org/webview/index.jsp?object=http://zacat.gesis.org/obj/fStudy/ZA4800 [10.04.2018].

27 Philpott, *Explaining the Political Ambivalence* (as n. 19), 507.

28 Ibid., 506–508.

29 Adapted from ibid., 508, table 1.

30 Ibid., 507; Hopkins, *Църква* (as n. 19), 278, 312–321.

conflicts in Serbia, mostly, but not exclusively over national issues in former Yugoslavia. In Bulgaria, the party-church conflicts were mostly related to the Bulgarian schism into two parallel church structures. The canonical Synod of the BOC was supported by the Bulgarian socialists, while the "Alternative Synod" enjoyed the support of the anti-communist reformists of the Union of Democratic Forces.[31] The current levels of differentiation were established relatively recently, namely in the mid-2000s, after more than a decade of negotiations, conflicts, and search for a mutually acceptable arrangement between the Orthodox Church and the state. Both countries regarded themselves as secular democracies and were eager to apply the "European standards" within their EU-accession agenda, all the while trying to restore something of their pre-communist past. By 2012, the resulting levels of differentiation in both countries were similar – moderately differentiated and consensual.

In Bulgaria, changes in church-state relations were followed by the BOC's assertion of its own autonomy – by dropping norms in its Constitution stipulating prerogatives of the state[32] and, unfortunately, reducing lay participation in church affairs.[33] The SOC's autonomy had been asserted already in 1947, when the state's prerogatives were removed from the text of its amended pre-war Constitution. Further, the Serbian Patriarch was to be chosen by lot (i.e., by chance), from among the three candidates who received the most votes. Together with several other limitations, this minimised the possible impact of the political involvement in the internal affairs of the SOC.[34] In Bulgaria, state intervention in the internal affairs of the BOC continued in the initial period of democratic transition. Only after 2004, the year in which the police was ordered to implement the recently adopted law on religion and expel the followers of the "Alternative Synod" from BOC properties, could the BOC effectively assert itself as legally autonomous

31 Monitor, "Единство на Българската православна църква: нихилистите от СДС създадоха разкола" [Unity of the Bulgarian Orthodox Church: The Nihilists of the SDS Created the Schism], *Interview with Stefan Penov*, 28.07.2004, URL: http://www.pravoslavieto.com/history/21/razkol/2004_razkola_penov.htm [10.04.2018]; Daniela Kalkandjieva, "The Bulgarian Orthodox Church", in Lucian Leustean (ed.), *Eastern Christianity and Politics in the Twenty-First Century*, London 2014, 114–139, here 133, note 15; Hopkins, *Църква* (as n. 19), 341–357. By the end of the 1990s, Săbev's schism had lost its relevance.

32 For example, a candidate for the office of Patriarch had to "enjoy the trust" of the government (Article 15 of *Устав на Българската православна Църква* [The Constitution of the Bulgarian Orthodox Church], 1950).

33 Changes were made in the Article 8. Compare *Устав 1950* with *Устав на Българската православна Църква: Приет от Шестия Църковно народен събор на 11 декември 2008 година* [The Constitution of the Bulgarian Orthodox Church: Adopted by the Sixth Church-People's Council on 11.12.2008].

34 Velibor Džomić, "Patrijarh po Božjoj volji i meri narodnoj" [Patriarch by the Will of God and according to the People's Measure], *Pravoslavlje: novine srpske patrijaršije* 1027-1028 (2010) 12–17, here 17.

from the state. This development was confirmed in its 2008 Constitution. The symphonic relationship cannot be established without either side enjoying at least some autonomy – and the new democracies eventually provided this opportunity for both the BOC and the SOC.

Secular Constitutions – Symphonic Intentions

In constitutional terms, both Serbia and Bulgaria are declaratory secular. Democratic constitutions have a certain symbolic dimension, aimed at embedding the political and participatory ethos into the local contexts. In this regard, the Bulgarian Constitution stipulates the importance of Orthodoxy for national identity, while the Serbian one is oriented towards proclaiming the multi-ethnic, multi-confessional, and multi-cultural character of the Serbian nation-state. This symbolic dimension is also concretely defined in the respective laws on religion:

> Eastern Orthodoxy […] has played a historic role in Bulgaria's statehood and has current meaning in its political life. Its spokesperson and representative is the autocephalous Bulgarian Orthodox Church.[35]

> The Serbian Orthodox Church has had an exceptional historical, state-building and civilisational role in forming, preserving and developing the identity of the Serbian nation.[36]

The Bulgarian Constitution from 1991 addresses the role of the church: "There shall be no political parties on ethnic, racial or religious lines, nor parties that seek violent seizure of state power." Moreover, the political parties are declared to be the exclusive participants in the political process, while trade unions and associations are excluded from it.[37] The article dealing with church-state relations declares both freedom of religion and Orthodoxy as the traditional religion: "The Eastern Orthodox denomination shall be considered as the traditional religion in the Republic of Bulgaria." It is further stipulated that "religious institutions shall be separated from the state" and that "religious institutions and communities, as well as religious beliefs shall not be used to political ends".[38] Freedom of religion and freedom to hold atheistic views are presented in the same article of the Constitution, with the prerogative of the state to "assist in the maintenance of tolerance and respect among the believers […] and between believers and non-

35 "Religious Denominations Act" (2002), Article 10.1. Translation from URL: http://www.legirel.cnrs.fr/spip.php?article540&lang=fr [10.04.2018].

36 "Zakon o Crkvama i verskim zajednicama" [Law on Churches and Religious Communities], *Službeni glasnik Republike Srbije* 36 (2006), Article 11.2.

37 "Конституция на Република България" [Constitution of the Republic of Bulgaria] (1991), Articles: 3, 11, 12.

38 Ibid., Article 13.

believers".[39] It might be argued that to some extent, the secular world-view got precedence over the religious one – as "religious and other convictions" cannot be seen as legitimate grounds for rejecting obligations prescribed by the Constitution and the laws of the Republic of Bulgaria.[40] In terms of identity, the Constitution gives much more weight to language than religion.[41]

The comeback of the symphonic tradition in Bulgaria was arguably marked by the Law on Religious Denominations. It was passed in 2002 and amended four times (2006, 2007, 2009 and 2013). Already in the preamble of the law, the parliament affirmed both the values of freedom of conscience and the historical role of the BOC in the development of Bulgarian spirituality and culture

According to Peter Petkoff, this law is ideologically based on the assumption that a liberal approach to the issue would eventually develop, following a short period in which communitarian principles are implemented. "The liberal agenda of the preamble of the statute almost stands in contrast with the text of the statute itself, which suggests that the BOC has the status of an established church".[42] One of the main arguments for claims that Bulgaria does have an established church lies within this law, which also stipulates who the legitimate representative of the BOC is. Going further than the Constitution, in which the *belief* was declared traditional (i.e., Eastern Orthodoxy), the law defines the BOC as the church led by the Synod and the Metropolitan of Sofia, who at the same time is the Bulgarian Patriarch.[43] From the onset of its implementation, it was clear that the state's intent was to end the schism within the BOC by supporting the canonical Synod (led by Patriarch Maksim) over the "Alternative" one. In 2004, the police evicted the "alternatives" from most of the property claimed by the BOC, and the losing side sued Bulgaria before the ECHR.[44] After the Court had reached the verdict condemning Bulgaria for its actions, not only the BOC and the Republic of Bulgaria, but also the representatives of other local Orthodox Churches rejected the verdict, by referring to the *symphonia* traditions of the Orthodox world[45] and by claiming that no Court could decide on this issue without taking into account the Orthodox canon law.[46]

39 Ibid., Article 37.
40 Ibid., Article 58.
41 Ibid., Article 36: "The study and use of the Bulgarian language shall be the right and obligation of every Bulgarian citizen."
42 Peter Petkoff, "Church-State Relations under the Bulgarian Denominations Act 2002: Religious Pluralism and Established Church and the Impact of Other Models of Law on Religion", *Religion, State & Society* 33/4 (2005) 315–336, here 315–316.
43 "Закон за вероизповеданията" [Law on Religious Denominations] (2002 – last amended 2013), Article 10.
44 Petkoff, "Church-State Relations" (as n. 42), 317–318.
45 Ghodsee, "Symphonic Secularism" (as n. 8), 229.
46 "Комюнике на Всеправославната работна среща София, 11–12 март 2009 г." [Communiqué of the Pan-Orthodox Working Meeting in Sofia, 11.-12.03.2009],

The Constitution of the Republic of Serbia, on the other hand, defined its scope simply as covering the "state of the Serbian people and all the citizens who live in it, based on the rule of law and social justice, principles of civil democracy, human and minority rights and freedoms, and commitment to the European principles and values".[47] The political parties and organisations, which through their actions aim at "[…] a forced overthrow of the constitutional system, violation of the guaranteed human or minority rights, inciting racial, national or religious hatred, shall be prohibited", as is the case with any individual aiming at the same.[48] Like in the Bulgarian case, several provisions aim at strengthening some of the elements of national identity. The Serbian language and the Cyrillic script are in official use, while the minority languages and scripts may be used according to the law. The Republic of Serbia has defined itself as a secular state, where no religion may be established as either state or mandatory religion.[49] The actual level of this separation is disputed. There has been a legal debate whether the Constitution bans any assistance, cooperation, and dialogue with religious organisations or not,[50] but since both the SOC and the state already tended to regard secularism with a cooperative church-state relationship as best suited to the Serbian situation, this in the end influenced the final interpretation of the norm.

The Serbian Law on Churches and Religious Communities declared the SOC, the Roman Catholic Church, the Slovak Evangelical Church (Augsburg confession), the Reformist Christian Church, the Evangelical Christian Church (Augsburg confession), the Islamic religious community, and the Jewish religious community as the traditional religions in Serbia. Other denominations were free to register in a procedure which required 71 signatures. The state can be called upon to assist in implementing the decisions of religious communities and offer them financial support. The law also proclaimed the right of religious communities to conduct religious education in public schools.[51] The freedom of religion in Serbia was defined as a corporate one, going beyond the individual level.[52] The lawmakers were careful not to imply that the law could establish any

---

Tsărkoven Vestnik 5 (2009) 5. See also Daniela Kalkandjieva, "Bulgarian Orthodoxy and the European Court of Human Rights: The Case of the Holy Synod of the Bulgarian Orthodox Church", in Alfons Bruening/Evert van der Zweerde (eds), *Orthodox Christianity and Human Rights*, Leuven 2012, 315–336.

47 "Устав Републике Србије" [Constitution of the Republic of Serbia], *Službeni glasnik Republike Srbije* 98 (2006), Article 1.

48 Ibid., Article 5.3.

49 Ibid., Articles 10, 11, 14, 43 and 49.

50 Vladimir Đurić, "Zakonsko uređivanje pravnog položaja crkava i verskih zajednica u Republici Srbiji: od osporavanja do unapređivanja" [The Legislative Regulation of the Legal Position of Churches and Religious Communities in the Republic of Serbia: From Contestation to Improvement], *Sveske za javno pravvo* 13 (2013) 43.

51 "Zakon o Crkvama" (as n. 36), Articles 4, 7, 8, 10, 11, 28 and 40.

52 Đurić, "Zakonsko uređivanje" (as n. 50), 47.

single religion. This was done by the simple recognition of the legal situation prior to 1941. Even if the notion of "traditional" denominations could be equated with "established religions", Serbia definitely (in formal terms) does not have the SOC as its (only) established church. In Serbian politics since 1990, there has been a tendency to reduce differentiation and strictly separate between church and state. The state accepted a series of SOC demands, which in general are not much different from those stated by the BOC in Bulgaria. These included restitution and renovation of confiscated property, religious education in public schools, closer cooperation with the state in the spheres of culture and public morality and re-establishing the office of army chaplains.

Arguably, most weight in the Serbian church-state relationship was given to re-introducing religious education in public schools. In Bulgaria, this idea was never accepted in a form to which the BOC could agree. One of the alleged fears of the Bulgarian state was that of growing religious radicalism.[53] Religious education was introduced as a facultative subject in some schools in the country, while the BOC and the Ministry of Education have not yet been able to find common ground for the concrete form of religious education.[54] According to BOC sources, less than one percent of the school children attend Orthodox religious education in public schools.[55] In Serbia, however, traditional religious communities have had the opportunity to spread their teachings in public schools since 2001. In order to avoid conflicts, participating religious communities can have insight in each other's curricula and intervene, if necessary.

Members of the Bulgarian armed forces may participate officially in religious ceremonies only outside their barracks. However, the number of public rituals with representatives of both the BOC and security forces is not small. Every year on St George's Day, the Bulgarian Patriarch performs water blessings and blessings of the army standards. Epiphany water blessings usually involve representatives of the river flotilla, naval forces, and local authorities. On the symbolical level, the most important sign of the newly established symphonic relationship is the presidential oath. The successive Bulgarian presidents, Georgi Părvanov, Rosen Plevneliev, and Rumen Radev, all took oath in the presence of

---

53 "Семейството, възпитанието, образованието и закрилата на подрастващите: Кръгла маса в рамките на Седмицата на православната книга 2012" [Family, Upbringing, Education and the Protection of Adolescents: Round Table within the Framework of the Week of the Orthodox Book 2012], *Tsărkoven Vestnik* 18 (2012) 1, 8.

54 A new proposal has recently been published in "Религия за обща култура ще се учи от I до XII клас като избираем предмет" [Religion as a Matter of General Culture will be Taught from 1st to 12th Grade], *Portal Verouchenie*, 20.04.2018, URL: https://www.verouchenie.com/религия-за-обща-култура-ще-се-учи-от-i-до-xii/ [21.04.2018].

55 Miroslava Ivanova, "Под 1% от децата се обучават на вероучение" [Less than 1 percent of Children Take Part in Religious Education], *Nova TV* 01.04.2018, URL: https://nova.bg/news/view/2018/04/01/211564/под-1-от-децата-се-обучават-на-вероучение [21.04.2018].

the Bulgarian Patriarch and also asked for his blessing. At the ceremonial level, there is at least a public display of the symphonic relationship, which according to journalist Goran Blagoev from the Bulgarian national broadcaster includes three reflections of Bulgarian statehood – the church, the army, and the head of state. The true source of this new *symphonia* in his view is the Bulgarian people,[56] represented through these institutions.

The Serbian Law on Churches and Religious Communities paved the way for re-introducing clergy in certain public service roles. The army was among the first institutions to start closer cooperation with the SOC after 2000, as it was deemed important for the overall troop morale. This change was reflected in the informal parts of the army rituals as well. The cadets of the Military Academy regularly end their graduation ceremony by making the sign of the cross, which illustrates the religious feelings of the new, desecularised generation of Serbian officers. The schools usually have portraits of St Sava in their premises, while health and education institutions may designate certain spaces for chapels. Religious communities can also propose candidates for the media regulatory body, the Broadcasting Agency of the Republic. One of the Serbian Bishops Porfirije (Perić) even presided over the Agency's Board between 2008 and 2014, before assuming the demanding office of Metropolitan of Zagreb and Ljubljana. Moreover, the traditional religious communities designate one member of the National Educational Council, and there is a tendency among them to delegate this task to the SOC. On the other hand, former mufti Muamer Zukorlić has since 2016 been the chairman of the Parliamentary Committee on Education.

Religious Policymaking in Serbia and Bulgaria

The fall of communism and the democratisation process brought both progressive and reactionary movements in the policymaking of these countries. Many of the pre-war political ideas have been "recycled" while being framed in the language of the "European standards", including those relevant for the church-state relationship. Both societal changes under communism (modernisation and secularisation of societies) and these countries' EU agenda are at least partly the reason why the symphonic equilibrium that has been established is a moderately differentiated one.[57] Integrationism was no longer a realistic option.

The symphonic relationship implies that the state should protect the canonical jurisdiction or at least the canonical order of its church. In the post-communist Balkans, this is almost always the rule. Bulgaria, as already mentioned, fought

56 Goran Blagoev, "Богоявленският водосвет: олицетворение на единството на Църква, държава и армия" [Epiphany Water-Blessings: Embodiment of the Church-State-Army Unity], *Tsărkoven Vestnik* 1 (2008) 1, 5.

57 Cf. Philpott, "Explaining the Political Ambivalence" (as n. 19), 506–508.

against the ECHR's verdict in favour of the "Alternative Synod" in 2009, while Prime Minister Sergey Stanishev (Bulgarian Socialist Party) promised to do "everything legally possible" to support the position of the BOC.[58] Prime Minister Borisov refused to meet the Ecumenical Patriarch after, in his opinion, the latter insulted Bulgaria by not referring to the BOC as an autocephalous church.[59] In his view, insulting the BOC demanded a strong reaction by the highest state officials. Similarly, tensions between the governments in Serbia and today's North Macedonia occasionally erupted over the conflict between the SOC and the canonically unrecognised Macedonian Orthodox Church. Both governments have defended the views of their church's hierarchies,[60] with Serbia even resorting to economic sanctions against its southern neighbour. The conflict of jurisdiction between the Romanian Orthodox Church and the SOC has also served as a pretext for the Romanian government to pressure Serbian authorities by threatening their EU-accession agenda.[61] At the same time, the Serbian practice of managing registration affairs of religious communities established a rule that any Orthodox community applying for registration had to obtain a concession from the SOC for using the term "Orthodox" in its name. In effect, several schismatic groupings (that of former Bishop Artemije and the zealotic "True Orthodox Church," for example) were thus denied registration,[62] while other canonical Orthodox Churches need the approval of the SOC for their operations in Serbia. The Romanian Orthodox Church in the Serbian Banat was declared "traditional" due to its agreement with the SOC, while the SOC rejected the registration of a Romanian church structure south of the Danube. The government in Belgrade did not ban the Romanian Church's activities in this region, nor did it employ radical measures. It simply followed the SOC's recommendation – in effect denying non-registered communities certain financial and property-related benefits without rendering their activities illegal.

Symphonia is also visible in the realm of foreign policy. The recently declared readiness of the government of (North) Macedonia to change its course in the relationship with Bulgaria was quickly followed by a gesture of goodwill from the BOC, which accepted the proposal of the Macedonian Orthodox Church to

58 "Официална среща на патриарх Максим с министър-председателя Станишев" [Official Meeting of Patriarch Maksim and PM Stanishev], *Tsărkoven Vestnik* 6 (2009) 2.

59 There were other problematic issues as well. See "Борисов: Не приех Вартоломей заради поведението му спрямо България" [Borisov: I did not receive Bartholomew because of his Conduct towards Bulgaria], *Standart*, 10.11.2015, URL: http://www.standartnews.com/balgariya/borisov_ne_prieh_vartolomey_zaradi_povedenieto_mu_spryamo_balgariya-309445.html [20.04.2018].

60 Cf. Aleksandar Raković, *Srbi i religijski intervencionizam 1991-2015* [The Serbs and Religious Interventionism 1991-2015], Belgrade 2015, 199–249.

61 Ibid., 289–318.

62 Ibid., 308–314.

declare the BOC as its "Mother Church".[63] Another trait of both Serbia and Bulgaria is that they readily employ their hierarchs in diplomacy geared towards Russia. To Serbia, which does not recognise the independence of Kosovo that was unilaterally declared, Russian (and Chinese) support in the Security Council of the UN is of paramount importance. The Kosovo issue is also one of the focal points of the activities of the SOC[64], which is why the Russian Patriarch Kirill felt it necessary to stipulate that "Kosovo is a holy place, a place of martyrdom".[65] The state-run Russian gas company "Gazprom" also financed a mosaic in the crypt of the St Sava Cathedral in Belgrade,[66] while the Serbian Patriarch thanked Russia for "everything it has done for us" during one of his visits to Moscow.[67] The BOC's connections to Moscow are also strong and traditional. On the eve of the Pan-Orthodox Council of Crete in 2016, the BOC was the first Orthodox Church to declare its non-participation. This was a clear concession to the Russian Church, which was uneasy about the Council, but did not want to be the first church to cancel participation. However, the BOC's engagement in Bulgarian diplomacy is less visible than in the Serbian case. Yet, the state sees the local autocephalous church as being useful for enhancing its "soft power"[68] among fellow Orthodox countries.

Another piece of this symphonic bargain is the church's attitude towards the government. As of 2000, neither church had disputed any election results, or

63 The text of the declaration on this matter from the BOC, which included the establishment of a committee of eight metropolitans to further act on the issue, does not reveal any concrete plan. See "РЕШЕНИЕ на Св. Синод по повод отправено писмо от Македонската православна църква" [DECISION of the Most Holy Synod on the further Path regarding the Letter from the Macedonian Orthodox Church], 27.11.2018, URL: http://www.bg-patriarshia.bg/news.php?id=249763 [20.04.2018].

64 Radmila Radić/Milan Vukomanović, "Religion and Democracy in Serbia since 1989: The Case of the Serbian Orthodox Church", in Sabrina Ramet (ed.), *Religion and Politics in Post-socialist Central and Southeastern Europe: Challenges since 1989*, Houndmills 2014, 180–211, here 183–185.

65 "Patrijarh Kiril: Kosovo je sveto mesto, mesto mučeništva" [Kosovo is a Holy Place, a Place of Martyrdom], *Radio-Televizija Srbije*, 13.09.2017, URL: http://www.rts.rs/page/stories/sr/story/125/drustvo/2868441/patrijarh-kiril-kosovo-je-sveto-mesto-mesto-muce nistva.html [20.04. 2018].

66 "'Gaspromnjeft' će finansirati izradu unutrašnjeg mozaika Hrama Svetog Save u Beogradu" [Gazpromneft shall Finance the Internal Mosaic in the St Sava's Cathedral in Belgrade], *NIS*, 30.08.2016, URL: https://www.nis.eu/lat/presscentar/gasprom-njeft-ce-finansirati-izradu-unutrasnjeg-mozaika-hrama-cvetog-save-u-beogradu [20.04.2018].

67 "Patrijarh Irinej zahvalio Putinu za sve što je Rusija uradila za Srbiju" [Patriarch Irinej thanked Putin for Everything Russia has done for Serbia], *Nova srpska politička misao*, 05.06.2017, URL: http://www.nspm.rs/hronika/patrijarh-irinej-zahvalio-putinu-za-sve-sto-je-rusija-uradila-za-srbiju.html?alphabet=l [20.04.2018].

68 More on the concept of "soft power": Joseph Nye, *Bound to Lead: The Changing Nature of American Power*, New York 1990.

engaged in scrutinising the fairness of the voting procedures. In the late 1980s and early 1990s, the relationship between the neo-communist Slobodan Milošević and the SOC seemed to become more agreeable than the one which the Serbian Church and the government had had in the decades before. However, by 2000, the relationship broke down almost entirely, as throughout the 1990s there were ecclesiastic circles favouring the non-communist opposition. There were official SOC statements denying legitimacy to the regime and even open SOC activities aimed at reconciling some opposition leaders with one another.[69] The SOC Synod even equated one of the most important turning points of contemporary Serbian history, namely Milošević's fall after the demonstrations of 5 October 2000, to the liberation of the Fatherland after World War II.[70]

After the electoral revolution in Serbia, the same bishops grew increasingly unhappy with the results. They were mostly concerned with the growing influence of different human rights NGOs,[71] which promoted LGBT rights, deconstructed Serbian national narratives, vehemently opposed religious education in public schools, and advocated expelling religion from the public sphere (usually by decrying "the church's meddling in politics"). Some bishops became openly disenchanted with the multi-party democracy and advocated a return to *sabornost*[72] instead. Others, like the very influential Bishop Irinej of Bačka (Novi Sad) expressed views resembling *symphonia* – the political parties should deal with everyday political issues, while the church should be allowed to voice its concerns over major problems.[73] Like in the age of symphonic monarchies, a government, which is not manifestly atheist (which is understood as "anti-Christian") and which does not openly insult the Orthodox Church by its deeds and actions, can be – from the church's point of view – a legitimate partner in the symphonic relationship.

The Orthodox activists and the SOC to a lesser extent responded to challenges from civil society by creating their own equivalent of such organisations. These

69 Ksenija Petrović, *Nationale Identität und Religion in Serbien und Kroatien im Vergleich*, Wiesbaden 2012, 223–227.

70 Marko Nikolić, "Stavovi Srpske pravoslavne crkve vezani za krizu u bivšoj Jugoslaviji i njen odnos prema evropskim integracijama" [Positions of the Serbian Orthodox Church in Regard to the Crisis in Former Yugoslavia and its Relationship towards the European Integration], in *Crkva u pluralističkom društvu* [The Church in a Pluralistic Society], Zrenjanin 2009, 89–116, here 106.

71 Radić/Vukomanović, "Religion and Democracy" (as n. 64), 180–211.

72 *Sabornost* represents a Serbian variation of the Orthodox political ideal also known by its Russian name *sobornost'*. Like in the Russian Slavophile tradition, it is regarded as an alternative to pluralistic democracy. In the Serbian case, it tends to regard traditional patriarchal communities of the region as a role model for the entire society. See also the contribution by Daniel Jianu in this volume.

73 Petrović, *Nationale Identität* (as n. 69), 147–148.

represented different ideological concepts,[74] and different political theologies, but usually gathered around Orthodoxy and nationalist or patriotic feelings. Some of these organisations served as the basis for the emergence of *Dveri,* the first successful post-communist pronouncedly Orthodox political party. Even before becoming a political party,[75] *Dveri's* members contributed to modernising the communication strategies of the SOC, when they took part in the editorial board of the SOC publication *Pravoslavlje* since 2004. When *Dveri* became a political party, this cooperation ended, yet the trajectory of the SOC's modernisation of communication continued. The SOC managed to create several other media outlets, including *TV Hram* [Temple TV][76] in 2015. The media advancement of the SOC in some areas was coupled with giving ground in some other. The SOC had vehemently argued against LGBT marches in Belgrade during the first decade of the 2000s, but this vehemence receded after Aleksandar Vučić, formerly known for his ultra-nationalist positions, became prime minister in 2014. The overwhelming majority of the SOC bishops did not publicly show any sign of opposition to Serbia's first openly homosexual prime minister either – Ana Brnabić, sworn into office on 29 June 2017.[77] The SOC engaged in conflicts with the state over the new government's Kosovo policies, and two bishops who opposed the "Brussels Agreements" between the governments in Belgrade and Priština even publicly prayed a "requiem" to the Lord for the government and the National Assembly of Serbia.[78]

Both the hegemony of the Serbian Progressive Party and internal scandals of sexual, criminal, or financial nature within the church have visibly reduced the SOC's influence. Paradoxically, the secular opposition to SOC influence diminished as well. In 2012, Tomislav Nikolić had to struggle to find excuses when questioned by the secularist journalists why he, as the newly elected President of a secular Republic, went to take the Patriarch's blessing.[79] In Vučić's

74 Some organisations, which ideologically leaned towards the ideas elaborated by the inter-war pro-fascist cleric Dimitrije Ljotić, were even banned by the Serbian authorities.

75 After deciding to participate in the elections, *Dveri* members left the editorial board of *Pravoslavlje*.

76 URL: http://www.tvhram.rs/ [20.04.2018]

77 Metropolitan of Montenegro and the Littoral Amfilohije (Radović) was a noteworthy exception and used Brnabić's sexual orientation to respond to criticism coming from Vučić's party rank-and-file. See "Đurić: Amfilohije na nedoličan način napao i Brnabić" [Đurić: Also Amfilohije Attacked Brnabić in an Indecorous Manner], *B92* 09.01.2018, URL: https://www.b92.net/info/vesti/index.php?yyyy=2018&mm=01&dd=09&nav_category=640&nav_id=1345005 [20.04.2018].

78 The media in Serbia have inflated the prayer, or rather the rhetorical figure, to a "requiem". The whole speech of Metropolitan Amfilohije (Radović) is still available (in Serbian) on YouTube, URL: https://www.youtube.com/watch?v=1LZuCLG5EAQ [20.04.2018].

79 "Nikolić išao kod patrijarha po blagoslov" [Nikolić went to the Patriarch for a Blessing], *Blic*, 04.06.2012, URL: http://www.blic.rs/vesti/politika/nikolic-isao-kod-patrijarha-po-blagoslov/fbefcs0 [29.09.2016].

Serbia, this is no longer the case. Vučić's 2016 statement that there is symphony in the relationship between the SOC and the government[80] did not cause any noteworthy backlash from the formerly vehemently secularist public intellectuals in Serbian mainstream media. On the other hand, the Serbian Progressive Party has already demonstrated that it is not going to put up with the SOC's complaints, if it does not stick to its part of the symphonic bargain and stay out of the field of everyday politics.

Several Orthodox civic and political opposition organisations, like the aforementioned *Dveri,* cannot rely on SOC support the way the Serbian opposition could prior to 2000. Serbian developments after 2012 are also offering several insights into conditions necessary for a symphonic relationship in democracy to work. The relative power of the church is partly a consequence of unwillingness or inability of the state to assert itself. When in 2013 two prominent SOC bishops celebrated a "requiem" on a protest rally in Belgrade, by asking the Lord to let the parliament and government of Serbia "rest in peace", Prime Minister Ivica Dačić stated that "nobody denies the right of the SOC, or anybody else, to express their views, but nobody has the right to threaten anybody or to act like in the age of Inquisition."[81] After Vučić's Serbian Progressive Party became the hegemonic party of the system, the need to employ gentle words when responding to individual SOC bishops became less pressing. In 2012, party leader Tomislav Nikolić was asking the Patriarch for a blessing before assuming the office of the President. Five years later, in 2017, Metropolitan Amfilohije (Radović) of Montenegro and the Littoral was verbally accused by Vučić's associates of engaging in "sorcery" after he expressed concerns that Vučić was about to "betray Kosovo".[82]

---

80 "Država i Crkva – svojevrsna simfonija" [The State and the Church – A Symphony of its own Kind], *B92* 25.03.2016, URL: https://www.b92.net/info/vesti/index.php?yyyy=2016&mm=03&dd=25&nav_category=11&nav_id=1111970 [29.09.2016].

81 "Dačić: čime je Bog zaslužio da ga ovakvi predstavljaju" [Dačić: What God has done to Deserve to be Represented like this], *Blic,* 10.05.2013, URL: https://www. blic.rs/vesti/politika/dacic-cime-je-bog-zasluzio-da-ga-ovakvi-predstavljaju-na-zemlji/27q54qe [29.09.2016].

82 "Kletve i vradžbine mitropolita Amfilohija" [Curses and Sorcery of Metropolitan Amfilohije], *Mondo*, 08.01.2018, URL: http://mondo.rs/a1070864/Info/Srbija/Amfilohije-Radovic-izjava-o-Vucicu-i-reakcije.html [20.04.2018]. Amfilohije responded by declaring that it is a "sorcery" when one grants the office of Prime minister to Ana Brnabić (an outed homosexual). "Mitropolit Amfilohije: Vradžbine su kada postaviš Anu Brnabić za premijera; Neprihvatljivo postizanje bilo kakvih obavezujućih sporazuma sa teroristima koji upravljaju okupiranim KiM" [Metropolitan Amfilohije: It is sorcery to appoint Ana Brnabić as the Prime Minister; Any agreement with the terrorists running the occupied Kosovo and Metohija is unacceptable], *Nova srpska politička misao* 08.01.2018, URL: http://www.nspm.rs/hronika/mitropolit-amfilohije-neprihvatljivo-postizanje-bilo-kakvih-obavezujucih-sporazuma-sa-teroristima-koji-upravljaju-okupiranim-kim.html [20.04.2018],

Yet, even the hegemonic party with the electoral support of 45 percent or above needs to take care not to engage in criticism of the SOC as a whole when tackling actions and statements of individual bishops. Having a dismissive attitude towards the SOC can still contribute to ending one's political career. Srđan Verbić, former Minister of Education, lost his post after attempting to re-organise or *de facto* abolish religious education in public schools.[83] While it was not regarded as his main error, the reaction of the SOC to his proposals was an item added to the list of other political failures.[84] According to the Serbian historian and Orthodox activist Aleksandar Raković, the Serbian authorities since 2012 are less willing to invest administrative resources in identity issues,[85] which, contrary to rhetorical announcements, might result in less *symphonia* in the future.

In Bulgaria, the Orthodox discourse normalised in situations when political leaders addressed BOC hierarchs. Being a respectful son/daughter of "our spiritual mother", as the BOC is frequently referred to, is often part of the image of a "good Bulgarian" that many high-ranking politicians try to convey. The BOC is also eager to reprint such statements in its official publications, as they convey the message that it is a respected partner to the state. The Bulgarian political discourse on the BOC would probably astonish many Serbian observers. Ever since Prime Minister and former monarch Simeon of Saxe-Coburg-Gotha decided to intervene in favour of the canonical Synod in 2002, most high-ranking Bulgarian politicians have openly demonstrated their commitment to the canonical BOC in their rhetoric. When Patriarch Maksim died in 2012, President Plevneliev stated that the late hierarch was "supporting the unity of the church and strengthening the Christian values and virtues in our society".[86] Prime Minister Borisov claimed that the Patriarch would be remembered in history as one of the "most principled and far-sighted leaders of the BOC", who enjoyed "trust and love of the Bulgarian people". The deputy Prime Minister Tsvetan Tsvetanov stated that the Patriarch was "a spiritual pillar of the statehood for decades". Similar statements came from other officials of the state. Chairman of

83 "Srđan Verbić: Želim da otvorim diskusiju o potrebi da se veronauka uči u školama – po meni bi bilo najbolje da imamo predmet u kome se đaci uče toleranciji" [Srđan Verbić: I want to open a Discussion on the Need to teach Religious Education in Schools – in my Opinion, it would be for the best to have a Subject Teaching Students Tolerance], *Nova srpska politička misao* 07.01.2016, URL: http://www.nspm.rs/hronika/srdjan-verbic-ne-ukidam-veronauku-vec-zelim-da-otvorim-diskusiju-o-potrebi-da-se-ona-uci-u-skolama.html?alphabet=l [20.04.2018].

84 "Sinod SPC zaprepašćen: Ministre, ne ukidajte veronauku" [The Synod of the SOC in Consternation: Minister, do not Abolish Teaching Religion], *Blic*, 25.12.2015 URL: https://www.blic.rs/vesti/drustvo/sinod-spc-zaprepascen-ministre-ne-ukidajte-veronauku-u-skolama/9xfm29b [20.04.2018].

85 Raković, *Srbi i religijski intervencionizam* (as n. 60), 9–10.

86 *Tsărkoven Vestnik* 21-22 (2012) 9–10. The entire issue was dedicated to the commemoration and the condolences on the occasion of Patriarch Maksim's death.

the Committee for Human Rights and Religious Denominations, Yordan Bakalov, even stated that by losing its spiritual father, the Bulgarian people became "orphans".

In a move that resembled the Emperor's participation in the medieval church councils, President Georgi Părvanov had decided to appear at the Sixth Church-People's Council of the BOC in 2008. Representatives of other parties attended this council as well.[87] Patriarch Maksim's 40th anniversary at the helm of the BOC was celebrated as a church-state ceremony, with receptions for the delegates of other Orthodox Churches in the premises of the highest-ranking officials of the state, representing both the left and the right of the political spectrum. President Părvanov and Prime Minister Boyko Borisov both expressed their "filial respect" in their addresses. Speaker of the National Assembly Tsetska Tsacheva vowed her support for the Patriarch's future initiatives. Addresses and greetings sent by the highest state officials containing phrases such as "I bow before You", "our spiritual Father", and "your Holiness" were commonplace on this occasion.[88] The most telling, however, was the formulation in a letter by the President: "According to the Constitution, church and state are separated, but historically and spiritually, they are inseparable. Because, how can one separate the state from its foundations (*ustoi*) and the people from its soul!"[89]

State policies can foster the "inclusion of ideas", like the inclusion of religious symbols in public places or as the symbols of the state, holidays or monuments.[90] In the Bulgarian case, public schools celebrate Ss. Cyril and Methodius, while state universities bear the names of the Bulgarian saints. Bulgarian legal documents introduce the possibility of celebrating certain Christian holidays on state level, with the BOC rituals underscoring their Christian character.[91] Army standards include St Andrew's cross and the motto "God is with us", while the coat of arms features a depiction of the medieval Bulgarian crown with cross. In Serbia, St Sava's day is celebrated as the foremost school holiday. While Serbian universities do not have saints' names, Orthodox symbols are present on another level. All official state symbols – flag, coat of arms, standards, and anthem – carry strong Orthodox symbolism. Prominent elements of the Serbian visual identity include the two-headed eagle of the Christian Roman Empire and the "Serbian cross". The national anthem since 2004 is "God of justice", with prayer-like lyrics. Furthermore, the Serbian cross figures on the army uniforms, car licence plates,

87 "Започна Шестият Църковно-народен събор" [The Sixth Church-State Council has Begun], *Dveri.bg*, 14.05.2008, URL: https://dveri.bg/au6rc [20.04.2018].

88 "Българските държавни институции изразиха почита си към предстоятеля на БПЦ" [Bulgarian State Institutions Expressed Respect to BOC's Patriarch], *Tsărkoven Vestnik* 14 (2011) 9–11.

89 Ibid., 10.

90 Jonathan Fox, "Do Democracies Have Separation of Religion and State?", *Canadian Journal of Political Science/Revue canadienne de science politique* 40/1 (2007) 1–25.

91 Petkoff, "Church-State Relations" (as n. 42), 317.

and as symbol of many other institutions. Public rituals in which clergy take part are numerous in both countries. Many Serbian institutions or associations have adopted their patron saint. Water-blessings take place on many occasions also in Bulgaria, including major construction projects of national importance.[92]

The strong presence of the Orthodox Church (and the visible influence of the Islamic communities in Muslim-majority areas) in public and political life did not stop the "Bertelsmann Transformation Index" (BTI)[93] from assessing the Bulgarian and Serbian political systems as "democratic" in 2018. Bulgaria remained in the group of "democracies in consolidation", Serbia after 2012 lost that status and reverted to the "defective democracy" camp. However, the Bulgarian democracy and constitutional framework enjoy an "undisputed" position according to the report (with distrust mostly targeting individual institutions),[94] whereas in Serbia citizens "generally approve" of democracy, although, less so since 2012.[95] The BTI assessors declared that in Bulgaria there is no (negative) influence of religious dogmas on political actors, while certain points of their criticism of SOC influence on Serbian politics could be disputed. Most issues listed in this part of the report cannot be considered democracy-related at all, like the SOC's opposition to Kosovo's independence and the idealisation of "the royalist Chetnik resistance movement of World War II". The lack of sufficient competence of the people assessing the BTI score for Serbia in this area can also be observed in the sentence that "the Serbian Orthodox Church has clearly put itself above the laws of the state, by confirming ongoing tax immunity",[96] although this very immunity was enabled by the Article 30 of the Serbian Law on Churches and Religious Communities. Other points of criticism could be applied to the presentation of the Bulgarian case by the BTI as well. It could be argued that with more competent assessors in the field of church-state relations, the Serbian score would exceed the current 8/10 and move closer to the Bulgarian 10/10. Aside from this, the BTI reports should be commended for demonstrating that the Orthodox Church is not the most likely threat to either of

---

92 "С водосвет пуснаха в експлоатация ЛОТ 4 на магистрала 'Струма'" [The Fourth Section of the "Struma" Highway put into Operation with Water Blessings], *Pik*, 10.09.2015, URL: http://pik.bg/с-водосвет-пуснаха-в-експлоатация-лот-4-на-магистрала-„струма"-news396931.html [20.04.2018]; "Откриха магистрала 'Люлин'" [The "Lylulin" Highway Opened for Use], *Gradăt*, 15.05.2011, URL: https://gradat.bg/infrastructure/2011/05/15/1089949_otkriha_magistrala_ljulin/ [20.04.2018].

93 When dealing with democracy-related issues, this index uses the theoretical framework of Wolfgang Merkel, "Embedded and Defective Democracies", *Democratization* 11/5 (2004) 33–58.

94 BTI 2018, "Bulgaria Country Report", URL: https://www.bti-project.org/en/reports/country-reports/detail/itc/BGR/ [20.04.2018].

95 BTI 2018, "Serbia Country Report", URL: https://www.bti-project.org/en/reports/country-reports/detail/itc/SRB/ [20.04.2018].

96 Ibid.

these democracies, as there are more pressing issues, which cannot be directly related to these countries' Orthodox heritage.

Conclusion – Symphonic Democracy: Its Applicability and the Limitations of the Concept

Symphonia is frequently used as a case in point that the Orthodox Church is unable to accept a modern, secular, and democratic church-state relationship.[97]While not reflecting the US standards in their policies towards religion,[98] both Serbia and Bulgaria count among the democracies, at least according to Freedom House and BTI. In both countries, there has been a tendency to idealise the pre-modern relationship between church and state. This includes the cooperative separation of church and state, namely the tendency of the state to protect the canonical prerogatives of its church, even when this means risking harsh criticism on the international level. Orthodox symbols, discourse and traditions have returned to public institutions, with political elites demonstrating their respect for Orthodox traditions in public.

Both churches tend to stay away from commenting on daily political issues and act only when they believe that there is a certain national emergency. Both the BOC and the SOC tend to legitimise the existing order through their participation in the new state rituals, without having major objections to its democratic, politically pluralist, and parliamentary character. Such arrangements reflect the attitudes of the general population as well. Serbia has, when compared to Bulgaria, a rather liberal law on religion, but is showing more favouritism towards the SOC. Both societies exert a relatively high level of social regulation of religion, which means that it is not the law which induces such an attitude into society, but rather the other way around.

The illiberal aspects of the relationship between church and state stem from the understanding that the primary beneficiaries of religious freedoms should be collectives, not the individuals. In Orthodox societies, based on their personalistic and communitarian anthropology, religious communities, rather than individuals, get the attention of lawmakers. Furthermore, there is a tendency to support a multi-cultural model of society, in which traditional religious communities and identities connected with them enjoy state support. The state benefits from this limited pluralism, which thus becomes manageable, while pressures connected to the Europeanisation process gradually, and thus manageably, increase the space

97 Vasilios N. Makrides, "Orthodoxes Christentum und Demokratie – inkompatible Größen?", *Ost-West-Gegeninformationen* 15/4 (2003) 16–22, here 17.

98 Kristen Ghodsee, "Secularism without Liberalism: Orthodox Churches, Human Rights and American Foreign Policy in Southeastern Europe", in Lucian N. Leustean (ed.), *Eastern Christianity and Politics in the Twenty-First Century*, London 2014, 754–776.

of religious freedom for the smaller and non-traditional communities as well. The verdict of the ECHR against Bulgaria, which posited that neither canon law nor the propagation of the majority views in the public sphere is the business of the state,[99] does not reflect the standards which emerged in several post-communist Orthodox democracies.

The two countries reached a similar church-state differentiation equilibrium from different starting positions, which raises the question whether a certain generalisation for Orthodox countries in similar democratisation situations is possible; in other words, whether Orthodox democracies tend to have specific differentiation levels. Based on the Bulgarian and Serbian examples, the claim that this kind of equilibrium might be specific for Orthodox societies is not far-fetched. Protection of the canonical jurisdiction of the local Orthodox Church is no special case of Bulgaria and Serbia alone. In other former Yugoslav countries, support of uncanonical structures (Macedonian Orthodox Church) or even structures of dubious Orthodox credentials (Montenegrin Orthodox Church) is a visible part of state policy.[100] This is a result of the specific experience of Orthodox church-state relations, where the local Orthodox Church was nationalised to the extent that both the nation-state and the nation-church reflect the same collective. Every citizen belongs to this collective, even if one does not share the church's faith. It does give these democracies a specific Orthodox flavour, even if it occasionally contradicts the views of the ECHR in terms of treatment of other communities claiming to be Orthodox.

Democracy is also a process, a never-ending project, a never finally determined ambition, rather than the institutional framework alone.[101] No democracy can survive in a society where the majority is not supportive of it, which is why one should welcome the readiness of the Orthodox Church to legitimise the democratic order. At this point, one cannot claim that the Orthodox support for democracy is expressed with the same vigour and enthusiasm as the romanticisation of the monarchies of bygone eras. Yet, one can safely argue that the Orthodox political theology as a whole is at a threshold in twenty-first century South Eastern Europe and that significant changes are to be expected in the future.

---

99 Kalkandjieva, "Bulgarian Orthodoxy" (as n. 46), 318–321.

100 Barbara Surk, "Milo Đukanović: Like it or not, Montenegro's going West", *Politico*, 20.05.2016, URL: http://www.politico.eu/article/milo-dukanovic-like-it-or-not-montenegros-going-west-interview-europe-nato-russia/ [26.03.2018]. See also the contributions by Nenad Živković and Emil Hilton Saggau in this volume.

101 Paul Blokker, *Multiple Democracies in Europe: Political Culture in New Member States*, Abingdon 2012, 52.

The Ecumenical Patriarchate of Constantinople: Power and Geopolitics

Nicolas Kazarian

The Ecumenical Patriarchate of Constantinople today faces a contradictory situation. Being the first Church within the communion of Orthodox Churches for centuries, this ecclesiastical institution has lost most of its territory and members over the course of the twentieth century.[1] After having sacrificed direct canonical jurisdiction over most of the Balkans a century before, the *Phanar* – shorthand for the Ecumenical Patriarchate – has seen its authority diminished as the Orthodox map evolved following a series of geopolitical events: the Russian Revolution (1917), the exchange of populations between Greece and Turkey (1923), the Ustasha massacres (1942-1944), the rise of communism in the Balkans (1945), the beginning of the modern conflicts in the Middle East (1948), the invasion and division of Cyprus (1974), the Lebanese Civil War (1975), the Yugoslav Wars (1991-2001), the collapse of the Soviet Union (1991), the invasion of Iraq (2003), the independence of Kosovo (2008), the Russo-Georgian War (2008), the Arab Spring (2010), and more recently the Syrian crisis (since 2011) and the conflict in Ukraine (since 2013).

On a more local level, the situation of the Ecumenical Patriarchate is no less uncomfortable. It is a religious minority in Turkey, with a controversial legal status and a decreasing population, while the Halki Theological Seminary, its only educational institution, is still closed. It also has to repeatedly negotiate with the Orthodox Church of Greece over its territorial jurisdiction in Greece, and the deep economic crisis of the latter drastically limited the financial and political support it was receiving from this country. On the other hand, the Pan-Orthodox Council of 2016 was seen as a chance for the Orthodox Church to fundamentally adapt

---

1 According to the protocol order, the Orthodox Church is composed of a communion of 14 Churches: The Ancient Patriarchates of Constantinople, Alexandria, Antioch, and Jerusalem; the "new" Patriarchates of Russia, Serbia, Romania, Bulgaria, and Georgia; and the other Autocephalous Churches of Cyprus, Greece, Poland, Albania, and Czech Lands and Slovakia. There is currently a disagreement between the Patriarchates of Constantinople and Moscow over the recognition of the Orthodox Church in America (OCA). Its autocephalous status was unilaterally granted by the Russian Church in 1970. In addition, in 2019, there was a break of communion between the Ecumenical Patriarchate of Constantinople and the Moscow Patriarchate due to the autocephaly granted by the former to the Orthodox Church of Ukraine, which still does not enjoy Pan-Orthodox recognition. This development further led to several changes in the jurisdictional status of Orthodox communities of the Russian tradition in Western Europe (e.g., in France). However, all these developments, which have a great geopolitical relevance, took place after the completion of the present chapter.

itself to the challenges of the modern world and created a strategic opportunity for the Ecumenical Patriarchate to overcome its local weaknesses by redefining its global power.

The concept of power is a central one in political science. In this chapter, I will draw on the theoretical framework developed by Thierry de Montbrial, a member of the French Academy of Political and Moral Sciences. According to de Montbrial, when talking about power, it is necessary to make the distinction between: a) power as "the ability to mobilise an entity's resources in determined directions", b) power as "the sum of goals potentially reachable by this mobilisation", and c) power as "the transition from virtuality to reality, that is to say, the passage to real action, which may include both discontinuity and choice".[2]

In light of this definition, the following questions may be posed: What are the resources of the Ecumenical Patriarchate that shape its power? How can it mobilise them? And finally, in which direction are these resources directed in order to visualise this power? In other words, how can geopolitics be an issue of power for the Ecumenical Patriarchate? The present chapter tries to answer these questions in three steps. First, it examines the notions of power and geopolitics in an Orthodox context that provide an idea of the resources available to the various actors. Second, it looks closely at the way the Ecumenical Patriarchate is attempting to deploy its sources of power and the challenges it faces thereby. Finally, it focuses on the issue of the Orthodox diaspora, which in the author's view is currently the main geopolitical resource of the Ecumenical Patriarchate.

Power and Geopolitics in Orthodoxy

The geopolitical dimension of Orthodoxy emerged in the field of political science, particularly in France, after the beginning of the Yugoslav Wars (1991-2001). The resurgence of this deadly conflict in South Eastern Europe quickly ruined hopes for a Hegelian "End of History". In fact, it was about a territorial fragmentation based on ethno-religious conflicts, a process vividly expressed by the negatively connoted term "Balkanisation". Following the fall of the Berlin Wall in 1989 and the end of the Cold War, Francis Fukuyama's *The End of History*[3] had namely predicted the decline of ideological conflicts in favour of global interconnections in which liberalism and capitalism would act as conflict regulators.

However, the bloody Yugoslav Wars demolished these arguments, and Samuel Huntington, the father of the *Clash of Civilisations*, quickly opposed them. History did not end in the early 1990s, because blood was still flowing, not

2 Thierry de Montbrial, "Qu'est-ce qu'une puissance au XXIe siècle?", 07.01.2013, URL: https://www.ifri.org/sites/default/files/atoms/files/questcequunepuissanceauxxisiecle.pdf [18.02.2016].

3 Francis Fukuyama, *The End of History and the Last Man*, New York 1992.

only in the Balkans, but also in Rwanda (1994). In a now famous article published in *Foreign Affairs*,[4] Huntington argued that ideological conflicts are indeed over in the wake of the collapse of communism as an alternative to liberal capitalism. Yet, large regions in the world will continue to compete around cultural dividing lines and generally along religious borders. Huntington proffered a list of different important civilisations, including the Western and the Eastern Orthodox ones, and gave priority to the religious solidarity within such large cultural units. In his view, religion was going to become the new influential background and the main driving force for future global conflicts. His conviction was clear: an appeal to solidarity in the West (the U.S. and Europe) under American leadership to face the Islamic threat or, worse, an unlikely "Islamic-Confucian" alliance. It should be noted that, according to Huntington, the Orthodox civilisational bloc – including the former Soviet Union, the former Yugoslavia (except Croatia and Slovenia), Bulgaria, Cyprus, Greece and Romania, as well as Armenia – is related to Islam in its opposition to Western Christianity and civilisation.

Orthodox Civilisation

According to Huntington, civilisations are differentiated on the basis of a process of otherness:

> First, differences among civilizations are not only real; they are basic. Civilizations are differentiated from each other by history, language, culture, tradition and, most important, religion. The people of different civilizations have different views on the relations between God and man, the individual and the group, the citizen and the state, parents and children, husband and wife, as well as differing views of the relative importance of rights and responsibilities, liberty and authority, equality and hierarchy. These differences are the product of centuries. They will not soon disappear. They are far more fundamental than differences among political ideologies and political regimes. Differences do not necessarily mean conflict, and conflict does not necessarily mean violence. Over the centuries, however, differences among civilizations have generated the most prolonged and the most violent conflicts.[5]

The homogeneous representation of blocs of civilisations is a recurrent criticism of Huntington's theory. A simple glance at the composition of the "Orthodox Civilisation" shows the diversity of cultural, not to say ethnic contexts that compose it and form distinct civilisational areas: Hellenic, Slavic, Georgian, Arabic, and so on. It very appropriately reflects, however, the role of religion in a sort of international partition of the world to which Orthodoxy has not remained completely foreign. Indeed, Patriarch Kirill of Moscow has been known to use the

---

4 Samuel P. Huntington, "The Clash of Civilizations?", *Foreign Affairs* 72/3 (Summer 1993) 22–49. See also Samuel P. Huntington, *The Clash of Civilizations and the Remaking of World Order*, New York 1996.

5 Huntington, "The Clash of Civilizations" (as n. 4), 25.

expression "Orthodox Civilisation", especially and vividly present in the foundation "*Russkiy mir*" (Russian World). This latter concept is a state-sponsored attempt to further Russian culture across the globe. It is not only a patriotic conception that identifies the cultural seeds of the Slavic world, but also the acknowledgement of religion as "the matrix […] which supports major ideological tendencies, now put forward by the political power over the community and collective identity […] In international circles, the Church defends a model of coexistence and dialogue of civilisations that is opposed to a unipolar world and defending the foreign policy of the State."[6]

At the same time, religion should not be reduced to its purely ideological dimension as the only factor explaining every modern conflict. One can even wonder whether civilisational theory and analysis apply to the Orthodox context at all. According to the French philosopher and Orthodox theologian, Jean-François Colosimo: "This theory does not seem obvious. It appears to depend excessively on the Occident-centrism of Spengler."[7] Oswald Spengler (1880-1936), an early twentieth-century German philosopher, inspired not only Huntington's theory of the clash of civilisations, but also Georges Florovsky's concept of "pseudomorphosis", which defined the true theological borders of the Orthodox Church in opposition to Western Latin influences since the sixteenth century.[8] According to Spengler, civilisations cannot hybridise and their process of growth and evolution guarantees their intrinsic homogeneity. However, "the Orthodox bloc, in the meantime, was dissolved before re-emerging: from 1991 to 2001, the new Balkan wars seemed to revive the lines running from Riga to Split which, since the eighth century, have separated Byzantine-Ottoman Europe from Frankish-Latin Europe. At the same time, Russia could not prevent Kosovo's secession from Serbia, nor the integration of Bulgaria and Romania into the European Union, putting a final end to Yugoslav and Pan-Slavic ideas as being Pan-Orthodox."[9]

Orthodoxy, Space, and Identity

The geopolitical reality of Orthodox Christianity first appears in the literature through an interdisciplinary approach, at the crossroads of Political Science and Geography, in the work of François Thual. Until the 2000s, he and Georges

6 Kathy Rousselet, "L'autorité religieuse en contexte post-soviétique: Regard sur le fonctionnement des paroisses russes orthodoxes", *Archives de sciences sociales des religions* 58 (2013) 15–36, here 16.

7 Jean-François Colosimo, "Métamorphose du divin", *Le Débat* 160 (2010) 79–93, here 84.

8 Oswald Spengler, *Der Untergang des Abendlandes,* Vols. 1-2, Wien/München 1918-1922; Georges Florovsky, *Пути русского богословия* [The Ways of Russian Theology], Paris 1937.

9 Colosimo, "Métamorphose" (as n. 7), 84.

Prévélakis, a geography professor at Paris I Panthéon Sorbonne, were the only scholars to analyse Orthodoxy as a key component of the geopolitical equation dividing the Balkans in the 1990s and as a constant form of power during the last years of the communist period in Russia. In this sense, their approach tended to examine the interaction between faith, identity, and territory. For Thual: "The geopolitics of the Orthodox world have shown us that religion, as a source of national ideology and collective legitimisation, is a matrix of the geopolitical representations that ultimately lead the world."[10]

If we can argue that Orthodoxy is a geopolitical reality, this is because it is about a religion that is deeply rooted in a territory, a territorial spirituality. At the intersection of its administrative organisation and its ecclesiology of communion, territory is an essential input to its canonical operation. The Orthodox Autocephalous Churches are territorial units modelled on historical administrative networks. Some of these churches date back to the period of the Roman Empire. Theologically speaking, the elaboration of an "ecclesiology of communion" during the twentieth century has strengthened the centrality of territorial borders as the canonical limits of communities gathered around one bishop as the guarantor of the only legitimate Eucharist celebrated in one circumscribed area, namely the diocese.[11] The meaning of territory is not only a canonical space, given that territory has gradually become a supporter of religious and ethno-national identities.[12]

The decline of the Ottoman Empire in the late nineteenth century led to a reassessment of religious identities. Consequently, these traditional community symbols have become the basis for modern nationalist and irredentist claims. The official status of the Orthodox Christians as the *Millet* (ethno-religious community) of the *Rum* in the Ottoman Empire did not call into question the universal dimension of the Christian tradition. The Patriarchate of Constantinople therefore remained an element of unity in the Ottoman Balkans until the emergence of the first stirrings of Greek nationalism. However, the growing political role of the Patriarch of Constantinople as a *millet-bashi* (ethnarch) of the Orthodox peoples altered the purely spiritual nature of his position and weakened the unity of his authority in the Orthodox world, resulting in the multipolar emergence of increasingly conscious ethno-national identities. The rise of these ideals within a Greek-speaking intelligentsia, which was increasingly polarised around the idea of territorial separation, had a huge impact on the self-representation of the Orthodox Church. Hence, the nationalist movements favoured the involvement of religious symbols in the process of building national

10 François Thual, *Géopolitique de l'orthodoxie,* Paris 1993, 121.

11 Nicolas Afanasiev, *L'Eglise du Saint-Esprit*, Paris 1975; John Zizioulas, *Eucharist, Bishop, Church – The Unity of the Church in the Divine Eucharist and the Bishop During the First Three Centuries*, Boston 2001.

12 Georges Prévélakis, *Balkans. Cultures et géopolitique*, Paris 1994.

identities. This development is clearly visible in the decision of Otto, King of Greece (1833-1862), in 1838 to establish a public national holiday on 25 March, celebrating the beginning of the Greek War of Independence and coinciding with the feast of the Annunciation. Orthodoxy became the cornerstone of nationalist constructs not only in Greece, but also in Serbia and Bulgaria during the same period. The administrative structure of the Orthodox Church loaned itself favourably to the nationalist agenda. According to Victor Roudometof, "although the institution of territorial autocephaly is part of the Eastern Orthodox tradition, the construction of national churches in the Balkans did not serve ecclesiastical purposes alone but, rather, provided the material and ideological infrastructure for the nationalizations of masses".[13] Alongside the nation-building process, we can also discern a similar and parallel phenomenon in religious terms, which could be described as church-building, with the creation of modern autocephalous Orthodox Churches (e.g., Greece in 1833, Serbia in 1832, Bulgaria in 1870, Romania in 1885). These changes took place at the expense of the Ecumenical Patriarchate's territorial authority; hence they were at times highly conflictual.

Far more problematic than the unilateral founding of the Greek Orthodox Church (1833) were the separatist tendencies of the Bulgarian Orthodox Exarch in Istanbul, who was not content with setting up a community on the canonical territory of the Ecumenical Patriarchate, but considered ethno-religious configurations as more important than the spiritual unity of the universal Orthodox world. The unilateral declaration of a Bulgarian Exarchate in 1870 caused the reaction of a Patriarchal Synod in Constantinople, which in 1872 officially condemned the tendency of *ethnophyletism* (i.e., nationalism).[14] Despite this condemnation, the portrayal of Orthodoxy as an essential symbol of national identity was not confined to Greece or Bulgaria alone, but established itself as a dominant paradigm throughout Eastern and South Eastern Europe from the nineteenth century onwards. This is not to say that Orthodoxy carried within itself the seeds of nationalism. It would be presumptuous to make such a generalisation, yet it appears that the Orthodox Church tends to respond to issues of collective identity by exploiting identity-based attachments to nationalist ideals.

These territorial reconfigurations have led to the creation of migration flows, as well as of transnational and even transcontinental networks. They are accompanied by a strengthening of identities, also organised in the context of the "Orthodox diaspora", that is to say outside the boundaries of the canonical territory of local Orthodox Churches (in Western Europe, America, Asia and

---

13 Victor N. Roudometof, "The Evolution of Greek Orthodoxy in the Context of World Historical Globalization", in Victor N. Roudometof/Vasilios N. Makrides (eds), *Orthodox Christianity in 21st Century Greece: The Role of Religion in Culture, Ethnicity and Politics*, Farnham 2011, 21–38, here 26.

14 Metropolitan Maximos of Sardes, *The Oecumenical Patriarchate in the Orthodox Church*, Thessaloniki 1976, 300–309.

Australia). This "de-territorialisation" of the Orthodox Churches is probably the more significant sign of the persistence of the particular ethno-religious synthesis fostered by the globalisation process today.[15] Some Orthodox communities continue to support the interests of their states of origin, serving as relays of influence. The respective Orthodox Church is considered as a part of the state's *soft power*, especially on the international level, underlining once more the strong ties between religion, state, and nation. François Thual once wrote that "the specificity of Orthodoxy is the symbiotic fusion between the national state and the religious".[16] The geopolitics of Orthodoxy seems to be influenced by the same phenomenon of fusion, which creates favourable conditions for further fragmentation among the Orthodox Churches.

Changing the Resources of Power

The case of the Ecumenical Patriarchate is symptomatic of an ongoing change in the global strategy of Orthodox Christianity. The Ecumenical Patriarch, *primus inter pares* (first among equals) in the Orthodox Church, seeks to overcome the current weakness of this historical institution. This is in many respects a clear oxymoron. In fact, this leading Orthodox Church has a very limited territory – Istanbul, most of Turkey, Mount Athos, Crete, part of northern Greece, the Dodecanese – and virtually no political support with the exception of Greece, whose diplomacy is limited by various constraints, however (e.g., the deep economic crisis in the 2010s). The Ecumenical Patriarchate's situation within Turkey is even worse. Its population is vanishing. Its legal status has been denied for decades. The Orthodox Seminary of Halki has been closed since 1971. The "Great Church of Constantinople" is treated as a marginalised minority within Turkish society (with less than 5000 people in Istanbul), despite its attempts to promote Turkey's integration into the European Union.[17]

The Ecumenical Patriarchate has responded to this *de facto* weakness by implementing a strategy of legitimisation based on strengthening its ecclesiastical authority over the entire Orthodox world and especially by promoting the Pan-Orthodox Council and asserting its ecclesiastical jurisdiction over the Orthodox diaspora globally. The Patriarchate of Constantinople also seeks to integrate multi-ethnic communities and to take root in parts of the world that do not fall under any particular Orthodox jurisdiction. The challenge of the diaspora is not,

15 Nicolas Kazarian, "Orthodoxie et mondialisation, une résistance en mouvement: étude des paradigmes grecs et russes", in Bérengère Massignon/Christophe Grannec (eds), *Les religions dans la mondialisation: entre acculturation et contestation*, Paris 2012, 125–146.

16 Thual, *Géopolitique* (as n. 10), 115.

17 Méropi Anastassiadou/Paul Dumont, *Les Grecs d'Istanbul et le patriarcat œcuménique au seuil du 21e siècle: une communauté en quête d'avenir*, Paris 2011.

however, limited to the process of integration. It denotes a much deeper shift within the spiritual vocation of each local church. The message of Christian salvation is a universal one, while at the same time theological and cultural particularities of each church become symbols of identity disseminated across the planet. In many cases, the bearers of the symbols no longer dissociate between religion and ethnicity. The transition from the one universal faith to particularist churches of global scope is effected through the *ethnicisation/nationalisation* of religious symbols. As a result, Orthodox Churches with a strong ethno-national identity tend to move beyond the boundaries of their canonical territory in order to better deploy their activities at the global level. In the Orthodox diaspora, thus, it seems that inter-Orthodox relations outside of traditional canonical territories are governed by a rationale based on ethno-national identities. For instance, the Orthodox Church of Cyprus maintains in its Statutory Charter (1980, art. 2) that its jurisdiction is not only over its insular territory – which creates the issue of the religious administration of the northern part of the island under Turkish control since 1974 –, but also over any person of Cypriot origin around the world. As this article entered directly into conflict with the claims of the Ecumenical Patriarchate over the religious management of the Greek-speaking Cypriot diaspora, particularly in Great Britain, it was never applied. The evasiveness of an ethno-national identification seems to be exacerbated by de-localisation, with the respective communities exhibiting the constituent elements of their imagery in order to combat any loss of their ethno-national identity.[18]

The Ecumenical Patriarchate ensures its dominant position in the context of the diaspora through the organisation and functioning of the Assemblies of Orthodox Bishops, instituted by the Fourth Pre-Conciliar Conference in Chambésy (Switzerland) in 2009. These temporal structures are chaired by the representatives of the Ecumenical Patriarchate in the various regions.[19] This gives them the opportunity to use their networks to transmit the claims of the Ecumenical Patriarchate and to reaffirm its primacy as a representative of the entire Orthodox world. In this way, the Greek American community and the Patriarchate of Constantinople continue to maintain close ties through the Greek Orthodox Archdiocese, which has its headquarters in New York since 1931. Moreover, the Association of the Archons of the Ecumenical Patriarchate exerts pressure on the American political sphere to contribute to the Patriarchate's survival in Turkey. In addition to providing substantial financial aid, the Archons also engage in international lobbying, particularly with European institutions, to bring the question of religious freedom in Turkey to the agenda as a major demand in favour of the protection of human rights. Their aim is to perpetuate the presence

---

18 See the contributions to Maria Hämmerli/Jean-François Mayer (eds), *Orthodox Identities in Western Europe: Migration, Settlement and Innovation*, Farnham 2014.

19 Nicolas Kazarian, "The Orthodox Church in France Facing French Secularism ('laïcité')", *Religion, State & Society* 43/3 (2015) 244–261.

of the Patriarchate by crystallising their demands around the re-opening of the Halki Seminary, which was closed by the Turkish state in 1971.

The Russian Orthodox Challenge

The Patriarchate of Moscow, in addition to a strong missionary spirit forged by the experience of the nineteenth century, today deploys its pastoral action by promoting the emergence of a collective spiritual identity, which is not only Russian, but Slavic too. It is implementing a twofold process of *de-territorialisation* not only by taking action outside the borders of the Russian Federation, but also by re-enhancing the value of the Orthodox imaginary, which is not so much an ethno-national as a cultural phenomenon, cementing an "Orthodox Civilisation", which excludes the West. Kathy Rousselet goes further: "Far from accepting a shrinking of its borders, the [Russian Orthodox] Church situates its mission within the framework of regional integration, whether by granting 'spiritual citizenship' to millions of Russians who are now situated beyond the borders of Russia, or by defending its jurisdictional territory."[20] This capacity of the Patriarchate of Moscow to project beyond the borders of both the Russian Federation and its own jurisdiction is an advantage that the country's political authorities do nothing to minimise and may even explicitly support by entrusting the Patriarchate with the management of the properties, which make up its religious architectural heritage outside Russia. The legal disputes over the ownership of the Russian Orthodox cathedral of Nice and the construction of a Russian Orthodox Cultural Centre in the heart of Paris should be understood in light of this situation. Hence, the political and spiritual spheres meet and collaborate around common interests, although their relationship remains somewhat ambiguous.

The territorial reconfiguration of the Orthodox world due to political instability and migration flows engenders symbolic changes, and communities are partitioned off when they should be united. This was the case of the Russian diaspora in France, for instance. The geopolitical upheavals of the Russian Revolution of October 1917 and the First World War shaped the Orthodox landscape in Western Europe. Many Russians fled to France to escape the Revolution. This migratory flow can be explained both by the traditional relationship between France and Imperial Russia and by the increased demand for labour in the 1920s. According to figures from the League of Nations, around 400,000 Russians settled in France. Small parish communities grew up in Paris and in major industrial areas such as Lorraine and the Northern Alps. Orthodox

20 Kathy Rousselet, "Globalisation et territoire religieux en Russie", in Jean-Pierre Bastian/ Françoise Champion/Kathy Rousselet (eds), *La Globalisation du Religieux*, Paris 2001, 183–196, here 194.

intellectuals clustered around the *Institut de Théologie Orthodoxe Saint Serge* in Paris.

However, the opposition to communism further complicated the jurisdictional mapping of the Orthodox world. The increasing harshness of the Soviet regime produced schisms within the Russian Church in the diaspora.[21] In 1926, the Russian Orthodox Church Abroad was founded. It was initially based in Sremski Karlovtsy (Yugoslavia) and only marginally present in France. Generally, it was characterised by conservatism. Metropolitan Evlogii, head of the Russian Orthodox diaspora in France, broke his ties with the Moscow Patriarchate and requested the diaspora's attachment to the Ecumenical Patriarchate of Constantinople, giving it the status of an Exarchate. This Exarchate brought together two-thirds of the Russian emigration, with the Cathedral of St Alexander Nevsky and the *Institut de Théologie Orthodoxe Saint Serge*, both in Paris, as its main centres. Only a small group remained faithful to the Moscow Patriarchate for ecclesiological reasons, refusing the right of the Patriarchate of Constantinople to govern the entire Orthodox diaspora.

For Vassilis Pnevmatikakis, following the lead of Nicolas Zernov, "the fragmentation of the Russian Orthodox diaspora into three different jurisdictions was the result of a crystallisation of three different approaches to the church and its relationship with the state".[22] These three approaches were reduced to two in 2007, when the Moscow Patriarchate and the Russian Orthodox Church Abroad signed a reconciliation agreement. This development defines the authenticity of the Russian Orthodox identity through an organic link with the Moscow Patriarchate. In order to respond adequately to this de-territorialised organisation, the Patriarchate of Moscow supports its own large Department for External Church Relations, which specifically deals with its affairs abroad. The current Patriarch Kirill spent years as the head of this Department, which is vital in structuring the diaspora and in proving the transnational character of the Moscow Patriarchate through its involvement in matters of international relations. For the tradition of the Exarchate, on the other hand, ecclesial identity could not be conditioned on the grounds of national identity. This historical tendency, however, was often challenged in post-communist times.[23]

---

21 Sebastian Rimestad, "The Russian Orthodox Church in Western Europe: one or many?", *Religion, State & Society* 43/3 (2015) 228–243.

22 Vassilis Pnevmatikakis, "La territorialité de l'Eglise orthodoxe en France, entre exclusivisme juridictionnel et catholicité locale", *Carnets de géographes* 6 (2013), URL: http://www.carnetsdegeographes.org/carnets_recherches/rech_06_04_Prevmatikakis.php [18.02.2016].

23 The unilateral decision by the Patriarchate of Constantinople to abolish its status as a non-territorial Exarchate in October 2018 happened after the completion of this chapter. The consequences of this decision, which led various Russian communities back to the jurisdiction of the Moscow Patriarchate, are not yet clear at the time of publication.

The Diaspora in the Context of the Holy and Great Council

The existence of Orthodox communities outside the boundaries of the canonical territory of the local churches creates a new dynamic for the Orthodox Churches in their pastoral care of migrants and the development of inter-Orthodox relations on the basis of a canonical compromise that the Archimandrite Grigorios Papathomas calls "multi-jurisdictional co-territoriality".[24] Furthermore, each local church takes a different approach to the concept of canonical territory and the definition of boundaries in the diaspora.

The Patriarchate of Constantinople bases all of its initiatives outside its canonical territory on considerations, which date back to the Council of Chalcedon (451). As discussed below in more detail, the Ecumenical Patriarchate's claims are, above all, linked to its status of *Protos* (first) or even *Primus inter pares* (first among equals) in the Orthodox world, as defined by Canon 28 of the Council of Chalkedon, granting it the right to act outside the borders of its canonical territory.[25]

The view of the Ecumenical Patriarchate on the issue of the Orthodox diaspora mirrors the principal stages of preparation for the Pan-Orthodox Council that was held on the island of Crete in June 2016. The Council was prepared through a series of Pre-Conciliar Conferences, meetings and consultations, in which the issues at stake had to be settled to avoid surprises during the Council itself. The first Pan-Orthodox Conference met in Rhodes in 1961, and in 1968 the Fourth Pan-Orthodox Conference (Chambésy) decided to hold *The Holy and Great Council of the Orthodox Church*, at which one of the first points on the agenda would be that of the Orthodox Diaspora.

The First Pan-Orthodox Pre-Conciliar Conference of Chambésy in 1976 confirmed the subject of the Orthodox Diaspora on the agenda of the Holy and Great Council. This choice followed a series of events that had made the topic unavoidable, especially the creation in 1970 of the autocephalous Orthodox

---

24 Grigorios Papathomas, "La relation oppositionnelle entre Eglise établie localement et 'Diaspora' ecclésiale (L'unité ecclésiologique face à la co-territorialité et à la multi-juridiction)", *Contacts* 57 (2004) 96–132.

25 Canon 28 reads: "Consequently, the metropolitans – and they alone – of the dioceses of Pontus, Asia and Thrace, as well as the bishops of the aforementioned dioceses who are among the barbarians, shall be ordained by the aforementioned most holy throne of the most holy Church of Constantinople. Each metropolitan of the aforementioned dioceses, along with his fellow-bishops of the province, ordains the bishops of the province, as has been provided for in the canons; but the metropolitans of the aforementioned dioceses, as has been stated, shall be ordained by the archbishop of Constantinople, after proper elections have been made according to custom and have been reported to him." Quoted from John Erickson, "Overview of History and Difficulties in Preparing for the Council", in George E. Matsoukas (ed.), *Orthodox Christianity at the Crossroads. A Great Council of the Church – When and Why?*, New York 2009, 19–40, here 22.

Church in America (OCA) by the Patriarchate of Moscow against the objections of the Ecumenical Patriarchate. It was deemed essential to address the issues related to the diaspora with the cooperation of all canonical Autocephalous Orthodox Churches and under the leadership of the Ecumenical Patriarchate in order to prevent further problems from arising. A transitory model for the pastoral care of the diaspora was then developed at the meetings of the Inter-Orthodox Preparatory Commission in November 1990 and November 1993 in Chambésy. An element of this solution was the creation of Episcopal Assemblies composed of the canonical bishops of each region. France was considered such a region, placed under the supervision of an Assembly of Canonical Bishops.

The specific example of the Orthodox Church in France neatly clarifies this development. The fragmentary and polymorphic nature of Orthodoxy in France is mitigated by the institutional contacts among the different bishops of varied ethno-national provenance. The relations among these Orthodox jurisdictions were first organised with the creation of an Inter-Orthodox Episcopal Committee in 1967.[26] This Committee, which became the Assembly of Orthodox Bishops of France (AEOF) in 1997, brings together all the bishops of the various canonical Orthodox jurisdictions. It constitutes an official body for dialogue not only with the public authorities, but also with civil society and other religious groups. The creation of the AEOF met the urgent need for coordination among various Orthodox communities in France. It did not constitute a uniquely French initiative, although it preceded the decisions of the Fourth Pan-Orthodox Pre-Conciliar Conference, held in Chambésy in June 2009, which was largely based on the French experience. According to Antoine Arjakovsky, a noted French historian, the importance of the Pre-Conciliar procedures lies in the ability of the Assemblies to bear witness to the unity of the Orthodox world through the unanimity of their members.[27] However, contrary to Arjakovsky's opinion, the 2009 decision did not oppose the "Mother Churches and the Local Churches",[28] but rather reflected a complex dialectical opposition and related tensions among the main Patriarchal seats. For example, the balance of power between the Patriarchates of Constantinople and Moscow after the fall of the Berlin Wall in

---

26 Pnevmatikakis, "La territorialité" (as n. 22). The oldest inter-episcopal Committee exists in the USA. It is the "Standing Conference of the Canonical Orthodox Bishops in the Americas" (SCOBA), which was founded in 1960. In 2010, it was renamed "Assembly of Canonical Orthodox Bishops of North and Central America", while since 2014 it is called "Assembly of Canonical Orthodox Bishops of the United States of America". Its history can be explained by the importance of the American continent for Orthodox Diasporas among different Patriarchates. See Alexei Krindatch, *Atlas of the American Orthodox Christian Churches*, Brookline/MA 2011.

27 Antoine Arjakovsky, "La question de la 'diaspora' au prochain Concile panorthodoxe", *Contacts* 243 (2013) 455–476, here 458.

28 In this case, "Local Churches" should be understood as communities or dioceses established in the diaspora.

1989 profoundly affected the question of primacy.[29] Thus, the tensions that have arisen around Estonia and Ukraine are characteristic of the opposition between symbolic power and demographic weight. These tensions can also be observed in the context of the diaspora, and other Orthodox Churches emphasise the transitory nature of the above solution. The document issued in June 2009 states that "[t]his Conference proposes that, for the transitional period where the canonical solution of the question will be prepared, […] 'Episcopal Assemblies' should be created that will bring together all the bishops of a region who are recognized as canonical, who will continue to remain subject to the same canonical jurisdictions as they do today".[30] In this regard, the AEOF crystallises the convergence of two phenomena: the tacit structural effects of French secularism or *laïcité* on the institutional representations of the major religious families and the transitory ecclesiological response to the problem through the creation of Episcopal Assemblies in the context of the Orthodox diaspora.[31]

Furthermore, the Episcopal Assemblies ensure the pre-eminence of the Patriarchate of Constantinople, which favours a canonical reading recognising its ecclesiastical jurisdiction over the entire Orthodox diaspora. Hence, the presidency of the Episcopal Assemblies follows the hierarchical protocol of the Orthodox Church: the presidency of these meetings is reserved for the representative of the Ecumenical Patriarchate.[32] The Presidency of the AEOF thus allows the Metropolitan of the Greek Orthodox Metropolis of France under Constantinople to secure a leading position as the guarantor of transitional Orthodox institutional unity, while also strengthening the symbolic authority of the Patriarchate of Constantinople and making it a key player both in political terms and on a purely religious level.[33] The Greek Orthodox Metropolis of France intends to play a leading role in the unification of the Orthodox Churches in the country. This would strengthen its authority despite its lack of political power compared to the Patriarchate of Moscow. The Metropolis is also about to be overtaken in demographic terms by the Patriarchate of Romania. The Ecumenical Patriarchate is thus seeking to *de facto* overcome its political and numerical weaknesses by implementing a strategy of legitimisation by strengthening its ecclesiastical authority over the entire Orthodox world, as well as by further promoting and establishing its position of *primus inter pares*.

---

29 Arjakovsky, "La question" (as n. 27), 461.

30 IV Pre-Conciliar Pan-Orthodox Conference, "The Orthodox Diaspora. Decision", Chambésy 2009, URL: http://www.goarch.org/archdiocese/documents/chambesy/decision [05.12.2015], §2.a.

31 Kazarian, "The Orthodox Church" (as n. 19).

32 IV Pre-Conciliar Pan-Orthodox Conference, "The Orthodox Diaspora" (as n. 30), §2.b.

33 Nikolaos A. Daldas, *Le Patriarcat œcuménique de Constantinople et le statut canonique de la "diaspora" orthodoxe de langue grecque: le cas de la France*, Athens 1999, 417.

To this purpose, the Ecumenical Patriarchate also reinvests the field of its "ecumenicity" by developing a global representation of Orthodoxy as a form of leverage, while at the same time highlighting the crucial issue of multiculturalism in the context of the diaspora.[34] The Greek Orthodox Metropolis of France includes a Georgian community and a Romanian community, as well as predominantly or even exclusively French-speaking communities. However, a sense of ethno-national identity has not completely vanished in them. According to Nikolaos Daldas, such a national tendency "will be encouraged for a long time [...] and it will advocate as model for the church organisation of the 'Orthodox diaspora' the right of every Autocephalous Church to administer its own 'diaspora'".[35]

In France, the power strategy of the Ecumenical Patriarchate is expressed through the appropriation of the institutional representation of Orthodoxy, as it is the case worldwide. It comes as no surprise that the administrative headquarters of the AEOF are also those of the Greek Orthodox Metropolis of France, and that the AEOF's main events, including the New Year's reception and the regular monthly meetings, are held there. The Metropolitan of the Ecumenical Patriarchate also represents Orthodoxy on the French national level, attending official events like the Bastille Day parade and meeting with political leaders. These privileges are identical to those of the leaders of all of France's major religions. However, in the case of the AEOF, they take on a unique dimension in light of the fact that unlike the majority of other religions, the Presidency of the AEOF is not a rotating one. It changes only with the replacement of the Metropolitan of the Ecumenical Patriarchate. This allows the Ecumenical Patriarchate to strengthen its networks and sustain its dominant position within French Orthodoxy. This also demonstrates the need for adjustments in order to ensure the compatibility of French law, which regulates the legal status of the AEOF, with Orthodox canon law. Interestingly enough, the question of a rotating presidency has been raised on the Pan-Orthodox level by the Patriarchate of Moscow. Due to the lack of consensus on the subject, the Russian Church has accepted the current practice, which follows the logic of the traditional protocol laid out in the Diptychs of the Orthodox Church.[36] The fact that the presidency is vested in the Metropolitan of the Ecumenical Patriarchate also allows the Patriarchate to promote its own claims, particularly with regard to the issue of religious freedom in Turkey.

34 Kazarian, "Orthodoxie" (as n. 15), 132–133.
35 Daldas, *Le Patriarcat* (as n. 33), 421.
36 The Diptychs regulate the protocol order within the Orthodox Church. See note 1.

Conclusion

Although the Ecumenical Patriarchate serves as the guarantor of unity and communion among the numerous autocephalous Orthodox Churches, it has been marginalised by the rise of the national Orthodox Churches, particularly that of the Patriarchate of Moscow. Using various theoretical perspectives, I have highlighted and analysed the efforts of the primate of the Orthodox Church to organise the Holy and Great Council as a crystallisation of its main, if not sole resource of power: diaspora. The ability of the Ecumenical Patriarchate to mobilise this issue is directly linked to its desire to counteract the diminution of its power in terms of territory and jurisdiction. Regarding the direction in which its resources are deployed, I argue that it is essentially a capitalisation of its power mainly through the symbols of authority. The multi-jurisdictional reality of the diaspora shows that the Ecumenical Patriarchate faces a challenging equation. This fact allows us to give another interpretation to the tensions between Constantinople and Moscow. The resistance facing the Ecumenical Patriarchate is also systemic: A communion of 14 local and canonical autocephalous Orthodox Churches implies a certain level of complexity in their mutual relations that creates limits on the primacy of Constantinople. The situation has become more complex after 2019 with the creation of the autocephalous Orthodox Church of Ukraine, which still does not enjoy Pan-Orthodox recognition and acceptance. The right balance between unity and diversity in the Orthodox world is thus at stake when we speak of the Ecumenical Patriarchate, the inter-Orthodox relations, as well as of the Pan-Orthodox process. One question remains, however, which is simultaneously a serious challenge: How can the Ecumenical Patriarchate effectively guarantee its power and implement its rights in the twenty-first century and in view of the continuous internal differentiation of the Orthodox world?

JURISDICTION

Using History as a Weapon: Jurisdictional Conflicts in Diverse Orthodox Contexts

Sebastian Rimestad

One of the fundamental teachings of the Orthodox Church is its emphasis on being the One, Holy, Apostolic and Catholic (i.e., all-embracing) Church of Christ that has remained faithful to the heritage of the Church Fathers of the first millennium until today. Unlike the Roman Catholic Church, which is more or less united organisationally under the Pope of Rome, the Orthodox Church is divided into several territorially defined administrative units, which are independent in practical matters, but united in faith. These units, called autocephalous churches, represent the fullness of the universal church and exist in a clearly delimited territory. Jurisdictional conflicts arise whenever these delimitations are contested, an issue that has become even more acute with the diminishing role of territoriality due to globalisation processes. This chapter attempts an analysis of several of these jurisdictional conflicts on the basis of how they employ historical narratives to prove their legitimacy.

The chapter is divided into five sections, beginning with a general overview over the notion of jurisdiction in the Orthodox Church. The three following sections analyse three different types of jurisdictional conflicts, called co-existence, secession, and protection. The jurisdictional conflicts in the areas outside the borders of the recognised autocephalous churches (the so-called diaspora) are not part of this chapter, although very similar conclusions can be drawn from these cases.[1] In the end, a small section attempts a general analysis of the topic and provides a few conclusions.

Jurisdiction

The term "jurisdiction" does not appear in the core texts of Orthodox canon law. Unlike in the Roman Catholic Church, where the term is hotly debated on a highly sophisticated theological level, the Orthodox Church discusses it only in relation to pragmatic issues. While the distinction between the power of ordination and the power of jurisdiction has worried Roman Catholic theologians at least since the twelfth century,[2] the Orthodox have resolved arising conflicts through

---

1 See Sebastian Rimestad, "The Russian Orthodox Church in Western Europe: One or Many?", *Religion, State & Society* 43 (2015) 228–243; Vassilis Pnevmatikakis, *La géopolitique de la diaspora orthodoxe en France: territoire, pouvoir, identité* (unpublished doctoral thesis), Paris 2014.

2 Laurent Villemin, *Pouvoir d'ordre et pouvoir de juridiction*, Paris 2003.

pragmatism and *oikonomia*.[3] Nevertheless, throughout history, the ecclesiology of the Orthodox Church has been much more affected by the question of jurisdiction than the Roman Catholic one, where all jurisdictional power emanates from the Pope. For, as Alexander Schmemann has argued, the ecclesiological reality of the Orthodox Church is the result of three layers of partly opposing canonical traditions.[4] The early church taught the absolute jurisdiction of the bishop within his diocese, which was the church universal in a concrete place. The bishops of a region, situated around a metropolitan bishop, regularly gathered together to consecrate new bishops and deal with the administrative and earthly matters of the church. These church "provinces" were grouped together in wider geographical areas, which again all accorded the primacy to the Bishop of Rome. This primacy, however, was not jurisdictional, but only one of honour and "solicitude".

According to Schmemann, this first and essentially Christian layer was gradually, from the fourth century onwards, supplemented by what he calls the "imperial" one. This layer was characterised by the inclusion of Christianity into the very political structure of the Roman Empire, soon to no longer include the western half of the Roman world and Rome itself. The main consequence of this development was that the structure of the church started to coincide with that of the empire, centred on its new capital – Constantinople. Schmemann argues that it was the imperial revaluation of the Christian hierarchy that enabled it to start talking about "jurisdiction" in the first place. The Bishop (Patriarch) of Constantinople was acknowledged theologically as *primus inter pares* – the first among equals –, while in the context of the Byzantine *symphonia*, he became the focal point of the church's jurisdictional power.

The third layer was the "national" one, which appeared from the nineteenth century onwards. According to Schmemann, the ideology of the "imperial" layer was being applied to the ethnically connoted new nations that emerged from the ailing Ottoman Empire. So, the Serbians, for example, when aiming for a secular, independent nation state, naturally perceived the need to also aim for its religious counterpart, an independent national church, which would have jurisdiction over all territories in the Serbian state. For Schmemann, it is important to keep in mind

3 Pierre L'Huillier, "Rapport entre pouvoirs d'ordre et de juridiction dans la tradition orientale", *Revue de droit canonique* 23 (1973) 281–289; John Erickson, "The 'Oikonomia' of Orders in Byzantine Canon Law", in Stephan Kuttner/Kenneth Pennington (eds), *Proceedings of the Sixth International Congress of Medieval Canon Law*, Vatican 1985, 259–270.

4 Alexander Schmemann, "A Meaningful Storm: Some Reflection on Autocephaly, Tradition and Ecclesiology", *St Vladimir's Theological Quarterly* 15 (1971) 4–27. Reprinted in idem, *Church, World, Mission: Reflections on Orthodoxy in the West*, Crestwood/NY 1979, 85–116.

> that this new "autocephalous" Church [...] is not a mere "jurisdictional" entity. Its main implication is not so much "independence" (for in fact it is usually totally dependent on the state), but precisely the national Church, or, in other words, the Church as the religious expression and projection of a nation, as indeed the bearer of national identity.[5]

The Russian Orthodox Church represents a prototype of this development, which was initialised before the rise of ethnic nationalism and thus slightly different from the later, more ethnically connoted national churches.

Whatever the merits of Schmemann's historical analysis in its details, it clearly shows that the notion of "jurisdiction" developed outside theological circles and has historically often been used by secular powers to project their political aims into the religious domain. Moreover, the original exclusive emphasis of territoriality in church structure has given way to an increased importance of identities. Especially in the modern globalising world, where the importance of distances is shrinking and processes of de-territorialisation and re-territorialisation across traditional geographical boundaries are occurring, it is not surprising that the idea of one church for one nation no longer carries a purely geographical meaning, but often alludes to the members of a nation, regardless of their geographical location.

At the same time, the theological discourse frantically tries to keep the focus on territorial delimitations. It is this oscillation between the territorial rhetoric and the national claim that is the cause of many jurisdictional conflicts, especially in the so-called diaspora, where each ethnically connoted church claims to speak on behalf of its co-nationals. But also in other cases, where a certain group of people feels misrepresented or left alone by the church they canonically belong to, this results in challenges to the jurisdiction of this church. These challenges exist in various forms, three of which are analysed in the following sections of this chapter. These three forms are ideal types, which are not mutually exclusive or even easily distinguishable.

The first form, "co-existence", is the case where two canonically valid jurisdictions co-exist on one and the same territory, both claiming to encompass this territory as a whole, but each catering essentially to a different social or national group. The most eminent examples of this form of jurisdictional conflict are Estonia and Moldova. Another form, called "secession", exists when one group, often inhabiting a specific territory, opts to secede from the church it canonically belongs to. This form is most clearly seen in (North) Macedonia and Montenegro, but also the ecclesiastical situation in Ukraine is an example of this type of conflict. The final form, "protection", is the case where a practically independent church needs protection or tutelage from a larger church in order to function. Yet, there is disagreement as to where this protection is to come from. This kind of conflict existed in Finland until 1957 and still latently exists in the

---

5 Schmemann, *Church, World, Mission* (as. n. 4), 97–99.

autocephalous Church of the Czech Lands and Slovakia. This is, moreover, the kind of conflict that is underlying most of the discussions concerning jurisdictional issues in the diaspora.

Co-Existence

As mentioned above, the paramount cases for this type of jurisdictional conflict are found in Estonia and Moldova. In both of these conflicts, the crux of the matter lies in the developments of the first half of the twentieth century. In the Estonian case, the key to the conflict lies in the periods 1917-1923 and 1940-1945. In the first period, the Orthodox community of Estonia emancipated itself from the tutelage of the Moscow Patriarchate, which underwent an extremely difficult period with the birth of the Soviet Union.[6] Even after having been granted wide autonomy by Patriarch Tikhon (Bellavin) of Moscow in 1920, the efforts for independence did not die, and the Estonian Orthodox leadership decided to join a Finnish state-sponsored Orthodox delegation heading to the Patriarchate of Constantinople to plead for full independence (i.e., autocephaly). This was not initially granted, but Patriarch Meletios IV (Metaxakis) of Constantinople offered to take the two autonomous churches into his jurisdiction due to the difficulties in communicating with the Patriarchate of Moscow at the time. The second period, 1940-1945, coincided with the integration of Estonia into the Soviet Union. This political integration was accompanied by an ecclesiastical integration, when Metropolitan Aleksander (Paulus) of Estonia was summoned to Moscow to publicly repent of the "schism" of 1923 and return to the jurisdiction of the Moscow Patriarchate.[7] During the German occupation of Estonia (1941-1944), Metropolitan Aleksander denied having consented to re-join the Moscow jurisdiction and continued to act as a Metropolitan of the Church of Estonia under Constantinople jurisdiction, even after having fled Estonia. He finally settled in Sweden and kept claiming he was the legitimate Metropolitan of all Estonia, while the Moscow Patriarchate had installed its own bishop there.

When the Soviet Union started to crumble in 1991, some disgruntled Orthodox clergymen in Soviet Estonia, together with the remaining clergy of the Estonian Orthodox Church in exile in Sweden, cherished the hope of a return to the inter-war autonomous church under Constantinople jurisdiction.[8] After the break-up of the Soviet Union, this group petitioned the Patriarchate of

6 Sebastian Rimestad, *The Challenges of Modernity to the Orthodox Church in Estonia and Latvia, 1917-1940*, Frankfurt/Main 2012, 73–96.

7 Daniela Kalkandjieva, *The Russian Orthodox Church, 1917-1948: From Decline to Resurrection*, Abingdon 2015, 122–125.

8 Sebastian Rimestad, "Orthodox Churches in Estonia", in Lucian N. Leustean (ed.), *Eastern Christianity and Politics in the Twenty-First Century*, London 2014, 295–311.

Constantinople to reinstate the decision of 1923, which had been declared ineffective in 1978. The result was the co-existence of two canonically valid jurisdictions of Constantinople and Moscow, both claiming to encompass the entire Estonian territory. Their co-existence has been extensively treated elsewhere,[9] so this chapter is only concerned with the deployment of historical arguments on both sides of the conflict.

The real history of the Orthodox Church in Estonia, as outlined above, is rather undisputed, but it is the significance of these historical actions that is at stake. For the supporters of the Church under Constantinople, the ethnic Estonians are the actors in the history of the church, and these actors emancipated themselves from Russian tutelage when Estonia became independent in the interwar period. During World War II, they became the victims of Russian and Soviet power politics, aimed at reinstating Russian dominance in the local Orthodox Church. This legacy of Russian custodianship continued even after the fall of the Soviet Union, and only with the return to the jurisdiction of Constantinople were the Estonian Orthodox again free to develop organically. For the proponents of belonging to the Moscow Patriarchate, the main actors are the Orthodox Russians of Estonia, who were sidestepped by aggressive Estonian nationalists during the interwar period. The interwar Estonian Orthodox Church was just an aberration, which in important respects left true Orthodoxy. The reintegration into the Russian "Mother Church" during World War II was simply a return to the true and correct order of things. After Estonian independence in 1991, history started to repeat itself, again with aggressive Estonian nationalists distracting from true Orthodoxy to achieve political goals.

These narratives have been extensively published in various languages.[10] Moreover, the publications are often conceived of as replies to the "attacks" of the other side. In order to suggest trustworthiness, most of these works include reproductions of archival documents, often with translations. The interesting point about this issue is that the documents provided in the pro-Moscow publications and those of the pro-Constantinople side do not always overlap. As an example, the second volume of the publication *Pravoslavie v Estonii* (Orthodox Faithful in

---

9 Ibid.

10 On the one hand, Grigorios D. Papathomas/Matthias H. Palli (eds), *The Autonomous Orthodox Church of Estonia*, Katérini 2002; Grigorios D. Papathomas, *Õnnetus olla väike kirik väikesel maal. Teoloogiline tõde Eesti Õigeusu Kiriku kohta* [The Misfortune of Being a Small Church in a Small Country. The Theological Truth about the Estonian Orthodox Church], Tallinn 2007; Stephanos (Charalambidis)/Jean-François Jolivalt, *La véritable histoire des Orthodoxes d'Estonie*, Paris 2012; and a special issue on Estonia of the French journal *Istina* 49 (2004). On the other hand, there is Igor Prekup, *Православие в Эстонии* [Orthodox Faithful in Estonia], Tartu 1998; Patriarch Aleksii II of Moscow, *Православие в Эстонии* [Orthodox Faithful in Estonia], Moscow 1999; Igor Prekup/ Nikolai Balashov (eds), *Православие в Эстонии* [Orthodox Faithful in Estonia], Vols. 1-2, Moscow 2010.

Estonia), published in Moscow in 2010, includes 234 documents, of which 71 pertain to the period prior to 1991. The English language publication of the Greek canon law specialist Grigorios Papathomas and the Estonian Orthodox priest Mattias Palli from 2001 includes 18 pre-1991 documents. However, only 13 of the documents are reproduced in both publications. In other words, there are five documents, which the pro-Moscow side deemed unnecessary to publish or unsuitable to underline their argument. The same goes the other way around. Neither side can credibly claim to neutrally describe the "true history", even if the last book to date in this controversy bears exactly this title: "The veritable history of Estonia's Orthodox".[11]

The Moldovan case is a very similar one, although it has received much less scholarly attention. This is probably because the stakes are not as high here. In this case, the two opposing Patriarchates are the Patriarchate of Moscow and that of Bucharest of the Romanian Orthodox Church. Both of them emerged anew in the post-communist world and regained their positions as strong and influential actors in church politics and beyond that. The fact that the Patriarchate of Constantinople does not have a stake in this conflict makes this case much less international than the Estonian one. The church in the territory of what is today the Republic of Moldova – historically called Bessarabia – has had a similarly disputed history as its Estonian counterpart.[12] Until 1812, Bessarabia was part of the Ottoman Empire, and the church was under the jurisdiction of the Patriarchate of Constantinople. Between 1812 and 1918, it was part of the Russian Empire, with the church reporting to Moscow. With the establishment of Greater Romania in 1918, Bessarabia was also incorporated into the new state while its church became the Metropolis of Bessarabia within the Romanian Orthodox Church. With Soviet occupation in 1940, and after a brief intermezzo again in 1944, the Metropolis ceased to exist and was turned into a mere Eparchy of the Russian Orthodox Church.

After the end of the Soviet Union and once Moldova had become an independent state, the Patriarchate of Bucharest started to work for a re-establishment of its Metropolis of Bessarabia as well. Already in December 1992, the Patriarchate declared the Metropolis as re-established, with Bishop Petru Păduraru at its helm. Bishop Petru had previously been a bishop of the Russian Orthodox Church, which defrocked him for transgressing the canonical norms of the church. However, this structure under Romanian jurisdiction was not recognised on the state level until after a decision from the European Court of Human Rights in 2001 obliged the Moldovan state to register it as a religious

11 Stephanos/Jolivalt, *La véritable histoire* (as n. 10). See also my review of the book in *Revue d'Histoire Ecclésiastique* 111/1-2 (2016) 340–343.

12 Andrei Avram, "Orthodox Churches in Moldova", in Lucian N. Leustean (ed.), *Eastern Christianity and Politics in the Twenty-First Century*, London 2014, 402–425.

organisation.[13] Currently, both structures continue to exist side by side and no solution to their conflict is in sight.

Again, as in the Estonian case, the objective side of history is rather undisputed, and it is the interpretation of important historical turning points that is at stake. In a statement published on the Moscow Patriarchate's website on the occasion of the Patriarchate of Bucharest's re-establishment of the three eparchies of the Metropolis of Bessarabia, the following narrative can be found:

> The current decision of the Holy Synod of the Romanian Church is a continuation and aggravation of its previous decision from 19 December 1992 on the "Re-activation of the Metropolis of Bessarabia in the Republic of Moldova". This structure, originally established by the Romanian Orthodox Church in 1918, after Romanian troops occupied the area between the Dniester and Prut rivers, which since 1813 had been the Kishinev diocese of the Russian Orthodox Church, was arbitrarily and unilaterally included in the Romanian Church under the name of "Metropolis of Bessarabia" and all bishops who disagreed with the decision were expelled from Bessarabia. Twice in 1918, St Tikhon, Patriarch of Moscow and All Russia, in his letters to the Holy Synod of the Romanian Church voiced his protest against this unlawful act, urging to resolve contentious religious issues through proper canonical relations between the Russian and Romanian Churches and with the participation of the clergy and people of the Kishinev diocese itself, but this fraternal appeal of the martyr saint remained unanswered. It was only in 1940 that the Kishinev Diocese was restored to the bosom of the Russian Orthodox Church.[14]

In the narrative of the Patriarchate of Bucharest, the events of 1918 are differently interpreted. The correspondence with Patriarch Tikhon of Moscow was regarded "as a sign that the Moscow Patriarchate church was open to bring together the Romanians", who saw "the will of the people" clearly on their side. [15] The obvious breach of the natural development occurred only in 1940 and again in 1944, when Soviet forces occupied Bessarabia and the church was forced to disappear.

According to the Tiraspol historian Viacheslav A. Sodol', historical research on Moldovan church history is "clearly politically motivated, openly anti-Soviet and at times even russophobic […] In fact, the priority for the researchers seems not to be the search for historical accuracy, but to serve the political interests of

13 Metropolitan Church of Bessarabia and Others v. Moldova (27.03.2002), Application No. 45701/99. The final ruling is available online at URL: http://hudoc.echr.coe.int/eng?i=001-59985 [17.03.2016].

14 "Заявление Священного Синода Русской Православной Церкви в связи с решением Румынской Православной Церкви об учреждении ее епархий на территории Молдавии и Украины" [Memorandum of the Holy Synod of the Russian Orthodox Church in Connection with the Decision by the Romanian Orthodox Church to Restore its Eparchies on Moldovan and Ukrainian Territories], 07.11.2007. URL: http://www.patriarchia.ru/db/text/318310.html [21.04.2017].

15 See Stelian Gombos, "Mitropolia Basarabiei" [The Metropolis of Bessarabia], 28.07.2009, section 7, URL: http://www.crestinortodox.ro/religie/mitropolia-basarabiei-135353.html [21.04.2017].

the unionists [i.e., the Romania-friendly Moldovans] in their fight with an unpleasant past".[16] Most certainly, it is possible to find similar strong condemnations of this "dominant" historiography from the Romanian side of the conflict as well.

The main difference between the Moldovan and Estonian case is not the issue of contention, which is virtually identical, but rather the scope of the conflict. In the Estonian case, the two most important patriarchates, Moscow and Constantinople, argue about a religious minority in an EU state. The Estonian state, although nominally neutral, is clearly leaning towards the Constantinople side, allowing the Patriarchate of Moscow to construct the conflict as one of the "West" vs. the "East". In Moldova, the Patriarchate of Moscow is up against the Patriarchate of Bucharest, which has less means and resources to influence and control the religious majority of a post-Soviet state on the edge of Europe. Moreover, the Moldovan state clearly leans towards the Moscow side. The polemic literature originating from the Estonian case is much more comprehensible and international than in the Moldovan case, although the historical narratives informing them remain remarkably similar.

Secession

The jurisdictional conflicts of the secession type relate to Orthodox communities intending to secede from what the Orthodox mainstream recognises as their canonical "Mother Church". Most often, this is because they do not feel represented by their "Mother Church", primarily for political reasons. The most prominent cases of this type of conflict are found in (North) Macedonia,[17] Montenegro and Ukraine, but also in Abkhazia and South Ossetia. There are similar autocephalist movements latently in Belarus and Latvia as well. Autocephaly is the full independence of an Orthodox Church from its canonical "Mother Church", a phenomenon that became fundamental in the Orthodox world following Schmemann's third layer of canonical tradition, namely nationalism. Its theological significance above the level of the individual diocese and the procedural question of its proclamation are still not fully clarified. However, as

---

16 Viacheslav A. Sodol', "Церковная история как орудие политической борьбы в историографии республики молдовы" [Church History as a Tool of the Political Struggle in the Historiography of the Republic of Moldova], in *Политическая фальсификация истории как барьер на пути демократического реформирования международных отношении на постсоветском пространстве* [The Political Falsification of History as a Hindrance on the Way to the Democratic Reform of International Relations in the Post-Soviet World], Tiraspol' 2009, 124–128, here 127.

17 The long-standing name dispute of this country with neighbouring Greece has been resolved by the Prespa Agreement of 2018. The unrecognised Orthodox Church in North Macedonia still bears the name "Macedonian Orthodox Church".

Schmemann pointed out, having an autocephalous church was vital for the national identity of the new states arising from the collapsing Ottoman and Russian Empires in the nineteenth and twentieth centuries.[18]

From a more recent perspective, this also seems to have been an important development after the break-up of Yugoslavia, when next to the Serbian Orthodox Church, which claims jurisdiction to all of the territory of former Yugoslavia, alternative church structures have appeared in (North) Macedonia and Montenegro.[19] Quite significantly, both of them can point to earlier historical and significant autocephalous churches – the Archbishopric of Ohrid (North Macedonia) and the Archbishopric of Cetinje (Montenegro). The autocephaly of the Archbishopric of Ohrid was abolished by the Patriarchate of Constantinople already in 1766, while the Montenegrin church autocephaly disappeared with the establishment of a common church jurisdiction for all Yugoslavia in 1920. In the case of the Macedonian autocephalists, their project dates back to the 1960s, when Yugoslavian leader Josip Broz Tito encouraged the creation of a separate Macedonian Church structure, which the hierarchy of the Serbian Church staunchly opposed. The conflict in Montenegro started in the 1990s, when Montenegrin nationalists founded a new church structure. Neither church has received canonical recognition by any of the other Orthodox Churches, which basically see in these cases inner-Serbian conflicts.

As far as the deployment of history in the argumentations of these church structures is concerned: It is not necessarily the wrongdoings of others that stand in the foreground, but rather one's own historical greatness. The Macedonian Orthodox Church uses the glorious history of the Archbishopric of Ohrid as an argument to its own existence today, eager to hush away its political activities in the twentieth century. For the Montenegrin Orthodox Church, the creation of a Duklja historical identity, where it holds a special place of honour, stands at the forefront of its ambitions.[20] As for the canonical guarantor of both of these churches, namely the Serbian Orthodox Church, on the other hand, the historical continuity cannot bypass its valid jurisdiction in both these areas, with the two church structures being nothing but the results of an unlawful rebellion. This is the opinion that most mainstream Orthodox authorities share, leaving little hope for either of the two churches to gain full recognition soon. For the Macedonian Orthodox Church, there have been negotiations giving hope for some kind of solution, but at this point in time this solution seems as far away as ever.[21]

---

18 Schmemann, "A Meaningful Storm" (as n. 4). See also Ernst Christoph Suttner, "Von 'Kirchennationen' zu Nationalkirchen", in idem (ed.), *Kirche in einer zueinander rückenden Welt*, Würzburg 2003, 685–700.

19 See also the contributions by Nenad Živković and Emil Hilton Saggau in this volume.

20 See esp. the contribution by Emil Hilton Saggau in this volume.

21 See the contribution by Nenad Živković in this volume.

The ecclesiastical situation in Ukraine is immensely complicated, as three different Orthodox Church structures have competed for the title of the Ukrainian Orthodox Church since the end of the Soviet Union. Since January 2019, the three structures have become two, as Patriarch Bartholomew of Constantinople accorded autocephaly to the Orthodox Church of Ukraine (OCU), essentially a merger of two of the previous structures.[22] Finally, the Ukrainian Greek Catholic Church (UGCC) of Byzantine Rite, but in union with the Roman Catholic Church, complicates matters even further.[23]

Each of these church structures has a specific historical narrative, which it deploys to legitimate itself. First, the Ukrainian Orthodox Church of the Moscow Patriarchate (UOC(MP)) was the sole canonically legitimate Orthodox Church in Ukraine for three decades. It claims continuity from the Baptism of the Kievan Rus' in 988 until today. Second, the Ukrainian Autocephalous Orthodox Church (UAOC), officially founded in the 1920s, also claimed this continuity, while accusing the Moscow Patriarchate of having unlawfully incorporated the Ukrainian lands into its jurisdiction in the seventeenth century. The third church structure, the Ukrainian Orthodox Church of the Kyiv Patriarchate (UOC(KP)),

---

22 The Ukrainian President Petro Proroshenko, with the backing of the Ukrainian Parliament, sent numerous letters to Patriarch Bartholomew of Constantinople, begging the latter – as the first among equals in the Orthodox Church – to resolve the difficult ecclesiastical situation in Ukraine. On 27 July 2018, Constantinople answered in a letter promising to investigate the issue. From this moment onwards, developments quickly succeeded. On 31 August 2018, Bartholomew met with Patriarch Kirill of Moscow in Istanbul, specifically to discuss the Ukrainian issue. Both patriarchs left the meeting claiming that it had been constructive, yet unresolving. Less than two weeks later, on 9 September 2018, Constantinople decided to send two of its American bishops with Ukrainian roots to Ukraine to investigate the local situation, an act which the Russian Orthodox Church immediately condemned. After about a month, on 11 October 2018, Constantinople declared the leaders of the two non-recognised Ukrainian Orthodox Churches canonical, namely Filaret (Denysenko) of the Kyiv Patriarchate and Makary (Maletich) of the Ukrainian Autocephalous Orthodox Church, thus overriding two and a half decades of tacit acknowledgement of their excommunication by Moscow. Moscow responded on 15 October 2018 by unilaterally breaking off the communion with the Patriarchate of Constantinople. A "Unification Council" was subsequently held in Kyiv on 15 December 2018, at which all Orthodox Bishops in Ukraine were invited, regardless of ecclesiastical affiliation and jurisdiction. However, only two bishops of the previously dominant church in Ukraine, the Ukrainian Orthodox Church (Moscow Patriarchate), officially participated in the council, which decided to dissolve the two formerly unrecognised church structures and create the Orthodox Church of Ukraine, with Metropolitan Epiphany (Dumenko, formerly Patriarchate of Kyiv) at its head. The official *tomos* from Constantinople, proclaimimg the Ukrainian autocephaly, was handed over to Metropolitan Epiphany on 07 January 2019, who was officially enthroned a month later.

23 A good overview is provided in Natalia Shlikhta, "The Ukrainian Greek Catholic Church" in Lucian N. Leustean (ed.), *Eastern Christianity and Politics in the Twenty-First Century*, London 2014, 623–655.

dated only from the early 1990s, when then Metropolitan of Kyiv, Filaret (Denisenko) refused to step down in favour of Metropolitan Volodymyr (Sabodan), who was designated by Moscow to take over. Their historical narrative is very similar to the one of the UAOC. The American scholar of Ukrainian origin Nicholas Denysenko characterised the developments since 1990 in this way:

> When political and societal upheaval created an opportunity for the Ukrainian Church to claim its independence, the Russian Church responded by granting the Ukrainians ecclesial autonomy. From the Russian perspective, this canonical act honored the Ukrainian desire to capture and reclaim its native religious identity without severing the bonds that had been deepened between Russia and Ukraine since the late sixteenth century. When the autocephalist Ukrainians took autocephaly outside of the canonical parameters of global Orthodoxy, Russians viewed this act as hostile, which could only be motivated by nationalism, which was foreign to Orthodox theology. The Russian Church responded to the autocephalist movement by labelling it as both uncanonical and schismatic, employing canonical and sacramental terms drawn from the repository of ecclesiastical history […]
> Obviously, the UGCC and the autocephalist Orthodox Ukrainians do not share the Russian view of ecclesial history. The autocephalist Orthodox Ukrainians believe that Russians have attempted to mute Ukrainian religious identity until it no longer exists. The process of restoring and reclaiming genuine Ukrainian religious identity can occur only under the aegis of complete ecclesiastical independence from Russia, which would stop the process of coercive Russification.[24]

In other words, the crux of the conflict once again lies not in the objective facts of history, but in their interpretation. From a Ukrainian autocephalist standpoint, the Russians have unduly interfered in Ukrainian religious affairs and organisation for half a millennium. The Russian standpoint, on the other hand, argues that Ukrainians and Russians belong together and cannot develop separately.[25] For the Patriarchate of Constantinople, the main incentive leading to the proclamation of Ukrainian autocephaly was a document from 1686 in which the transfer of direct authority over the Metropolis of Kyiv was determined. According to the canonists, this document stated that the Moscow Patriarch was entitled to name the Metropolitan of Kyiv, even though the latter still recognised the Patriarchate of Constantinople as his "Mother Church".[26] The autocephalists

24 Nicholas Denysenko, "Intra-Christian Conflict in Ukraine: Historical Foundations and a Theological Proposal", URL: https://www.academia.edu/12890997/_Intra-Christian_Conflict_in_Ukraine_Historical_Foundations_and_a_Theological_Proposal_ [21.04. 2017].

25 See also Alfons Brüning, "Orthodoxie als Element ukrainischer nationaler Identität", in Thomas Bremer (ed.), *Religion und Nation. Die Situation der Kirchen in der Ukraine*, Wiesbaden 2003, 11–23.

26 Cyril Hovorun, "Комментарии к Константинопольским синодальным грамотам 1686 года" [Comments on Constantinople's Synodal Decision of 1686], 06.11.2018, URL: https://www.linkedin.com/pulse/комментарии-к-константинопольским-синодальным-грамотам-cyril-hovorun/ [22.02.2019]. The Greek original of the document itself was published in Vera G. Tchentsova, "Синодальное решение 1686 г. о Киевской

welcomed this interpretation, allowing the Patriarchate of Constantinople to reaffirm its legitimate duties as "Mother Church" to settle the conflict. For the UOC(MP) and the Moscow Patriarchate, the 1686 document was obsolete, as it had not been enforced for centuries and reflected a long-gone *status quo*, not providing any legitimacy to the aspiring role of Constantinople in Ukraine.

As Denysenko has argued, the churches of Ukraine do not so much engage in a constructive historiographical exercise, but rather "play the blame game", mutually accusing each other of fundamental theological and historical wrong-doings.[27] The Ukrainian case is further exacerbated by the war-like conflict dividing the country since 2013, which renders mutual understanding among the various church entities very difficult indeed.[28] The proclamation of autocephaly was followed by a unilateral break in communion between the Russian Orthodox Church and Constantinople. It is too early to say what this means for Orthodoxy in Ukraine, which is more torn than ever before, and worldwide.[29] At the time of writing, no other Orthodox Church has officially followed the Russian Church in de-legitimising Constantinople. Although some Orthodox Churches (e.g., the Orthodox Church of Greece, the Patriarchate of Alexandria) have officially recognised Ukrainian autocephaly and backed Constantinople's policies, most of them still refrain from doing so and keep a rather cautious and tactful attitude towards both conflicting parties. Hence, the whole issue will stay with the Orthodox world in the future, given that the stakes are so high.[30]

Two more cases that belong to the secession type are the Churches of Abkhazia and South Ossetia, which have declared their independence from the Georgian Orthodox Church.[31] Both of these churches claim historical continuity to previously existing entities in their respective territories, but neither of them carries any political weight or has been able to achieve canonical recognition from another Orthodox Church. The historical narratives of each of these church

---

митрополии" [The Synodal Decision of 1686 about the Kyiv Metropolis], *Древняя Русь. Вопросы медиевистики* 2/68 (2017) 89–110.

27 Denysenko, "Intra-Christian Conflict" (as n. 24), 15–16.

28 See also the contribution by Oleg Kyselov in this volume.

29 See the analysis by Iannis Carras, "Moscow, Kyiv, Constantinople: What Happens after the Ukrainian Church Crisis?", *Open Democracy* 21.02.2019, URL: https://www.opendemocracy.net/od-russia/iannis-carras/moscow-kyiv-constantinople-what-happens-after-ukrainian-church-crisis [22.02.2019].

30 In this context, the independent Russian analyst Sergei Chapnin talked about the hesitant responses from the rest of the Orthodox world: Sergei Chapnin, "Рождение третьей силы?" [The Birth of a Third Force?], *colta.ru*, 22.02.2019, URL: https://www.colta.ru/articles/media/20550-rozhdenie-tretiey-sily [22.02.2019]. English translation: URL: https://www.facebook.com/panorthodox.synod/posts/2366230423608460?__tn__=K-R [22.02.2019].

31 Kimitaka Matsuzato, "Orthodox Churches in Abkhazia, South Ossetia and Transnistria", in Lucian N. Leustean (ed.), *Eastern Christianity and Politics in the Twenty-First Century*, London 2014, 387–401.

entities are probably similar to those in Ukraine, with strenuous continuities and mutual accusations of previous wrongdoings. The same can be argued in the case of Latvia, where individual clerics, mostly suspended from their duties, wage a war against the established hierarchy of the local Russian Orthodox Church in order to re-establish the Latvian Orthodox Church under the jurisdiction of the Patriarchate of Constantinople that existed briefly before World War II.[32]

Protection

This final type of jurisdictional conflict occurs over churches that are already recognised as autocephalous. In fact, if the Orthodox Church had taken its ecclesiology more seriously, this kind of conflict should never have occurred. However, several instances of this kind of conflict have happened over the course of the last century; most recently, following the demission of Archbishop Kryštof (Pulec) of Prague, Metropolitan of the Czech Lands and Slovakia in April 2013 after allegations of illicit relations with women.[33] The tiny Orthodox Church of the Czech Lands and Slovakia, numbering about 75,000 faithful, is nevertheless recognised by all other Orthodox Churches as an autocephalous church. Consequently, it should have been able to legitimately assure its own succession.

However, complications arose during the meeting of the Czech and Slovak Synod in December 2013, summoned to elect a new Bishop of Prague and select the new Metropolitan. This was because two representatives of the Russian Orthodox Church appeared next to the two observers from the Patriarchate of Constantinople that had been invited by the acting head of the church, Archbishop Simeon (Jakovlević). With the intervention of the Russia side, Simeon was deposed, and Archbishop Rastislav (Gont) of Prešov and Slovakia was designated to replace him. Moreover, a young monk, which Simeon had deemed unsuitable,

32 The most prolific of such writers is Jānis Kalniņš, *Latvijas Pareizticīga Baznīca Vēstures komentars* [The Latvian Orthodox Church – A Historical Commentary], Riga 2007. See also Inese Runce/Jelena Avanesova, "The Latvian Orthodox Church", in Lucian N. Leustean (ed.), *Eastern Christianity and Politics in the Twenty-First Century*, London 2014, 370–386.

33 "Предстоятель Православной Церкви Чешских земель и Словакии подал в отставку" [The Primate of the Orthodox Church of the Czech Lands and Slovakia resigned], 13.04.2013, URL: http://www.bogoslov.ru/text/3222110/index.html [21.04.2017]; Stanislav Matveev, "Contemporary Influence of the Russian Orthodox Church within the 'Autocephalous' Orthodox Church of the Czech Lands and Slovakia", *Kremlin Watch Report*, 04.10.2018, 12, URL: https://www.kremlinwatch.eu/userfiles/contemporary-influence-of-the-russian-orthodox-church-within-the-autocephalous-orthodox-church-of-the-czech-lands-and-slovakia.pdf [22.02.2019].

was elected new Bishop of Prague.[34] Simeon went on to consider himself the only canonical bishop left in the Czech Lands and Slovakia, while Rastislav was official named Metropolitan in January 2014. The Patriarchate of Moscow welcomed Rastislav as the new head of the Czechoslovak Orthodox Church, while the Patriarchate of Constantinople clung to Simeon and refused to recognise Rastislav. The situation remained unresolved until Rastislav sent a letter of repentance to Patriarch Bartholomew I of Constantinople in January 2016, who decided to formally recognise him and end the latent schism.[35]

This conflict of jurisdiction therefore occurred over the legitimate succession within an autocephalous church. The conflict was about which of the two most powerful Patriarchates in the Orthodox World had the right to influence the decision-making in the weak Czechoslovak Orthodox Church – the Patriarchate of Constantinople or that of Moscow. Officially, each autocephalous church has the right to decide on its own, but there obviously exist newly founded and small churches, which are less capable of doing so. Hence, there is a conflict of historiographies also in this case, since the Moscow-friendly bishops in this church prefer to see the year 1951 as the birth date of the Czechoslovak Church, when the Moscow Patriarchate formally granted it autocephaly.[36] Archbishop Simeon, on the contrary, dates this autocephaly only since 1998, namely when the Patriarchate of Constantinople signed a new *tomos* of autocephaly.[37]

These two opposing views of history do not only concern the date of achieving autocephalous status. An anonymous historical overview, obviously written by someone with an affiliation to the Moscow Patriarchate, heavily criticises the Constantinople *tomos* of historical insensitivity:

34 "Patriarcha Bartoloměj je zděšen!!!" [Patriarch Bartholomew is horrified !!!], 31.12.2013, URL: http://www.pravoslavnacirkev.info/aktuality/zpravodajstvi/740-patriarcha-bartolomej-je-zdesen-arcibiskup-simeon-byl-odvolan-nikoliv-kanonickym-postupem-ale-spise-nepruhlednymi-a-neprijatelnymi-zpusoby-synod-funguje-nezdrave-a-svevolne-usneseni-synodu-jsou-neplatna-arcibiskup-simeon-zustava-metropolitnim-spravcem [21.04.2017]; "Statement of Archbishop Simeon", 09.12.2013, URL: http://pravoslavi.cz/church-in-schisma.htm [20.03.2016].

35 "Le Patriarcat œcuménique a reconnu le métropolite Rostislav, primat de l'Église orthodoxe des Terres tchèques et de Slovaquie", 14.01.2016, URL: http://orthodoxie.com/le-patriarcat-oecumenique-a-reconnu-le-metropolite-rostislav-primat-de-leglise-orthodoxe-des-terres-tcheques-et-de-slovaquie/ [21.04.2017].

36 Kalkandjieva, *The Russian Orthodox Church* (as n. 7), 337; Vladimir Bureha, "Чехословацкая Православная Церковь: путь к автокефалии" [The Czechoslovak Orthodox Church: The Road to Autocephaly", 05.12.2001, URL: http://www.pravoslavie.ru/orthodoxchurches/39938.htm [21.04.2017]; Matveev, "Contemporary Influence" (as n. 33), 9.

37 "Patriarcha Bartoloměj je zděšen!!!" (as n. 34); Bureha, "Чехословацкая Православная Церковь" (as n. 36); Matveev, "Contemporary Influence" (as n. 33), 10.

> Describing the Christianisation of the Great Moravian Empire, the authors of the *tomos* mention the mission of Saints Cyril and Methodius who came here from Constantinople. But they do not take into account the subsequent history of Christianity in the Czech Lands. We find no mention here that Saint Methodius was consecrated bishop in Rome and until his death remained in the jurisdiction of the Archbishop of Rome. Nothing is said about the fact that the successor of Saint Methodius – Saint Gorazd I – had to leave Moravia for Serbia. Generally, the *tomos* is silent about everything that happened in the Czech Lands between the death of Saint Methodius and the consecration of Archbishop Sawatij.[38] The *tomos* does not include a single mention of the personality and activity of the Holy Martyr Gorazd.[39] It also omits the fact of the many years' obedience to Serbian jurisdiction over the Czech lands. The granting of autocephaly to the Church of Czechoslovakia in 1951 is also not mentioned, but from the context of the document, one almost certainly can assume that the authors have a negative attitude to this historical fact.[40]

In fact, as a sober historiographical treatment of interwar Orthodoxy in Czechoslovakia would show,[41] the situation here very much resembles the current conflict in Estonia, where one Patriarchate claims territorial continuity, while parts of the local Orthodox community prefer to turn to Constantinople. The Czechoslovak conflict of the 1920s ended when Bishop Sawatij, formally under Constantinople jurisdiction, was pushed to the margins and Bishop Gorazd under Serbian jurisdiction became the only face of Czechoslovak Orthodoxy.[42] Russian Church involvement started only after World War II, when Bishop Gorazd had been executed by the Germans and Sawatij had disappeared into oblivion, since "his" church officially never had existed.[43] In this vacuum, the Moscow Patriarchate found a place to enter the scene and actively integrated the

38 Sawatij of Prague and all Czechoslovakia became the first Czechoslovak Bishop in 1923, when Constantinople granted autonomy to his church. Pavel Marek/Jurij Danilec, "Contribution to the Knowledge of Archbishop Sawatij's Activities in Subcarpathian Ruthenia in the First Half of the 20th Century", *Kultúrne dejiny* 5 (2014) 58–79, here 61; Matveev, "Contemporary Influence" (as n. 33), 9.

39 Gorazd was Bishop of Moravia and Silesia in the interwar period. He remained under the jurisdiction of the Church of Serbia throughout his life and was executed by German Nazis in 1942. See Kalkandjieva, *The Russian Orthodox Church* (as n. 7), 219; Matveev, "Contemporary Influence" (as n. 33), 8.

40 Bureha, "Чехословацкая Православная Церковь" (as n. 36).

41 There is such a work available in Czech language (Pavel Marek/Volodymyr Bureha, *Pravoslavní v Československu v letech 1918-1953* [The Orthodox Faithful in Czechoslovakia in the years 1918-1953], Brno 2008). Since then, the two authors have published shorter works in Russian and English regarding specific aspects of this history. In addition, Sergei Matveev from the Russia-critical think-tank *Kremlin Watch* has provided an analysis of the current conflict: See Matveev, "Contemporary Influence" (as n. 33).

42 Marek/Danilec, "Contribution" (as n. 38), 65.

43 Marek/Bureha, *Pravoslavní* (as n. 41), 444–445.

Czechoslovak Church in Moscow-friendly church structures, before granting this re-formed church autocephaly in 1951.[44]

The current jurisdictional conflict is thus again one between the Patriarchates of Constantinople and Moscow, who use historical narratives and omissions to underscore the legitimacy of their tutelage, while other facts are also used to discredit the respective opponent. A very similar development can be observed in the case of the Polish Orthodox Church, although there is no jurisdictional conflict in this case. The Polish Orthodox Church, similarly to the other Orthodox Churches in the countries emanating from the fall of the Russian Empire, sought for ways to legitimise its independence in the 1920s.[45] The Polish secular authorities strongly pressed for a solution not involving Moscow, which was regarded as an oppressor and arch-rival. The bishops then turned to the Patriarchate of Constantinople, which eventually granted the Polish Church autocephaly in 1924. After World War II, with the expansion of the Soviet sphere of influence also over Poland, the Patriarchate of Moscow pressured the Polish Church into officially repenting the 1924 jurisdictional switch and returning to the bosom of the Russian "Mother Church" in 1948.[46] Concurrently with this humiliation, the Polish Church was anew granted autocephaly, but this time from Moscow. In the Polish Orthodox Church today, there is disagreement as to its correct date of birth – 1924 or 1948 –, but so far, no conflict. This can be attributed either to the more sizeable Polish Orthodox community, which does not need outside assistance, or to the fact that the Constantinople *tomos* came first and claims temporal priority over the Russian involvement.

Another church where the Moscow Patriarchate has attempted to regain its influence after having lost it is the Church of Finland. This church had left Moscow for Constantinople together with the Estonian Church back in 1923. The negotiations for a return to Moscow jurisdiction initiated after World War II, however, were not crowned with success.[47] Hence, the Patriarchate of Moscow grudgingly recognised the Constantinople autonomy of the Finnish Church in 1957. In the case of the Orthodox Church of Georgia, its ancient autocephaly (fifth century) had been abolished after the Russian expansion into Georgia in 1811 and was re-established only in 1943.[48] The Patriarchate of Constantinople officially acknowledged this autocephaly with a *tomos* in 1990. Since the *tomos* makes numerous references to the ancient roots of Georgian autocephaly, it has not

---

44 Kalkandjieva, *The Russian Orthodox Church* (as n. 7), 218–224; Matveev, "Contemporary Influence" (as n. 33), 9.

45 Antoni Mironowicz, *Kościół prawosławny na ziemiach polskich w XIX i XX wieku* [The Orthodox Church in the Polish Lands in the 19th and 20th Centuries], Białystok 2005, 84–124.

46 Ibid., 245–249; Kalkandjieva *The Russian Orthodox Church* (as n. 7), 226–231.

47 Kalkandjieva, *The Russian Orthodox Church* (as n. 7), 231–233.

48 Ibid., 186–187.

provoked any conflict so far. Furthermore, the relationship between the Georgian and Russian Churches is troubled with many other issues, such as the Abkhazian and South Ossetian question.

Finally, the situation of the Orthodox Church in Hungary, and more generally in the so-called Orthodox Diaspora communities, existing outside the canonically recognised borders of the various autocephalous churches, also often fit into this kind of conflicts. Without going into too much detail here, some of these communities do not have a "Mother Church" as such, and therefore try to use historical arguments to justify one or another jurisdictional affiliation. A prime example is the Archdiocese of Orthodox Parishes of Russian Tradition in Western Europe – Exarchate of the Patriarchate of Constantinople. This exarchate, which traces its origins back to the Russian emigration to France in the 1920s, left the jurisdiction of the Moscow Patriarchate in 1931, after demands from the latter that its bishop should openly support the Soviet regime, and switched to the jurisdiction of the Patriarchate of Constantinople.[49] The further history of the Exarchate includes several attempts of the Constantinople Patriarchate to usher it back to its Russian "Mother Church". Each time, however, influential voices argued historically against such a move by reference to the unique historical path of the Exarchate in the Russian emigration as the only church community fully embracing the spirit of the Moscow Council of 1917/18. However, this situation changed in recent years, especially since Patriarch Bartholomew decided in November 2018 to dissolve the Exarchate in the context of the establishment of the autocephalous Ukrainian Orthodox Church.[50] The Exarchate tried for more than a year to dispute this decision, yet unsuccessfully. In the course of 2019, the Exarchate parishes joined various church jurisdictions, often following internal splits.

Conclusion

In most of these cases, history serves as a tool to achieve an underlying objective of church politics, be it seeking for the support of certain nationalists or legitimating and enhancing one's own position in the hierarchy. For many of the conflicts, several such objectives are closely intertwined and do not lend themselves to an easy analysis. Additionally, the sometimes-significant language pluralism inherent in these incidents – language being the main distinguishing factor for many of these projects – does not simplify their analysis. In any case, the conflicts can be analysed from a purely secular point of view, in which one runs the risk of forgetting that the church conceives of itself as a divinely inspired,

---

49 Ibid., 44–48.

50 Rimestad, "The Russian Orthodox Church" (as n. 1). See also Carras, "Moscow, Kyiv, Constantinople" (as n. 29).

but human-built structure. For many ordinary believers, the quarrels at the level of church hierarchy do not bear much significance, as long as they can go to a church on Sunday and participate in a familiar liturgy with a local priest they know. The questions of jurisdiction, church autocephaly, as well as the canonical order of the church structures and their hierarchy carry little significance for them.

For those employed by the church or serving it as clergy, these questions sometimes take on existential significance, since they are dependent on the recognition of the church structure they work for to receive their wages and social security. In modern states, where there normally exists a separation between church and state, regardless of its specific form, this is less often the case, given that the state usually does not intend to interfere with internal ecclesiastical issues. This was the case in Ukraine until mid-2018, for example, where the state refused to take sides in the ecclesiastical conflict, treating all religious organisations equally, although it changed its policy later on and actively supported Ukrainian autocephaly. In the cases where Orthodox Christianity is a minority religion, the political influence on the Orthodox Church is also not very important. In the case of (North) Macedonia with a majority Orthodox Church, for example, state interference is clear-cut and official. However, in the areas without international recognition, such as Abkhazia or Eastern Ukraine, the situation is obviously even more precarious.

As a result, most of these conflicts amount to inner-Orthodox quarrels, which the actors more or less successfully link with theological argumentation. Their political impact is limited, although some secular actors try to utilise them for their political aims. This is especially the case in (North) Macedonia and to some extent in Ukraine.[51] The inclusion of historical arguments complements this political exploitation, yet it acquires different meanings on the theological and political levels. This is perhaps because the general Orthodox discourse is very much concerned with the historical tradition and tries to discover theological truth in the historical road of the church. Therefore, it appears vital to determine the historical trajectory through which the theology of the church comes to the fore. On a theological level, then, historical narratives about the church as a living organism that experiences decline and advancement are considered as important parts of the entire corpus of the Christian truth. However, as soon as these narratives start referring to other Orthodox Churches and Christians as opponents, this unavoidably leads to dissonances, which subsequently can be easily superimposed on more geopolitical and demographic fault lines. As a result, this situation inevitably leads to intra-Orthodox jurisdictional conflicts of the different kinds discussed above.

51 See also the contributions by Nenad Živković and Oleg Kyselov in this volume.

Autonomy or Autocephaly, Recognition or Isolation? A Comprehensive Approach to the Macedonian Schism in the Serbian Orthodox Church

Nenad Živković

In the second half of the twentieth century, the Serbian Orthodox Church (SOC) was affected by two notable schisms. The first broke out in 1964 in North America but was eventually overcome in the aftermath of the dissolution of Yugoslavia (1991) and its communist regime. The schism in the Republic of (North) Macedonia,[1] where since 1967 officially, but effectively since 1945, the Macedonian Orthodox Church (MOC) acts independently, unrecognised by other canonical autocephalous Orthodox Churches, and survives to this day.

In 2002, the delegations from the Serbian and Macedonian Churches signed an agreement, which was supposed to resolve the schism from 1967. It envisaged ecclesiastical autonomy for the Macedonian Church within the Serbian Patriarchate and left the decision on its future status to the forthcoming Pan-Orthodox council. When the agreement failed to be ratified in (North) Macedonia, the Patriarchate in Belgrade, encouraged by the fact that one bishop from the MOC was willing to accept unity with the SOC, decided to establish its own autonomous church in this region. Since 2004, the ecclesiastical situation in (North) Macedonia exhibits a paradoxical dimension, since the main Orthodox Church in the country, the MOC, remains unrecognised by worldwide Orthodoxy. Instead, the Orthodox Churches recognise the autonomous Orthodox Archbishopric of Ohrid (OAO), which is a part of the SOC. The OAO, on the other hand, is small in number and remains unrecognised by (North) Macedonia.

---

1 Since 2019 North Macedonia is the internationally accepted name of this ex-Yugoslav Republic in the wake of the Prespa Agreement of 2018, which resolved the related, long-standing dispute with Greece. This Agreement distinguished the Slavic Macedonian people, nation, and language from the ancient Macedonia of Hellenic culture and heritage, claimed by modern Greece and Greek Macedonians. The still unrecognised, non-canonical Orthodox Church in North Macedonia bears the name "Macedonian Orthodox Church". The above agreement, however, did not end the differences between North Macedonia and Bulgaria, such as those regarding the "Macedonian language". More importantly, as we shall see below, Bulgaria is also involved and interested in the Macedonian Church schism. Historically, the territory of today's North Macedonia was also referred to as Vardar Macedonia. Geographically, however, the region of Macedonia includes, in addition to Vardar Macedonia, the south-western parts of modern Bulgaria (Pirin Macedonia), the northern and north-eastern parts of modern Greece (Aegean Macedonia), as well as small portions of southern Serbia and eastern Albania. See Fikret Adanır, *Die makedonische Frage. Ihre Entstehung und Entwicklung bis 1908*, Wiesbaden 1979, 2–3.

There are several aspects, usually intertwined, which are deeply rooted in this ecclesiastical conflict. The historical dimension, that is, the evolution of the ecclesiastical conflict in (North) Macedonia, deserves to be discussed in the first place, since the argumentations of those involved in this conflict primarily draw on the interpretation of historical events. Relevant, even central for this issue, is the struggle of the people of (North) Macedonia for national recognition, in which the role of the second Yugoslavia (1945-1991) was indispensable.[2] The state-building dimension of post-Yugoslav (North) Macedonia, particularly the controversies regarding the failure of the agreement on ecclesiastical unity from 2002, proved to be of a great significance to the contemporary developments of the schism. Beside these mainly internal Macedonian aspects and the relations between the SOC and the MOC, there is also an inter-orthodox aspect of the Macedonian ecclesiastical dispute, which must not be overseen. Often, all or most of these aspects are intertwined, which is why it is important not to treat them separately from one another. Instead, a combined approach is suggested in this chapter. Since neither the scope of this chapter nor the necessary spatial limitations allow for a detailed presentation of every aspect of the Macedonian ecclesiastical dispute, several relevant points within each of the above defined dimensions are presented instead. At the end, a short summary follows, and the future perspective of this dispute is addressed in the concluding remarks.

History Revisited – The Evolution of the Macedonian Ecclesiastical Question

Historical arguments are equally being applied by either side of this schism in the efforts to prove their own and refute the position of the opposing side. Moreover, studies dealing with this issue usually concentrate on its historical dimension and are, as a rule, written in order to support a particular position.[3] The problem is,

---

2 It has been pointed out that the Yugoslav communist leadership had good reasons to support the Macedonian process of nation-building and include the region of Vardar Macedonia as a separate federal unit in post-war Yugoslavia. This contributed, among other aspects, to securing control over this region and averting the aspirations from the Bulgarian side. See Stefan Troebst, "Yugoslav Macedonia, 1943-1953: Building the Party, the State, and the Nation", in Edgar Hösch/Konrad Clewing (eds), *Das makedonische Jahrhundert. Von den Anfängen der nationalrevolutionären Bewegung zum Abkommen von Ohrid, 1893-2001. Ausgewählte Aufsätze*, München 2007, 241–258, here 243. See also ibid., 248–254 on some decisive aspects of the nation-building process.

3 Among Macedonian authors: Doné Ilievski, *The Macedonian Orthodox Church: The Road to Independence*, Skopje 1973; Jovan Belčovski, *Историските основи за автокефалноста на македонската православна црква* [Historical Foundations of the Autocephaly of the Macedonian Orthodox Church], Skopje 1985; Slavko Dimevski, *Историја на македонската православна црква* [History of the Macedonian Orthodox

however, that there is usually not one single history, but rather many, at least as many as there are actors involved. Having this in mind, we can at best speak of *entangled histories* in this context.[4]

Christianity and the institutionalised church were present on the territory of the modern-day Republic of North Macedonia since the early Middle Ages. Originally under the jurisdiction of the Church of Rome, it was subdued to the Patriarchate of Constantinople in the eighth century. From the second half of the ninth century, with the rise of the Bulgarian and afterwards the Serbian medieval states, the conjunction changed, since each of these states ruled over the Macedonian territory at some point of time. One should also bear in mind that the territorial meaning of the designation "Macedonia" kept changing throughout history. Technically speaking, the Archbishopric of Ohrid was a remnant of the First Bulgarian Empire, which ceased to exist after 1018, when it was conquered by the Byzantine Emperor Basil II.[5] It seems that he did not abolish the already existing Bulgarian Patriarchate of Ohrid, but degraded it to the rank of Archbishopric, setting down the rule that all future archbishops must be appointed by the emperor.[6] Subsequently, this Archbishopric retained some sort of

---

Church], Skopje 1989 (first published in a much shorter version in 1965). Among Serbian authors: Djoko Slijepcević, *Македонско црквено питање* [The Macedonian Church Issue], Munich 1969 (a shorter version was published in 1959); Predrag Puzović, *Раскол у Српској православној цркви – македонско црквено питање* [The Schism in the Serbian Orthodox Church – the Macedonian Church Issue], Belgrade 1997; Veljko Đorić Mišina, *Герман Ђорић: Патријарх у обезбоженом времену* [German Djorić: Patriarch in a Godless Time], Slanci 2012 (one subchapter deals with the Macedonian Orthodox Church).

4 See the first volume from the series on this topic: Roumen Daskalov/Tchavdar Marinov (eds), *Entangled Histories of the Balkans. Volume One: National Ideologies and Language Policies*, Leiden 2013.

5 Before it was finally subdued by the Byzantine Emperor Basil II, the First Bulgarian state was ruled by one of the Cometopuli brothers, Samuel (effectively since 976; as emperor 997-1014). The post-1945 Macedonian historiography sees Samuel's medieval state as Macedonian and not as Bulgarian, as it is generally regarded by the existing scholarship. See Ulf Brunnbauer, "Historiography, Myths and the Nation in the Republic of Macedonia", in idem (ed.), *(Re)Writing History – Historiography in South East Europe after Socialism*, Münster 2004, 165–200, here 179. On the Macedonian national interpretation of the medieval period, including Samuel's state, see also Irena Stefoska, "Nation, Education and Historiographic Narratives: The Case of the Socialist Republic of Macedonia (1944-1990)", in Ulf Brunnbauer/Hannes Grandits (eds), *The Ambiguous Nation. Case Studies from Southeastern Europe in the 20th Century*, Munich 2013, 195–225, here 213–220.

6 The capital of the First Bulgarian state consecutively moved westwards from the city of Preslav and after a short period in Sofia (then known as Sredets) and subsequently Voden, Moglen and Prespa, it finally settled at the city of Ohrid, along with the Patriarchal seat. Cf. Georg Ostrogorsky, *Geschichte des byzantinischen Staates*, München 1980, 253, 262; Ivan Snegarov, *История на Охридската архиепископия. Том 1: От основаването и*

autocephaly (or autonomy), absorbing gradually many dioceses in the Balkans and continued to exist until 1767, when it was finally abolished by the Ottomans. Simultaneously, the Patriarchate of Peć (until 1346 with the rank of an Archbishopric) of the Serbian medieval state spread its jurisdiction at the expense of the Archbishopric of Ohrid but was finally abolished in 1766 after being renewed in 1557. The dioceses of both Ohrid and Peć were then taken over by the Patriarchate of Constantinople.

The nineteenth century marked the beginning of national liberation movements, along with the rise of national churches: 1831 in Serbia, 1833 in Greece, 1864 in Romania, and 1870 in Bulgaria.[7] With exception of Romania, the region of current North Macedonia was claimed ecclesiastically as well as nationally by all these actors. Although the Patriarchate of Constantinople had jurisdiction over it, since 1874 the Bulgarian Orthodox Exarchate also started to appoint bishops and established a parallel church hierarchy there. This was, in fact, made possible by the infamous Article 10 of the sultan's firman on the foundation of the Bulgarian Exarchate (1870) through a schism from the Patriarchate of Constantinople. More specifically, this article provided for the establishment of the Exarchate parishes there if two thirds of the population expressed this wish.[8] However, during 1890-1892 the Exarchate's Bishop of Skopje, Teodosij (Gologanov), actually tried, contrary to the pro-Bulgarian policy of the Exarchate, to re-establish the Archbishopric of Ohrid as an independent Macedonian Church. Not surprisingly, this attempt was favourably regarded by the Greek side.[9] Towards the end of the century, following several pleas of the Serbian state and church (Metropolitanate of Belgrade), the Patriarchate of Constantinople agreed to appoint several Serbian bishops instead of Greeks there, which was the usual practice until then. In a similar manner as their Bulgarian

---

до завладяването на Балканския полуостров от Турците [The History of the Ohrid Archdiocese, Volume 1: From the Foundation until the Turkish Conquest], Sofia 1995 [1924], 12–14.

7 On the historical background of and tendency to nationalisation of the Orthodox Churches, see Vasilios N. Makrides, "Why are Orthodox Churches Particularly Prone to Nationalization and Even to Nationalism?", *St Vladimir's Theological Quarterly* 57/3-4 (2013) 325–352. In the case of the Bulgarian Exarchate, the "national" church was formed even before the foundation of the Bulgarian state (1878). In fact, the Exarchate's existence contributed to the later delineation of the political borders of Bulgaria.

8 "Ферман за Българската Екзархия (27 февруари 1870 г.)" [Ferman on the Bulgarian Exarchate (27.02.1870], in Hristo Matanov *et al.* (eds), *Подбрани извори за българската история. Том трети. Българските земи под османска власт. Българско възраждане* [Selected Sources for Bulgarian History. Vol. 3. The Bulgarian Lands under Ottoman Rule. The Bulgarian Revival], Sofia 2008, 413–414.

9 Tchavdar Marinov, "Famous Macedonia, the Land of Alexander: Macedonian Identity at the Crossroads of Greek, Bulgarian and Serbian Nationalism", in Tchavdar Marinov/ Roumen Daskalov (eds), *Entangled Histories of the Balkans. Volume One: National Ideologies and Language Policies*, Leiden 2013, 273–330, here 288.

counterparts, they engaged in opening schools and influencing the building of a Serbian national self-awareness among the population.[10] After the Balkan Wars (1912-1913), the region was annexed to Serbia, and the clergy of the Exarchate was expelled. Officially, however, the ecclesiastical jurisdiction was granted to the re-established Patriarchate of Peć – the Serbian Orthodox Church – only after the First World War, when the Kingdom of Serbs, Croats and Slovenes, comprising the region of Vardar Macedonia, was formed.[11]

This jurisdiction effectively lasted only until 1941, when, following the dissolution of the Kingdom of Yugoslavia, the region of Vardar Macedonia was occupied by Bulgarian forces. In the same way, its ecclesiastical administration was taken over by the Bulgarian Orthodox Church (BOC), which did not, however, send bishops to any of the sees there. Instead, the dioceses in Vardar Macedonia were merely administrated.[12] After the occupation was over, the communist Yugoslav authorities did not allow the two bishops of the SOC, who had been expelled at the beginning of occupation, to return to their posts in Macedonian territories. Instead, in October 1944 the *Initiative Committee for the Organisation of Church Life in Macedonia* was formed only to grow into the *Initiative Committee for the Foundation of the Independent Church in Macedonia and the Renewal of the Archbishopric of Ohrid* towards the beginning of 1945.[13] The neutralisation of the higher leadership of the SOC by the communists presented a convenient occasion for the proclamation of the independent Macedonian Church, envisaged as the restored Archbishopric of Ohrid. This proclamation took place gradually on three clergy-laity councils, starting already in 1945. At the *First Clergy-Laity Council* held in Skopje on 4 March 1945, with the support and in the presence of the new local as well as federal authorities, albeit in absence of bishops, the MOC was proclaimed autocephalous, but the decision was soon changed to an autonomous status within the SOC.[14] For the next 13 years, the Macedonian Church would remain without bishops.

---

10 Victor Roudometof, *Collective Memory, National Identity and Ethnic Conflict: Greece, Bulgaria and the Macedonian Question*, Westport/CT 2002, 91–93.

11 See Radmila Radić, "Serbian Christianity", in Ken Parry (ed.), *The Blackwell Companion to Eastern Christianity,* Malden/MA 2007, 231–248, here 235–236.

12 Björn Opfer-Klinger, *Im Schatten des Krieges. Besatzung oder Anschluss, Befreiung oder Unterdrückung? Eine komparative Untersuchung über die bulgarische Herrschaft in Vardar-Makedonien 1915-1918 und 1941-1944*, Münster 2005, 285.

13 See Jure Zečević Božić, *Die Autokephalieerklärung der Makedonischen Orthodoxen Kirche*, Würzburg 1994, 27–28; Radmila Radić, *Држава и верске заједнице, 1945-1970. Део 2: 1954-1970* [The State and Religious Communities, 1945-1970. Part 2: 1954-1970], Belgrade 2002, 284.

14 The article 7 of the final declaration of this Council foresaw that the MOC would, together with "the other Orthodox Churches in Yugoslavia", enter into unity with the envisaged "Yugoslav Orthodox Church," once this is formed. Cf. Puzović, *Раскол* (as n. 3), 8; Ilievski, *The Macedonian Orthodox Church* (as n. 3), 75–76.

The *Second Clergy-Laity Council*, which was convened in October 1958 in the presence of several prominent figures from the political establishment, declared the restoration of the Archbishopric of Ohrid and chose the vicar bishop Dositej Stojković for its first archbishop, but remained in eucharistic unity with the Patriarchate of Belgrade.[15]

Despite the fact that the Council was conducted without its consent, the Patriarchate of Belgrade accepted almost all its decisions, and after two new bishops were consecrated for the MOC during the Patriarchal visit in 1959, the issue was considered resolved. The Patriarchate also clearly understood the MOC to be autonomous, whereas some actions of the hierarchy of the MOC, such as organising Macedonian parishes abroad – primarily in Australia and Canada – showed that the understanding of the nature of its status was subject to various interpretations.[16] Such differences in understanding the position and the authority of the MOC eventually led to further alienation. When the Episcopal Assembly of the SOC chose not to grant autocephaly[17] to the MOC in May 1967,[18] the *Third Clergy-Laity Council* was convened in July of the same year, again in Ohrid. On

15 There was a lot of controversy around Bishop Dositej and why he was determined to go to Ohrid despite the objection and even the direct prohibition of the new Patriarch German (Djorić) to do so. Dositej stated that there were details, which he was unable to reveal, that forced him to go to the planned Clergy-Laity Council at Ohrid, regardless of his intentions. Cf. Puzović, *Раскол* (as n. 3), 51.

16 See Ilievski, *The Macedonian Orthodox Church* (as n. 3), 106–107; Jovan Vraniškovski, *Brief History of the Ohrid Archbishopric* (transl. by Elena Vitanova and Valeria Kjulumova), Ohrid 2008, 74.

17 Extensive pressure from the political establishment on the SOC was at work to recognise the MOC as autocephalous. See Marko Nikolić/Duško Dimitrijević, "'Macedonian Orthodox Church' in former Yugoslav State", *Politikologija religije/Politics and Religion/Politologie des Religions* 8/1 (2013) 193–214, here 195–202; Ljupčo S. Risteski quotes a statement made by Krste Crvenkovski, a prominent Macedonian communist leader at the time, that he was present at the meeting with some of the most important Yugoslav (federal) political leaders (among others, Petar Stambolić, Veljko Vlahović and Edvard Kardelj), when it was decided to "support the creation, i.e., the renewal, of the Macedonian autocephalous church": Ljupčo S. Risteski, "Recognition of the Independence of the Macedonian Orthodox Church (MOC) as an Issue Concerning Macedonian National Identity", *ЕтноАнтропоЗум/EthnoAnthropoZoom* 6 (2009) 145–185, here 163–165.

18 The Assembly stated the reasons for not granting autocephaly at length, among them: The MOC hierarchy does not suffice in numbers, since there are only 3 bishops, while 4 are required in order to form an autonomous metropolitan bishopric (Canon 4 of the First Ecumenical Council); the MOC does not have any kind of theological school at its disposal; and the Macedonian hierarchy is in violation of Orthodox canon law in more than one way since it does not refer to any canon whatsoever in affirming its unilaterally declared autonomy/autocephaly, and not only relies, but also invokes state and political intervention. See Dimitrios S. Constantopoulos, "Die 'autokephale orthodoxe Kirche von Mazedonien'", *Kanon II: Jahrbuch der Gesellschaft für das Recht der Ostkirchen* (1974) 28–38.

18 July 1967 it declared the MOC autocephaly, an event which coincided with the 200-year anniversary of the abolishment of the Archbishopric of Ohrid. As a reaction, the SOC declared the MOC a schismatic organisation, aborted liturgical communion with it, and instructed an ecclesiastical canon law process against all involved persons.[19]

In the aftermath of these events, the SOC retained its categorical position not to recognise the autocephaly of the MOC. Every further attempt to negotiate the status of the MOC failed. It was only in the late 1990s that a round of negotiations led to a mutually acceptable agreement. On 17 May 2002 in the southern Serbian city of Niš the two ecclesiastical delegations signed the *Draft Agreement on Establishing Church Unity*. It envisaged the MOC as an autonomous Church within the SOC under the official name Archbishopric of Ohrid – not the Macedonian Orthodox Church – and left the final resolution to the future Pan-Orthodox Council.[20] Although the Macedonian delegation accepted it, the agreement was not ratified by the Synod of the MOC. This instigated the SOC, encouraged by the fact that metropolitan Bishop of the Diocese of Povardarie (the MOC), Jovan Vraniškovski, was willing to accept the agreement and enter into eucharistic unity with the SOC, to proceed and implement the agreement by appointing Bishop Jovan as Exarch of the Patriarch in the Republic of (North) Macedonia, thus creating a parallel Church to the MOC. Since 2005, Bishop Jovan acts as the Archbishop of the Orthodox Archbishopric of Ohrid, which is autonomous under the SOC and is, in that way, in ecclesiastical terms the only recognised Church in (North) Macedonia, albeit unrecognised by the state.

The Struggle for National Recognition

The struggle for the recognition of the Macedonian national authenticity exhibits an extremely high level of complexity. To address this question in detail here would not only be virtually impossible; it would also exceed the spatial as well as the thematic frame of this chapter. Instead, three points are taken into account: the irredentist policies of the Bulgarian, Greek, and Serbian states in the nineteenth and the first half of the twentieth century vis-à-vis the Macedonian heritage, the

19 Puzović, *Раскол* (as n. 3), 84. The canonical character of the MOC, especially of its unilateral proclamation of autocephaly, has ever since been denied, primarily by the SOC. Analysing the canons invoked by the MOC, which are based on the territorial adaptation of the ecclesiastical to the civil administration, Günter Prinzing came to conclusion that the external (political) conditions for acquiring autocephaly were indeed met after 1991 in the case of the MOC. See Günter Prinzing, "Die umstrittene Selbstständigkeit der Makedonischen Orthodoxen Kirche in historischer Sicht" *Aus der Südosteuropa-Forschung* 10 (1999) 31–43, here 37–39.

20 "Draft Agreement on Establishing Church Unity", in Borjan Vitanov (ed.), *Заради идното Царство, Том I/For the Kingdom to come, Vol. I*, Ohrid 2005, 106–113.

emergence of the Internal Macedonian Revolutionary Organisation, and finally the role of the communist establishment of the Second Yugoslavia.

During the nineteenth century, the peoples of the Balkans engaged in the struggles for liberation from the Ottoman rule as well as in efforts for national affirmation. These processes can clearly be observed in the cases of the Greek, Serbian, Bulgarian and Romanian peoples. However, some other groups of peoples, usually smaller in number, were politically, culturally and religiously dominated by their larger, more powerful and nationally more articulate neighbours. These smaller peoples were considered lacking their own history and language, on which grounds they were also denied national authenticity.[21] Such was the case of the whole geographical region of Macedonia (Aegean, Pirin, and Vardar Macedonia), where throughout the nineteenth and the first half of the twentieth century assimilatory actions had been undertaken by Bulgaria, Greece and Serbia equally. Two very common tools used to achieve this objective were educational institutions and the church. To be a member of one church meant consequently to belong to its respective nation – Bulgarian, Greek or Serbian.[22] In the same way, the presence of a certain church and its clergy endorsed the territorial (i.e., automatically national) claims of the late nineteenth and early twentieth century in the Macedonian area.[23] Naturally, these irredentist policies excluded any kind of either ethnic or national authenticity of the Slavic Macedonian population. For the three competing actors, the Slavic-speaking population in the Macedonian region was, in the best case, an amorphous mass. It is difficult to oversee that precisely these three nationalisms – Bulgarian, Greek, and Serbian – largely contributed, however paradoxical it may be, to the formation of a specific national identity of the Macedonians, and, in more practical terms, to the struggle against such influences.[24]

One of the main hallmarks of the Macedonian struggle for national recognition was the Internal Macedonian Revolutionary Organisation (IMRO), founded in Thessaloniki in 1893. It aimed to establish an autonomous Macedonian state, which would distance itself from the competing claims over its people and territory by the three neighbouring states. Initially, it was a small size organisation, but in cooperation with the Bulgarian nationalists, who again saw in IMRO the opportunity for spreading Bulgarian objectives, it grew into a strong

---

21 Pedro Ramet refers to Macedonians, Byelorussians and Ukrainians. See Pedro Ramet, "Autocephaly and National Identity in Church-State Relations in Eastern Christianity: An Introduction", in idem (ed.), *Eastern Christianity and Politics in the Twentieth Century*, Durham/NC 1988, 3–19, here 4–5.

22 Roudometof, *Collective Memory* (as n. 10), 91.

23 Violeta Duklevska Schubert, "'My Faith, my Nation': Exploring the 'Natural' Affinity between Orthodox Christianity and National Identity in Macedonia", in Victor C. de Munck/Ljupcho Risteski (eds), *Macedonia – the Political, Social, Economic and Cultural Foundations of a Balkan State*, London 2013, 65–88, here 72–74.

24 Marinov, "Famous Macedonia" (as n. 9), 276–328.

organisation, which also launched violent attacks.[25] This eventually led to the Ilinden Uprising in 1903, during which the activists managed to capture the town of Kruševo and declare independence.[26] Although short-lived, this event and its relation to the IMRO remained a crucially important moment in the national liberation narrative and would be "re-enacted" towards the end of the Second World War. Nevertheless, after the failure of the Ilinden Uprising, the organisation faced ideological divisions between left and right, leading to internal struggles and assassinations, and, eventually to the dissolution of the IMRO in 1908.[27]

The two Balkan Wars as well as the First World War and their aftermaths affected the Macedonian national question extensively.[28] This was the case because after the Second Balkan War, in the summer of 1913, most of the region of Vardar Macedonia – including Ohrid, Štip, Kočani, and Bitola – was, in accordance with the Treaty of Bucharest, annexed to Serbia. Although it may have been an exaggeration, the extent of the Serbian ecclesiastical and civil influence there led prominent geographer and geologist Jovan Cvijić at the time to affirm that had it not been for the First World War (1914-1918), Macedonia would have most certainly been completely Serbian (i.e., the locals would identify themselves as Serbians).[29] Nevertheless, he also noted that there was an occasional dissatisfaction in the eastern part of Macedonia, on the border with Bulgaria, where the Serbian authorities had not enjoyed as much success.

The constellations of the First World War brought Macedonia in the hands of Bulgaria, which during its control over the lands implemented the same assimilation measures that were being used earlier under Serbian control. With the formation of the Kingdom of Serbs, Croats and Slovenes (since 1929 Yugoslavia) after the war, Macedonia was again under Serbian rule. The very name of the state reveals that it essentially recognised only those three nations.

---

25 Marinov extensively elaborates "how deeply intertwined Macedonian nationalism was in its initial phases with its Bulgarian counterpart," precisely on the example of the initial IMRO. The lack of national clarity in its beginnings was also a proof for other actors involved in the Macedonian question that a separate Macedonian nationality does not exist. Ibid., 299–303.

26 Roudometof, *Collective Memory* (as n. 10), 93. The development of the Macedonian question before the two Balkan Wars and the First World War is thoroughly discussed in Adanır, *Die makedonische Frage* (as n. 1).

27 This ideological division bore an additional burden. Put in a simplified manner, the leftists envisaged a truly self-governed Macedonia, while the right wing preferred unification with or even annexation to Bulgaria. See Andrew Rossos, *Macedonia and the Macedonians: A History*, Stanford/CA 2008, 117–121.

28 On the situation in (North) Macedonia during the First World War, see: Björn Opfer, "Das bulgarisch-orthodoxe Exarchat und die Okkupationsverwaltung in Vardar-Makedonien 1915-1918", *Zeitschrift für Religions- und Geistesgeschichte* 54/2 (2002) 154–170.

29 Jovan Cvijić, *Балканско полуострво* [The Balkan Peninsula], Belgrade 1991 [1918-1922], 431.

The Macedonian revolutionary activists of the right wing and largely pro-Bulgarian IMRO saw such a state of affairs as another occupation and, in the period 1921-1934, launched numerous armed attacks against the armed forces of the state.[30] Their actions culminated with the assassination of King Alexander Karadjordjević in Marseille in October 1934. However, the hopes of the revolutionaries were shattered during the hostile Bulgarian occupation of the Second World War, which applied even more aggressive techniques of assimilation than their Serbian and Greek opponents in the earlier years. As a result, Victor Roudometof affirms, this finally led to more widespread support for the communist partisan resistance forces, since they were promising freedom and national recognition within the new state of Yugoslavia.[31]

Thus, when the foundations of Second Yugoslavia as a federal state were laid in 1943 at the second session of the Anti-Fascist Council for the National Liberation of Yugoslavia (AVNOJ), Macedonia was, for the first time, envisaged as a self-governed federal political unit, while the Macedonian nation was openly recognised.[32] In 1944, on Saint Elijah's day (*Ilinden*), celebrated on 2 August, the first session of the Anti-Fascist Council for the National Liberation of Macedonia (ASNOM) took place. The date of the session resonated with the symbolism of national liberation, being scheduled on the anniversary of the 1903 Ilinden Uprising. The first session of the ASNOM effectively established the People's Democratic Republic of Macedonia within federal Yugoslavia and, among other things, proclaimed the Macedonian language as the official language of the Republic.[33] The significance of these actions was enormous for the national affirmation of the Macedonians, but it is important to emphasise that the idea of Macedonian statehood was not invented at the Second Session of the AVNOJ in November 1943 or at the first session of the ASNOM in August 1944. These

30 In fact, as a result of the previous split between the right and the left, in the early 1920s two separate organisations under the name IMRO appeared: the IMRO of the right orientation, usually termed as Autonomist, and the IMRO United, which was of the left orientation and as such recognised by the Communist International (Comintern) and the Communist Parties of Bulgaria, Greece and Yugoslavia. The former aimed for a self-governed Macedonia, while the latter anticipated a wider union of the Balkan (Slavic) peoples. The right oriented IMRO operated from Pirin Macedonia, where it had its stronghold, and was largely pro-Bulgarian. It was this IMRO that carried out violent attacks. For more about the ideological differences, including the influences of left and right ideologies of the period on the two organisations, see Rossos, *Macedonia and the Macedonians* (as n. 27), 155–177.

31 Roudometof, *Collective Memory* (as n. 10), 104.

32 See Radić, *Држава* (as n. 13), 282–283.

33 See Rossos, *Macedonia and the Macedonians* (as n. 27), 196–197.

decisions finally gave legitimacy to national claims by legally recognising a separate Macedonian nation for the first time in history.[34]

Naturally, the Macedonian struggle for national recognition cannot be reduced to these three points alone. They can, however, be taken as representative, since they point to some of the most important factors that shaped, influenced and, finally, legitimised this struggle. The nature of the ecclesiastical issue at play here, especially the circumstances in which it emerged in the aftermath of the Second World War, as presented in the previous section, indicates that the Macedonian struggle for national recognition extended into the ecclesiastical field as well.[35] This aspect and its contemporary implications are further discussed in the following section.

The Macedonian Ecclesiastical Question in the Contemporary Context

As long as Yugoslavia existed, other aspects of the Macedonian question – such as Greece's disapproval of the usage of the name Macedonia or Bulgaria's contestation of the Macedonian language and hence the Macedonian nation – were in a way frozen. When the Yugoslav era ended and Macedonia moved on as an independent Republic, this rapidly changed.[36] In addition to the church, which was already unrecognised, now the very name of the state, as well as the language, were internationally contested. The 2002 agreement on ecclesiastical unity between the SOC and the MOC, also known as the Niš Agreement, exhibits a special place within this context. This agreement combines, in a certain manner, the national (including the name issue) with the church aspect. This section therefore discusses the provisions of the Niš Agreement, the implications of its failure, that is, its diverse interpretation and implementation, as well as the latest developments.

34 These facts and their later implications are probably the reasons why there is a common understanding that the Macedonian nation "is a product of Yugoslav communism". See Marinov, "Famous Macedonia" (as n. 9), 275–276.

35 This does not mean that the possibility of an independent Macedonian Church was envisaged only in the communist era. Krste P. Misirkov, one of the most important figures of the Macedonian struggle for national recognition, in his 1903 work *On Macedonian Matters* wrote that one of the first tasks of the Macedonian intelligentsia should be to establish a separate, independent church, i.e., to re-establish the Archbishopric of Ohrid as the "Archbishopric of all Macedonia". See Krste P. Misirkov, *За македонцките работи* [On Macedonian Matters], Sofia 1903, 22–23.

36 The most indicative example is that between 1993 and 2019 the internationally recognised name of the state was "Former Yugoslav Republic of Macedonia" (FYROM), following an interim agreement with Greece under the auspices of the United Nations. As already mentioned, with the Prespa Agreement of 2018 the long-standing dispute with Greece was resolved and the officially recognised name since 2019 is "Republic of North Macedonia". However, the differences with Bulgaria on a number of issues still exist.

The Draft Agreement on Establishing Church Unity, as it is officially known, envisaged "broad church *independence*, that is, broadest church *autonomy*" for the Church in Macedonia, which would, as a result of its unity with the SOC, be recognised by the community of the worldwide Orthodox Church.[37] The agreement itself consists of the preamble, in which autonomy is granted, seventeen articles defining the organisation and the rights of the Church in Macedonia, and, lastly, a short agreement on pastoral cooperation with the SOC. While most of the provisions of the agreement set regulations in regard to the common ecclesiastical order (e.g., the right to its own Constitution, to a primate and a synod of bishops, to form new and redistribute the existing dioceses, to elect and consecrate new bishops), the problems arose due to the articles regarding the *name* of this church. This issue was tackled in the articles fourteen and fifteen, which declared that the official name of the church, "in accordance with the ancient Church Tradition and historical practice" should be the Archbishopric of Ohrid, and hence the title of its primate should be "Archbishop of Ohrid and Metropolitan of Skopje".[38] Nevertheless, the same articles also stated that in the "internal official communication" with the Patriarchate in Belgrade the already existing and earlier established name and title of the archbishop – *Macedonian* – may be used in the same way as before.

As Ljupče S. Risteski pointed out, the real problem within this agreement seems to have been that, whatever proposal for the name would have been made (e.g., Orthodox Church in Macedonia), "the signifier of the national background of the Church", which was from the political perspective of state-building of paramount importance, was missing.[39] This is why accepting this solution was understood by political agents as the loss of statehood, an attack on their identity, and finally subjection to either the Great Serbian or Greek aspirations over Macedonia.[40] As a result, after enormous public pressure – carried out by government officials and through the media,[41] the Holy Synod of the MOC

37 *Draft Agreement* (as n. 20), 106 (No emphasis in the original).

38 Ibid., 110.

39 Risteski, "Recognition" (as n. 17), 177.

40 See Todor Cepreganov/Maja Angelovska-Panova/Dragan Zajkovski, "The Macedonian Orthodox Church", in Lucian N. Leustean (ed.), *Eastern Christianity and Politics in the Twenty-First Century*, London 2014, 426–438, here 428; Zoran Bojarovski, "Macedonia: Church Deal Bishops Accused of Treason", *Religioscope* 07.06.2002 (reposted 08.07.2002), URL: http://www.religioscope.com/notes/2002/025_macedonia_back.htm [05.03.2016].

41 For instance, the *Government Committee for Religious Communities* met the day before the Synod's decisive session. Its assertive conclusions and recommendations not only that the MOC should not accept the Agreement, but that it should also punish the bishops who signed it, were published on the day of the Synod's session. See Nenad Živković, "Улога медија у Скопљу у одбацивању Нишког споразума 2002. Године" [The Role of the Print Media in Skopje in the Rejection of the Niš Agreement in 2002], in Vladimir

rejected the agreement on 6 June 2002. Prior to this session and after being publicly accused of treason, the three bishops, who, as members of the official delegation, had earlier signed it, publicly defended both the proposed agreement and themselves. In a joint press conference, held on 28 May, they insisted that it was the best proposal that had ever been made by the SOC and that it would most certainly lead toward recognition of an autocephalous status in the near future. As for the problematic solution of the name, it was their opinion that it is a small compromise, met in order to avoid resistance from the bloc of the Greek-controlled churches, compared to the gain of finally being received in the communion of the worldwide Orthodox Church, i.e., not being isolated as a schismatic church anymore.[42]

When the Synod of the MOC dismissed the agreement, Jovan Vraniškovski, Bishop of Povardarie, contacted the Patriarchate in Belgrade after consultations with several bishops of the MOC, as he personally testifies, wishing to find a new way towards a solution. He himself had not been present at the session where the decision to reject the proposal was taken.[43] Thereupon, then Patriarch Pavle openly addressed all bishops, clergy and faithful people in the Republic of (North) Macedonia, calling them to enter into sacramental unity with the Patriarchate and through it with the entire Orthodox world. Bishop Jovan was, together with some of his clergy, the only one to accept this appeal. As a result, in September 2002 the Patriarchate in Belgrade decided to appoint him Exarch of the Serbian Patriarch in the Republic of (North) Macedonia, as well as Archbishop of Ohrid. In 2004, two new bishops were elected and consecrated by the SOC for posts in (North) Macedonia, and after the synod of the autonomous Orthodox Archbishopric of Ohrid (OAO) was formed, Bishop Jovan was, in 2005, confirmed as its Archbishop.

There were two major consequences of these actions. First, they had profound impacts on the ecclesiastical set-up in (North) Macedonia. Instead of overcoming it, the schism was, in fact, deepened and rendered even more complicated by the

---

Vukašinović (ed.), *Зборник радова – Међународна конференција Српска православна црква у штампаним медијима 2003-2013, Београд, 20-21. октобар 2015* [International Conference "The Serbian Orthodox Church in Print Media 2003-2013", Belgrade, 20-21.10.2015], Belgrade 2015, 129–140; Saško Dimevski, "Владиците-потписници црковно да се казнат и да се покајат" [The Bishops who Signed should be Ecclesiastically Punished and Repent], *Утрински весник*, 06.06.2002, URL: http://star.utrinski.com.mk/?pBroj=885&stID=12046&pR=2 [04.03.2016].

42 "'Автономна охридска архиепископија' ја води црквата до автокефалност" [The 'Autonomous Ohrid Archdiocese' and its Road to Autocephaly], *Дневник*, 29.05.2002, URL: http://star.dnevnik.com.mk/?pBroj=1860&stID=3136 [04.03.2016]. One of those bishops, Petar, stated in a television interview in January 2015 that the three of them were tricked into signing a false agreement in 2002. See "VO CENTAR Jovan Pop bez zemja", URL: https://www.youtube.com/watch?v=qj9sqjkyJ5o [04.03.2016].

43 Vraniškovski, *Brief History* (as n. 16), 88.

creation of a parallel hierarchy. The (North) Macedonian state does not recognise the OAO in any way, while it is the only recognised church in its territory in ecclesiastical terms, although small in number of adherents. The OAO is also generally portrayed in the Macedonian public discourse as a sect and, more importantly, a traitorous organisation to the Macedonian nation, financed by both Serbs and Greeks.[44] The MOC, on the other hand, enjoys the status of the official church in the country as well as that of one of the most important national symbols, yet it remains unrecognised by the other Orthodox Churches. At the same time, the MOC sees the actions of the SOC in a very hostile manner and as a clear violation of canon law – usurping the "natural" jurisdiction of an already existing church. Furthermore, this situation could threaten to undermine, or destabilise, the symbolic significance of the MOC in the post-Yugoslav Macedonian state-building context.

Second, the implementation of the Niš Agreement on behalf of the SOC caused severe consequences for the hierarchy and the adherents of the OAO: Archbishop Jovan has since 2004 been repeatedly convicted and imprisoned, lastly being released in February 2015 after more than three years in prison.[45] He was originally convicted of instigating ethnic, racial and religious hatred (2004), and then, on two occasions (in 2006 and 2009 in absence), accused of having embezzled funds while still a bishop of the MOC. Moreover, higher clergymen of the SOC were delayed and in some cases denied entry to the Republic of (North) Macedonia,[46] a monastery in construction was demolished,[47] and possessions

44 B. G., "Српскиот егзарх имал и други финансиери покрај српскиот буџет" [The Serbian Exarch had other Sponsors besides the Serbian Budget], *Утрински весник*, 09.03.2006, URL: http://star.utrinski.com.mk/?pBroj=2026&stID=63993&pR=3 [05.03.2016].

45 In 2009, Archbishop Jovan was detained in Bulgaria when he tried to cross the Bulgarian-Serbian border. The Court of Appeals in Sofia ruled that he was being persecuted on political and religious grounds and expressed the opinion that his return to (North) Macedonia would pose serious threat to both himself and his adherents, on which grounds the court decided not to extradite him. See "Булгарска неће изручити владику Јована" [Bulgaria will not Extradite Bishop Jovan], *Вечерње новости*, 04.01.2011, URL: http://www.novosti.rs/vesti/naslovna/aktuelno.69.html:313775-Bugarska-nece-izruciti-vladiku-Jovana [05.03.2016].

46 "International Religious Freedom Report 2004: Macedonia", URL: http://www.state.gov/j/drl/rls/irf/2004/35470.htm [07.03.2016]; "International Religious Freedom Report 2005: Macedonia", URL: http://www.state.gov/j/drl/rls/irf/2005/51567.htm [07.03.2016].

47 "International Religious Freedom Report 2005: Macedonia". Mentioning that the object was in fact built without a permit, the report emphasised that the OSCE was not able to obtain a copy of the decision by the competent ministry authorising the monastery's destruction, which was conducted by policemen.

were confiscated.[48] According to several sources, Archbishop Jovan was mistreated in prison,[49] and there are ongoing court trials against other bishops, monks, and some lay people of the OAO.

Although some developments and most prominently the release from prison of Archbishop Jovan on 2 February 2015 sent a signal of a good will for the resolution of this issue, such resolution did not take place yet. The Assembly of Bishops of the SOC decided in May 2015 to accept the continuation of further negotiations with the MOC, under the condition that the legal prosecution against the hierarchy and members of the OAO is aborted and the renewed process against Archbishop Jovan is resolved in his favour.[50] The close links between the state and the MOC may have led to such open demands from the SOC.[51] However,

48 In May 2012, the Holy Assembly of Bishops of the SOC addressed the public stating that the police broke into several monasteries and private homes of the clergy and monastics of the OAO, confiscating computers and other material property and arresting two nuns and one monk. See "Public Announcement Regarding the Latest State-Police Persecution of the Members of the Orthodox Ohrid Archbishopric", 25.05.2012, URL: http://spc.rs/eng/public_announcement_regard_latest_statepolice_persecution_members_orthodox_ohrid_archbishopric [07.03.2016].

49 For instance, after serving one third of their sentence, a convict is legally entitled to weekend-release, which was denied to Archbishop Jovan, even after he had already served two thirds of his sentence, without any explanation from the prison warden. He was also denied having visits from anyone other than his 76-year-old mother and his sister. See "Соопштение" [Announcement], 01.12.2014, URL: http://www.poa-info.org/arhiepiskop/soopstenija/20141203.html [07.03.2016].

50 "Одлука Светог Архијерејског Сабора о почетку новог дијалога са Македонском православном црквом која је у расколу" [Decision of the Holy Episcopal Council on the Beginning of a New Dialogue with the MOC in Schism], 27.05.2015, URL: http://spc.rs/sr/odluka_svetog_arhijerejskog_sabora_o_pochetku_novog_dijaloga_sa_makedonskom_pravoslavnom_crkvom_koja [08.03.2016].

51 These links have been observed on several occasions, including in the International Religious Freedom Report, published annually by the State Department of the United States. The close relations between the MOC and the state can also be observed when one bears in mind the attempts of the OAO to be registered before the state as a religious community, so that it could avoid future prosecution on the grounds of illegal operations. In 2004, and again in 2009, the application of the OAO to register was rejected. Whereas in 2004 the law contained a disputed regulation "one confession – one religious community", which prevented the legitimisation of a second Orthodox Church in the country, this was not the case in 2009 – the law on religious communities having been altered in 2007. In its ruling from 2009, the court referred to the expertise from the MOC, which objected to the name proposed by the OAO for registration: 'Greek-Orthodox Ohrid Archbishopric of the Patriarchate of Peć'. The objection was substantiated by the emphasis that the designation 'Patriarchate of Peć' was, according to its statute, a part of the official name of the SOC. It was further asserted that the SOC did not have jurisdiction over the MOC or over the territory of the Republic of (North) Macedonia. See "Решение" [Decision], 28.07.2009, 2, 9, URL: http://www.poa-info.org/mk/istorija/sovremena/Resenie_za_odbivanje_na_registracija_na_POA.pdf [12.12.2018].

releasing Archbishop Jovan from prison did not come simply as a sign of good will from the Macedonian side, regardless of how often the SOC emphasised that in order to continue the negotiations the Archbishop had to be released. This action, as well as its further implications were carried out after a mediation of the Russian Orthodox Church (ROC), which is further discussed in the next section.

The Macedonian Church Schism on the Pan-Orthodox Level

This dispute has not only involved other individual Orthodox Churches, primarily the neighbouring Bulgarian and Greek Churches; it has also, especially in the recent years, played a role in a wider Orthodox context. This is particularly the case in regard to the somewhat ambivalent relations between the Patriarchates of Constantinople and Moscow, since numerous appeals from the MOC to the other autocephalous churches for recognition of its autocephaly have provoked reactions from these two Patriarchates too.[52] Several illustrative occasions of an inter-Orthodox character, as well as the latest developments in the Pan-Orthodox context concerning the Macedonian ecclesiastical dispute are presented here.

In 1996, the alternative National Church Council of the Bulgarian Orthodox Church (BOC) elected an alternative Patriarch, thus causing a schism within the BOC. Among the delegates from other Churches, all of them non-canonical, representatives from the MOC were present.[53] Having in mind that the alternative Bulgarian Patriarch Pimen then supported the MOC, three priests belonging to his branch celebrated a liturgy in 1998 in Skopje with the MOC.[54] Contrary to this, the canonical Bulgarian Patriarch at the time, Maxim, believed that the question ought to be resolved between the SOC and the MOC, which is why he strongly opposed the joint celebration of a liturgy in Vratsa (Bulgaria) between the Bulgarian Metropolitans Neofit (now Patriarch of the BOC) and Kalinik of Vratsa with Metropolitans Petar and Timotej and Bishop Jovan of the MOC.[55] During the period of Patriarch Maxim of Bulgaria, the official contacts with the MOC were relatively aloof, but this changed since the election of Neofit as Patriarch of the BOC in 2013. For instance, in May 2014, Archbishop Stefan of the MOC participated in a celebration of Saint Cyril and Methodius in Sofia, together with

52 See Cepreganov *et al.*, "The Macedonian Orthodox Church" (as n. 40), 428–429.

53 At this council, no presence from any canonically recognised Orthodox Church was noted. See James L. Hopkins, *The Bulgarian Orthodox Church: A Socio-historical Analysis of the Evolving Relationship between Church, Nation and State in Bulgaria*, New York 2009, 231.

54 Janice Broun, "The Bulgarian Orthodox Church: The Continuing Schism and the Religious, Social and Political Environment" *Religion, State & Society* 32/3 (2004) 209 – 245, here 213.

55 Ibid.

Patriarch Neofit.[56] There was no combined liturgical celebration this time, but one could interpret this action as a message that the BOC could change its position and would be willing to intercede in resolving the Macedonian ecclesiastical issue.[57]

In addition, the Greek Orthodox Church had played a role in initiating the negotiations that had led to the infamous Niš Agreement. More specifically, it was the late Archbishop Christodoulos who mediated between the SOC and the MOC.[58] After the failure of the agreement, the relations and contacts between the Greek Church and the MOC have been almost non-existent at an official level. For instance, the MOC delegation was denied participation in the funeral ceremony for Archbishop Christodoulos in 2008 in Athens.[59] However, in a 2013 interview, Metropolitan Petar of the MOC said that even after the failure of the Niš Agreement there had been diplomatic contacts with almost all autocephalous churches, including the Greek one.[60] On another occasion, the same bishop expressed his persuasion that "the solution for the MOC is in the hands of the two

56 Radmila Zaverska, "МПЦ може да очекува помош од БПЦ" [The MOC can Expect Help from the BOC], *Нова Македонија*, 13.05.2014, URL: http://www.novamakedonija.com.mk/NewsDetal.asp?vest=51314737355&id=9&setIzdanie=23172 [12.03.2016].

57 In addition to the Bulgarian Metropolitans, the following example shows the occasionally unclear situation concerning the Eucharistic communion with other recognised Orthodox Churches. As reported on the website of the MOC, in June 2013 in the Romanian city of Constanţa, the dean of the Theological Faculty in Skopje, Aco Girevski, as well as hieromonk Grigorij Nasteski, both from the MOC, took part in a liturgy celebrated by the Archbishop Teodosii (Petrescu) of Tomis (Constanţa) of the Romanian Orthodox Church. The Macedonian ambassador, who was present at the liturgy, described the event as a "miracle", "historical", and for him yet unseen, emphasising that the joint celebration with "the second largest Orthodox Church in the world – the Romanian Orthodox Church – *de facto* implies the recognition of our Church". See "Архијерејска божанствена литургија во Констанца на Вознесение Господово" [Episcopal Divine Liturgy in Constanţa on Ascension Day], 20.06.2013, URL: http://mpc.org.mk/vest.asp?id=5715 [12.03.2016].

58 In his *Brief History of the Ohrid Archbishopric*, Archbishop Jovan claims that it was his initiative to resume the negotiations, which he launched upon his election to the episcopacy in 1998. It was through him that then Archbishop of Athens Christodoulos agreed to appear as a mediator between the SOC and the MOC. See Vraniškovski, *Brief History* (as n. 16), 86–87.

59 S. K. D., "Забранет влез на МПЦ за погребот на Христодулос" [The MOC Banned from Christodoulos' Funeral], *Вест*, 31.01.2008, URL: http://star.vest.com.mk/default.asp?id=146790&idg=8&idb=2286&rubrika=Makedonija [12.03.2016].

60 "Г. Петар: МПЦ во 1945 требаше да бара признање од друга црква, а не од СПЦ" [Bishop Petar: In 1945 the MOC should have Asked for Recognition from some other Church, and not from the SOC], *Press 24*, 04.05.2013, URL: http://press24.mk/gpetar-mpc-vo-1945-trebashe-da-bara-priznavanje-od-druga-crkva-ne-od-spc [12.03.2016].

churches – the Greek and the Serbian –, the issue is political, and it depends on the solution of the name of the Macedonian state".[61]

On the other hand, the ongoing rivalry between the Patriarchates of Constantinople and Moscow seemingly found the MOC–SOC dispute a suitable arena as well. The two Patriarchs on several occasions declared their positions concerning this ecclesiastical issue, offered mediatory help or somehow implied that they would have the ability or power to mediate between the two sides. Worth noting is that both Patriarchates addressed the issue from the point of view that it is *not* resolved.

For example, in January 2004, a month after the formation of the Synod of the OAO, Archbishop Stefan of the MOC gave an interview to the Moscow journal *Izvestiia*.[62] In this interview, he emphasised the close cultural, linguistic and religious connections between the two nations, stating that, for instance, when Metropolitan Kirill (since February 2008 Patriarch of Moscow, i.e., head of the Russian Orthodox Church – ROC) visited (North) Macedonia he was able to understand the language without translation.[63] When asked why the MOC, as of late, has more frequently and openly asked for Russian Orthodox assistance in clarifying its ecclesiastical status, he answered, among other things, that Metropolitan Kirill offered his help on the ROC's behalf, which was later confirmed by Patriarch Alexii II in a conversation with the Macedonian Prime Minister.[64]

In an interview that he gave to the Serbian newspaper *Blic* in January 2008, Patriarch Alexii II expressed his willingness to mediate between the SOC and the

---

61 "МПЦ: Решење за МПЦ у рукама грчке и српске цркве" [MOC: The Solution for the MOC in the Hands of the Greek and Serbian Church], *RTV*, 02.05.2012, URL: http://www.rtv.rs/sr_ci/drustvo/mpc-resenje-za-mpc-u-rukama-grcke-i-srpske-crkve_316610.html [12.03.2016].

62 Iurii Sigov, "Архиепископ Стефан: 'Македония может стать форпостом России на Балканах'" [Archbishop Stefan: 'Macedonia Might Become an Outpost of Russia in the Balkans], *Известия*, 27.01.2004, URL: http://izvestia.ru/news/286260 [13.03.2016]; Branco Blahović, "МПЦ ја барат помош од Руската црква" [The MOC Asks for Help from the Russian Church], *Утрински весник*, 29.01.2004, URL: http://star.utrinski.com.mk/?pBroj=1383&stID=6419&pR=3 [13.03.2016].

63 Sigov, "Архиепископ Стефан" (as n. 62). Later, in one article commenting on the election of Kirill as the Patriarch of Moscow in February 2009, a reference was made to this visit to Macedonia. He was, the article stated, quite sceptical regarding the possibility of solving the ecclesiastical problem in Macedonia through the formation of a parallel hierarchy, such as the OAO. In addition, the article reported that two Metropolitans of the MOC were present at the ceremony of enthronisation of the new Patriarch. See Biljana Jovanovska, "Патријархот Кирил од прва рака ги знае состојбите во МПЦ" [Patriarch Kirill Knows the Situation in the MOC Firsthand], *Утрински весник*, 05.02.2009, URL: http://www.utrinski.mk/?ItemID=5D6D893D0FFE364A856D09D9E2173B3C [13.03.2016].

64 Ibid.

MOC. Pointing out that it was in the same way that the ROC succeeded in overcoming the schism with the Russian Orthodox Church Outside Russia (ROCOR), he argued that the only exit from the rather difficult situation would be to renew negotiations between the churches in the spirit of utmost tolerance and compromise, all the while not neglecting the holy canons.[65] He finally said that the ROC was willing to share its experience and offer its help in the dialogue.

The position that the late Patriarch took in this interview strongly indicated that for the ROC the question of the Church in Macedonia was not resolved. In addition, he did not mention the OAO at all, although at that time it had actively existed for over four years. Although Patriarch Alexii's reference to the ecclesiastical issue in (North) Macedonia had an overall neutral tone, his offer of mediation in the process of solving this issue created the impression that the ROC possessed a certain ambition and power in this issue.

Soon afterwards, at the funeral ceremony for the late Serbian Patriarch Pavle in November 2009, Ecumenical Patriarch Bartholomew of Constantinople took advantage of the opportunity to deliver a eulogy to mention that the new Patriarch of the SOC would need to deal with the ecclesiastical conflict in the Republic of (North) Macedonia.[66] It was unusual and unexpected from the Ecumenical Patriarch to address this matter at such a gathering. Bearing in mind that also a delegation of the MOC was present at the funeral ceremony, while the Moscow Patriarch was not, one could draw the conclusion that Patriarch Bartholomew seized the opportunity not only to remind the high clergy of the SOC that the ecclesiastical situation in the Republic of (North) Macedonia remains unresolved, but also that the Ecumenical Patriarchate closely follows its development.

Since 2014, however, the Moscow Patriarchate, with the support of the Russian state, played a significant role in loosening the tensions the imprisonment of Archbishop Jovan caused. In February 2014, in the course of a visit by the President of the Republic of (North) Macedonia to Moscow, Patriarch Kirill said that the ecclesiastical situation in that country ought to be resolved and offered his help in this matter.[67] According to the press release of the Moscow Patriarchate, the Patriarch reminded that the Russian Empire had always endeavoured to protect the Macedonian people, as well as some important

65 Tanja Vasiljević, "Kosovske svetinje nisu za političku trgovinu" [Kosovo sacred objects are not for political trade], *Blic*, 11.01.2008, URL: http://www.blic.rs/Vesti/Drustvo/26312/Kosovske-svetinje-nisu-za-politicku-trgovinu- [13.03.2016].

66 Biljana Jovanovska, "Што кажа Вартоломеј од Белград?" [What did Bartholomew say in Belgrade?], *Утрински весник*, 20.11.2009, URL: http://www.utrinski.mk/default.asp?ItemID=059D7BD9031D7148A2CE3BD8A467395B [14.03.2016].

67 "Рускиот патријарх ќе помага за МПЦ" [Russian Patriarch will Provide Help to the MOC], *Утрински весник* 09.02.2014, URL: http://www.utrinski.mk/?ItemID=1D0DC3517B2765449189408963D46AEA [14.03.2016].

Orthodox places, now situated in the Republic of (North) Macedonia.[68] Addressing the canonical status of the MOC he referred to this problem as "weakening Orthodoxy" and emphasise that "the restoration of the canonical status of the Macedonian Orthodox Church will be a factor that, more than any other, will ensure the preservation of the Macedonian national, cultural, and religious identity".[69]

In December 2014, Metropolitan Hilarion (Alfeyev) of the ROC, head of the ROC's Department for External Church Relations, visited Archbishop Jovan in a hospital in Skopje, where he had been transferred for this occasion.[70] The visit of this second most important hierarch of the ROC did in fact send a strong message to the public, as well as to both civil and ecclesiastical authorities. Metropolitan Hilarion, together with the ambassador of the Russian Federation to the Republic of (North) Macedonia, first met with the President, Prime Minister and Foreign Minister of the country, that is, with its highest representatives, and afterwards with Archbishop Stefan of the MOC. Two days after this visit, the MOC issued a statement, thankfully accepting the initiative of the ROC to mediate in the dialogue with the SOC, at the same time addressing the Macedonian authorities to have mercy on imprisoned Archbishop Jovan.[71] Less than two months later, In February 2015, he was released from prison, and on the following day it was reported that he will visit Russia for medical treatment at the invitation of the Moscow Patriarch. The next week, he was in Saint Petersburg. In fact, according to the joint statement of the SOC's Press service and the Department for External Church Relations of the ROC, all of this had already been discussed in November 2014 during the official visit of Patriarch Kirill to Belgrade.[72] Archbishop Jovan stayed for three months in the Russian Federation and has been enjoying freedom

68 "Святейший Патриарх Кирилл встретился с Президентом Македонии Георге Ивановым" [Patriarch Kirill met with Macedonian President George Ivanov], 09.02.2014, URL: http://www.patriarchia.ru/db/text/3562435.html [14.03.2016].

69 Ibid. The reference of the Moscow Patriarch to the preservation of national identity through the restoration of the canonical status appears quite illustrative, being made from one of the highest offices within Slavic Orthodoxy. It should be pointed out, however, that, according to this press release, Patriarch Kirill did not mention autocephaly *per se*, but spoke rather of "the restoration of the canonical status". Such a construction, being less concrete, could involve different solutions. He also mentioned that this problem should be solved in "a brotherly dialogue with the Serbian Orthodox Church".

70 "Саопштење за јавност" [Press release], 23.12.2014, URL: http://spc.rs/sr/saopshtenje_za_javnost_13 [18.03.2016].

71 "Соопштение" [Announcement], 22.12.2014, URL: http://www.mpc.org.mk/vest.asp?id=6310 [18.03.2016].

72 "Саопштење Службе за комуникацију Одељења спољних црквених веза Московске Патријаршије и Информативне службе Српске Православне Цркве" [Communiqué of the Department for External Church Relations of the Moscow Patriarchate and the SOC Press Service], 03.02.2015, URL: http://spc.rs/sr/oslobodjen_iz_zatvora_arhiepiskop_ohridski_jovan_vranishkovski [18.03.2016].

ever since upon his return to the Republic of (North) Macedonia. He is, however, still under prosecution, together with the Bishops Marko and David from the OAO.

At the controversial Pan-Orthodox Council that was held on the island of Crete between 16 and 26 June 2016, the MOC was not invited, since its ecclesiastical status is still unrecognised. Moreover, the topic "Autocephaly and the way of granting it", which would directly affect the current ecclesiastical situation in the Republic of (North) Macedonia, was not part of the discussions of the Council, although it is one of the crucial issues for the coordination of the entire Orthodox world today. One could argue that the Russian pressure on (North) Macedonia was undertaken with regard to positioning itself before the Council. The mediation of the Moscow Patriarchate in Skopje obviously had a successful outcome. One way to interpret this success would be to understand it as a message to the entire Orthodox world that the Moscow Patriarchate, and not Constantinople, has the ways and means, or at least, the potential to mediate in the unresolved conflicts in the Orthodox world. In the run-up to the Pan-Orthodox Council, a letter addressing the primates of the autocephalous Orthodox Churches, in which the Council was asked to recognise the MOC, was sent on the behalf of the monastics of the MOC.[73] The strict regulations of the Council in Crete, however, did not allow for such a request to be discussed.[74]

These few examples serve to demonstrate that the Macedonian Church schism with all its implications plays a role not only in the bilateral inter-Orthodox relations, but on the Pan-Orthodox level as well. The fact that, to use a more lapidary expression, almost everyone appears as or assumes authority, while practically no one fully possesses it in reality, shows that the Orthodox world appears unable to manifest organisational accord. Precisely in this context, some churches, such as the Patriarchates of Constantinople and Moscow, occasionally use the Macedonian ecclesiastical dispute as a proxy arena for their own struggle for primacy.

73 "Македонските монаси во активна црковна дипломатија за признавање на автокефалноста" [Macedonian Monks in Active Diplomacy for the Recognition of Autocephaly], *Religija.mk*, 09.04.2016, URL: http://religija.mk/makedonskite-monasi-vo-aktivna-crkovna-diplomatija-za-priznavanje-na-avtokefalnosta/ [07.06.2016].

74 A similar request by the Ukrainian Parliament to accord the Orthodox Church in Ukraine autocephaly was also not discussed at the Council. Yet, in the wake of further developments, the Patriarchate of Constantinople finally granted autocephaly to the Ukranian Church in 2019, a step that led the Moscow Patriarchate to break off its relations with Constantinople.

Concluding Remarks

In addition to a purely ecclesiastical, i.e. canonical, view the Macedonian ecclesiastical dispute manifests several other aspects as well. In fact, they are not separable from each other. Among them are the issues concerning modern Macedonian national identity, in the centre of which is the problematic of the nation's and state's name. The terminological solutions of the so-called Niš Agreement on liturgical unity between the SOC and the MOC proved an insurmountable obstacle for restoring this unity. The failure of this attempt led thus to an even more deepened conflict, which remains to this day. In the middle of this conflict is the autonomous Archbishopric of Ohrid, which was formed under the auspices of the SOC. The Archbishop of the OAO had been imprisoned on several occasions, whereas some other members of the hierarchy and lay adherents have been prosecuted as well on various accusations.

This dispute is not only present within bilateral inter-Orthodox relations. It has also gained a certain amount of significance on a Pan-Orthodox level. Various signals from the Patriarchates of Constantinople and Moscow that they are willing to mediate in order to overcome the Macedonian Church schism have been addressed and they present a case in point in this matter. Nevertheless, the ecclesiastical situation in the Republic of (North) Macedonia still remains complex and unresolved despite the fact that the release from prison of Archbishop Jovan presented a certain new hope in this regard. The Pan-Orthodox Council of Crete from 2016 did not address one of the essential questions of the Orthodox Church of our time, namely the issue of autocephaly, consequently depriving, for the time being, the MOC and some other non-canonical Orthodox Churches of the possibility of resolving the issue of their status in an institutional manner on the Pan-Orthodox level. The MOC has since tried to obtain recognition from the Bulgarian Orthodox Church, which it would, in return, recognise as its "Mother Church". This did not occur, although, as an answer to this request, the BOC formed a joint commission with the MOC in order to further examine the possibilities for the solution of the MOC's status. As long as other Orthodox Churches recognise the SOC as the only relevant and legitimate address for resolving the Macedonian Church schism, it will be difficult for the MOC to undertake any steps for canonical recognition, which would not include the SOC. At the same time, this means that the OAO, irrespective of its position in society and its legal status in the country, must be part of the equation as well. It is, however, questionable if the MOC would, in an event of a renewed reconciliation attempt, accept the position of the OAO and if so, in what form. All this is, as already stated above, only then conceivable, if the Orthodox consensus on the SOC's position in this dispute remains unchanged.

Finally, the overall issue here is not simply the dispute between the MOC and the SOC. It is a much larger and a grave problem for the unity of the Orthodox world and concerns the question of a national self-confirmation through the formation of a separate, independent – *autocephalous* – national church. In other words, the model that was established in the nineteenth century – establishing an independent church (from the Patriarchate of Constantinople, which was still under the Ottoman rule) as a certain continuation of the state-building process – survived in the twentieth and the twenty-first centuries. The Macedonian ecclesiastical question is a case in point here, but it is by no means unique, as the example of the Ukrainian Orthodox Church, its autocephaly in 2019, and the subsequent schism between Constantinople and Moscow show. After solving its problems with Greece with the Prespa Agreement, North Macedonian politicians have officially approached the Patriarchate of Constantinople in order to inquire about the possibilities of accepting the MOC in the family of the canonical Orthodox Churches. It remains to be seen how the Patriarchate of Constantinople will act in this situation, considering the problems that the recent recognition of the Ukrainian Church autocephaly by Constantinople has created in the Orthodox world. Needless to say, a solution of the Macedonian Church schism cannot be found without the involvement and the consent of the SOC, whereas the potential role of the BOC in this process is also still open. All in all, the above complex situation reveals the current inability of the Orthodox world to address the issue of nationalisation (i.e., of the particular nationalisations) of the church in a critical, self-reflective, and consensual way. As long as this situation lingers on, there will be in all probability new canonical recognitions or non-canonical declarations of church autocephaly in the near future. This could easily pave the way not only for further similar disputes and schisms, but also for a growing disunity within the universal Orthodox Church. In turn, this underlines the pressing need to reach a Pan-Orthodox consensus on crucial issues pertaining to the effective communication and operation of the entire Orthodox world.

The Return of Duklja: The Montenegrin Orthodox Church's Recasting of History

Emil Hilton Saggau

A picture printed in 2012 in *Lučindan*, the Montenegrin Orthodox Church's (henceforth MoOC) magazine, shows a religious procession. In it, two men carry icons of two local medieval magnates and behind them walks Metropolitan Mihailo, the head – or "Vladika" – of the MoOC (secular name: Miras Dedić).

This picture shows a central religious transformation, which started in the early 1990s within the Montenegrin state. Montenegro has been the scene for the revitalisation of a MoOC after a bitter feud between pro-independence Montenegrins and the Serbian Orthodox Metropolitanate of Montenegro and the Littoral (in Serbian: *Mitropolija Crnogorsko-Primorska*) during the breakup of Yugoslavia. The MoOC has tried to transform, adapt, and rewrite the history of Montenegro to fit into its claim for an independent religious status detached from the Patriarchate of Belgrade and the Serbian Orthodox Church (SOC). This reshaping is partly based on the revival of a "Dukljan" religious identity linked to the medieval Slavic state known as Duklja (in Latin: *Dioclea*),[1] which is claimed to have been religiously and culturally independent from the Serbian medieval state known as Raška. This claim is bluntly put across in the picture as the two icons depict Prince Jovan Vladimir and Count Ivan Crnojevići, who were both rulers of the historical region of Duklja. In the picture, they are elevated into sainthood and portrayed as the cultural and religious medieval pillars of the MoOC's "Dukljan" identity.

---

1 The state Duklja, known in Greek as Διοκλεία and in Latin as *Dioclea*, was originally a Roman city, founded outside the current Montenegrin capital Podgorica in the Zeta valley. An archbishop resided in the city Dioclea that was destroyed during several wars between 700 and 1000. The last recorded bishop left the city after its destruction in 980. The Archdiocese of Diokleia is today a titular Metropolis in the Eastern Orthodox Church under the Ecumenical Patriarchate of Constantinople, currently held by Metropolitan Kallistos Ware. See Vojislav D. Nikčević, *Monumenta Montenegrina – Arhiepiskopije Duklja i Prevalitana* [Montenegrin Monuments – The Archbishopric of Duklja and Prevalitana], Podgorica 2001, 240–242.

A Montenegrin Orthodox procession in 2012.[2] The two icons display St Vladimir and St Ivan Crnojevići.

This claim and the new Montenegrin "Dukljan" Orthodox identity is not straightforward and is certainly contested. The term "Duklja" in itself refers to the above mentioned Roman-Slavic region, but nowadays it has also increasingly become a Serbian derogative slur, which is used to describe the overstated Montenegrin national movement's claims of past glory and territory from a Serbian nationalist point of view. On the other hand, the name of "Duklja" is celebrated and held high within Montenegrin nationalist intellectual circles, because it refers to a Montenegrin past untouched by Serbs. The term was therefore strategically used by these intellectuals when they established the first pro-Montenegrin academy, namely the Duklja Academy of Science and Arts. The term hence contains both extremely negative and positive connotations depending on the context in which it is used.

The name of the MoOC is likewise problematic insofar as it attests three pro-Montenegrin claims. The use of "Montenegro" as one all-encompassing title, instead of using "Montenegro and the Littoral" as the SOC does, is a demonstration that the state of Montenegro is considered as a single coherent territorial, civic, and national unit as opposed to a state encompassing a number of regional differences. This claim of unity is expanded through the use of the term "Church" and even its description of being an "Orthodox" Church. This is because the MoOC is not canonically recognised as an Orthodox Church by the main canonical Orthodox Churches. The use of "Church" and "Orthodoxy" as labels is therefore also problematic, because it attests that the MoOC belongs to a

2 The photo is reproduced from *Lučindan* 45 (2012) 2.

special family of Christian Churches, which its Serbian counterpart, however, categorically rejects.[3]

The contestation is perhaps not surprising when one takes into account that the Balkan Peninsula is in every way a region of *entangled history*. The programmatic theoretical reflection of *histoire croisée*, suggested by Michael Werner and Bénédict Zimmermann, is much needed here.[4] The sources and materials mentioned in this study are currently embedded into various national contexts, and it is therefore necessary to remember this entanglement between states, nationalities, and ethnicities when they are treated. This article, thus, consist of two main sections: The first and most thorough section focuses on the pro-independence Montenegrins, as well as on the terminology and the approach of the MoOC uses to portray and analyse the "Duklja" identity. Moreover, it investigates the basis for the historical claims that form the roots of this identity. The second section turns to a much more Serbian-orientated approach centred on the SOC and discusses both points of view and the cultural, religious, and national entanglement of which they are proof in order to outline the reception mechanisms and historiographical practices in the two churches and the communities around them.

The Reshaping of Montenegrin Nationhood

The MoOC's historical claims and the reconstruction of the Montenegrin national identity are not a unique process, but follow an already known trajectory in a similar fashion as in the other former Yugoslav Republics. Klaus Buchenau correctly notes that all former Yugoslav states experienced an increased "sacralisation of the nation" during the early 1990s.[5] The return of the Duklja identity in Montenegro is one of many South Eastern European examples of how this process of sacralisation takes place within various institutional, political, and cultural settings. The process of sacralisation of a nation, as Buchenau refers to it, is the religiously based process in which the nationhood of one nation is bolstered and strengthened through references to an external power (e.g., God). The nation becomes something more than a mere community, because it is elected, chosen,

3 For a more detailed discussion of this ecclesiological aspect of the MoOC, see Emil Hilton Saggau, "The Self-proclaimed Montenegrin Orthodox Church – A Paper Tiger or a Resurgent Church?", in Mirko Blagojević/Zlatko Matić (eds), *Religion in Contemporary Society/Религия и современное общество*, Belgrade 2017, 31–54.

4 Michael Werner/Bénédicte Zimmermann, "Beyond Comparison: *Histoire Croisée* and the Challenge of Reflexivity", *History and Theory* 45/1 (2006) 30–50, here 31–32.

5 Klaus Buchenau, "Religion und Nation in Serbien, Bulgarien und Rumänien: Drei verschiedene Wege in Südosteuropa", in Alojz Ivanišević (ed.), *Re-Sakralisierung des öffentlichen Raums in Südosteuropa nach der Wende 1989?*, Frankfurt am Main 2012, 61–84, here 62.

and anointed by a divine power. A definition of a nation in an Eastern and Central European context is the following:

> The nation is a particular positioning in the political, cultural, historic, and spiritual universe; it is a cosmic entity. It refers – in ways that differ from country to country – to specific (real or imagined) sources and heritage, and it determines communal belonging, goals, and values.[6]

The sacralisation transforms the *particular positioning*, to use Miklós Tomka's term, into a community based on external references to a religion. The imagined, delimited, and sovereign connection between the members of the nation (community) is then not only natural or organic, but one that is divinely selected.[7]

The process of sacralisation of the nation in the Yugoslav Republics was not only a revival of national categories (Serbs, Croats, Montenegrins etc.), but also a revival of the religious traditions associated with them.[8] The former Yugoslav communist government was aware of the mobilising ideological powers vested in the concept of nationhood and tried to create a Yugoslav *civil religion* and civil citizenship, without any references to a Christian God or an ethnic nation, but with the same sort of ritual, liturgical, and symbolic power. Civil religion is, since Robert N. Bellah's 1967 article on *Civil Religion in America*, and later his book from 1975 called *The Broken Covenant*, often described as the societal effort to create a nationhood without divine implications, but with a numinous sound.[9] The project of a common Yugoslav civil religion massively failed for many reasons, paving the way for the revival of the pre-Yugoslav nationalities and the religious communities linked to them – all anxious for a possible return to power. This was most visible in the revival of Croatian and Serbian nationalism, where the political establishment forged a close alliance with the Catholic and Orthodox religious communities respectively.[10] The Montenegrin communists and other pro-Montenegrin non-governmental organisations were very much aware of the potential nation-building and enforcing powers to be found in religion from early on. This is exemplified in the discussions over the heritage of Metropolitan and

---

6 Miklós Tomka/Réka Szilárdi, "Religion and Nation", in András Máté-Tóth/Gergely Rosta (eds), *Focus on Religion in Central and Eastern Europe: A Regional View*, Berlin 2016, 75–111, here 82.

7 For an elaboration on the sacralisation of nations in South Eastern Europe, see Emil Hilton Saggau, "Unblocking the Sacred: New Perspectives on the Religious Revival in South Eastern Europe", *Journal for Religion and Society in Central and Eastern Europe* 11/1 (2018) 39–55.

8 For a thorough introduction to the connection between religion and nationalism in former Yugoslavia, see Pål Kolstø (ed.), *Strategies of Symbolic Nation-building in South Eastern Europe*, London 2014.

9 Robert N. Bellah, "Civil Religion in America", *Dædalus* 96/1 (1967) 1–21; Robert N. Bellah, *The Broken Covenant: American Civil Religion in Time of Trial*, New York 1975.

10 John R. Lampe, *Yugoslavia as History*, Cambridge 2000, 332–364.

secular ruler of Montenegro, Petar II Petrović-Njegoš (1813-1851), which took place from the 1960s and onwards. This partly explains the effort to support the MoOC and the reluctance to accept the SOC in Montenegro.[11]

The British historian Andrew Hastings provides a concrete example of how religious communities help shape these national formations in his work on nationhood.[12] Hastings identifies the concrete process and the core factors that can be activated in order to create a nation. He argues that the nationhood has to draw on traditions, events, and heritage that go beyond the immediate present, because this provides the nation with legitimacy. Religious communities in particular play an important role in the nation-building process through various factors, such as 1) a sanctification of the starting point, 2) a mythologisation and commemoration of national threats, 3) the social role of the clergy, 4) the production and supervision of vernacular literature, 5) the use of the Biblical narrative as a model for nations, 6) an independent national church, and 7) a national destiny for which it is chosen.[13] This can be seen in the shaping of a Montenegrin nation based on the Dukljan identity. Hastings' identification of factors can be used as a tool to analyse the MoOC and the Duklja identity.

The Political Change: Montenegro from 1990 until Today

The current rekindling of the Duklja identity has been slower than other national awakenings in the rest of former Yugoslavia. The new Montenegrin identity had to be created by differentiating it from the Serbian one, although the two constitute a quite homogenous Slavic speaking population with same the religion – unlike in Bosnia and Croatia, for example. The challenge only became possible because the Montenegrin society has seen a drastic economic, political, and ideological shift in the last twenty-five years, slightly delayed from the transformation elsewhere in the former Yugoslav Republics. The religious transformation and creation of a new nationhood are definitely part of this shift and follow the same trajectory as the state's ideological and cultural transformation.[14] The shift was a necessary step due to the slow dissolution of socialist Yugoslavia and the subsequent civil wars. The process in Montenegro differs, among other things,

---

11 Emil Hilton Saggau, "A Shrine for the Nation: The Material Transformation of the Lovćen Site in Montenegro", *Journal of Balkan and Near Eastern Studies* 20/5 (2018) 495–512.

12 Andrew Hastings, *The Construction of Nationhood – Ethnicity, Religion and Nationalism*, Cambridge 1997.

13 Ibid., 187–188.

14 For a throughout study of this transformation, see Florian Bieber, "Montenegrin Politics since the Disintegration of Yugoslavia", in idem (ed.), *Montenegro in Transition*, Baden-Baden 2003, 11–41.

from the rest of Yugoslavia, because Montenegro's political elite was closely associated with its Serbian counterpart from 1989 to 1996.[15]

The period of crisis from the 1980s until the end of the Kosovo War in 1999 provided a window of opportunity for a distinct Montenegrin nationalist movement, which began to fortify its position in the Montenegrin society in the early 1990s – as its sister movements did in Croatia, Serbia, Bosnia, and Macedonia. The primary objective of the early Montenegrin national movement (*Liberalni Savez Crne Gore*) was a detachment of the former Socialist Republic of Montenegro from the Serbian one in order to protect the Montenegrin identity (people) against what they called the Serbian "aggressor".[16] This national movement was at first rather small unlike the groups in Croatia and did only reach a broader part of the population after 1996.

As several social scientists have observed, one of the reason for its popularisation was that religion in Yugoslavia in the late 1980s became one of the bearing arches in the emerging nationalist movements.[17] This was also true in the Montenegrin Republic where the Montenegrin nationalistic movement identified the local branch of the Serbian Orthodox Church, the Metropolitan of Montenegro and the Littoral, as the Serbian "aggressor". The Montenegrin nationalist movement and their supporters in the old cultural capital of Montenegro, Cetinje, clashed with the Serbian Orthodox Church and its supporters on several occasions in the early 1990s – including during a celebration of the local saint Petar in 1992. These events persuaded parts of the movement to form (or revive) the MoOC in 1993.[18]

Along with the formation of this religious organisation, a whole branch of Montenegrin political and cultural institutions emerged such as *Matica Crnagorska* ("The Cradle of Montenegro", founded in 1993) and the *Dukljanska Akademija Nauka i Umjetnosti (*Dukljan Academy of Science and Arts, founded in 1999). These organisations were created during a dramatic shift in Montenegrin politics in 1996-1997 when the now Socialist (formerly Communist) monolithic Party that had ruled Montenegro exclusively since the Second World War split into two groups, one pro-Montenegrin and the other pro-Serbian. The pro-Montenegrin wing was led by Prime Minister Milo Đukanović and has been

15 Kenneth Morrison, *Montenegro – A Modern History*, London 2009, 81–88.

16 Ibid., 91–98.

17 Lampe, *Yugoslavia* (as n. 10), 343–344

18 I do not focus here on the struggle itself in detail. The political and concrete manifestation of the conflict are described at length by Stefan Kube, "Wer repräsentiert die Orthodoxie in Montenegro? Kirchliche Konflikte um den öffentlichen Raum", in Alojz Ivanišević (ed.), *Re-Sakralisierung des öffentlichen Raums in Südosteuropa nach der Wende 1989?*, Frankfurt am Main 2012, 115–131; Morrison, *Montenegro* (as n. 15), 142–168; František Šistek, "Clericalization of Nationalism", in András Máté-Tóth/Cosima Rughinis (eds), *Spaces and Borders: Current Research on Religion in Central and Eastern Europe*, Berlin 2010, 118–130.

successful in keeping itself in power since 1996. It led a broad alliance of Montenegrin parties and civil society towards independence. Following a referendum, the Montenegrin Republic was declared independent from Serbia in 2006.[19]

Religion has been a key battleground in the cultural and political struggle between the pro-Montenegrin and pro-Serbian parts of Montenegrin society, especially since the political divide in 1996. The MoOC therefore plays a vital role in this conflict for the pro-Montenegrin side. The church was officially condemned as a nationalist sect by the SOC and several others of the canonical Orthodox Churches but has been supported by the Montenegrin nationalist movement. Today, there are close links between the MoOC and the Montenegrin nationalist cultural, political, and communication centres. The last phase of the conflict concerns a new law on "Freedom of Religion or Beliefs and Legal Status of Religious Communities", adopted on 27 December 2019 by the Parliament of Montenegro and in force since 8 January 2020. This law basically supports the greater nationalisation of the Orthodox Church in Montenegro in favour of the MoOC and is in many respects discriminatory towards the SOC. The latter has subsequently reacted with massive protests and voiced serious concerns about this development, while it also received wide support from the canonical Orthodox Churches, as well as political backing from Serbia. After all, Ecumenical Patriarch Bartholomew, in a letter to the President of the Republic of Montenegro Milo Đukanović on 21 June 2019, had made clear that he recognises only the Holy Metropolitanate of Montenegro under the SOC as the canonical church in the country.

The Content of the Duklja Identity

The MoOC constructed the Dukljan identity through a series of historical and religious claims. These claims are supported through various lines of argument that dwell on different aspects of the church, its contested history, its religious and cultural identity, and its theological and legal foundations. The arguments are presented to the fullest of their extent in the MoOC's main publication *Lučindan*. This church magazine features articles where the main spokespersons of the MoOC address their congregation as well as discuss several themes relating to the church. The magazine often features articles with historical content or references of particular interest in relation to our topic. Some examples of these are Aleksander Radoman's article about Bodin Vojislavljević and the state of Duklja (spanning from the ninth to the eleventh centuries) from 2013 or Novak Adzić's article about Đurađ II Balšić and the Zeta state (in the fourteenth and fifteenth

19 Morrison, *Montenegro* (as n. 15), 205–221.

centuries) from 2012.[20] Radoman and Adzić's articles could best be described as popular historical articles, which explain and dramatise the life of historical persons such as Bodin or Đurađ. A notable feature of these texts is that their authors spend a great deal of energy investigating the family and the various relationships of the person in question in order to demonstrate which other local nobles Đurađ or Bodin were related to. This endeavour has an underlying target that rarely reaches the surface of the text. Both writers try to show how Bodin and Đurađ were not associated to the great noble families or bloodlines of the Bulgarian, Serbian, and Albanian medieval realms. In fact, they want to demonstrate that they belong to a unique Dukljan-Slavic line of blood.

Lučindan also features articles of another type, in which the historical content becomes a premise embedded into other topics or discussions of a particular theme. Examples of such articles include the treatment of the so-called *Rumija* case, such as the articles of R. Rotković, S. Vucinić, and Z. L. Đurović from 2011-2012.[21] The *Rumija* case, in short, is a discussion of the ownership of the *Rumija* mountain in Montenegro. The mountain has since 2005 been a key battleground between Serbian, Montenegrin, and Albanian interests. The discussion over the site erupted after representatives of the SOC in 2015, with the use of two Serbian military helicopters, placed a pre-fabricated tin church on the top of the mountain in order to claim the site as a holy place for the SOC. The action of the SOC thereby excluded the local Albanians and Montenegrins according to their parties, organisations, and the MoOC.[22] The religious significance of *Rumija* is based on the heritage of St Jovan Vladimir, who is claimed as a local saint by not only the SOC and MoOC, but also by several other Eastern Orthodox Churches, such as the Bulgarian, Macedonian, Albanian, and Greek ones. *Rumija* occupies a central place in the hagiography of the saint. This case is discussed in the articles mentioned above, often leading the authors to postulate a series of claims about Jovan Vladimir, his family, and his connection to the Vojislavljević house.

The essence of these articles in regard to the past independence of Montenegro is summarised in an editorial note, which states the following:

---

20 Aleksander Radoman, "Bodinoc olovni pečat zlatnog sjaj" [Bodin's Lead Seal has a Golden Glow], *Lučindan* 46 (2013) 56–63; Novak Adzić, "Đurađ II Balšić i Kosovoski boj 1389. godin" [Đurađ II Balšić at the Battle of Kosovo Field 1389], *Lučindan* 45 (2013) 29–35.

21 R. Rotković, "SPC traži tomos od CPC iako ga ni ona sama nija imala" [The SOC asks for a Tomos from the MoOC, even though it did not need to], *Lučindan* 41 (2011) 45–49; S. Vučinić, "Đe dukljansko-barsko arcibskupija?" [Is Duklja-Bar an Archbishopric?], *Lučindan* 40 (2011) 49–51; Z. L. Đurović, "Sveti Vladimir Dukljanski" [Saint Vladimir of Duklja], *Lučindan* 40 (2011) 152–154.

22 See Đorđe Pavićević/Srđan Đurović, "Relations between Montenegro and Serbia from 1991-2006: An Analysis of Media Discourse", in Pål Kolstø (ed.), *Media Discourse and the Yugoslav Conflicts*, London 2012, 129–154, here 145–146.

> These are the truths; the Montenegrins form an independent, indigenous, and historical nation that originated and evolved in its own millennial ethnic and historical past [...] created in the struggle for freedom and attained freedom that was constituted and preserved in their state Duklja – Zeta – Montenegro [...] This state is not created by the SOC in Montenegro since the Montenegrin state is older than the Serbian state and church, because the Dukljan Montenegrin ruler, Mihailo Vojislavljević, and his country were internationally recognised, and he was crowned 140 years before the first Serbian ruler.[23]

It is further elaborated in a press release printed in the same magazine, which argues that "Montenegro was liberated from the Serbian occupation of the Nemanja dynasty in 1360, during the reign of the Balšić, the country's second dynasty".[24]

As shown in these two quotes, the MoOC clearly states that the historical Slavic state of Duklja under the Vojislavljević rule and the Zeta state under the Balšić (and later Crnojevići) house were independent from Byzantium, as well as medieval Bulgaria and Serbia according to their point of view. The independence of these states is taken as a sort of guarantee that the churches of these states were also in fact independent and under the supervision of these rulers. This is a rather vital point because it stresses that the churches and the traditions that originated in Duklja are something completely different from the Serbian Church founded under the Nemanja house. The Nemanja house and the Serbs are in general portrayed as alien to the Duklja tradition. In the quote, the MoOC speaks of a "Serbian occupation under the Nemanja dynasty", which is, in other words, a portrayal of the Serbs and their medieval kings as enemies that subverted the Montenegrin Church, people, and state. An underlying premise in this claim is that Duklja was the cradle for a people, in ethnic terms, that were to become Montenegrins and that they differed significantly from the Serbian "ethnicity". This people created a state and church of their own, which then came to be oppressed by the foreign Serbian ruler. The press release puts it bluntly:

> One of the most obvious pieces of evidence of this [the Serbian occupation, E.H.S.] is the destructive and subversive act of oppression on the Dukljan-Montenegrin cult of prince St Vladimir, whose dynasty, Vojislavljević, was repressed under the Serbian-Nemanja occupation of Montenegro from 1186 onwards.[25]

---

23 Montenegrin Orthodox Church, "Nije SPC nego CPC gradila I učvršćivala Crnu Gore" [It is not the SOC, but the MoOC that forms and strengthens Montenegro], *Lučindan* 43 (2012) 10–13, here 10.

24 Montenegrin Orthodox Church, "Poništenje odluka Podgoričtenje skupštenje omogućava ostvarenje prava Crne Gore i CPC" [The Annulment of the Decisions of the Podgorica's Assembly Enabling the Exercise of Montenegro's Rights and the MoOC], *Lučindan* 43 (2012) 20–23, here 20.

25 Ibid.

The press release argues that the Serbian occupation oppressed the cult of St Jovan Vladimir (d. 1016), who is claimed to be both a true Montenegrin (Dukljan) and a member of the Vojislavljević dynasty.

The releases, articles, and editorial notes in *Lučindan* constitute a series of claims in which a distinct historical narrative and Dukljan identity emerge. This identity is based on an independent religious tradition that unfolded and existed within the independent Duklja and Zeta states under the ruling houses of Vojislavljević, Balšić, and Crnojevići. This independent tradition is, according to the MoOC, best expressed in the cult of St Jovan Vladimir, who is a member of the Vojislavljević family and an indigenous member of the Duklja Slavic kin. The independence of these states and houses is regarded as a sort of historical proof of the indigenous character of the Montenegrin people and church as descendants of these states.

Figure 1: References to central geographical terms and names from Montenegro's medieval past in *Lučindan*, 2009-2014 (nos. 33-47, except nos. 34 and 44).

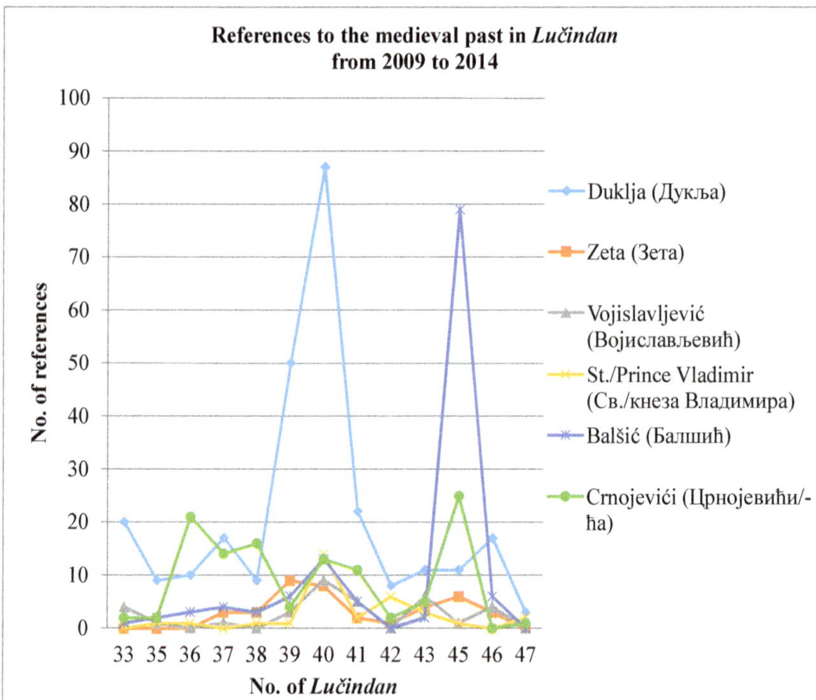

Figure 1 displays how often these names of geographical units and rulers are mentioned in *Lučindan* between 2009 and 2014, which is on average 48 references per issue. Each magazine is roughly one hundred pages long and features around 20 articles, which – on average – means that for every two pages there is one reference to these medieval terms. This is interesting because most of the references are not to religious leaders or landmarks, such as St Jovan Vladimir, which one could expect a church magazine to be writing about. In fact, references to St Jovan Vladimir only make up around 5 percent of all the medieval references during the period. These basic calculations reveal the extent and volume of this "Duklja" theme in the MoOC's main outlet.

In the pro-Montenegrin magazine of *Matica Crnagorska*, the same structures exist. *Matica Crnagorska* describes itself as "an independent non-governmental organization of intellectuals, founded at Cetinje in 1993".[26] The organisation is devoted to a pro-Montenegrin stance and publishes a journal with political, scientific and cultural content. It pays special attention to the promotion of the Montenegrin identity and the MoOC. Its programme from 2014 states:

> Montenegro is a political and cultural community with a millennium long statehood tradition. Since the foundation of the independent state of Duklja in the mid-11th century, […] Montenegro, despite periods of shorter or longer occupation, always managed to reconstitute its independence.[27]

And it continues:

> The Montenegrin Orthodox Church was one of the rare churches not to succumb to earthly benefits and desire to rule the people. As the Western Church had its own archbishopric in Duklja, so Constantinople supported some dioceses._The reality of coexistence of Eastern and Western churches on the territory of modern Montenegro has a long tradition that resulted in rarely recognized examples.[28]

In *Matica Crnagorska*'s pro-Montenegrin programme, the organisation highlights the long tradition of church and state independence as a significant backdrop of the Montenegrin identity and modern state. These two independent institutions are closely interlinked and therefore form the backbone of the Montenegrin cultural, religious, and political identity in their view. There are two important historical claims in this "backbone" of Montenegrin identity. The first one is that there existed an independent Slavic state called Duklja in the eleventh century with its own cultural traditions that differed significantly from the Slavic Serbian community and the Serbian medieval kingdom that emerged from the province of

26 Matica Crnagorska Website: URL: http://www.maticacrnogorska.me/aboutus.html [13.02. 2016].

27 "The Programme of Matica Crnogorska – Montenegro on its European Path" (translated by Milena Filipović, 2014) 11, URL: http://www.maticacrnogorska.me/files/MATICA%20CG%20PROGRAM%20ENG.pdf [13.02.2016].

28 Ibid., 30.

Raška. Second, the organisation emphasises that the Montenegrin territory was split between allegiance to the Western Latin and Eastern Orthodox Churches, which led to a rare example of co-existence. In the background of this dual religiosity, it claims that the Church in Montenegro developed its own unique tradition. Vojislav D. Nikčević, a Montenegrin historian, has written two major works on the formation and ecclesiastial history of the provinces of Duklja and Pravalitana, which complement several smaller treatments of the topic.[29]

In *Matica Crnagorska*'s journal, other historical themes resurface, such as the medieval historical past in a series of articles published between 2010 and 2014. One of the main themes under scrutiny is the complex political history of the principality of Zeta during the rule of the Balšić and Crnojevići house after the fall of the Serbian Empire (ca. 1362-1514). This theme seems vital for the authors because of the unique religious blend of Latin and Eastern Orthodox Christianity. Moreover, in the former Montenegrin capital Cetinje, several monasteries and castles were founded during this period. Božidar Šekularac, an author in *Matica*, points out that the borders of modern-day Montenegro were formed at this time.[30] The Balšić and Crnojevići era of Zeta is therefore central in the eyes of these pro-Montenegrin authors, because the borders, as well as the cities and cultural heritage of Montenegro were formed during that period. It therefore becomes clear that the political status, religious orientation, and cultural origin of the Crnojevići are also a vital part of the Montenegrin identity along the same line as an independent Duklja in the eleventh century.[31] The main sources of the Montenegrin discourse on the Balšić and Crnojevići period of Zeta are two anthologies and an additional volume published by *Matica Crnagorska*.[32]

This analysis of the MoOC's publications and its close cultural ally *Matica Crnagorska* reveals four main points regarding the medieval past of Montenegro. These four points are the central pillars of the Dukljan identity and are used both combined and individually to argue for a significant independent religious and cultural tradition in Montenegro that differs from Serbia proper:

---

29 Vojislav D. Nikčević, *Duklja i Pravalitana*, Podgorica 2012; Nikčević, *Monumenta* (as n. 1).

30 Božidar Šekularać, "Crnojevići u izvornoj građi matica" [Crnojevici at the Original Cradle City], *Matica* (2010) 551–562.

31 For a thorough introduction to and analysis of the stance of pro-Montenegrin intellectuals regarding Montenegrin identity, history, and language, which is not completely overlapping with that of the MoOC, see Hans-Michael Miedlig, "Zur Frage der Ethnizität und Identität der Montenegriner in Geschichte und Gegenwart", *Zeitschrift für Balkanologie* 42 (2006) 146–165.

32 See Josip Jelčić, *Zeta i dinastija Balšića* [Zeta under the Balšić Dynasty] Podgorica 2010; Čedomir Drašković *et al.*, *Zeta / Crna Gora u doba Balšići (1360-1421)* [Zeta/Montenegro at the Time of the Balšić (1360-1421)], Podgorica 2012; Čedomir Drašković *et al.*, *Crnojevići* [The Crnojevići House], Podgorica 2010.

1. The region that encompasses Montenegro was an independent kingdom called Duklja under the Vojislavljević house before Serbia (Raška) emerged.
2. The region had its own independent church history before the Serbian takeover.
3. The region was also an independent entity called Zeta after the fall of the Serbian Empire under the rule of the Balšić and Crnojevići houses.
4. The region therefore has its own distinct and significant medieval religious and cultural tradition.

In the following section, these claims and how they frame the history of the region is examined, followed by a discussion of the reasoning behind them.

Claim 1: The Significance of Duklja

The first claim concerns Duklja and contains a series of intertwined points. First of all, these points are bound up with the claim that the Slavic inhabitants of medieval Duklja were different from the Serbs. Importantly, the house of Vojislavljević is regarded as a family with a significant identity as Dukljan.

Duklja was originally a Roman colony or polis, likely to have been established under Emperor Flavian in the late second century in the later Eastern Roman province of Praevalitana.[33] The area is later mentioned as a separate province called Dioclea in the Byzantine text *De Administrando Imperio* dating from the mid-tenth century. In this text, the Byzantine Emperor Constantine VII Porphyrogenitus describes the land as "Diokleia" (in Greek: Διοκλεία). The text points out that Diokleia is a specific area along the line of Croatia, Dalmatia, Zamulje, and Serbia. Unlike the description of Croatia, Serbia and even the province of Zamulje, towards the beginning of the text, the author does not describe in precise terms the ethnic belonging of the inhabitants.[34] What is known as *The Chronicle of the Priest of Duklja (CPD)* provides a more detailed description of the area and its local Slavic magnates from the ninth to the tenth century. It is probably written in the eleventh century, according to most studies.[35] CPD is divided into three main sections and claims in the first section that the region was in fact called "Croatia rubera" (red Croatia) and led by its own Slavic nobles, mentioned by name, partly under Byzantine or Bulgarian supremacy. However, there are no other sources or remains that support this list of rulers as

33 Marjeta Šašel-Kos, "Ananca: Greek Ananke worshipped at Dioclea (Dalmatia)", in Werner Eck/Bence Fehér/Péter Kovács (eds), *Studia Epigraphica in Memoriam Géza Alföldy*, Bonn 2013, 295–306.

34 Constantine VII, "De Administrando Imperio", in Guyla Moravcsik (ed.), *Corpus Fontium Historiae Byzantinae*, vol. 1, Washington/DC 1967, 162–163.

35 Norman W. Ingham, "The Martyrdom of Saint John Vladimir of Dioclea", *International Journal of Slavic Linguistics and Poetics* 35–36 (1987) 199–216.

well as the name for the region suggested in CPD. The main point of the CPD is, nevertheless, that the ruling house of the Duklja region was of Slavic-Croatian descent and under Latin influence. This "Latin" claim on Duklja seems to be intended due to the fact that the CPD's main intention is to declare the port city of Bar as a long-standing Latin centre worthy to be a Western Archbishopric.[36] After all, the historical value of CPD is highly criticised by the medieval scholars Norman Ingman and Paul Stephenson.[37]

Probably the first and most well-documented independent rulers of Duklja seem to have been the family of Voislav or Vojislavljević that ruled the principality from about 1030 onwards. The first ruler is often identified as Stefan Voislav, described as a Byzantine governor (in Greek: ἄρχων) in the Byzantine sources.[38] The Vojislavljević family was able to claim independence under Mihailo (ca. 1050-1081) and his son Constantin Bodin (ca. 1072-1108), who raised their province to a kingdom that was recognised by Rome. Bodin was moreover successful in securing the promotion of the port city of Bar to a Western Archbishopric in 1089. During this period, a Norman crusade went through the region. Crusaders seem to have passed through Bodin's kingdom, to whom their chronicles simply refer as the "Slavic King".[39] In fact, the Byzantine sources do not completely align with CPD and the Western sources. They do recognise the limited independence of Mihailo's rebellious realm, but at the same time state that Bodin was solely a Byzantine governor (in Greek: δούξ), which does seem to have been the case for his family from 1108 onwards following his death and a later Byzantine invasion. The Byzantine account written by John Skylitzes describes the rebellion under Stefan and Mihailo in the 1030s as a "Serbian" uprising.[40]

All in all, this short survey of the sources from this period and the literature available shows that the status of Duklja and the "ethnicity" of its inhabitants is not an easy question to answer. The medieval historian John Fine concludes in that spirit that all the contemporary sources of Byzantium, the Normans and even the Arabs on Duklja did not seem to have been interested in differentiating between various Slavic tribes, realms, and traditions.[41] The sources often just refer to them simply as Slavs. This is quite important regarding the Dukljan identity, because it reveals that the MoOC's claim is based on two points of view. First of all, the MoOC applies modern-day categories, such as ethnicity and nations, to

36 Paul Stephenson, *Byzantium's Balkan Frontier: A Political Study of the Northern Balkans 900-1204*, Cambridge 2006, 119.

37 See ibid.; Ingham, "The Martyrdom" (as n. 35), 201.

38 John Fine, *The Early Medieval Balkans: A Critical Survey from the Sixth to the Late Twelfth Century,* Ann Arbor/MI 1991, 36.

39 Ibid., 36–37.

40 Ingham, "The Martyrdom" (as n. 35), 202.

41 John Fine, *When Ethnicity did not Matter in the Balkans: A Study of Identity in Pre-Nationalist Croatia, Dalmatia, and Slavonia in the Medieval and Early-Modern Periods*, Ann Arbor/MI 2006.

old sources and texts that simply lack such categories. Secondly, the MoOC simply disregards all sources that contradict their interpretation, such as the Byzantine ones. It is rather noticeable that all external sources to Duklja – except the Papal ones – do not regard Duklja as much more than a rebellious region ruled by a tribe of Serbs. The only account that describes the region as independent and having an "ethnicity" of its own is the CPD, which is a very questionable source with its own agenda and probably even written fairly long after the events had taken place. The CPD is the only internal source and is therefore valuable. However, the way it is treated as representing the complete truth on this matter with modern categories applied to it reveals that the MoOC's modern-day agenda is the basis of their interpretation of Duklja.

Claim 2: The Independent Church

There are no doubts that there in fact was a functioning church structure in the Roman city of Dioclea (Duklja) from the early fourth century onwards. The Roman Pope addressed a bishop based in Duklja in some letters from the seventh century before the Avar invasion and destruction of the city. There also seems to have been an ongoing contact between the Western Church and some of the coastal dioceses and the Bishopric of Bar, which were under Slavic rule from the ninth century onwards.[42]

The CPD contains a short and elaborative Life (*vita*) of St Jovan Vladimir, a local pious ruler murdered around 1016 in a church by his brother-in-law, the newly crowned Bulgarian Emperor, during an internal struggle over succession to the Bulgarian throne. This *vita* bears resemblance to the Western and Eastern traditions of lives of saints (*vitae sanctorum*) and contains some familiar topics, such as a betrayal modelled on the Judas story. The *vita* reveals that there was a significant and strong ecclesial base present in and around Duklja and that its members were powerful enough to produce a *vita* and interpret Jovan Vladimir's death into the familiar martyrdom scheme. Moreover, it also shows that the secular power in the area was probably aware of the value of promoting a local saint, especially one that was associated with the ruling family. The CPD claimed Jovan to be the uncle of Stefan Voislav and therefore an obvious patron saint for the Vojislavljević dynasty and state. This connection might also explain the unwillingness of the later Orthodox Church under the Serbian Nemanja rule to accept Jovan Vladimir as a saint. He might simply have been a symbol of a rival family and principality, which they had no reason to promote further. In the *vita*, Jovan Vladimir is portrayed as merely a local ruler under the supremacy of Byzantium and later of Bulgaria. The Byzantine John Skylitzes, however, in his

42 Francis Dvornik, *Byzantine Missions among the Slavs*, New Brunswick/NJ 1970, 17.

historical chronicle from the thirteenth century, describes him as the ruler of all of Serbia.[43]

The close interconnection between the ruling elite and the ecclesiastical community under the Vojislavljević dynasty is also very much visible elsewhere than in the CPD. Both Mihailo and Bodin seem to have used the East-West split strategically as a way to bolster their claims to kinghood. Duklja was, as the Byzantine sources describe, regarded as a Byzantine region, and the Constantinopolitan Patriarch would therefore never have accepted the area's status as a local independent kingdom. The Western Latin Church, on the other hand, might have been more willing to do so in order to manifest its power in the region in a way that was yearned for in the CPD. Mihailo and Bodin must have turned to the Western Latin Church, because it would have been the most accessible way to form an independent kingdom and subsequently a local Archbishopric under their rule, as John Fine suggests.[44]

The sources therefore point to interesting ecclesiastical circumstances in the Montenegrin area that might provide some historical context to the narrative of an independent church. This is mainly because the area was situated right in the middle between the Eastern and Western Churches and that their rulers, both secular as well as ecclesiastical, used this to their advantage in order to promote or advance their region. The strategical use of the East-West split is, however, not uncommon for the region and was exploited by the ruling elites of both Serbia, the Nemanja, and Albania, the Skanderbeg.[45]

In this strategical game, the Bishopric of Bar was central. It had lost its status as an Archbishopric shortly after the decline of the Duklja state, while in 1142 it came under the supremacy of the Latin Archbishopric of Dubrovnik (Ragusa). Both the ruling house, Nemanja, of old Serbia, the Raška state, and the magnates in the Serbian province of former Duklja tried on several – often less successful – occasions to use Bar's role as an ecclesiastical centre to bolster their own power base in the region and in relation to the Western Latin world. One of these occasions was when a member of Raška's ruling dynasty, Vukan Nemanja, ruled Duklja and tried to challenge both of his younger brothers. One of his brothers ruled all of Raška and the other one, later known as St Sava, had introduced the Eastern Orthodox faith at full scale to the Serbian Kingdom. Vukan was able to restore Bar as a Latin Archbishopric in 1199. He later overthrew his brothers in 1202 with Hungarian help with the promise of turning Serbia and Duklja into a Latin Christian realm. The local Latin clergy was after 1202 gathered in Bar in order to make the new Latin Archbishopric coherent. The remaining sources from this re-structuring of the ecclesiastical rule reveal that there seems to have been a

43 See Ingham, "The Martyrdom" (as n. 35), 199–201.

44 Fine, *The Early Medieval Balkans* (as n. 38), 215–216.

45 John Fine, *The Late Medieval Balkans: A Critical Survey from the Sixth to the Late Twelfth Century*, Ann Arbor/MI 1994, 3.

local mixture of Eastern and Western traditions within that local branch of the Latin Church. A following war with Bulgaria, which Vukan lost, returned his brother to power over Raška, who subsequently restored Eastern Orthodoxy in Duklja.[46] The local powers in Bar and Zeta were, however, overshadowed by the fast growing power of Venice (and later of the Habsburgs) that came to control most of the coastline of today's Montenegro and its Latin Church until the end of the First World War.[47]

Another central historical root is the local history of the Eastern Metropolitanate of Zeta, which was originally founded as a Bishopric under the Nemanja-controlled Church by St Sava in 1220 to counter the influence of the Latin Church along the coast, after Vukan's failed attempt to take control over all of Duklja and Raška. The anti-Catholic trait of the local Eastern Orthodox Church in the Serbian realm became distinct and is also visible in the Code of the later Nemanja ruler, Serbian Emperor Stefan Dušan (1331-1355), which condemned the "Latin heresy". The Bishopric of Zeta was later raised to a Metropolitanate after the Nemanja Church was turned into the Peć Patriarchate in 1346. Remarkably, the Metropolitanate of Zeta was the *de facto* landowner of the coastline including Bar, as well as of larger regions inland during the Serbian Empire. This highlights the strong power base into which the eastward oriented Metropolitanate of Zeta was growing during the late medieval period under the Nemanja rule.[48]

It is thus noticeable that for the Montenegrin (Duklja-Zeta) region, the independence of the ecclesiastical structures was closely intertwined with the independence of the state. The ecclesiastical structures (Eastern and Western) seem to have been there and able to support any secular claim for independence, as they did in the CPD and under Vukan Nemanja. Whether or not this in itself constitutes the described independent church structure, seems a bit less clear. However, there seems to have been a specific trait inherent to the ecclesiastical culture of the region that is less common for the church in general, which is the mixture of Eastern and Western influences. This trait is uncommon in a broader church historical context, but nevertheless seems to have been common for specific areas in the Balkans, as this mixture is also noticeable in Albania and Bosnia.[49]

---

46 Ibid., 44.
47 Ibid.
48 Ibid., 45–46.
49 See, for example, Alexis P. Vlasto, *The Entry of the Slavs into Christendom*, Cambridge 1970, 187–207; John Fine, *The Bosnian Church: Its Place in State and Society from the Thirteenth to the Fifteenth Century. A New Interpretation*, New York 1975.

Claim 3: Independent Zeta

Unlike the early medieval period of Montenegro, the later eras are described in more detail in the available sources. The region, which was known as Zeta, included much of the coastal region and the mountainous hinterland along the Zeta valley and river and was a constituting part of the Serbian Kingdom. In short, the general history of Duklja-Zeta during this period is that the local noble house of Balšić was able to secure in 1362 a large degree of autonomy for the province from the other Serbian principalities that had plunged into internal strife under the weak rule of the last Serbian Nemanja ruler, Emperor Uroš (1336-1371). The Balšićs were later ousted by their rivals, the noble house of Crnojevići, who ruled Zeta until the final Ottoman takeover in 1514. The Crnojevići were devoted to Eastern Orthodoxy and ended much of the Latin Church's influence, which had flourished under the Balšić house.[50] The "ethnic" belonging of both these noble houses is ambiguous and debatable to a large extent. However, there seems to have been a stronger polarisation in the late period between the Latin Catholics, centred on the Venetian controlled coastline, and the Orthodox in the formerly Serbian controlled hinterland. This problematic constellation resurfaces, for example, in the diplomatic negotiations between the Serbian Empire and Venice in the 1420s and 1440s.[51]

Crnojevići Zeta eventually succumbed to the Ottomans and was ruled by an Islamised member of the Crnojevići house while other members preferred exile in Venice.[52] The main legacy of this period was left by Ivan Crnojevići who ruled from 1465 to 1490 and was forced by the Venetians to leave the former Zeta capital in Skadar for the mountains. In these mountains he founded the fortress city of Zablajk and the city of Cetinje that, along with Ivan's newly built monastery, became the seat of the Metropolitan of Zeta. The metropolitan later became the secular and religious leader of the clans in what became known as the Black Mountain (Montenegro). Ivan thus played a key role as his legacy, including his heraldry, a double headed golden eagle, became the centre of Montenegrin statehood in the following period.

The crucial question about the Zeta rulers, the Balšićs and Crnojevići, is whether or not these rulers were in actual fact autonomous and able to recreate the region as an independent state. There is not any easy or clear answer to this claim. It is very evident that the entire region was ravaged by the local magnates' struggles for power under pressure from the Venetians along the coast, the Hungarians in the North, and the rising Ottoman power in the South during the decline of the Serbian Empire. The multitude of alliances, noble hostages, and

50 Elizabeth Roberts, *Realm of the Black Mountain – A History of Montenegro,* New York 2007, 99–102.

51 Fine, *The Late Medieval Balkans* (as n. 45), 502.

52 Roberts, *Realm of the Black Mountain* (as n. 50), 95–99.

diplomatic relations under the Balšićs and Crnojevići reveals that they were nothing more nor less than feudal lords attempting to advance their own interests in the region. This was done through alliances and submissions to foreign powers, such as Ivan's submission to the Venetians, and it is therefore clear that Zeta was not a completely autonomous region and certainly not a very coherent state, even by medieval standards. The region was, as many other medieval principalities, a feudal holding belonging to a noble house capable of swearing allegiance to other noble houses, kings, and states or even of advancing their own house to the level of kingship. The nobles of Zeta never got that far and should not be considered more than noblemen.[53] The independence or autonomy of the region in the late medieval period is not visible without confusing the medieval feudal system with modern state structures.[54] The region was as independent as any feudal holding during a breakup of a central authority and the subsequent power vacuum, but this does not mean that the region was autonomous. With that said, one needs to underline that this does not devalue the heritage of the Balšićs and Crnojevići, but rather puts it into the correct historical context of the medieval era and the turmoil in the Balkans during the period from the decline of the Serbian Empire to the final Ottoman takeover. The Balšićs and Crnojevići heritage was crucial for the region's culture and its further development, but it simply did not include a complete and coherent period of autonomous statehood.

Claim 4: A Significant Religious and Cultural Tradition

As the historical survey has shown, there is definitely an independent local cultural and religious heritage in Duklja and Zeta that differs from that of Serbia-Raška. The emerging kingdom of Duklja, the feudal independence of the principality of Zeta, and the formation of a Western and Eastern Archbishopric in the region are all part of this heritage. The question is rather whether or not this heritage actually constitutes a significant tradition or origin on which a national narrative could be based. Each of the parts described above can be downplayed, as they actually have been throughout the Yugoslav period in order to enforce a coherent Serbian or Yugoslav identity to Montenegro's population.[55]

The "Duklja" identity in the MoOC's discourse, as analysed above, shows a series of the aforementioned Andrew Hasting's core factors that could be activated in order to form a new nationhood. First, the emphasis on Jovan Vladimir and Ivan Crnojevići is an attempt to sanctify the starting point for an ethno- and ecclesio-genesis. Second, the constant references to the threat posed

---

53 Ibid., 99–102.

54 Miedlig, "Zur Frage" (as n. 31), 155.

55 František Šistek, "Regimes of Historicity, Identity and Temporality in Montenegro, 1905-45", in Diana Mishkova/Balázs Trencsényi/Marja Jalava (eds), '*Regimes of Historicity' in Southeastern and Northern Europe, 1890-1945*, London 2014, 82–100.

by the medieval Nemanja-ruled Serbia and the SOC in Serbia today amount to a mythologisation and commemoration of national threats. The Serbs are portrayed as aliens and a destructive force from outside trying to spoil the "pure" Duklja-Zeta-Montenegrin realm. Finally, it is crucial for the MoOC to show that it is not only older than the SOC, but that it was an independent national church even from early medieval times. All three claims are disputable, but play a role in the formation a separate national and religious identity detached from Serbia and the SOC.

In the following section, the alternative viewpoints on the Montenegrin past are briefly outlined in order to better discuss the multiplicity of perspectives regarding the Montenegrin population's religious identity.

A Serbian-Coloured Viewpoint on the Montenegrins

Petar Vlahović from the Serbian Academy of Sciences and Arts draws up an alternative Montenegrin identity in a text from 1995. He raises the question of the tribal or ethnic affiliation of the Duklja magnates, which he claims to be Serbian just as the Nemanja house. He portrays the Vojislavljević family as Serbs and characterises them as a rivalling Serbian noble house to the Nemanja dynasty. Second, he questions the validity of the CPD with good reason and a fair use of historical arguments.[56] Vlahović also notes

> that many Montenegrin clans derive their origin from some real or imaginary ancestor. They often connect themselves, whether they have real grounds or not, to the Nemanja and the heroes of the Kosovo battle.[57]

Slavenko Terzić, also a member of the Serbian Academy of Sciences and Arts, takes his point of view a step further regarding the CPD and the interpretation of the Duklja magnates. Terzić claims that the pro-Montenegrin interpretation in fact is a fascist-Catholic construction, created in order to weaken the Serbian nation and de-attach Montenegro from Serbia.[58] The construction of the Duklja identity, which Terzić calls the "Diokletian Red Croat" identity, originated in the interwar period and the writings of a Montenegrin writer, Savić Marković Štedimlija (1906/7-1970). In 1937, Štedimlija wrote a pamphlet titled *Crvena Hrvatska* (Red Croatia) and a book based on it titled *Osnovi crnogorskog nacionalizma* (The Foundations of Montenegrin Nationalism).[59] In these texts, Štedimlija argued that

56 Petar Vlahović, "The Serbian Origins of the Montenegrins", in *The Serbian Question in the Balkans*, Belgrade 1995, 157–168, URL: http://www.njegos.org/past/vlahovic.htm [21.03.2016].

57 Ibid., 159.

58 Slavenko Terzić, "Savić Marković Štedimlija – Ideologist of 'Red Croatia'", URL: http://www.njegos.org/past/stedimlija.html [21.03.2016].

59 Ibid.

Montenegrins were not Serbians, but in fact former Catholics and "red" Croatians, as the CPD suggests, who were forced to convert to Orthodoxy and Serbianised by the Nemanja rulers. Terzić characterises this as a pro-Croatian and Catholic fascist interpretation of Montenegro's history and further claims that this point of view was adopted by the anti-Serbian communists, who wanted to weaken Serbia and create a separate and independent Montenegro as part of the re-organisation of Yugoslavia after the Second World War.[60]

The SOC in Montenegro also views the history of Montenegro very differently from the narrative presented by the MoOC. The SOC sees the Western influence along the coast as a part of the Venetian and Catholic domination of Dalmatia, which was countered by St Sava, who according to the SOC restored "true" Christianity in the region. In the eyes of the SOC, there would have been no Montenegro and no Orthodoxy in the region if it were not for the efforts of St Sava and the Nemanja dynasty. The early partial independence of the ecclesiastical structures in Duklja is overlooked as some minor event within the broad Christian world before the split between East and West in 1054. The Montenegrin Metropolitan and the Crnojevići state are therefore also regarded as something created by Sava and the Nemanja dynasty and hence as a continuation of the tradition rather than an opposition to it.[61]

The very title of the Metropolitan of the SOC expresses this view on history because its full name is the "The Metropolitan of Montenegro and the Littoral". "Montenegro", in this title, refers to most of the Crnojevići state in the hinterland and along the Zeta valley, while "the Littoral" refers to the coastal and Latin-dominated region of modern-day Montenegro. These two regions are regarded as something different from each other, and not as something that together constitutes Montenegro throughout history, as the pro-Montenegrins claim.

The Ambiguous Montenegrin Nationhood

The pro-Serbian interpretation of the Duklja-Zeta past, in which Duklja was a Serbian proto-state and the Crnojevići were a continuation of the Serbian tradition, was in fact also the general understanding of the past in the late period of the Montenegrin Kingdom (1889-1918) according to František Šistek's analysis.[62] Šistek argues that the Montenegrin King Nikola I Petrović-Njegoš (1841-1921) saw Montenegro as the Piedmont of the Serbs and therefore deployed the Montenegrin identity into the broader history of the Serbs in order to

60 Ibid.

61 Orthodox Metropolitanate of Montenegro and the Littoral, "Brief History of the Orthodox Metropolitanate of Montenegro and the Littoral" (2000), URL: http://www.njegos.org/past/metrohist.htm [13.02.2016].

62 Šistek, "Regimes" (as n. 55), 82–100.

ideologically support his effort to be the head of all South Slavs. After the First and Second World War, this specific interpretation of the Montenegrin identity and past was not favoured by the Yugoslav authorities. The Communist Party in charge in Yugoslavia after the Second World War and its main Montenegrin spokesperson Milovan Đilas took a more balanced stand on Montenegrin national identity. Đilas argued that the Montenegrin was both Serbian and something else. This approach allowed the Montenegrin identity to contain an ambiguous character, in which a specific republican Montenegrin nationhood, nurtured by the communist state, existed along a more Serbian-based ethnicity and language.[63]

The pro-Serbian viewpoint on the Montenegrin identity was, however, revived by the Serbian nationalist movement in the late 1980s under President Slobodan Milošević – such as it appears in the writings of Terzić and Vlahović. This revival coincided with the reappearance of the contemporary pro-Montenegrin construction of the Duklja identity by the MoOC and *Matica Crnagorska*. The MoOC and *Matica Crnagorska*'s interpretation of the Duklja past does bear much resemblance to Štedimlija's interpretation from 1937. They both focus on the CPD and the "non-Serbian" features of the Duklja-Zeta past. A quite important point is therefore that both the pro-Serbian and the pro-Montenegrin positions are traceable back to the formation and discussion of the Montenegrin national identity in the late nineteenth and early twentieth century. The two viewpoints are in fact shaped as the ideological, cultural, and religious backdrop and cultural heritage of the Montenegrin civil war in 1918-1920 between the pro-Serbian Whites and the pro-Montenegrin Greens. The religious and cultural conflict portrayed in this article is therefore not merely a modern phenomenon, but rather a continuation of the discussion of the embattled and ambiguous identity of the Montenegrins. The MoOC's revival of the Dukljan identity is not without a history of its own.[64]

What is remarkable in this process is how these historical themes were in fact revived and re-interpreted in the church-, state-, and nation-building processes of Montenegro within the MoOC. The ambiguous religious, ethnic, and national symbolism of St Jovan Vladimir and Ivan Crnojevići is dismantled to pave the way for a new sort of symbolic value. "St Ivan" is used as a sort of guardian saint for the MoOC and put forward as the name-giver to its new church in Cetinje, which was built in 2013-2014. Ivan, as the founder of Cetinje, is therefore simply occupied or used as a religious symbol by the MoOC, which enforces the religious and cultural claim that the MoOC has on the city and its monastery. What we observe here is a process of transformation and utilisation of historical saints, rulers, events, and sites that underpin and support the argument that Montenegro and its population are something different than Serbia. The identity of the region

63 Srda Pavlović, "Who are the Montenegrins? Statehood, Identity and Civic Society", in Florian Bieber (ed.), *Montenegro in Transition*, Baden-Baden 2003, 83–106.

64 Ibid., 90–91; Morrison, *Montenegro* (as n. 15), 14–26.

is detached from the Nemanja dynasty, which is often portrayed as brute invaders and autocratic rulers of Duklja, and therefore from the grand narrative of Serbia. The contemporary pro-Montenegrin agents thereby fabricate a process reverse to that of Yugoslavia; they downplay the Nemanja period and highlight the non-Serbian parts, such as the Duklja state and church. Returning to Andrew Hastings' points regarding the construction of nationhood, it becomes clear that the MoOC activates the core factors he identified. The MoOC tries to sanctify a starting point of "Montenegrinness", exemplified by the sanctification of Jovan Vladimir and Ivan Crnojevići, as well as the church mythologising of the Nemanja rule as a threat to Montenegro. It is therefore apparent that the Duklja identity and the logic embedded in it constitute a distinct recasting of the specific Montenegrin nationhood.

A second and problematic aspect of this recasting is, however, the use of the concepts of church, state, and nation. It is clear that the MoOC uses modern-day concepts when interpreting its own past. The church and state of Duklja are subsequently regarded as the same as the modern state and church of Montenegro. This is a problematic approach, because the contemporary ideology of nationalism, the organisational and cultural state structures, and the church's ecclesiology are projected back into a past that lacks such structures. There are structures at the surface of Montenegro's history that resemble those of a modern-day church, nation, and state, but to conclude that they are exactly the same seems a bit too hasty – even when one takes Hastings' anti-modernist interpretation of nationalism into account. Hastings argues that there are concepts of states, nations, and peoples in the medieval past, which contemporary nations could be based on, but he admits that the medieval structures are not the exact same as the contemporary ones.[65]

A central point regarding Montenegrin identity is the historical hypothesis that there existed independent Duklja and Zeta states with a specific Montenegrin "ethnos" – and this hypothesis "is unsustainable" according to Hans Miedlig.[66] Miedlig's conclusion underlines that what is regarded as state or ethnic structures could very well simply be allegiance to kin, clans or tribes. The Byzantine sources speak of the Duklja state as a sort of tribal federation. It is therefore likely that the Vojislavljević state was a federation held together by kinship allegiance, as John Fine suggests.[67] Likewise, this state structure is transferable to the Balšić and Crnojevići state, where kin seems to have mattered most. The external powers, such as Venice and the Ottomans, were aware of that and therefore deployed the various members of the Crnojevići family as local rulers in order to pacify the region. These sorts of allegiance or family bonds seem to have been central in the

65 Hastings, *The Construction of Nationhood* (as n. 12), 25–26.

66 Miedlig, "Zur Frage " (as n. 31), 157, 161.

67 This is one of the central points in his work on ethnicity in the Balkans. See Fine, *When Ethnicity did not Matter* (as n. 41).

shaping of the Montenegrin region from the seventh to the sixteenth century. Likewise, Montenegrin society in the seventeenth and eighteenth centuries was formed around clans, and it was the allegiance to these clans that mattered most, according to Srda Pavlović's analysis of the Montenegrin identity.[68]

In light of this, it is interesting that a key strategy and underlying argument of the MoOC is that the church itself is also founded on the basis of tribal allegiance. As unfolded elsewhere, the MoOC views each church building and parish as something that belongs to a "family" or specific clan.[69] According to a spokesperson, the organisational structure and ownership of the church were therefore based on kin. This "ecclesiology of kinship" seems to reach beyond the modern-day world and the modern organisation of states. Such a structure is perhaps a much more genuine tradition of allegiance in Montenegrin society. However, such a conception of identity – both in religious and national terms – implicitly shows that Montenegro is still socially organised in clans and is therefore a tribal state. I would therefore like to stress that the point is not that Montenegro is still a tribal society, but that we might better understand the Duklja identity not as a specific ethnos or nationhood, but rather as an identity of kinship that survived within the clan structures of Montenegro and has been revived today. Even the pro-Serbian author Vlahović identified in his text the clan system and the tribal structures as quite important factors in Montenegro. In his opinion, this is the explanation of Montenegrin identity, which he claims is a clan-identity unlike the Serbian identity, which is an ethnic one.[70]

The Serbian-Montenegrin word for people (*narod*, *narodnost*) bears reference to that as well, because it also refers to a broader concept of family or blood bond between kin and clan.[71] A Montenegrin religious identity based on such a concept of kinship is not far from nationalism, because it is still based on the idea that all members belong to a delimited and sovereign connected community, which is the central part of the classic constructivist definition of a nation.[72] This discussion is of course much broader and comes down to the question of what a nation or people is, and whether it makes sense to expect a complete ethnogenesis thereof.[73]

68 Pavlović "Who are the Montenegrins?" (as n. 63), 84–86.

69 For a thorough discussion of the connection between church, kin, and clan in Montenegro, see Saggau, "Unblocking the Sacred" (as n. 7), 48–49.

70 Vlahović, "The Serbian Origins" (as n. 56), 157–168.

71 See Florin Curta, *The Making of Slavs*, Cambridge 2007, 17.

72 Tomka/Szilárdi, *Religion and Nation* (as n. 6), 81–85.

73 For a detailed discussion of such issues in the research history on the Slavs, see Curta, *The Making of Slavs* (as n. 71), 6–35.

The Return of Duklja

On this basis, I would argue that the MoOC's revival of the Dukljan identity must be seen as several interlinked processes. It is first and foremost a continuation of the pro-Montenegrin traditions in Montenegro that date back to the civil war of 1918-1920, but also a nation-building process in which a specific religious sacralisation of history takes place. The process of church- and nation-building within the MoOC and *Matica Crnagorska* that was laid out is a sort of cultural and political process of differentiation whereby the church and the nation are claimed to be holy. The process of differentiation is a hermeneutical strategy, where the differences in the factual history of Montenegro and Serbia in general are highlighted and used as milestones that mark the difference rather than the bond. The mutuality and the long period of the medieval Serbian Kingdom are rejected as something external, threatening, and hostile to the Montenegrins, wherefore the Nemanja rulers are labelled as "violent" and "autocratic". This process resembles to a large degree how Hastings argues that nationhood is constructed by ecclesiastical agents. The differentiation process and revival of the Duklja identity have resulted in not just a re-interpretation of history, but a "sacralised" history (to use Klaus Buchenau's term). History describes a sort of transcendent holiness, in which the nation, the church, and the state are turned into eternal categories – as Goran Sekulović puts it: "A holy and free Montenegrin trinity – the Montenegrin historical unity of people, state, and church."[74]

---

74 Goran Sekulović, "Crnogorska identitetska prava i slobode" [Montenegrin Identity Rights and Freedom], *Matica* (2010) 7–74, here 6, URL: http://www.maticacrnogorska.me/files/44/01%20goran%20sekulovic.pdf [19.02.2019].

Notes on Contributors

Daniel Jianu is a PhD candidate at the Department of Religious Studies at the University of Erfurt, Germany. His research interests focus on secularism, international relations theory and religion, as well as the relationship between Orthodox Christianity and the foreign policy in predominantly Orthodox countries of South Eastern Europe. His recent publications include the chapter "Symphonia and the Historical Relationship between State and Church: Legacies from Byzantine Times until today", in Tobias Köllner (ed.), *Orthodox Religion and Politics in Contemporary Eastern Europe: On Multiple Secularisms and Entanglements*, London: Routledge, 2018, 17–33.

Anna Karpathakis is Professor of Sociology at Kingsborough Community College, City University of New York, USA. She holds a PhD from Columbia University, New York, with a thesis entitled *Sojourners and Permanent Settlers: Greek Immigrants of Astoria, New York.* She researches in the areas of Greek immigrants, racialisation, transnationalism, and sociology of religion, in which she has published extensively. Among her book publications: *Greek American Families: Traditions and Transformations* (New York: Pella, 1999), co-edited with Sam J. Tsemberis and Harry J. Psomiades; and *New York Glory: Religions in the City* (New York: New York University Press, 2001), co-edited with Tony Carnes.

Rev. Protopresbyter **Nicolas Kazarian** was born in France, where he pursued his undergraduate degree at the Institute of Orthodox Theology Saint Serge in Paris, graduating with a BA. He continued his studies at the University of Cyprus, Nicosia, and at the University of Thessaloniki, Greece, before moving to Switzerland to start an MA in Orthodox Theology at the Orthodox Theological Institute of Chambésy, Switzerland. He completed his PhD at the Sorbonne. Currently, he is a professor at the Institute of Orthodox Theology Saint Serge and a research associate at the French Institute for International and Strategic Affairs in Paris. He also teaches at the Catholic University of Paris. He is the author of numerous publications about the Orthodox Church, ecumenical dialogue, interfaith relations, and geopolitics in various languages. His most recent book publication is *L'orthodoxie: une introduction de référence à l'histoire, à la foi, aux rites et à la spiritualité* (Paris: Eyrolles, 2019).

Frances Kostarelos is Full Professor at Governors State University, Chicago, Illinois, in the Department of Anthropology and Sociology. She studied Political Science and Cultural Anthropology at the University of Chicago. Her doctoral research focused on the development of African American storefront churches in the context of race discrimination and economic dislocation in Chicago. She currently researches religious pluralism with a focus on race, ethnicity, and social class as they shape the lived experience of Orthodox Christians in North America. In recent years, she has directed attention to a growing culture of spiritual elders and monastic institutions among Orthodox Christians in the United States.

Oleg Kyselov is Senior Researcher at the Institute of Philosophy at the H.S. Skovoroda National Academy of Sciences of Ukraine in Kyiv. He studied Philosophy and Religious Studies at Taras Shevchenko Kyiv National University, Ukraine, and received his PhD there with a thesis on Christian ecumenism. He is currently working on his *Habilitation* thesis on scientific atheism in Soviet Ukraine. His main research areas include sociology of religion, church-state relations, religious tolerance, interfaith relations, and ecumenism, in which he has published numerous articles.

Vasilios N. Makrides studied in Athens, Harvard, and Tübingen and has been Professor of Religious Studies (specialising in Orthodox Christianity) at the Faculty of Philosophy of the University of Erfurt, Germany, since 1999. His research interests include the comparative religious and cultural history and sociology of Orthodox Christianity; the religious and cultural relations between Eastern and Western Europe; and Greek Orthodox diasporic communities. Among his recent publications: *Orthodox Christianity and Modern Science: Tensions, Ambiguities, Potential* (Turnhout: Brepols Publishers, 2019), co-edited with Gayle E. Woloschak; and the special thematic issue "Christianisme orthodoxe et économie dans le sud-est européen contemporain", *Archives de sciences sociales des religions* (Paris) 64, No. 185 (janvier-mars 2019), co-edited with Katerina Seraïdari.

Sebastian Rimestad is Senior Researcher in the Department of Religious Studies at the University of Erfurt, Germany. He studied Political Science, International Relations, and Religious Studies in Aberdeen, Tartu, and Erfurt. He holds a PhD degree in Religious Studies (published as *The Challenges of Modernity to the Orthodox Church in Estonia and Latvia, 1917-1940*, Frankfurt am Main: Peter Lang, 2012) and is in the process of publishing his second book on Orthodox Christians in Western Europe, which is based on his *Habilitation* at the University of Erfurt, completed in 2019. He has also published numerous articles and book chapters in scholarly journals and collective volumes on the Baltic States, Orthodox Christianity, and religion in modernity.

Emil Hilton Saggau holds an MA in Theology and Balkan Studies and is currently working as a PhD student at the section for Church History of the University of Copenhagen, Denmark. Prior to his PhD enrolment, he worked at the Centre for European Islamic Thought. His main interests lie in the interferences between religion, nationalism, and politics in South Eastern Europe. He has published several articles in this area and especially concerning the Orthodox Church in Montenegro, which is also the topic of his dissertation. He received the Miklós Tomka Award from ISORECEA in 2018 for his paper on nationalism and religion in Montenegro and the Elite Research Prize for young researchers from the Danish Ministry for Higher Education and Science in 2019.

Dragan Šljivić holds a PhD in Religious Studies from the University of Erfurt. He studied Political Science, International Relations, and Management at the University of Belgrade, Serbia. His PhD thesis entitled *Between the Vox Populi and the Vox Dei: The Orthodox Church and Embedding Democracy in Bulgaria and Serbia, 2007-2012* will be published in 2020. His key areas of interest are the relationship between Orthodoxy and democracy in the Balkans and church-state relations in the post-communist states of South Eastern Europe. His recent publications include the article, co-authored with Nenad Živković, "Self-Ruled and Self-Consecrated Ecclesiastic Schism as a Nation-Building Instrument in the Orthodox Countries of South Eastern Europe", *Genealogy* 2020, 4(2), 52, URL: https://doi.org/10.3390/genealogy4020052.

Georgios E. Trantas is a Marie Skłodowska-Curie Individual Fellow at Aston University, Birmingham, UK. He holds a PhD in Religious Studies from the University of Erfurt. His interdisciplinary expertise involves the politics of religion and cultural diplomacy, soft power, self-perception, nationhood, citizenship, and cultural-political identity. Moreover, his research pertains to intra-European migration and the formation of religioscapes thereof, with a focus on religious art and culture as spatial markers of migrant communities in the public sphere and as symbolic constellations of being and belonging. He has published extensively in the above areas including the book *Being and Belonging: A Comparative Examination of the Greek and Cypriot Orthodox Churches' Attitudes to 'Europeanisation' in Early 21st Century* (Berlin: Peter Lang, 2018).

Rev. **Nenad Živković** studied Orthodox Theology in Belgrade, Serbia, and completed his Master's Degree in Religious Studies at the University of Erfurt, Germany. He is currently working on his PhD that deals with the role of autocephaly in the nation-building processes of (North) Macedonia and Montenegro from a comparative perspective. He has published various articles in Serbian, English, and German on the ecclesiastical schism, canonical order, and identity issues in (North) Macedonia and the Serbian Orthodox Church. His recent publications include the chapter "Surrendering to Public Pressure: The 'Macedonian Orthodox Church' and the Rejection of the Niš Agreement in 2002", in Tobias Köllner (ed.), *Orthodox Religion and Politics in Contemporary Eastern*

Europe: On Multiple Secularisms and Entanglements, London: Routledge, 2018, 214–232; and the article, co-authored with Dragan Šljivić, "Self-Ruled and Self-Consecrated Ecclesiastic Schism as a Nation-Building Instrument in the Orthodox Countries of South Eastern Europe", *Genealogy* 2020, 4(2), 52, URL: https://doi.org/10.3390/genealogy4020052.

Erfurter Studien zur Kulturgeschichte des Orthodoxen Christentums

Herausgegeben von / Edited by
Vasilios N. Makrides

Band 1 Vasilios N. Makrides (Hrsg.): Religion, Staat und Konfliktkonstellationen im orthodoxen Ost- und Südosteuropa. Vergleichende Perspektiven. 2005.

Band 2 Klaus Buchenau: Kämpfende Kirchen. Jugoslawiens religiöse Hypothek. 2006.

Band 3 Angelos Giannakopoulos: Tradition und Moderne in Griechenland. Konfliktfelder in Religion, Politik und Kultur. 2007.

Band 4 Kristina Stoeckl: Community after Totalitarianism. The Russian Orthodox Intellectual Tradition and the Philosophical Discourse of Political Modernity. 2008.

Band 5 Nicolai Staab: Rumänische Kultur, Orthodoxie und der Westen. Der Diskurs um die nationale Identität in Rumänien aus der Zwischenkriegszeit. 2011.

Band 6 Sebastian Rimestad: The Challenges of Modernity to the Orthodox Church in Estonia and Latvia (1917-1940). 2012.

Band 7 Łukasz Fajfer: Modernisierung im orthodox-christlichen Kontext. Der Heilige Berg Athos und die Herausforderungen der Modernisierungsprozesse seit 1988. 2013.

Band 8 Alexander Agadjanian: Turns of Faith, Search for Meaning. Orthodox Christianity and Post-Soviet Experience. 2014.

Band 9 Thomas Heinzel: *Weiße Bruderschaft* und *Delphische Idee*. Esoterische Religiosität in Bulgarien und Griechenland in der ersten Hälfte des 20. Jahrhunderts. 2014.

Band 10 Mihai-D. Grigore: Neagoe Basarab – Princeps Christianus. Christianitas-Semantik im Vergleich mit Erasmus, Luther und Machiavelli (1513-1523). 2015.

Band 11 Vasilios N. Makrides / Jennifer Wasmuth / Stefan Kube (Hrsg.): Christentum und Menschenrechte in Europa. Perspektiven und Debatten in Ost und West. 2016.

Band 12 Alena Alshanskaya: Der Europa-Diskurs der Russischen Orthodoxen Kirche (1996-2011). 2016.

Band 13 Stamatios Gerogiorgakis: *Futura contingentia, necessitas per accidens* und Prädestination in Byzanz und in der Scholastik. 2017.

Band 14 Alexander Ponomariov: The Visible Religion. The Russian Orthodox Church and her Relations with State and Society in Post-Soviet Canon Law (1992-2015). 2017.

Band 15 Isabella Schwaderer: Platonisches Erbe, Byzanz, Orthodoxie und die Modernisierung Griechenlands. Schwerpunkte des kulturphilosophischen Werkes von Stelios Ramfos. 2018.

Band 16 Georgios E. Trantas: Being and Belonging. A Comparative Examination of the Greek and Cypriot Orthodox Churches' Attitudes to 'Europeanisation' in Early 21st Century. 2018.

Band 17 Julia Anna Lis: Antiwestliche Diskurse in der serbischen und griechischen Orthodoxie. Zur Konstruktion des „Westens" bei Nikolaj Velimirović, Justin Popović, Christos Yannaras und John S. Romanides. 2019.

Band 18 Sebastian Rimestad / Vasilios N. Makrides (eds): Coping with Change. Orthodox Christian Dynamics between Tradition, Innovation, and *Realpolitik*. 2020.

www.peterlang.com

www.ingramcontent.com/pod-product-compliance
Ingram Content Group UK Ltd.
Pitfield, Milton Keynes, MK11 3LW, UK
UKHW022222051026
15624UKWH00002B/293

9 783631 671467